Handbook of Recidivism Risk/Needs Assessment Tools

Handbook of Recidivism Risk/Needs Assessment Tools

*Edited by Jay P. Singh, Daryl G. Kroner, J. Stephen Wormith,
Sarah L. Desmarais, and Zachary Hamilton*

WILEY Blackwell

Registered Office(s)
John Wiley & Sons, Inc., 111 River Street, Hoboken, NJ 07030, USA
John Wiley & Sons Ltd, The Atrium, Southern Gate, Chichester, West Sussex, PO19 8SQ, UK

Editorial Office
The Atrium, Southern Gate, Chichester, West Sussex, PO19 8SQ, UK

For details of our global editorial offices, customer services, and more information about Wiley products visit us at www.wiley.com.

Wiley also publishes its books in a variety of electronic formats and by print-on-demand. Some content that appears in standard print versions of this book may not be available in other formats.

Library of Congress Cataloging-in-Publication Data Is Available

ISBN 9781119184287 (cloth)
ISBN 9781119184294 (paper)
ISBN 9781119184263 (ePUB)
ISBN 9781119184270 (ePDF)

Cover Design by Wiley
Cover Image: © Koron/Gettyimages

Set in 10/12pt Warnock Pro by SPi Global, Chennai, India
Printed in Singapore by C.O.S. Printers Pte Ltd

10 9 8 7 6 5 4 3 2 1

To Mom, Dad, Anj, Josh, and Erik for sticking out a long journey
To Norma Raycraft
To Amelita Bayani and Donnie Wormith
To my husband, Richard, and our girls, Grace and Mireille
To Robert 'Barney' Barnoski, Tim Brennan, and my wife, Sarah

Contents

Notes on Contributors

Antonio Andrés-Pueyo, PhD, is Professor and Chair of the Clinical Psychology and Psychobiology at the University of Barcelona (Spain). He is a member of the Advanced Studies of Violence Group (GEAV) and co-author of the RisCanvi. His research interests include violence risk assessment and management in correctional settings.

Karin Arbach-Lucioni, PhD, is Professor at the School of Psychology of National University of Cordoba (Argentina) and Researcher at the National Council of Scientific and Technological Research of Argentina. She has co-authored the RisCanvi. She is an expert in violence risk assessment and management in psychiatric and correctional facilities.

Christopher Baird is currently Chairman of the Board of Directors of the National Council on Crime and Delinquency (NCCD). Before retiring in 2012, he spent 28 years with NCCD, serving as Research Director, Vice President, and President. He authored dozens of research articles and reports and received several national awards for his work.

James Bonta received his PhD in Clinical Psychology from the University of Ottawa in 1979. Upon graduating, Dr Bonta was the Chief Psychologist at the Ottawa-Carleton Detention Centre, a maximum security remand centre for adults and young offenders. During his 14 years at the Detention Centre he established the only full-time psychology department in a jail setting in Canada. In 1990 Dr Bonta joined Public Safety Canada where he was Director of Corrections Research until his retirement in 2015. Throughout his career, Dr Bonta has held various academic appointments, professional posts, and he was a member of the Editorial Advisory Boards for the *Canadian Journal of Criminology* and *Criminal Justice and Behavior*. He is a Fellow of the Canadian Psychological Association, a recipient of the Criminal Justice Section's Career Contribution Award for 2009, the Queen Elizabeth II Diamond Jubilee Medal, 2012, the Maud Booth Correctional Services Award (2015), and the 2015 Community Corrections Award, International Corrections and Prisons Association. Dr Bonta has published extensively in the areas of risk assessment and offender rehabilitation. His latest publications include a book co-authored with the late D. A. Andrews entitled *The Psychology of Criminal Conduct* now in its sixth edition (with translations in French and Chinese). He is also a co-author of the Level of Service offender risk-need classification instruments which have been translated into six languages and are used by correctional systems throughout the world.

Tim Brennan is Chief Scientist at Northpointe Institute. His work has appeared in the *Journal of Quantitative Criminology*, *Criminology and Public Policy*, *Criminal Justice and Behavior*, and others. His research interests are in quantitative methods for offender classification, machine learning, risk assessment, sentencing decision-making, and open dynamic systems modeling. He was recipient of the Warren-Palmer award from the Corrections and Sentencing Division of the American Society of Criminology.

Thomas H. Cohen is a social science analyst at the Administrative Office of the United States Courts (AOUSC), Probation and Pretrial Services Office. His work includes analyzing risk assessment at the post-conviction and pretrial levels and authoring reports on how the AOUSC integrates the risk principle into its operational practices. His recent research has appeared in *Criminology and Public Policy*, *Criminal Justice Policy Review*, *Federal Probation*, *Law and Human Behavior*, and *Psychological Services*. Moreover, he has authored several technical reports on criminal court case processing at the state and federal levels through his prior work at the Bureau of Justice Statistics.

Sarah L. Desmarais, PhD is an Associate Professor and Coordinator of the Applied Social and Community Psychology Program at North Carolina State University. Her current research focuses on the assessment and treatment of justice-involved adolescents and adults and the assessment of risk for terrorism. She has more than 100 peer-reviewed publications on topics including violence and mental illness, behavioral health and risk assessment strategies, and domestic violence. Dr. Desmarais is co-author of the Short-Term Assessment of Risk and Treatability (START) and the Short-Term Assessment of Risk and Treatability: Adolescent Version (START:AV). She has conducted trainings worldwide on risk assessment and serves on local, state, and federal behavioral health and criminal justice policy taskforces.

William Dieterich is Director of Research at Northpointe Institute. His work has appeared in *Prevention Science*, *Journal of Quantitative Criminology*, *Criminal Justice and Behavior*, and others. His interests focus on risk model development and validation, survival modeling, and related methods.

Jérôme Endrass studied psychology, psychopathology, and philosophy at the University of Zurich. He received his habilitation at the University of Zurich in 2008. Since 2011, he has been an APL professor at the University of Constance and is currently head of the forensic psychology research group. Since October 2013, he has served as deputy head of the Department of Mental Health Services, and prior to that, between 2003 and September 2013, he led the Research Department.

Leonel C. Gonçalves studied forensic psychology at the University of Minho, School of Psychology, Portugal, where he completed his Master (2008) and PhD degrees (2014). Since November 2014, he has been working as a researcher at the Department of Mental Health Services of the Zurich Office of Corrections, in the Research and Development Division. His research interests include inmate adjustment to prison life and the assessment of offenders.

Zachary Hamilton, PhD, is currently an Associate Professor of Criminal Justice and Criminology at Washington State University, the Director of the Washington State Institute of Criminal Justice (WSICJ). He is the primary developer of the Static Risk Offender Needs Guide – Revised (STRONG-R), the Modified Positive Achievement Change Tool (M-PACT) for juveniles, the Spokane Assessment for Evaluation of Risk (SAFER) for pretrial defendants, and the Nebraska Department of Correctional Services Infractions Risk and Prison Classification Instrument. His current work focuses on risk and needs assessment and identifying responsive populations for treatment matching. Recent publications have appeared in *Criminology and Public Policy*, *Experimental Criminology*, *Justice Quarterly*, *Journal of Substance Abuse Treatment*, *Criminal Justice & Behavior*, *Sex Abuse*, *Victims and Violence*, and *Offender Rehabilitation*.

Philip Howard, PhD, is a Principal Research Officer in the Analytical Services Directorate of the United Kingdom's Ministry of Justice. His current research interests include modeling recidivism and prison safety risks, and the integration of risk assessment into prison and probation operational practice. His recent research has been published in journals including *Criminal Justice and Behavior, Law and Human Behavior,* and *Sexual Abuse,* and he frequently contributes to guidance issued to prison and probation officers.

Kiersten L. Johnson, PhD received her doctorate in psychology from North Carolina State University. She currently works at the RAND Corporation.

Natalie J. Jones holds a PhD and an MA in Psychology from Carleton University in Ottawa, Canada, both with a forensic specialization. In 2011, she was awarded the Canadian Psychological Association Certificate of Academic Excellence for Best Doctoral Dissertation. Upon completing her doctoral work, Dr Jones joined Orbis Partners as Director of Research. In this capacity, she is responsible for managing justice-related research projects including the validation of risk assessment tools, program evaluations, and the provision of research services to clients across the United States and Canada. Her specific research interests lie in the development of strengths-based and gender-informed risk assessment and intervention strategies for justice-involved populations. In addition, Dr Jones has several peer-reviewed publications in investigative psychology spanning the areas of offender profiling, linkage analysis, indicators of suicide note authenticity, and diagnostic decision-making in policing contexts.

Daryl G. Kroner, PhD, is a Professor at the Department of Criminology and Criminal Justice at Southern Illinois University (SIU). He has more than 20 years of experience in the field as a correctional psychologist. During this time, he worked at maximum, medium, and minimum facilities delivering intervention services to incarcerated men. Dr Kroner has consulted on prison management and release issues, including with the Council of State Governments Justice Center and the UK's National Offender Management System. Dr Kroner is the past-chair of Criminal Justice Psychology of the Canadian Psychological Association and past-chair of the Corrections Committee for the American Psychology and Law Society. He is also a fellow of the Canadian Psychological Association. In collaboration with Dr Jeremy Mills he has developed several instruments, including the Measures of Criminal Attitudes and Associates (MCAA); Depression, Hopelessness and Suicide Scale (DHS); Criminal Attribution Inventory (CRAI); Transition Inventory (TI); and the Measures of Criminal and Antisocial Desistance (MCAD). In 2008, Dr Kroner joined the Department of Criminology and Criminal Justice at SIU. Current research interests include risk assessment, measurement of intervention outcomes, interventions among offenders with mental illness, and criminal desistance.

Edward J. Latessa received his PhD from Ohio State University and is Director and Professor of the School of Criminal Justice at the University of Cincinnati. Dr Latessa has published over 170 works in the area of criminal justice, corrections, and juvenile justice. He is co-author of eight books including *What Works (and Doesn't) in Reducing Recidivism, Corrections in the Community,* and *Corrections in America.* Professor Latessa has directed over 195 funded research projects including studies of day reporting centers, juvenile justice programs, drug courts, prison programs, intensive supervision programs, halfway houses, and drug programs. He and his staff have also assessed over 1,000 correctional programs throughout the United States, and he has provided assistance and workshops in 48 states. Dr Latessa served as President of the Academy of Criminal Justice Sciences (1989–90). He has also received several awards including: Marguerite Q. Warren and Ted B. Palmer Differential Intervention Award presented by the Division of Corrections and Sentencing of the American Society of Criminology (2010), Outstanding Community Partner Award from the Arizona Department of Juvenile Corrections (2010), Maud Booth Correctional Services Award in recognition of dedicated service and leadership presented by the Volunteers of America (2010), Community Hero Award presented by Community Resources for Justice, (2010), the Bruce Smith Award for outstanding contributions to criminal justice by the Academy of Criminal Justice Sciences (2010), the George Beto Scholar, College of Criminal Justice, Sam Houston State University, (2009), the Mark Hatfield Award for contributions in public policy research by The Hatfield School of Government at Portland State University (2008), the Outstanding Achievement Award by the National Juvenile Justice Court Services Association (2007), the August Vollmer Award from the American Society of Criminology (2004), the Simon Dinitz Criminal Justice Research Award from the Ohio Department of Rehabilitation and Correction (2002), the Margaret Mead Award for dedicated service to the causes of social justice and humanitarian advancement by the International Community Corrections Association (2001), the Peter P. Lejins Award for Research from the American Correctional Association (1999); ACJS Fellow Award (1998); ACJS Founders Award (1992); and the Simon Dinitz award by the Ohio Community Corrections Organization. In 2013 he was identified as one of the most innovative people in criminal justice by a national survey conducted by the Center for Court Innovation in partnership with the Bureau of Justice Assistance and the U.S. Department of Justice.

Brian K. Lovins is the Assistant Director for Harris County Community Supervision and Corrections Department. He earned his PhD in Criminology from the University of Cincinnati, School of Criminal Justice. Prior to coming to Houston, his work at the School of Criminal Justice included developing a state-wide juvenile risk assessment (Ohio Youth Assessment System, OYAS) and adult risk assessment (Ohio Risk Assessment System, ORAS), as well as redesigning juvenile and adult correctional programs to meet evidence-based standards. Dr Lovins has been invited to present to over 150 agencies and routinely trains agencies in the principles of effective intervention, risk assessment, and the delivery of cognitive-behavioral interventions. In addition, he has published articles on risk assessment, sexual offenders, effective interventions, and cognitive-behavioral interventions.

Christopher T. Lowenkamp received his PhD in Criminal Justice from the University of Cincinnati (UC). He has served as the director of the Center for Criminal Justice Research and the associate director of The Corrections Institute at UC. He has also served as a probation officer and jail emergency release coordinator in Summit County Ohio and as a probation administrator with the Office of U.S. Probation and Pretrial Services. Dr Lowenkamp is currently a social science analyst at the Administrative Office of the United States Courts (AOUSC), Probation and Pretrial Services Office. He has co-authored over 75 articles and book chapters. In an effort to close the knowing-doing gap, Dr Lowenkamp has been involved in training thousands of correctional staff in effective practices and risk assessment.

Wagdy Loza is a licensed psychologist in Ontario. He was the Chief Psychologist at Kingston Penitentiary before he retired from the Correctional Service of Canada after 30 years of service. He is currently a member of the Ontario Review Board which is responsible for determining whether criminals who were found "not criminally responsible due to mental illness" were well enough to be released into the community. Dr Loza has developed two widely used psychological tests. The first is used to predict whether criminals will reoffend violently or non-violently. The second is designed to measure Middle-Eastern extremism and terrorism. Dr Loza is also an Adjunct Assistant Professor (Psychiatry, Queen's University) and ex. Adjunct Professor (Psychology, Carleton University). He has over 40 publications and offers training, workshops, and presentations in several countries around the world.

Jennifer L. Lux is a Research Associate at the University of Cincinnati Corrections Institute (UCCI). She earned her PhD in Criminal Justice from the University of Cincinnati, School of Criminal Justice in 2016. Her research interests include the assessment of correctional programs, the science of implementation and knowledge transfer, and more generally correctional treatment and rehabilitation. She has co-authored publications and served as a project director on several correctional projects. Specific topics of research and service include an evaluation study of juvenile programs in the state of Ohio and the implementation and rollout of the Texas Risk Assessment System in partnership with the Texas Department of Criminal Justice. For the last five years, the majority of Dr Lux's experience has been with risk assessment instruments, from training to coaching to ensure agencies are using the tools with fidelity and integrity, to working with the University of Cincinnati Information Technology Solutions Center to develop and maintain various correctional agencies' automated risk assessment systems.

Xiaohan Mei is a PhD candidate in criminal justice and criminology at Washington State University and senior research associate of the Washington State Institute for Criminal Justice (WSICJ). His most recent publications on validation of measurement instruments appeared in the *Prison Journal*. His research interests include the study of deviance and criminology, risk-needs assessment instrument validation, core correctional practices and program fidelity, management in corrections and organizational studies, quantitative methodology, and psychometric analytic approaches. His work has also appeared in *Journal of Offender Rehabilitation* and *International Journal of Offender Therapy and Comparative Criminology*.

Holly A. Miller holds a PhD in Clinical Psychology from Florida State University and currently is the Associate Dean and a Professor in the College of Criminal Justice at Sam Houston State University. She is the author of the Miller Forensic Assessment of Symptoms Test (M-FAST) and the Inventory of Offender Risk, Needs, and Strengths (IORNS). Dr. Miller's teaching, research, and practice interests include forensic assessment and working with individuals who have sexually offended. She is a licensed clinical psychologist and sex offender treatment provider who consults with various agencies providing expertise on evaluation, treatment, and research.

John Monahan, a psychologist, holds the John S. Shannon Distinguished Chair in Law at the University of Virginia, where he is also Professor of Psychology, and Professor of Psychiatry and Neurobehavioral Sciences. He is a member of the National Academy of Medicine and serves on the National Research Council. In 2016, Monahan was elected a Fellow of the American Academy of Arts and Sciences.

Santiago Redondo, PhD, is Professor and Chair of the Advanced Studies of Violence Group at the University of Barcelona. He has co-authored the RisCanvi. Dr Redondo has a long experience in applied research with sexual and violent offenders and is an expert in criminology.

Charles Robinson has nearly 20 years of experience in community supervision. He currently works for the United States Probation Office in the District of New Hampshire and previously served as the Travis County Community Supervision and Corrections Department (adult probation) chief probation officer. He has co-authored publications, served as a trainer, and developed programs for criminal justice clients.

David Robinson holds a PhD in psychology from Carleton University and has engaged in the development, validation, and implementation of criminal justice assessments for more than 30 years. From 1988 to 1997, he was a senior research manager with Correctional Service Canada. After his tenure in government, he began consulting work and became a founding member of Orbis Partners in 2001. He has directed program evaluations on correctional interventions including cognitive skills, substance abuse, drug courts, boot camps, programs for women/girls, case management models, and juvenile diversion. Dr Robinson conducted validation studies on numerous assessment devices and worked on early validation efforts with the LSI and YLS. Over the past 20 years, he managed 12 state-wide implementations of assessment and case management tools, along with work in numerous county and non-government organizations. His current research focuses on measurement and validation of strengths in risk/need assessments.

Astrid Rossegger studied psychology and criminology at the University of Constance. Since 2000, she has worked as a researcher for the Department of Mental Health Services of the Canton of Zurich and has served as head of the Research Department since October 2013. She is a member of the executive board of the Department of Mental Health Services and since 2007 has taught at the University of Zurich and the University of Constance.

Douglas Routh is a PhD candidate in criminal justice and criminology at Washington State University and senior research associate of the Washington State Institute for Criminal Justice (WSICJ). His most recent publications on offender typologies, offender reentry, and offender rights have appeared in Justice Quarterly, Journal of Offender Rehabilitation, and International Journal of Offender Therapy and Comparative Criminology. His research interests include corrections, risk assessment, evidence-based practices, problem-solving courts, and quantitative methodology.

Jay P. Singh, PhD, PhD, is a Fulbright Scholar and the internationally award-winning Founder and Chairman of the Global Institute of Forensic Research. Former Senior Clinical Researcher in Forensic Psychiatry and Psychology for the Department of Justice of Switzerland and fellow of the Mental Health Law and Policy Department at the University of South Florida, he completed his graduate studies in psychiatry at the University of Oxford and clinical Psychology at Universitat Konstanz. He was promoted to Full Professor at Molde University College in Norway in 2014 and is currently affiliated with the Department of Psychiatry and the Wharton School of Business at UPenn. Dr. Singh has been the recipient of awards from organizations including the prestigious 2015 Saleem Shah Early Career Excellence Award from the American Board of Forensic Psychology and 2015 Early Career Professional Award from APA Division 52. Additional bodies of recognition have included the American Psychology-Law Society, the Royal College of Psychiatrists, the European Congress on Violence in Clinical Psychiatry, the Society for Research in Child Development, and the Society for Research in Adolescence.

Faye S. Taxman, PhD, is a University Professor in the Criminology, Law and Society Department and Director of the Center for Advancing Correctional Excellence at George Mason University. She is recognized for her work in the development of systems-of-care models that link the criminal justice system with other service delivery systems, as well as her work in reengineering probation and parole supervision services and in organizational change models. She developed the RNR Simulation Tool (www.gmuace.org/tools) to assist agencies to advance practice. Dr. Taxman has published more than 190 articles and several books including "Tools of the Trade: A Guide to Incorporating Science into Practice." and "Implementing Evidence-Based Community Corrections and Addiction Treatment" (Springer, 2012 with Steven Belenko). She is co-Editor of the Health & Justice. The American Society of Criminology's Division of Sentencing and Corrections has recognized her as Distinguished Scholar twice as well as the Rita Warren and Ted Palmer Differential Intervention Treatment award. She received the Joan McCord Award in 2017 from the Division of Experimental Criminology. She has a Ph.D. from Rutgers University's School of Criminal Justice.

J. Stephen Wormith received his PhD from the University of Ottawa in 1977. Since then he has worked as a psychologist, researcher, and administrator at various correctional facilities in the Correctional Service of Canada and as Psychologist-in-Chief for the Ontario Ministry of Community Safety and Correctional Services. Currently, he is a professor in the Psychology Department at the University of Saskatchewan, where he is also the Director of the Centre of Forensic Behavioural Science and Justice Studies. Dr Wormith's research activities have concentrated on the assessment, treatment, and therapeutic processes of offenders. He co-authored the Level of Service/Case Management Inventory (2004) with D. A. Andrews and J. Bonta, and participates internationally in research and training on risk assessment. He consults with the corrections departments in federal and provincial governments across Canada and serves in court as an expert witness on matters of offender assessment and treatment. He is on the editorial board of a number of criminal justice and psychology journals. Dr Wormith is a Fellow of the Canadian Psychological Association (CPA) and represents CPA on the National Associations Active in Criminal Justice. He is a recipient of the International Association of Correctional and Forensic Psychology's Edwin I. Megargee Distinguished Contribution Award and the American Psychological Association's Division 18 Leadership in Education Award.

Preface: Recidivism Risk Assessment in the 21st Century

John Monahan

The *Handbook of Recidivism Risk Assessment* could not be appearing at a more propitious time. Sentencing and parole authorities around the world are turning to behavioral science for guidance in triaging offenders into those who require rehabilitative interventions in institutional settings and those who can more effectively be treated in the community. Drs Singh, Kroner, Wormith, Desmarais, and Hamilton have gathered together an A-list of leading international scholars and practitioners to portray and probe the field of recidivism risk assessment. The possibilities occasioned by this book for cross-fertilization across instruments and across jurisdictions are difficult to exaggerate.

I will not attempt to summarize the myriad insights found between the covers of this remarkable book. Instead, let me briefly put three issues addressed in these chapters into the larger context of criminal sentencing: the theory of sentencing that animates or proscribes recourse to recidivism risk assessment, the diverse roles that recidivism risk assessment may play in sentencing, and conundrums that recur whenever recidivism risk informs sentencing (Monahan & Skeem, 2016).

The Role of Recidivism Risk Assessment in Hybrid Systems of Sentencing

Almost all jurisprudential scholars of sentencing distinguish between two broad and polar opposite approaches to the allocation of criminal punishment. One of these approaches is usually termed retributive and the other utilitarian. Adherents of the retributive approach believe that an offender's moral culpability for crime committed in the past should be the sole consideration in determining his or her punishment. In the best-known retributive theory, known as "just deserts," offenders should be punished "because they deserve it, and the severity of their punishment should be proportional to their degree of blameworthiness" (Frase, 2013, p. 8) for the crime they have committed in the past, and to nothing else.

In stark contrast, advocates of the utilitarian approach believe that punishment is justified solely by its ability to decrease future criminal acts by the offender or by deterring other would-be offenders from committing—or continuing to commit—crime.

Many legal scholars have argued that any workable theory of sentencing must address *both* retributive *and* utilitarian concerns, rather than just one of them. The most influential hybrid theory of sentencing is that developed by Norval Morris (1974) which he called "limiting retributivism." In Morris's theory, retributive principles can only set an upper (and perhaps also a lower) limit on the severity of punishment, and within this range of what he called "not undeserved" punishment, utilitarian concerns—such as the offender's risk of recidivism—can be taken into account.

The risk of recidivism has a central function in utilitarian theories of punishment, an important function (along with perceptions of blameworthiness) in hybrid theories of punishment, and no function (or a very limited one) in retributive theories of punishment.

The Roles of Recidivism Risk Assessment

Within the theoretical constraints described above lie three important roles for risk assessment in sentencing:

Informing Decisions Regarding the Imprisonment of Higher Risk Offenders

Risk assessment can provide an empirical estimate of whether an offender has a sufficiently high likelihood of again committing crime to justify a larger "dose" of incapacitation. That is, within a range of severity set by moral concerns about the criminal act of which the offender has been convicted, risk assessment can assist in determining whether, on utilitarian crime-control grounds, an offender should be sentenced to the upper bound of that range.

Informing Decisions Regarding the Supervised Release of Lower Risk Offenders

Risk assessment can provide an empirical estimate of whether an offender has a sufficiently low likelihood of again committing crime to justify an abbreviated period of incapacitation, supervised release (probation/parole), or no incapacitation at all. Within a range of severity set by moral concerns about the criminal act of which the offender has been convicted, risk assessment can assist in determining whether, on utilitarian crime-control grounds, an offender should be sentenced to the lower bound of that range.

Informing Decisions Designed to Reduce the Risk Posed by Offenders

Risk assessment can also inform correctional strategies to reduce an offender's level of risk, even if the length of a sentence is set by purely retributive concerns. Any valid tool can be used to identify higher risk offenders for more intensive interventions, placing others at appropriately lower levels of intervention. Programs that match the intensity of correctional interventions to offenders' risk level have been shown to reduce recidivism (Cohen, Lowenkamp, & VanBenschoten, 2016).

Risk assessment instruments differ in the sentencing goal(s) they are meant to fulfill: some are designed exclusively to predict recidivism (assess "risk" to fulfill Roles 1 and 2 above), whereas others are meant to inform risk reduction (assess "needs" to fulfill Role 3 above).

Recurring Conundrums When Recidivism Risk Informs Sentencing

Four difficult problems frequently accompany the introduction of recidivism risk assessment into the criminal sentencing process.

Conflating Risk and Blame

The task of assigning blame for an offender's past crime and the task of assessing an offender's risk for future crime are orthogonal aspects of sentencing. Dealing simultaneously with the independent concerns of blame and risk in sentencing is not unduly problematic when a given variable bears on both concerns to similar effect, e.g., when both concerns point in the direction of raising or both point in the direction of lowering the severity of a sentence otherwise imposed. But dealing with the separate concerns of blame for past crime and risk for future crime at the same time becomes problematic when a given variable bears importantly on one of the two concerns, but is irrelevant to the other. And dealing simultaneously with the orthogonal concerns of blame and risk becomes highly contested when a given variable bears on each of the two concerns, but to opposite effect.

First, consider variables that affect perceptions of blame and assessments of recidivism risk in similar ways. The clearest example of a variable that has comparable effects on perceptions of blame and on assessments of risk is involvement in crime. It has long been axiomatic in the field of risk assessment that past crime is the best predictor of future crime. All recidivism risk assessment instruments described in this book reflect this empirical truism.

Second, consider variables that affect either perceptions of blame or assessments of recidivism risk, but not both. Demographic and life history variables that characterize an offender may have significant predictive validity in assessing his or her likelihood of recidivism, but no bearing on the ascription of blame for the crime of which he or she was convicted. In terms of demography, race (Skeem & Lowenkamp, 2016), gender (Skeem, Monahan, & Lowenkamp, 2016), and (adult) age (Monahan, Skeem, & Lowenkamp, 2017) all correlate significantly with criminal recidivism. However, neither race nor gender nor (adult) age bear on an offender's blameworthiness for having committed crime in the past—as a class, offenders who are of one race are no more (and no less) blameworthy than offenders who are of another race, offenders who are women are no more (and no less) blameworthy than offenders who are men, and (adult) offenders of one age are no more (and no less) blameworthy than (adult) offenders who are of another age. The same is true of life history variables: educational attainment and employment status do not bear on an offender's blameworthiness for having committed crime. A high school drop-out is no more (and no less) blameworthy than a high school graduate when he or she decides to commit a crime. The same can be said of people with and without a job.

Finally, consider variables that affect perceptions of blame and assessments of risk in contrary ways. The clearest example of a variable that has contrary effects on perceptions of blame and on assessments of recidivism risk is combat-induced trauma. Numerous studies have found that combat-induced post-traumatic stress disorder (PTSD) is a significant risk factor for a soldier's future commission of serious violence to others in civilian life (e.g., Elbogen et al., 2014), and thus could serve as a valid risk factor for recidivism among offenders with combat-induced PTSD. According to the United States Supreme Court, however, such trauma could also function to mitigate the offender's blameworthiness for the commission of crime, and therefore could serve to reduce the severity of a criminal sentence otherwise given. In *Porter v. McCollum* (2009), the Court stated: "Our Nation as a long tradition of according leniency to veterans in recognition of their service. [T]he relevance of [the defendant's] extensive combat experience is [t]hat the jury might find mitigating the intense stress and mental and emotional toll that combat took on [the defendant]" (p. 44).

Group Data and Individual Inferences

One issue that has generated much controversy in the field of risk assessment in recent years is whether accurate inferences about an individual person—in this case, the recidivism risk of a convicted offender—can be drawn from data derived from groups of people (in this case, the recidivism risk that characterizes groups of convicted offenders). Some scholars have taken the position that "on the basis of empirical findings, statistical theory, and logic, it is clear that predictions of future offending cannot be achieved, with any degree of confidence, in the individual case" (Cooke & Michie, 2010, p. 259).

This view has been vigorously contested. For example, Hanson and Howard (2010) state that Cooke and Michie's (2010) argument that individual inferences cannot be derived from group data "if true, . . . would be a serious challenge to the applicability of any empirically based risk procedure to any individual for anything" (p. 277). Mossman (2015, p. 99) offers a medical analogy: "Suppose a 50-year-old man learns that half of people with his diagnosis die in five years. He would find this information very useful in deciding whether to purchase an annuity that would begin payouts only after he reached his 65th birthday."

The debate among scientists on the legitimacy of making individual inferences from group data appears to be subsiding. In the recent words of two eminent statisticians (Imrey & Dawid, 2015, p. 40):

> If groups of individuals with high and low propensities for violence recidivism can be distinguished, and courts act upon such distinctions, recidivism will decline to the extent that groups most prone to violence are incapacitated, and infringements upon those least so prone are minimized.

Assessing Risk or Reducing Risk?

Although, as the chapters of this book amply illustrate, a wealth of empirical guidance is available for assessing adult offenders' risk of recidivism, far less guidance is available for reducing that risk. Validated "causal" risk factors—i.e., variable risk factors that, when changed through intervention, can be shown to change recidivism risk—are in short supply. High quality adult correctional services, in the United States at least, are even more rare. Based on a cohort of California prisoners, Petersilia and Weisberg (2010) found that substance abuse treatment (of any sort) was offered to 10% of those with substance abuse problems, and basic anger control treatment was offered to one-quarter-of-one-percent of those with anger problems. "Evidence-based" treatment programs and principles are even more scarcely implemented in adult correctional settings. As Lipsey and Cullen (2007, p. 315) state: "The greatest obstacle to using rehabilitation treatment effectively to reduce criminal behavior is . . . a correctional system that does not use the research available and has no history of doing so."

Risk Assessment and Racial Disparity

In the United States, according to data from the Bureau of Justice Statistics (Carson, 2014), young (i.e., 18–19-year-old) black males are over nine times more likely than young white males to be imprisoned. As Frase (2013) has stated:

> Even when such disparity results from the application of seemingly appropriate, race-neutral sentencing criteria, it is still seen by many citizens as evidence of societal and criminal justice unfairness; such negative perceptions undermine the legitimacy of criminal laws and institutions of justice, making citizens less likely to obey the law and cooperate with law enforcement. (p. 210)

Does the use of recidivism risk assessment in sentencing affect racial disparities in imprisonment. Former U.S. Attorney General Eric Holder (2014) believes that it does: Although risk assessments "were crafted with the best of intentions, I am concerned that they may inadvertently undermine our efforts to ensure individualized and equal justice."

Whether risk assessment affects racial disparities in sentencing is an important empirical question. Risk assessment could exacerbate racial disparities in sentencing, as Holder hypothesizes. But risk assessment could also reduce or have no effect on disparities. Disparities associated with the use of risk assessment may vary as a function of both the baseline sentencing context and the risk assessment instrument chosen.

First, in terms of the baseline sentencing context, the question is "risk assessment compared to what?" The effect of risk assessment on disparities depends on what practices risk assessment is replacing. Common denominators include (a) judges' unstructured and informal consideration of offenders' likelihood of recidivism, which is less transparent, less consistent, and less accurate than evidence-based risk assessment, and (b) sentencing guidelines that heavily rely on criminal history and therefore heavily contribute to racial disparities.

Second, the effect of risk assessment on disparities may depend on the specific risk assessment instrument chosen. Any instrument used to inform sentencing must be shown to predict recidivism with similar accuracy across groups, i.e., the instrument must be free of predictive bias. However, given a pool of instruments that are free of predictive bias, some instruments will yield greater mean score differences between groups than others (Skeem & Lowenkamp, 2016). Much more research is needed to define the conditions under which risk assessment affects sentencing disparities. Studies are needed to determine, for example, how strongly different instruments correlate with race, which risk factors drive that correlation, and what (if anything) can be done to reduce that correlation without compromising predictive utility. If policymakers blindly eradicate risk factors from a tool because they are contentious, they risk reducing predictive utility and exacerbating the very racial disparities they seek to ameliorate.

Recidivism Risk Assessment in the 21st Century

Developments in sentencing theory that justify reliance upon recidivism risk assessment, changes in sentencing policy that emphasize identifying offenders at high risk or at low risk of recidivism or that emphasize how to reduce offenders' recidivism risk, and the resolution of several persistent conundrums will determine the degree of progress that can be expected in incorporating recidivism risk into criminal sentencing. The *Handbook of Recidivism Risk Assessment* will be an essential source in guiding these developments.

References

Carson, E. (2014). *Prisoners in 2013*. Washington, DC: Bureau of Justice Statistics. Retrieved from https://www.bjs.gov/content/pub/pdf/p13.pdf

Cohen, T., Lowenkamp, C., & VanBenschoten, S. (2016). Does change in risk matter? Examining whether changes in offender risk characteristics influence recidivism outcomes. *Criminology and Public Policy, 15*, 263–296. doi:10.1111/1745-9133.12190

Cooke, D. J., & Michie C. (2010). Limitations of diagnostic precision and predictive utility in the individual case: A challenge for forensic practice. *Law and Human Behavior, 34*, 259–264. doi:10.1007/s10979-009-9176-x

Elbogen, E., Johnson, S., Wagner, H., Sullivan, C., Taft, C., & Beckham, J. (2014). Violent behaviour and post-traumatic stress disorder in US Iraq and Afghanistan veterans. *British Journal of Psychiatry, 204*, 368–375. doi:10.1192/bjp.bp.113.134627

Frase, R. S. (2013). *Just sentencing: Principles and procedures for a workable system.* New York, NY: Oxford University Press.

Hanson, K. R., & Howard, P. D. (2010). Individual confidence intervals do not inform decision-makers about the accuracy of risk assessment evaluations. *Law and Human Behavior, 34,* 275–281. doi:10.1007/s10979-010-9227-3

Holder, E. (2014). Attorney General Eric Holder Speaks at the National Association of Criminal Defense Lawyers 57th Annual Meeting. Retrieved from http://www.justice.gov/opa/speech/attorney-general-eric-holder-speaks-national-association-criminal-defense-lawyers-57th

Imrey, P., & Dawid, P. (2015). A commentary on statistical assessment of violence recidivism risk. *Statistics and Public Policy, 2,* 25–42. doi:10.1080/2330443X.2015.1029338

Lipsey, M., & Cullen, F. (2007). The effectiveness of correctional rehabilitation: A review of systematic reviews. *Annual Review of Law and Social Science, 3,* 97–320. doi:10.1146/annurev.lawsocsci.3.081806.112833

Monahan, J., & Skeem, J. L. (2016). Risk assessment in criminal sentencing. *Annual Review of Clinical Psychology, 12,* 489–513. doi:10.1146/annurev-clinpsy-021815-092945

Monahan, J., Skeem, J., & Lowenkamp, C. (2017). Age, risk assessment, and sanctioning: Overestimating the old, underestimating the young. *Law and Human Behavior.* Advance online publication. doi:10.1037/lhb0000233

Morris, N. (1974). *The future of imprisonment.* Chicago, IL: University of Chicago Press.

Mossman, D. (2015). From group data to useful probabilities: The relevance of actuarial risk assessment in individual instances. *Journal of the American Academy of Psychiatry and the Law, 43,* 93–102.

Petersilia, J., & Weisberg, R. (2010). The dangers of pyrrhic victories against mass incarceration. *Daedelus, 130,* 124–133. doi:10.1162/DAED_a_00028

Porter v. McCollum, 558 U.S. 30 (2009).

Skeem, J. L., & Lowenkamp, C. (2016). Risk, race, and recidivism: Predictive bias and disparate impact. *Criminology, 54,* 680–712. doi:10.1111/1745-9125.12123

Skeem, J., Monahan, J., & Lowenkamp, C. (2016). Gender, risk assessment, and sanctioning: The cost of treating women like men. *Law and Human Behavior, 40,* 580–593. doi:10.1037/lhb0000206

Part I

Introduction

1

Performance of Recidivism Risk Assessment Instruments in U.S. Correctional Settings*

Sarah L. Desmarais, Kiersten L. Johnson, and Jay P. Singh

The rates of correctional supervision and incarceration in the United States are staggering. To demonstrate, almost seven million people—or one in 35 adults—were under the supervision of correctional systems in the United States at the end of 2013 (Glaze & Kaeble, 2014). This includes approximately one in 51 adults on probation or parole and one in 110 adults incarcerated in prison or jail. These are rates higher than seen anywhere else in the world. As a point of comparison, the rate of incarceration in the United States is more than four times the rate of incarceration found in the majority of the world's countries (Walmsley, 2013). In fact, even though the United States has less than 5% of the global population, it has close to one-quarter of the world's prisoners (Walmsley, 2013). Clearly, there is a pressing need for efforts to reduce mass incarceration in the United States, including treatment to reduce recidivism and diversion of lower risk offenders to alternative settings and punishments. Indeed, not all offenders are at equal risk of recidivating (Langan & Levin, 2002) and, accordingly, may not require the same levels of supervision and intervention (Monahan & Skeem, 2016). Additionally, in contrast with the traditional "one-size-fits-all" criminal justice approach, research shows that the most effective strategies for reducing recidivism are those delivered to offenders at greater risk of recidivism that target individual needs (Andrews & Bonta, 2010). Consequently, psychologists and other professionals working in U.S. correctional agencies face mounting pressures to differentiate between offenders at greater and lower risk of recidivism and to guide decisions regarding treatment and supervision (Jung, Brown, Ennis, & Ledi, 2015; Monahan & Skeem, 2016).

In recent years, risk assessment has come to be recognized as a key component of criminal justice reform and evidence-based corrections in the United States (Casey, Warren, & Elek, 2011). There is overwhelming evidence that risk assessments completed using structured approaches produce estimates that are more reliable and more accurate than unstructured risk assessments (Ægisdóttir et al., 2006; Grove, Zald, Lebow, Snitz, & Nelson, 2000). Risk assessments completed using structured approaches also have been shown to lead to better public safety outcomes (Mamalian, 2011). For these reasons, instruments designed to predict risk of general recidivism, including committing a new crime and violating conditions of probation or parole, are increasingly required and being implemented in correctional agencies in the United States (Miller & Maloney, 2013; Monahan & Skeem, 2014; Monahan & Skeem, 2016). Despite the many different risk assessment instruments available, relatively little is known regarding the performance, and inter-rater reliability and predictive validity specifically, of recidivism risk assessments completed on adult offenders in U.S. correctional settings. Though there have been several high-quality reviews of risk assessment instruments to date, the ability

Handbook of Recidivism Risk/Needs Assessment Tools, First Edition. Edited by Jay P. Singh, Daryl G. Kroner, J. Stephen Wormith, Sarah L. Desmarais, and Zachary Hamilton.
© 2018 John Wiley & Sons, Ltd. Published 2018 by John Wiley & Sons, Ltd.

of their findings to inform decisions regarding which recidivism risk assessment instrument to implement in U.S. correctional settings is limited in three crucial ways.

First, these reviews have focused primarily on instruments designed to predict specific forms of recidivism, notably violent or sexually violent offending, rather than predicting general recidivism more broadly (e.g., Fazel, Singh, Doll, & Grann, 2012; Gendreau, Goggin, & Little, 1996; Hanson & Morton-Bourgon, 2009; Singh, Grann, & Fazel, 2011; Tully, Chou, & Browne, 2013; Yang, Wong, & Coid, 2010). Violent and sexually violent offenders, however, comprise a relatively small proportion of the U.S. inmate population overall (Carson & Sabol, 2012). As such, the assessment of general recidivism risk is a more common task. Second, prior reviews have included a relatively short list of risk assessment instruments, typically fewer than 10, rather than including a comprehensive list of risk assessment instruments that are being used in practice. Third, and finally, prior reviews have examined the performance of risk assessments in studies conducted in multiple countries, with the predominance of studies conducted in Canada and the United Kingdom. Assessment instruments—risk assessment or otherwise—do not have reliability and validity that are transportable across populations and settings (AERA, APA, & NCME, 2014). There may be meaningful differences between offenders, assessors, and services in U.S. correctional settings and those in other jurisdictions that affect the reliability and validity of risk assessments (Monahan & Skeem, 2016).

To advance knowledge, we conducted a systematic review of studies conducted in correctional settings in the United States that have examined the predictive validity of assessments completed on adult offenders using instruments designed to predict risk of general recidivism. Our goal was to synthesize findings of the American validation research to help policymakers, psychologists, and other professionals working in U.S. correctional settings choose from among the potentially overwhelming list of risk assessment instruments available. In the sections that follow, we discuss characteristics of risk assessment instruments, samples, and studies that may affect the performance of assessments, and that, as such, we will examine in our review.

Characteristics of Risk Assessment Instruments

Recidivism risk assessment instruments may be distinguished in terms of their approach, item type, and item content. First, there are two broad categories that distinguish between approaches used by risk assessment instruments: actuarial and structured professional judgment. The actuarial approach represents a mechanical model of risk assessment in which offenders are scored on a series of items that were most strongly associated with recidivism in the development samples. Then, total scores are cross-referenced with actuarial risk tables (Hilton, Harris, & Rice, 2006). In contrast, the structured professional judgment approach guides assessors to consider a set number of factors that are empirically and theoretically associated with the outcome of interest. Though individual items are scored, assessors ultimately make a categorical judgment of risk level (e.g., low, moderate, or high) based on their professional judgment rather than using total scores (Guy, Packer, & Warnken, 2012). Risk assessment instruments also can be differentiated by the type and content of their items, such as risk, protective, static, and dynamic factors. Risk factors are characteristics that are associated with increases in the likelihood of recidivism, whereas protective factors are characteristics associated with decreases in the likelihood of recidivism (de Ruiter & Nicholls, 2011). Risk and protective factors can either be static or dynamic in nature. Static factors are historical (e.g., history of antisocial behavior) or otherwise unchangeable characteristics (e.g., sex, race/ethnicity), whereas dynamic factors are characteristics that may change over time and/or when targeted in treatment (e.g., substance abuse) (Douglas & Skeem, 2005).

Characteristics of Samples and Studies

Beyond the characteristics of the instruments, performance of risk assessments may differ as a function of the characteristics of the research samples and study designs. For instance, offender race/ethnicity and sex are potentially important sources of assessment bias (Scurich & Monahan, 2016). In fact, Former U.S. Attorney General Eric Holder recently spoke *against* the use of risk assessments to inform sentencing decisions due to concerns over bias against racial/ethnic and other minorities (Holder, 2014). Some reviews of personality assessment tools and violence risk assessment instruments support his perspective, finding that assessments may be more accurate for White offenders compared to those of other racial/ethnic backgrounds (Leistico, Salekin, DeCoster, & Rogers, 2008; Singh et al., 2011). However, other studies have failed to identify such racial/ethnic biases (e.g., Guy, Edens, Anthony, & Douglas, 2005). No reviews, to our knowledge, have explored racial/ethnic biases in assessments of risk for general recidivism. With respect to offender sex, meta-analytic research suggests that we may expect risk assessment instruments to differ in their predictive validity for male compared to female offenders (Leistico et al., 2008). Again, however, the research is mixed (e.g., Holtfreter & Cupp, 2007; Singh et al., 2011; Smith, Cullen, & Latessa, 2009). Given the higher proportion of female prisoners in the United States (8.8%) compared to other jurisdictions, such as the United Kingdom (5.4%) and Canada (5.1%) (Walmsley, 2012), and the overrepresentation of racial/ethnic minorities among U.S. inmates (Carson & Sabol, 2012), there is a need to examine findings across studies conducted in U.S. correctional settings.

In addition to the characteristics of the offenders, there are aspects of the design of the studies themselves that may impact the reliability and validity of assessments completed using the recidivism risk assessment tools under investigation. For instance, much of the extant knowledge stems from research-based studies, in which researchers can carefully train and monitor assessors. However, these conditions are not necessarily present or realistic in routine practice (Desmarais et al., 2012; Desmarais, Van Dorn, Telford, Petrila, & Coffey, 2012; Douglas, Otto, Desmarais, & Borum, 2012; Vincent, Guy, Fusco, & Gershenson, 2012). Though there has been considerable discussion regarding the reliability of risk assessments completed in routine practice compared to the reliability of those completed in research studies, we are not aware of any research reviews that have specifically examined the predictive validity of risk assessments—predicting general recidivism or other outcomes—completed in the context of research versus routine practice.

The Current Review

Herein we report findings of a systematic review of the U.S. research examining the validity of assessments completed using instruments designed to predict general recidivism among adult offenders. We sought to provide a comprehensive summary of the state of science and practice in the United States, acknowledging that, by design, our review focused on the context of the American penal system. Differences in the characteristics of offenders in the United States compared to those of offenders in other countries, combined with the remarkably high rate of incarceration in the United States, suggested the need for a review of the American empirical evidence and reflected recent calls for such data from clinicians tasked with conducting risk assessments in U.S. correctional settings and policymakers alike (Holder, 2014). Our specific aims were to: (1) identify and describe the characteristics and content of risk assessment instruments designed to predict general recidivism that have been validated in the United States; (2) summarize the characteristics of the studies that have been conducted in U.S. correctional settings; and (3) synthesize the findings regarding the inter-rater reliability and predictive validity of risk assessments completed using these instruments on adult offenders in the United States.

Method

Review Protocol

We used the Preferred Reporting Items for Systematic Reviews and Meta-Analyses (PRISMA) Statement (Moher, Liberati, Tetzlaff, & Altman, 2009), a 27-item checklist of review characteristics, to enable a transparent and consistent reporting of results.

Search Strategy

Identification of recidivism risk assessment instruments

We identified risk assessment instruments designed to predict the likelihood of general recidivism, including new offenses and the violation of probation or parole conditions, in adult offenders by searching PsycINFO, the U.S. National Criminal Justice Reference Service Abstracts, and Google using combinations of the following keywords: *risk assessment, instrument, tool, general, recidivism, offending, parole violation,* and *prediction.* We located additional instruments using references in related systematic reviews (e.g., Fazel et al., 2012; Gendreau et al., 1996), surveys of clinicians (e.g., Singh et al., 2014; Viljoen, McLachlan, & Vincent, 2010) and through discussion with risk assessment experts. We restricted the search to instruments whose calibration studies (for actuarial instruments) or manuals (for structured professional judgment instruments) had been published by December 31, 2012. We excluded instruments if they: (a) were designed to predict specific forms of recidivism or criminal behavior (e.g., violence, sexual violence, or domestic violence); (b) were intended for guiding the assessment of juvenile offenders; (c) had not been validated in the United States; or (d) were developed for use in a specific jurisdiction or institution and had not been implemented elsewhere.

We also excluded violence risk assessment instruments (e.g., Historical, Clinical, Risk Management-20, Webster, Douglas, Eaves, & Hart, 1997; Violence Risk Appraisal Guide, Quinsey, Harris, Rice, & Cormier, 2006); clinical and behavioral inventories (e.g., Beck Depression Inventory, Beck, Steer, & Carbin, 1988; Lifestyle Criminality Screening Form, Walters, White, & Denney, 1995; Novaco Anger Scale, Novaco, 1994); personality assessment tools (e.g., Personality Assessment Inventory, Morey, 1991; Psychopathy Checklist-Revised, Hare, 2003;); and criminal thinking scales (e.g., TCU Criminal Thinking Scales, Knight, Garner, Simpson, Morey, & Flynn, 2006; Psychological Inventory of Criminal Thinking, Walters, 1995). Though often used to aid in the risk assessment process, these instruments were not designed to assess risk of general recidivism per se. Moreover, systematic reviews of their predictive validity have been reported elsewhere (Gendreau et al., 1996; Singh et al., 2011; Walters, 2012).

Using these inclusion and exclusion criteria, we identified the 19 assessment instruments or systems designed for predicting risk of general recidivism that are listed in Table 1.1. We also identified 47 instruments designed for use in specific jurisdictions or institutions. Detailed review of the latter is beyond the scope of the current analysis.

Table 1.1 Characteristics of 19 Recidivism Risk Assessment Instruments Implemented and Validated in the United States

		Characteristics			
Instruments	**k**	**Number of Items**	**Target Population**	**Target Outcome**	**Administration Time (minutes)**
Correctional Offender Management Profile for Alternative Sanctions (COMPAS; Brennan et al., 2009)	3	70	All Offenders	Any Recidivism	10–60
Inventory of Offender Risks, Needs, and Strengths (IORNS; Miller, 2006)	1	130	All Offenders	Any Recidivism	15–20
Level of Service Inventory–Revised (LSI-R; Andrews & Bonta, 1995)	25	54	All Offenders	Any Recidivism	30–40
Level of Service Inventory–Revised: Screening Version (LSI-R:SV; Andrews & Bonta, 1998)	2	8	All Offenders	Any Recidivism	10–15
Ohio Risk Assessment System-Pretrial Assessment Tool (ORAS-PAT; Latessa, Smith, Lemke, Makarios, & Lowenkamp, 2009)	3	7	All Offenders	New Offenses	10–15
Ohio Risk Assessment System-Community Supervision Tool (ORAS-CST; Latessa et al., 2009)	1	35	All Offenders	New Offenses	30–45
Ohio Risk Assessment System-Community Supervision Screening Tool (ORAS- CSST; Latessa et al., 2009)	1	4	All Offenders	New Offenses	5–10
Ohio Risk Assessment System-Prison Intake Tool (ORAS-PIT; Latessa et al., 2009)	1	31	All Offenders	New Offenses	—
Ohio Risk Assessment System-Reentry Tool (ORAS-RT; Latessa et al., 2009)	1	20	All Offenders	New Offenses	—
Federal Post Conviction Risk Assessment (PCRA; Johnson, Lowenkamp, VanBenschoten, & Robinson, 2011)	2	30	All Offenders	Any Recidivism	15–30
Risk Management System (RMS; Dow, Jones, & Mott, 2005)	2	65	All Offenders	New Offenses	—
Self-Appraisal Questionnaire (SAQ; Loza, 2005)	2	72	All Offenders	New Offenses	15
Salient Factor Score: Salient Factor Score-1974 Version (SFS74; Hoffman & Beck, 1974)	3	9	Parolees	New Offenses	—
Salient Factor Score-1976 Version (SFS76; Hoffman & Beck, 1980)	4	7	Parolees	New Offenses	—
Salient Factor Score-1981 Version (SFS81; Hoffman, 1983)	8	6	Parolees	New Offenses	—
Service Planning Instrument-Women (SPIn-W; Millson, Robinson, & Van Dieten, 2010)	2	100	All Offenders	New Offenses	—

(Continued)

Table 1.1 (Continued)

			Characteristics		
Instruments	**k**	**Number of Items**	**Target Population**	**Target Outcome**	**Administration Time (minutes)**
Static Risk and Offender Needs Guide (STRONG; Barnoski & Drake, 2007)[a]	1	26	All Offenders	New Offenses	—
Wisconsin Risk and Needs (WRN; Baird, Heinz, & Bemus, 1979)	9	53	All Offenders	New Offenses	—
Wisconsin Risk and Needs-Revised (WRN-R; Eisenberg, Bryl, & Fabelo, 2009)	1	52	All Offenders	New Offenses	—

Notes: k = number of samples; All Offenders = inmates, probationers, and/or parolees; New Offenses = new charge, arrest, conviction, or incarceration; Violations = violations of conditions of probation or parole; Any Recidivism = new offenses or violations; Time = as reported in the instrument manual; – Data not provided.
a)   The STRONG includes three parts; table values reflect only the first part, which is used to assess risk of recidivism.

Identification of U.S. validation studies

We identified studies conducted in the United States investigating the predictive validity of the 19 recidivism risk assessment instruments through the same search engines and secondary sources as above, using both the acronyms and full names of the instruments as search criteria (see Figure 1.1). Investigations published in peer-reviewed journals were considered for inclusion, as were government reports, Master's theses, and doctoral dissertations. We included studies if their titles, abstracts, or methods sections described evaluations of validity in predicting general recidivism, including new offenses and violations of probation or parole conditions, conducted in U.S. correctional settings. When multiple instruments were administered to the same participants, we extracted predictive validity estimates for each instrument separately. When samples overlapped, we included the predictive validity estimate from the sample with the most participants to avoid double-counting. When predictive validity estimates were reported for more than one outcome, we included the estimate from the most sensitive outcome; for example, if a study reported predictive validity estimates for both arrest and incarceration, we included the arrest estimate in our analyses. We excluded studies if they only examined predictive validity of select items or scales of an instrument.

Using this search strategy, we filtered an initial total of 173 records to a final count of 53 studies (*k* samples = 72), including 26 journal articles (*k* = 30), 16 government reports (*k* = 31), two master's theses (*k* = 2), and nine doctoral dissertations (*k* = 9). References for the 53 included studies are marked with an asterisk in the reference list. As no validation studies investigating the Correctional Assessment and Intervention System (National Council on Crime and Delinquency, 2006), Community Risk/Needs Management Scale (Motiuk & Porporino, 1989), Dynamic Factor Identification and Analysis (Brown & Motiuk, 2005), Level of Service/Case Management Inventory (Andrews, Bonta, & Wormith, 2004), Level of Service/Risk-Need-Responsivity (Andrews, Bonta, & Wormith, 2008), Level of Service Inventory (Andrews, 1982), Offender Group Reconviction Scale (Copas & Marshall, 1998), Offender Assessment System (HM Prison Service and National Probation Directorate, 2001), Recidivism Risk Assessment Scales (Van der Knaap & Alberda, 2009), Risk of Reconviction (Bakker, Riley, & O'Malley, 1999), Salient Factor Score–1998 (United States Parole Commission, 2003),

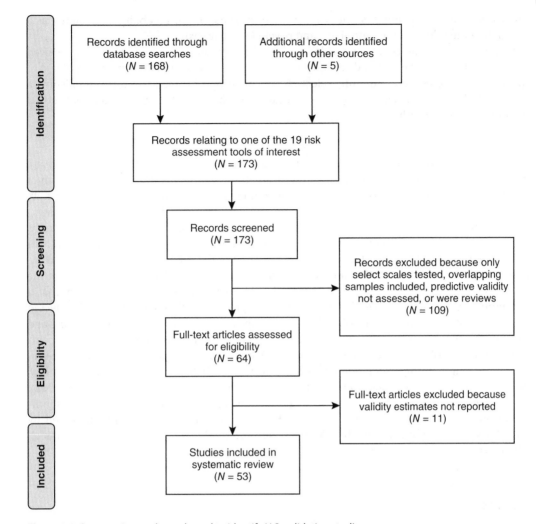

Figure 1.1 Systematic search conducted to identify U.S. validation studies.

Statistical Information of Recidivism Scale (Nuffield, 1982), or Service Planning Instrument (Van Dieten & Robinson, 2007) met our inclusion criteria at the time of data analysis, we excluded these instruments from further review.

Data extraction
Three research assistants enrolled in a doctoral program in psychology extracted the following information from each study: (1) demographics and design characteristics, including characteristics of the study samples (population, sample size, sex, race/ethnicity, age, psychiatric diagnoses); the assessment process (setting, timing, format, assessor, sources of information used to administer, amount of time needed to administer and score); and study designs and procedures (geographic location, research or practice context, temporal design, outcome, length of follow-up); (2) characteristics of the risk assessment instruments (assessment approach, number of items, types of items, domains measured, intended population, and predicted outcome); and (3) performance of the risk assessments (estimates of inter-rater reliability and

predictive validity). Where possible, we collected information on reliability and validity as a function of offender sex, race/ethnicity, and psychiatric diagnosis.

The research assistants were provided with a standardized extraction sheet and received training in its use by the first and second author. As a measure of quality control, 11 (20.8%) of the included studies were randomly selected and coded by all three assistants, establishing a high level of inter-rater reliability (κ = .88; Landis & Koch, 1977). Disagreements were settled by consensus of the authors.

Data analysis

First, sample, study design, and instrument characteristics were descriptively analyzed using measures of central tendency and dispersion parameters. Second, the item type and content of the instruments was summarized. Third, median inter-rater reliability and predictive validity estimates for total scores and risk classifications were calculated and compared across instruments, where possible. Predictive validity was assessed for any recidivism, new offenses only, and violations only as outcomes. Extracted predictive validity estimates included the area under the receiver operating characteristic curve (AUC), the point-biserial correlation coefficient (r_{pb}), the odds ratio (OR), and Somer's d, the indices most commonly reported in the field (Singh, Desmarais, & Van Dorn, 2013). Briefly, AUC represents the probability that a randomly selected recidivist would have received a higher risk rating than a randomly selected non-recidivist; r_{pb} represents the direction and strength of association between risk rating and recidivism; OR represents the ratio of the odds of a lower risk rating in those who did not recidivate to the odds of a higher classification in those who did; and Somer's d represents the direction and strength of the association between an ordinal predictor (e.g., estimate of risk as low, moderate, or high) and a dichotomous outcome (e.g., recidivating vs. not) (see Singh, 2013). A supplemental table providing guidance regarding benchmarks and equivalency across indices of predictive validity is available online. Finally, subgroup analyses were conducted by offender sex, race/ethnicity, psychiatric diagnosis, and study context (research or practice), when possible.

Results

Characteristics and Content of Instruments

Table 1.1 describes the characteristics of instruments included in this review. The number of items ranged widely across instruments, from four for the ORAS-CSST to 130 for the IORNS, with an average of 41.00 (SD = 35.08, Range = 4–130). All instruments were intended for use across offender populations, with the exception of the SFS74, SFS76, and SFS81, which were intended for use with parolees, specifically. Most (n instruments = 14, 73.7%) were designed to assess risk of new offenses, excluding violations. Estimated administration time was reported in the manuals of about half of the instruments (n = 9, 47.4%) and when reported, ranged from 5–10 minutes for the ORAS-CSST up to 60 minutes for the COMPAS. All instruments used the actuarial approach to risk assessment.

The type and content of items included in the 19 recidivism risk assessment instruments are summarized in Table 1.2. Only two instruments, the IORNS and the SPIn-W, included protective factors; all others included risk factors exclusively. The majority of instruments (n = 15, 78.9%) included a combination of static and dynamic factors, with the exception of the SFS instruments and the STRONG, both of which only included static factors. None of the instruments were comprised uniquely of dynamic factors. All instruments included

Table 1.2 Type and Content of Items Included in the 19 Recidivism Risk Assessment Instruments Implemented and Validated in the United States

Instruments	Types				Content Domains									
	Risk	Protective	Static	Dynamic	Attitudes	Associates/ Peers	Antisocial Behavior	Personality Problems	Relationships	Work/School	Leisure Activities	Substance Use Problems	Mental Health Problems	Housing Status
COMPAS	X		X	X	X	X	X	X	X	X	X	X	X	X
IORNS	X	X	X	X	X	X	X	X	X	X		X	X	
LSI-R	X		X	X	X	X	X	X	X	X	X	X	X	X
LSI:SV	X		X	X	X	X	X		X	X		X	X	
ORAS-PAT	X		X	X			X			X		X		X
ORAS-CST	X		X	X	X	X	X	X	X	X	X	X		X
ORAS-CSST	X		X	X		X	X			X		X		
ORAS-PIT	X		X	X		X	X	X	X	X	X	X	X	X
ORAS-RT	X		X	X	X		X	X	X	X		X	X	
PCRA	X		X	X	X	X	X		X	X		X		
RMS	X		X	X	X	X	X	X	X	X		X	X	X
SAQ	X		X	X	X	X	X	X				X		
SFS74	X		X	X			X			X		X		X
SFS76	X		X	X			X			X		X		
SFS81	X		X	X			X					X		
SPIn-W	X	X	X	X	X	X	X		X	X	X	X	X	X
STRONG	X		X	X	X		X					X		
WRN	X		X	X	X	X	X		X	X		X	X	
WRN-R	X		X	X	X	X	X		X	X		X	X	

items assessing history of antisocial behavior and substance use problems. Items assessing leisure activities, in contrast, were included relatively infrequently (*n* instruments = 5, 26.3%). Overall, the COMPAS and the LSI-R included items that captured the most content domains. The ORAS-CST, ORAS-PIT, RMS and SPIn-W evaluated all but one of the 10 domains; the exception varied for each instrument (see Table 1.2). The SFS81 and STRONG instruments considered the fewest of the domains, at two each.

Sample and Study Characteristics

Characteristics of the 72 included samples can be found in Table 1.3. Risk assessments were completed by professionals in correctional settings for over three-quarters of the samples (81.9%); the remainder were conducted by the researchers (15.3%) or self-administered (2.8%). Assessments were most often completed in prison (27.8%) or community corrections (37.5%) settings, but also were conducted in jail (9.7%), a clinic or hospital (4.2%), or at other settings (5.6%). Setting was unstated or unclear for the remaining 11 samples (15.3%). In terms of timing, approximately one-third of samples (36.1%) included assessments conducted during community supervision, one-fourth of samples included assessments completed prior to release (26.4%), and the remaining reported assessments conducted either prior to incarceration (11.1%) or upon admission (9.7%). Timing was unstated or unclear for the remaining 12 samples (16.7%). File reviews were used to complete assessments in 24 samples (33.3%), interviews in 12 samples (16.7 %), and offender self-report in two samples (2.8%).

More than two-thirds of samples (69.4%) were investigated using a prospective study design. The average length of follow-up was almost two years (*M* = 23.5 months, *SD* = 6.3, Range = 6-138). Samples were most frequently drawn from Midwestern states (37.5%) followed by southwestern and northeastern states (11.1% each). For the majority of samples (69.4%) any recidivism as the outcome; roughly one-quarter (26.4%) reported on a variety of recidivism outcomes; and the remainder (18.1%) focused specifically on violations. The operational definition of recidivism varied, but arrest was used most frequently (30.6%), followed by conviction (12.5%), incarceration (9.7%), revocation of probation or parole (4.2%), and charge (2.8%). Assessments for the majority of samples (65.3%) were conducted in the context of routine practice rather than for the purposes of research. Nearly one-third of samples (30.6%) were from studies conducted by an author of the tool under investigation. For five instruments—the IORNS, the PCRA, the ORAS instruments, the STRONG, and the WRN-R—all studies included in our review were completed by an author of the instrument under investigation. For another three instruments—the RMS, the COMPAS, and the SFS family of instruments—at least half of the studies were completed by an author of the instrument under investigation.

More than one-third of samples (40.3%) comprised inmates and roughly one-quarter (22.2%) comprised probationers; the remainder included either parolees only (11.1%), inmates and parolees (6.9%), or probationers and parolees (11.1%). Offender legal status was not reported in six samples (8.3%). The average sample size after attrition was 5,032 (*SD* = 12599; Range = 49–51,648). The average offender age at the time of risk assessment was 33.5 years (*SD* = 10.0). In samples where sex was reported (83.3%), the majority of offenders (85.5%) were male. In samples where race/ethnicity was reported (76.4%), almost two-thirds of offenders (60.8%) were White and close to one-third (28.3%) were Black, with 13.6% identified as Hispanic. Psychiatric diagnoses were very rarely reported: Only five studies reported on the prevalence of major mental disorders, substance use disorders, or personality disorders in their samples. Each of these studies used different diagnostic categories, precluding comparisons of findings across subgroups.

Table 1.3 Characteristics of 72 Samples Investigating the Predictive Validity of Recidivism Risk Assessment Instruments in the United States

Category	Group	Number of $k = 72$ (%)
Assessment process		
Risk assessor	Researcher	11 (15.3)
	Professional	59 (81.9)[a]
	Self-administered	2 (2.8)[b]
Risk assessment setting	Jail	7 (9.7)
	Prison	20 (27.8)
	Clinic/Hospital	3 (4.2)
	Community	27 (37.5)
	Other	4 (5.6)
	Unstated/Unclear	11 (15.3)
Timing of risk assessment	Pre-incarceration	8 (11.1)
	At admission	7 (9.7)
	Pre-release	19 (26.4)
	During community supervision	26 (36.1)
	Unstated/Unclear	12 (16.7)
Source of information	File review	24 (33.3)
	Interview	12 (16.7)
	Self-report	2 (2.8)
	Mixed	18 (25.0)
	Unstated/Unclear	16 (22.2)
Study design		
Study context	Research	25 (34.7)
	Practice	47 (65.3)
Temporal design	Prospective	50 (69.4)
	Retrospective	22 (30.6)
Geographical region	Northwest	2 (2.8)
	Southwest	8 (11.1)
	Midwest	27 (37.5)
	Northeast	8 (11.1)
	Southeast	5 (6.9)
	Non-continental	1 (1.4)
	Mixture	1 (1.4)
	Unstated/Unclear	20 (27.8)
Population	Inmates (pre-release)	29 (40.3)
	Probationers	16 (22.2)
	Parolees	8 (11.1)
	Inmates + parolees	5 (6.9)
	Probationers + parolees	8 (11.1)
	Other	6 (8.3)

(Continued)

Table 1.3 (Continued)

Category	Group	Number of k = 72 (%)
Type of outcome	General recidivism	50 (69.4)
	Violation/Breach of conditions	13 (18.1)
	Mixed	19 (26.4)
Length of follow-up (months)	Mean (SD)[d]	23.5 (6.3)
Source of outcome detection	Arrest	22 (30.6)
	Charge	2 (2.8)
	Conviction	9 (12.5)
	Incarceration	7 (9.7)
	Violation of terms	3 (4.2)
	Mixed	29 (40.3)
Sample demographics[c]		
Sample size after attrition	Mean (SD)	5,032 (12,599)
Male participants (per sample)	Mean (SD)	3,256 (8,965)
White participants (per sample)	Mean (SD)	1,879 (6,148)
Black participants (per sample)	Mean (SD)	906 (2,524)
Hispanic participants (per sample)	Mean (SD)	685 (1,792)
Age at risk assessment (in years)	Mean (SD)[d]	33.5 (10.0)

Notes: k = number of samples; *SD* = standard deviation. Percentages may not sum to exactly 100% due to rounding.
a) Correctional officer (k = 35, 48.6%), parole service associate (k = 2, 2.8%), probation officer (k = 1, 1.4%), other trained staff (k = 14, 19.4%), unstated/unclear (k = 7, 9.7%).
b) The SAQ, the only included instrument designed to be self-administered, was not be administered by either a researcher or professional.
c) Of those eight (11.1%) samples for which demographic characteristics were reported for samples before participant attrition, five (6.9%) had more than 25% attrition during follow-up (Dow et al., 2005; Fass, Heilbrun, DeMatteo, & Fretz, 2008; Holland, Holt, Levi, & Beckett, 1983; Miller, 2006; Millson et al., 2010).
d) Fixed-effects mean.

Performance of Recidivism Risk Assessment Instruments

Inter-rater reliability

Inter-rater reliability was evaluated in only two studies that met inclusion criteria, one examining the LSI-R (Simourd, 2006) and the other, the LSI-R:SV (Walters, 2011). In both studies, inter-rater reliability was excellent: 90% agreement and intra-class correlation coefficient = .80, respectively. Assessments in these studies were conducted by professionals rather than research assistants, providing strong evidence of inter-rater reliability in the field, specifically.

Predictive validity

Table 1.4 presents the median validity estimates by instrument for the prediction of any recidivism (i.e., new offenses and/or violations), collapsed across total scores and risk classifications. Overall, no one instrument stood out as producing more accurate assessments than the others, with validity varying with the indicator reported. Specifically, the instruments that produced the risk assessments with the highest AUCs were the STRONG, SPIn-W, and PCRA.

Table 1.4 Predictive Validity Estimates Produced by Total Scores or Risk Classifications for Any Recidivism

| | Predictive Validity Estimates | | | | | | | | | | | |
| | AUC | | | r_{pb} | | | OR | | | Somer's *d* | | |
Instruments	K	Mdn	IQR	k	Mdn	IQR	k	Mdn	IQR	k	Mdn	IQR
COMPAS	3	0.67	0.64–0.69	1	0.31	—	1	1.3	—	—	—	—
LSI-R	5	0.64	0.60–0.71	21	0.25	0.11–0.28	6	1.10	1.04–1.09	2	0.26	0.23–0.28
LSI:SV	1	0.57	—	1	0.27	—	—	—	—	—	—	—
ORAS-PAT	—	—	—	5	0.24	0.22–0.27	—	—	—	—	—	—
ORAS-CST	—	—	—	1	0.37	—	—	—	—	—	—	—
ORAS-CSST	—	—	—	1	0.38	—	—	—	—	—	—	—
ORAS-PIT	—	—	—	1	0.36	—	—	—	—	—	—	—
ORAS-RT	—	—	—	1	0.36	—	—	—	—	—	—	—
PCRA	2	0.71	0.71–0.71	—	—	—	—	—	—	—	—	—
RMS	3	0.67	0.64–0.94	—	—	—	—	—	—	—	—	—
SFS74	—	—	—	—	—	—	—	—	—	2	0.34	0.32–0.36
SFS76	—	—	—	1	0.40	—	—	—	—	2	0.36	0.34–0.37
SFS81	—	—	—	4	0.44	0.39–0.46	2	3.00	0.76–5.23	5	0.41	0.38–0.52
SPIn-W	1	0.73	—	—	—	—	1	0.91	—	—	—	—
STRONG	1	0.74	—	—	—	—	—	—	—	—	—	—
WRN	3	0.67	0.61–0.74	6	0.19	0.10–0.21	1	0.98	—	—	—	—
WRN-R	1	0.66	—	—	—	—	—	—	—	—	—	—

Notes: k = number of samples; *Mdn* = median; *IQR* = inter-quartile range; AUC = area under the receiver operating characteristic curve; r_{pb} = point-biserial correlation coefficient; OR = odds ratio. Estimates were calculated using either total scores or risk classifications.

The instruments that produced the risk assessments with the highest r_{pb} values were the SFS81 and the SFS76. The instrument that produced the risk assessments with the highest OR was the SFS81. Finally, the instrument that produced the risk assessments with the highest Somer's *d* value was the SFS81 (see Table 1.4).

Table 1.5 presents the median validity estimates for total scores in predicting any recidivism, new offenses, and violations, in turn. Validity varied by outcome and indicator. For any recidivism (i.e., new offenses and/or violations), for example, the instrument that produced the risk assessments with the highest OR for any recidivism was the SFS81, whereas the instruments that produced the risk assessments with the highest r_{pb} values were the SFS76 and SFS91 (see Table 1.5). For new offenses, the instrument that produced the risk assessments with the highest AUC value was the STRONG. The instruments that produced the risk assessments with the highest r_{pb} values were the ORAS-CST and ORAS-CSST. While the r_{pb} value and OR for risk assessments completed using the LSI-R were poor for the prediction of new offenses, the Somer's *d* and AUC values were stronger (see Table 1.5). For violations, the AUC value for risk assessments completed using the WRN was higher than for those completed using any other instrument (see Table 1.5).

Table 1.5 Predictive Validity Estimates Produced by Total Scores for Any Recidivism, New Offenses, and Violations

Outcomes and Instruments	Predictive Validity Estimates											
	AUC			r_{pb}			OR			Somer's d		
	K	*Mdn*	*IQR*	*k*	*Mdn*	*IQR*	*k*	*Mdn*	*IQR*	*k*	*Mdn*	*IQR*
Any recidivism				2	0.28	0.27–0.28	1	1.09	—	—	—	—
LSI-R	—	—	—	1	0.23	—	—	—	—	—	—	—
ORAS-PAT	—	—	—	1	0.40	—	—	—	—	—	—	—
SFS76	—	—	—	3	0.45	0.34–0.47	2	3.00	0.76–5.23	1	0.55	—
SFS81	—	—	—	—	—	—	1	0.91	—	—	—	—
SPIn-W	—	—	—									
New offenses												
COMPAS	3	0.67	0.66–0.70	1	0.31	—	1	1.30	—	—	—	—
LSI-R	4	0.66	0.61–0.71	17	0.16	0.11–0.26	5	1.08	1.04–1.10	1	0.28	—
LSI:SV	1	0.57	—	1	0.27	—	—	—	—	—	—	—
ORAS-PAT	—	—	—	2	0.23	0.21–0.24	—	—	—	—	—	—
ORAS-CST	—	—	—	1	0.37	—	—	—	—	—	—	—
ORAS-CSST	—	—	—	1	0.38	—	—	—	—	—	—	—
ORAS-PIT	—	—	—	1	0.36	—	—	—	—	—	—	—
ORAS-RT	—	—	—	1	0.36	—	—	—	—	—	—	—
PCRA	2	0.71	0.71–0.71	—	—	—	—	—	—	—	—	—
RMS	1	0.67	—	—	—	—	—	—	—	—	—	—
STRONG	1	0.74	—	—	—	—	—	—	—	—	—	—
WRN	2	0.64	0.61–0.67	5	0.19	0.10–0.21	1	0.98	—	—	—	—
WRN-R	1	0.66	—	—	—	—	—	—	—	—	—	—
Violations												
COMPAS	1	0.61	—	—	—	—	—	—	—	—	—	—
LSI-R	1	0.62	—	4	0.24	0.16–0.30	1	1.09	—	1	0.23	—
ORAS-PAT	—	—	—	2	0.27	0.26–0.28	—	—	—	—	—	—
RMS	1	0.64	—	—	—	—	—	—	—	—	—	—
WRN	1	0.74	—	—	—	—	—	—	—	—	—	—

Notes: k = number of samples; *Mdn* = median; *IQR* = inter-quartile range; AUC = area under the receiver operating characteristic curve; r_{pb} = point-biserial correlation coefficient; OR = odds ratio.

Table 1.6 presents the median validity estimates for risk classifications in predicting any recidivism. Overall, risk classifications were found to produce robust levels of predictive validity. Specifically, RMS and SPIn-W produced risk assessments with excellent AUC values, and strong Somer's *d* values were reported for risk assessments completed using the SFS74, SFS76, and SFS81 (see Table 1.6). The instrument that produced the risk assessments with the highest r_{pb} value was the SFS81, while the r_{pb} value for risk assessments completed using the WRN was much lower (see Table 1.6). There were too few studies to examine predictive validity of

Table 1.6 Predictive Validity Estimates Produced by Risk Classifications for Any Recidivism (including New Offenses and Violations)

| | Predictive Validity Estimates | | | | | | | | |
| | AUC | | | r_{pb} | | | Somer's *d* | | |
Instruments	*k*	*Mdn*	*IQR*	*k*	*Mdn*	*IQR*	*k*	*Mdn*	*IQR*
RMS[a]	1	0.94	—	—	—	—	—	—	—
SFS74	—	—	—	—	—	—	2	0.34	0.32–0.36
SFS76	—	—	—	—	—	—	2	0.36	0.34–0.37
SFS81[a]	—	—	—	1	0.43	—	4	0.40	0.38–0.45
SPIn-W	1	0.73	—	—	—	—	—	—	—
WRN[a]	—	—	—	1	0.18	—	—	—	—

Notes: *k* = number of samples; *Mdn* = median; IQR = inter-quartile range; AUC = area under the receiver operating characteristic curve; r_{pb} = point-biserial correlation coefficient. Odds ratios were not calculated for any samples using risk classifications to measure predictive validity. The risk classifications evaluated were those recommended by instrument authors.

a) One or more estimates exclude technical violations as an outcome.

new offenses to the exclusion of violations. No studies that met our inclusion criteria reported on the validity of risk classifications in predicting violations to the exclusion of new offenses.

Table 1.7 presents the median validity estimates for risk assessments in predicting any general recidivism by offender sex. When validity estimates were reported by offender sex, instruments generally produced similar predictive validity estimates for men and women. However, predictive validity was slightly better for men than women for risk assessments completed using the LSI-R:SV and ORAS-CST, whereas the reverse was true for assessments completed using the ORAS-RT (see Table 1.7). Comparisons of predictive validity by offender race/ethnicity were possible only for assessments completed using the COMPAS and LSI-R. For COMPAS assessments, predictive validity was found in a single study to be identical for White and Black offenders (AUCs = .69; Brennan, Dieterich, & Ehret, 2009). For LSI-R assessments, predictive validity also was similar across offender race/ethnicity in the two studies reporting this data (White: r_{pb} = .22; OR = 1.04, Cramer's *V* = .13; Black: OR = 1.03, Cramer's *V* = .09; Hispanic: OR = 1.03, Cramer's *V* = .10; Non-White: r_{pb} = .24; Lowenkamp & Bechtel, 2007; Kim, 2010).

Finally, comparisons between the predictive validity of risk assessments completed in the context of research or routine practice were possible for the LSI-R, RMS, SPIn-W, and WRN. Table 1.8 presents the median validity estimates for risk assessments completed using these instruments in predicting any recidivism by study context. Whereas both LSI-R and WRN total scores performed comparably whether conducted in the context of research or practice, RMS risk classifications demonstrated better predictive validity when completed by researchers than by practitioners (see Table 1.8). In contrast, SPIn-W assessments performed better in the context of practice than research (see Table 1.8), though the former estimate was for total scores and the latter for risk classifications. No comparisons were possible for risk assessments completed using the COMPAS IORNS, SFS76, and SFS81 because they were only evaluated in the context of practice. Conversely, risk assessments completed using the LSI-R:SV, ORAS tools, PCRA, SAQ, SFS74, STRONG, and WRN-R were only evaluated in the context of research.

Table 1.7 Predictive Validity Estimates Produced by Total Scores for Male and Female Offenders in U.S. Correctional Settings

	Predictive Validity Estimates														
	AUC					r_{pb}					OR				
Instruments	k	Mdn_Men	IQR_Men	Mdn_Women	IQR_Women	K	Mdn_Men	IQR_Men	Mdn_Women	IQR_Women	k	Mdn_Men	IQR_Men	Mdn_Women	IQR_Women
COMPAS	1	0.67	—	0.69	—	1	0.32	—	0.32	—	—	—	—	—	—
LSI-R	—	—	—	—	—	7	0.25	0.18–0.32	0.23	0.26–0.30	2	1.06	1.03–1.09	1.03	—
LSI:SV	1	0.57	—	—	—	1	0.29	—	0.22	—	—	—	—	—	—
ORAS-CST	—	—	—	—	—	1	0.37	—	0.30	—	—	—	—	—	—
ORAS-CSST	—	—	—	—	—	1	0.36	—	0.37	—	—	—	—	—	—
ORAS-PIT	—	—	—	—	—	1	0.32	—	0.35	—	—	—	—	—	—
ORAS-RT	—	—	—	—	—	1	0.30	—	0.44	—	—	—	—	—	—
SFS76	—	—	—	—	—	1	0.40	—	—	—	—	—	—	—	—
SFS81	—	—	—	—	—	1	0.34	—	—	—	1	5.23	—	—	—
SPIn-W	1	—	—	0.73	—	—	—	—	—	—	1	—	—	0.91	—
STRONG	1	0.74	—	0.72	—	—	—	—	—	—	—	—	—	—	—
WRN	—	—	—	—	—	1	0.21	—	—	—	—	—	—	—	—

Notes: k = number of samples; *Mdn* = median; *IQR* = inter-quartile range; *AUC* = area under the receiver operating characteristic curve; r_{pb} = point-biserial correlation coefficient; OR = odds ratio. Somer's *d* was not calculated for any samples reporting sex-specific estimates.

Table 1.8 Predictive Validity Estimates Produced by Total Scores or Risk Classifications by Study Context

Study Context and Instruments	Predictive Validity Estimates											
	AUC			r_{pb}			OR			Somer's *d*		
	k	*Mdn*	*IQR*	*k*	*Mdn*	*IQR*	*k*	*Mdn*	*IQR*	*k*	*Mdn*	*IQR*
Research												
LSI-R	1	.74	—	3	.14	.11–.16	—	—	—	—	—	—
RMS	1	.94	—	—	—	—	—	—	—	—	—	—
SPIn-W	—	—	—	—	—	—	1	.91	—	—	—	—
WRN	—	—	—	3	.19	.08–.21	—	—	—	—	—	—
Practice												
LSI-R	4	.63	.60–.66	18	.25	.10–.28	6	1.09	1.04–1.09	2	.26	.23–.28
RMS	2	.66	.64–.67	—	—	—	—	—	—	—	—	—
SPIn-W	1	.73	—	—	—	—	—	—	—	—	—	—
WRN	3	.67	.61–.74	3	.18	.10–.21	1	.98	—	—	—	—

Notes: k = number of samples; *Mdn* = median; *IQR* = inter-quartile range; AUC = area under the receiver operating characteristic curve; r_{pb} = point-biserial correlation coefficient; OR = odds ratio. Estimates were calculated using either total scores or risk classifications.

Discussion

With staggering numbers of adults under correctional supervision in the United States, ending mass incarceration has been identified as a national priority (Obama, 2015). Efforts are underway across the United States to adopt evidence-based correctional approaches that will more appropriately and effectively incapacitate and rehabilitate offenders at greater risk of recidivism, while diverting lower risk offenders to alternative settings and punishments. Risk assessment figures prominently in many of these strategies (Casey et al., 2011). As a result, psychologists and other professionals working in U.S. correctional settings are increasingly being required to use risk assessments to inform decisions regarding incarceration, diversion, and release, and to guide the development of interventions to reduce recidivism risk (Monahan & Skeem, 2016). However, relatively little is known regarding the accuracy and reliability of recidivism risk assessments completed on adult offenders in U.S. correctional settings. Instead, prior research reviews have been characterized by relatively short lists of instruments designed to predict specific forms of recidivism, namely violent and sexually violent offending, or studies conducted in other jurisdictions, notably Canada and the United Kingdom. This review summarized the state of science and practice in the United States with respect to the performance of risk assessments completed using instruments designed to predict general recidivism, including committing a new crime and violating conditions of probation or parole, among adult offenders.

Our literature review identified 19 risk assessment instruments that had been evaluated in 53 studies published between January 1970 and December 2012 representing 72 unique samples of adult offenders in U.S. correctional settings. The risk assessment instruments varied widely in the number, type, and content of their items, but generally were characterized by static risk factors to the exclusion of dynamic risk factors and protective factors. For most instruments, predictive validity had been evaluated in one or two studies that met our inclusion criteria. Those studies often were completed by the developers of the instrument under investigation. Perhaps one our most striking findings, only two of the 53 studies reported on the inter-rater reliability of the risk assessments. These two studies revealed very high rates of field reliability for the LSI-R and LSI-R:SV. Whether risk assessments completed using the other 17 instruments are consistent across assessors in U.S. correctional settings was not addressed in the reviewed literature, though findings of recent research are promising (e.g., Lowenkamp, Johnson, Holsinger, VanBenschoten, & Robinson, 2013). Inter-rater reliability is relevant to any forensic assessment involving the rating or coding of items (Douglas et al., 2012) and a necessary criterion for validity (Douglas, Skeem, & Nicholson, 2011; Gottfredson & Moriarty, 2006). Consequently, there is a critical need for data on the inter-rater reliability of recidivism risk assessments completed on adult offenders in U.S. correctional settings.

No one instrument emerged as producing the "most" accurate risk assessments in U.S. correctional settings; however, findings of our review suggest that some instruments may perform better in predicting particular outcomes compared to others. Risk assessments completed using the SFS instruments, for example, performed especially well in predicting any recidivism (i.e., new offenses and/or violations), whereas risk assessments completed using the ORAS-CST, ORAS-CSST, PCRA, and STRONG performed especially well in predicting new offenses. WRN assessments stood out in the prediction of violations. These findings suggest that certain risk assessment instruments may be appropriately used to inform at least some sentencing decisions, such as the allocation of probation conditions and frequency of contact. However, the more widespread use of risk assessment instruments in the sentencing process is a topic of continued debate (Monahan & Skeem, 2016).

Additionally, findings of our review suggest that some instruments produced risk assessments that perform better for male compared to female offenders in U.S. correctional settings. In particular, the LSI instruments produced assessments with only fair validity for female offenders, though predictive validity was generally good for male offenders. In contrast, a large meta-analytic review of LSI assessments reported similar effect sizes for male and female offenders (Smith et al., 2009), suggesting that our findings may be specific to the two studies that met our inclusions criteria. Other instruments, such as the COMPAS, ORAS, and STRONG, produced risk assessments with good validity for both male and female offenders. That said, our findings regarding parity or differences in the predictive validity of risk assessments for male and female offenders in U.S. correctional settings are limited by the small number of studies that provided sex-specific validity estimates. Given the rising numbers of women in U.S. jails (Glaze & Kaeble, 2014), continued efforts are needed to evaluate the validity of instruments being used to predict recidivism risk among female offenders in U.S. correctional settings.

Due to data restrictions, we were unable to systematically compare performance of risk assessments as a function of race/ethnicity, a topic receiving considerable attention in contemporary public, political, and academic discourse (Hamilton, 2015; Holder, 2014; Scurich & Monahan, 2016; Starr, 2014). We found some evidence suggesting comparable predictive validity of COMPAS and LSI-R for White and non-White offenders. However, only three studies conducted in the United States at the time of our review provided estimates of predictive validity by racial/ethnic group: one for risk assessments completed using the COMPAS and two for risk assessments completed using the LSI-R. Findings of prior reviews and studies of individual risk assessment instruments have found evidence of racial bias in the effectiveness of risk assessments (e.g., Chenane, Brennan, Steiner, & Ellison, 2015; Leistico et al., 2008; Singh et al., 2011). Conversely, other studies have failed to find differences in risk assessment accuracy as a function of offender race (e.g., Lowenkamp, Holsinger, & Cohen, 2015; Miller, 2006b).

As the use and consequences of risk assessments in the American penal system continue to grow, there is a pressing need for research that investigates potential racial disparities in assessments of risk for general recidivism.

Finally, no studies that met our inclusion criteria provided estimates of predictive validity as a function of mental disorders, substance use disorders, or personality disorders. Even when the diagnostic characteristics of the study samples were reported, predictive validity estimates were not provided by subgroup. Recent research suggests that mentally disordered and non-disordered offenders share many of the same predictors of recidivism (Skeem, Winter, Kennealy, Louden, & Tatar, 2014), suggesting that risk assessments also may perform comparably across these subgroups of offenders. Yet, this remains an empirical question to be answered through further research.

Limitations

The methodology of our review limits its findings in three ways. First, our review focused on the state of risk assessment science and practice in United States. Our search strategy resulted in the exclusion of some recently revised versions of well-known risk assessment instruments that either had not been validated in the United States within our search time frame or that were not identifiable by their current name, but that show very positive results, such as the Level of Service/Case Management Inventory (Andrews, Bonta, & Wormith, 2004) and the Women's Risk/Need Assessment (Van Voorhis, Wright, Salisbury, & Bauman, 2010). Our interest in risk assessments completed on adult offenders in U.S. correctional settings also resulted in the exclusion of studies conducted in other jurisdictions. There have been several evaluations of the inter-rater reliability and predictive validity of assessments completed in other jurisdictions, most often Canada and the United Kingdom, or that have been published since the time of our literature review (e.g., Lowenkamp et al., 2015).

Second, our intent was to present a representative sample of all the U.S. validation research available on a comprehensive list of risk assessment instruments. Accordingly, we used an inclusive selection strategy and did not conduct a systematic assessment of study quality. For this reason, we did not undertake a formal meta-analysis and did not compute inferential statistics, but rather compared the effect sizes reported across studies descriptively. Third, although we strove to include all studies conducted in the United States published in both the peer-reviewed and grey literatures between January 1970 and December 2012, our review was still subject to publication bias. There also may be studies that met inclusion criteria but were inadvertently and unintentionally excluded by our search strategy.

Conclusions

Despite these limitations, this review represents a comprehensive summary of the inter-rater reliability and validity of risk assessments in predicting general recidivism in adult offenders in the United States. With efforts underway across the United States to reduce mass incarceration through evidence-based criminal justice practices, our overarching goal was to provide information that would assist clinicians and policymakers alike in selecting from the many different risk assessment tools available for implementation in U.S. correctional settings. Instead of identifying one instrument that produced the "best" or "most accurate" risk assessments, our findings suggest that predictive validity may vary as a function of offender characteristics, settings, and recidivism outcomes. Our review also identified important gaps in the U.S. validation research, such as limited reporting of inter-rater reliability and few comparisons of predictive validity between offender subgroups. In light of these findings, decisions regarding which recidivism risk assessment instrument to use should be guided by the empirical evidence—or lack thereof—supporting the instrument's use with a given population (e.g., inmates, probationers, parolees) and for the outcome of interest (e.g., new offenses, violations). Practical issues should be taken into consideration as well, such as the sources of information needed to complete the assessments (e.g., self-report, interview, review of official records), instrument length and administration time, instrument cost, and training requirements. These issues may impact the feasibility of implementing recidivism risk assessment instruments, even those that have been well-validated in a given jurisdiction and population, with fidelity (Monahan & Skeem, 2016).

Author Note

This project was funded by the Council of State Governments Justice Center. The content is solely the responsibility of the authors and does not necessarily represent the official views of the sponsor. We gratefully acknowledge the research assistance and contributions of Krystina Dillard, Rhonda Morelock, and Grace Seamon. We also thank David D'Amora, Fred Osher, and other Council of State Governments Justice Center staff for their support and feedback on this project.

* Sections of this chapter are reprinted with permission from Desmarais, S. L., Johnson, K. L., & Singh, J. P. (2016). Performance of recidivism risk assessment instruments in U.S. correctional settings. *Psychological Services, 13*, 206–222. https://doi.org/10.1037/ser0000075

References

References marked with an asterisk indicate studies included in the systematic review.

Ægisdóttir, S., White, M. J., Spengler, P. M., Maugherman, A. S., Anderson, L. A., Cook, R. S., et al. (2006). The meta-analysis of clinical judgement project: Fifty-six years of accumulated research on clinical versus statistical prediction. *Counseling Psychologist, 34*, 341–382. doi:10.1177/0011000005285875

American Educational Research Association (AERA), American Psychological Association (APA), & National Council on Measurement in Education (NCME). (2014). *Standards for educational and psychological testing.* Washington, DC: American Psychological Association.

Andrews, D. A. (1982). *Level of Service Inventory.* Toronto, ON: Ontario Ministry of Correctional Services.

Andrews, D. A., & Bonta, J. (1995). *Level of Service Inventory–Revised.* North Tonawanda, NY: Multi-Health Systems.

Andrews, D. A., & Bonta, J. L. (1998). *Level of Service Inventory–Revised: Screening Version (LSI-R:SV): User's manual.* Toronto, ON: Multi-Health Systems.

Andrews, D. A., Bonta, J., & Wormith, S. J. (2004). *The Level of Service/Case Management Inventory (LS/CMI).* Toronto, ON: Multi-Health Systems.

Andrews, D. A., Bonta, J., & Wormith, S. J. (2008). *The Level of Service/Risk-Need-Responsivity (LS/RNR).* Toronto, ON: Multi-Health Systems.

Andrews, D. A., & Bonta, J. (2010). Rehabilitating criminal justice policy and practice. *Psychology, Public Policy, and Law, 16*, 39–55. doi:10.1037/a0018362

Baird, C., Heinz, R., & Bemus, B. (1979). *The Wisconsin Case Classification/Staff Deployment Project.* Madison, WI: Wisconsin Department of Corrections.

Bakker, L., Riley, D., & O'Malley, J. (1999). *Risk of Reconviction: Statistical models predicting four types of re-offending.* Wellington, New Zealand: Department of Corrections Psychological Service.

*Barnoski, R., & Aos, S. (2003). *Washington's Offender Accountability Act: An analysis of the Department of Corrections' risk assessment.* Olympia, WA: Washington State Institute for Public Policy.

*Barnoski, R., & Drake, E. K. (2007). *Washington's Offender Accountability Act: Department of Corrections' static risk assessment.* Olympia, WA: Washington State Institute for Public Policy.

Beck, A. T., Steer, R. A., & Carbin, M. G. (1988). Psychometric properties of the Beck Depression Inventory: Twenty-five years of evaluation. *Clinical Psychology Review, 8,* 77–100. doi:10.1016/0272-7358(88)90050-5

*Blomberg, T., Bales, W., Mann, K., Meldrum, R., & Nedelec, J. (2010). *Validation of the COMPAS risk assessment classification instrument.* Tallahassee, FL: Center for Criminology and Public Policy Research.

*Brennan, T., Dieterich, W., & Ehret, B. (2009). Evaluating the predictive validity of the COMPAS risk and needs assessment system. *Criminal Justice and Behavior, 36,* 21–40. doi:10.1177/0093854808326545

Brown, S. L., & Motiuk, L. L. (2005). *The Dynamic Factor Identification and Analysis (DFIA) component of the Offender Intake Assessment (OIA) process: A meta-analytic, psychometric, and consultative review* (Research Report R-164). Ottawa, ON: Correctional Service Canada.

Carson, E. A., & Sabol, W. J. (2012, December). *Prisoners in 2011* (NCJ 239808). Washington, DC: Bureau of Justice Statistics.

Casey, P. M., Warren, R. K., & Elek, J. K. (2011). *Using offender risk and needs assessment information at sentencing: Guidance for courts from a national working group.* Williamsburg, VA: National Center for State Courts. Retrieved from http://ncsc.contentdm.oclc.org/cgi-bin/showfile.exe?CISOROOT=/criminal&CISOPTR=196

*Castillo, E. D., & Alarid, L. F. (2011). Factors associated with recidivism among offenders with mental illness. *International Journal of Offender Therapy and Comparative Criminology, 55*(1), 98-117. doi:10.1177/0306624X09359502

Chen, H., Cohen, P., & Chen, S. (2010). How big is a big odds ratio? Interpreting the magnitudes of odds ratios in epidemiological studies. *Communications in Statistics – Simulation and Computation, 29,* 860–864. doi:10.1080/03610911003650383

Chenane, J. L., Brennan, P. K., Steiner, B., & Ellison, J. M. (2015). Racial and ethnic differences in the predictive validity of the Level of Service Inventory–Revised among prison inmates. *Criminal Justice and Behavior, 42,* 286–303. doi:10.1177/0093854814548195

Cohen, J. (1988). *Statistical power analysis for the behavioral sciences.* Hillsdale, NJ: L. Erlbaum.

*Connolly, M. M. (2003). *A critical examination of actuarial offender-based prediction assessments: Guidance for the next generation of assessments.* Unpublished doctoral dissertation, University of Texas at Austin, Austin, TX.

Copas, J., & Marshall, P. (1998). The Offender Group Reconviction Scale: The statistical reconviction score for use by probation officers. *Journal of the Royal Statistical Society, Series C, 47,* 159–171. doi:10.1111/1467-9876.00104

*Davidson, C. (2012). *2012 Iowa Board of Parole risk assessment validation.* Des Moines, IA: Department of Human Rights, Division of Criminal and Juvenile Justice Planning.

*Davidson, J. (2007). *Risky business: What standard assessments mean for female offenders.* Unpublished doctoral dissertation, University of Hawaii at Manoa, Manoa, HI.

de Ruiter, C., & Nicholls, T. L. (2011). Protective factors in forensic mental health: A new frontier. *The International Journal of Forensic Mental Health, 10,* 160–170. doi:10.1080/14999013.2011.600602

Desmarais, S. L., Sellers, B. G., Viljoen, J. L., Cruise, K. R., Nicholls, T. L., & Dvoskin, J. A. (2012). Pilot implementation and preliminary evaluation of START:AV assessments in secure juvenile correctional facilities. *The International Journal of Forensic Mental Health, 11*, 150–164. doi:10.1080/14999013.2012.737405

Desmarais, S. L., Van Dorn, R. A., Telford, R. P., Petrila, J., & Coffey, T. (2012). Characteristics of START assessments completed in mental health jail diversion programs. *Behavioral Sciences and the Law, 30*, 448–469. doi:10.1002/bsl.2022

Douglas, K. S., Otto, R., Desmarais, S. L., & Borum, R. (2012). Clinical forensic psychology. In I. B. Weiner, J. A. Schinka, & W. F. Velicer (Eds.), *Handbook of psychology, volume 2: Research methods in psychology* (pp. 213–244). Hoboken, NJ: John Wiley & Sons.

Douglas, K. S., & Skeem, J. (2005). Violence risk assessment: Getting specific about being dynamic. *Psychology, Public Policy, and Law, 11*, 347–383. doi:10.1037/1076-8971.11.3.347

Douglas, K. S., Skeem, J. L., & Nicholson, E. (2011). Research methods in violence risk assessment. In B. Rosenfeld & S. D. Penrod (Eds.), *Research methods in forensic psychology* (pp. 325–346). Hoboken, NJ: John Wiley & Sons, Inc.

*Dow, E., Jones, C., & Mott, J. (2005). An empirical modeling approach to recidivism classification. *Criminal Justice and Behavior, 32*, 223–247. doi:10.1177/0093854804272892

*Eaglin, J., & Lombard, P. (1982). *A validation and comparative evaluation of four predictive devices for classifying federal probation caseloads.* Washington, DC: Federal Judicial Center.

*Eisenberg, M., Bryl, J., & Fabelo, T. (2009). *Validation of the Wisconsin Department of Corrections risk assessment instrument.* New York, NY: Council of State Governments Justice Center.

*Evans, S. E. (2009). *Gender disparity in the prediction of recidivism: The accuracy of LSI-R modified.* Master's thesis, University of Alabama, Tuscaloosa, AL.

*Farabee, D., & Zhang, S. (2007). *COMPAS validation study: First annual report.* Los Angeles, CA: Department of Corrections and Rehabilitation.

*Farabee, D., Zhang, S., Roberts, R. E. L., & Yang, J. (2010). *COMPAS validation study: Final report.* Los Angeles, CA: Department of Corrections and Rehabilitation.

*Fass, T. L., Heilbrun, K., DeMatteo, D., & Fretz, R. (2008). The LSI-R and the COMPAS: Validation data on two risk-needs tools. *Criminal Justice and Behavior, 35*, 1095–1108. doi:10.1177/0093854806298468

Fazel, S., Singh, J. P., Doll, H., & Grann, M. (2012). The prediction of violence and antisocial behaviour: A systematic review and meta-analysis of the utility of risk assessment instruments in 73 samples involving 24,827 individuals. *British Medical Journal, 345*, e4692.

*Flores, A. W., Lowenkamp, C. T., Smith, P., & Latessa, E. J. (2006). Validating the Level of Service Inventory–Revised on a sample of federal probationers. *Federal Probation, 70*(2), 44–48.

Gendreau, P., Goggin, C., & Little, T. (1996). *Predicting adult offender recidivism: What works!* (Cat. No. JS4-1/1996-7E). Ottawa, ON: Public Works and Government Services Canada.

Glaze, L. E. & Kaeble, D. (2014, December). *Correctional population in the United States, 2013* (NCJ 248479). Washington, DC: Bureau of Justice Statistics.

Gottfredson, D. S., & Moriarty, L. J. (2006). Statistical risk assessment: Old problems and new applications. *Crime & Delinquency, 52*, 178–200. doi:10.1177/0011128705281748

*Gould, L. (1991). *A comparison of models of parole outcome.* Unpublished doctoral dissertation, Louisiana State University, Baton Rouge, LA.

Grove, W. M., Zald, D. H., Lebow, B. S., Snitz, B. E., & Nelson, C. (2000). Clinical versus mechanical prediction: A meta-analysis. *Psychological Assessment, 12*, 19–30. doi:10.1037/1040-3590.12.1.19

Guy, L. S., Edens, J. F., Anthony, C., & Douglas, K. S. (2005). Does psychopathy predict institutional misconduct among adults? A meta-analytic investigation. *Journal of Consulting and Clinical Psychology, 73*, 1056–1064. doi:10.1037/0022-006X.73.6.1056

Guy, L. S., Packer, I. K., & Warnken, W. (2012). Assessing risk of violence using structured professional judgment guidelines. *Journal of Forensic Psychology Practice, 12*, 270–283. doi:10.1080/15228932.2012.674471

HM Prison Service and National Probation Directorate. (2001). *The Offender Assessment System: User manual*. London, England: Home Office.

Hamilton, M. (2015). Risk-needs assessment: Constitutional and ethical challenges. *American Criminal Law Review, 52*, 231.

Hanson, R., & Morton-Bourgon, K. E. (2009). The accuracy of recidivism risk assessments for sexual offenders: A meta-analysis of 118 prediction studies. *Psychological Assessment, 21*, 1–21. doi:10.1037/a0014421

Hare, R. D. (2003). *The Hare Psychopathy Checklist-Revised* (2nd ed.). Toronto, ON: Multi-Health Systems.

*Harer, M. (1994). *Recidivism among federal prison releasees in 1987: A preliminary report*. Washington, DC: Federal Bureau of Prisons Office of Research and Evaluation.

*Henderson, H. M. (2006). *The predictive utility of the Wisconsin Risk Needs Assessment in a sample of Texas probationers*. Unpublished doctoral dissertation, Sam Houston State University, Huntsville, TX.

Hilton, N., Harris, G. T., & Rice, M. E. (2006). Sixty-six years of research on the clinical versus actuarial prediction of violence. *The Counseling Psychologist, 34*, 400–409. doi:10.1177/0011000005285877

*Hoffman, P. (1983). Screening for risk: A revised Salient Factor Score (SFS 81). *Journal of Criminal Justice, 11*, 539–547. doi:10.1016/0047-2352(83)90006-5

*Hoffman, P. (1994). Twenty years of operational use of a risk prediction instrument: The United States Parole Commission's Salient Factor Score. *Journal of Criminal Justice, 22*, 477–494. doi:10.1016/0047-2352(94)90090-6

*Hoffman, P., & Adelberg, S. (1980). The Salient Factor Score: A nontechnical overview. *Federal Probation, 44*, 44–52.

Hoffman, P., & Beck, J. (1974). Parole decision-making: A Salient Factor Score. *Journal of Criminal Justice, 2*, 195–206. doi:0.1016/0047-2352(74)90031-2

*Hoffman, P., & Beck, J. (1980). Revalidating the Salient Factor Score: A research note. *Journal of Criminal Justice, 8*, 185–188. doi:10.1016/0047-2352(80)90025-2

*Hoffman, P., & Beck, J. (1985). Recidivism among released federal prisoners: Salient Factor Score and five-year follow-up. *Criminal Justice and Behavior, 12*, 501–507. doi:10.1177/0093854885012004007

Holder, E. H. (2014). *Attorney General Eric Holder Speaks at the National Association of Criminal Defense Lawyers 57th Annual Meeting and the 13th State Criminal Justice Network conference*. August 1, 2014. Retrieved from http://www.justice.gov/opa/speech/attorney-general-eric-holder-speaks-national-association-criminal-defense-lawyers-57th

*Holland, T., Holt, N., Levi, M., & Beckett, G. (1983). Comparison and combination of clinical and statistical predictions of recidivism among adult offenders. *Journal of Applied Psychology, 68*, 203–211. doi:10.1037/0021-9010.68.2.203

*Holsinger, A. M., Lowenkamp, C. T., & Latessa, E. J. (2004). Validating the LSI-R on a sample of jail inmates. *Journal of Offender Monitoring, 17*, 8–9.

Holtfreter, K., & Cupp, R. (2007). Gender and risk assessment: The empirical status of the LSI-R for women. *Journal of Contemporary Criminal Justice, 23*, 363–382. doi:10.1177/1043986207309436

Howard, B. (2007). *Examining predictive validity of the Salient Factor Score and HCR-20 among behavior health court clientele: Comparing static and dynamic variables*. Unpublished doctoral dissertation, Palo Alto University, Palo Alto, CA.

*Johnson, J. L., Lowenkamp, C. T., VanBenschoten, S. W., & Robinson, C. R. (2011). The construction and validation of the Federal Post Conviction Risk Assessment (PCRA). *Federal Probation, 75*, 16–29.

Jung, S., Brown, K., Ennis, L., & Ledi, D. (2015). The association between presentence risk evaluations and sentencing outcome. *Applied Psychology in Criminal Justice, 11*, 111–125.

*Kelly, B. (2009). *A validation study of Risk Management Systems*. Master's thesis, University of Nevada, Las Vegas, NV.

*Kelly, C. E., & Welsh, W. N. (2008). The predictive validity of the Level of Service Inventory–Revised for drug-involved offenders. *Criminal Justice and Behavior, 35*, 819–831. doi:10.1177/0093854808316642

*Kim, H. (2010). *Prisoner classification re-visited: A further test of the Level of Service Inventory–Revised (LSI-R) intake assessment*. Unpublished doctoral dissertation, Indiana University of Pennsylvania, Indiana, PA.

Knight, K., Garner, B. R., Simpson, D. D., Morey, J. T., & Flynn, P. M. (2006). An assessment for criminal thinking. *Crime & Delinquency, 52*, 159–177. doi:10.1177/0011128705281749

Landis, J. R., & Koch, G. G. (1977). The measurement of observer agreement for categorical data. *Biometrics, 33*, 159–174.

Langan, P. A., & Levin, D. J. (2002). *Recidivism of prisoners released in 1994* (NCJ 193427). Washington, DC: Bureau of Justice Statistics.

*Latessa, E., Smith, P., Lemke, R., Makarios, M., & Lowenkamp, C. (2009). *Creation and validation of the Ohio Risk Assessment System: Final report*. Cincinnati, OH: Authors.

Leistico, A. R., Salekin, R. T., DeCoster, J., & Rogers, R. (2008). A large-scale meta-analysis relating the Hare measures of psychopathy to antisocial conduct. *Law and Human Behavior, 32*, 28–45. doi:10.1007/s10979-007-9096-6

*Listwan, S., Piquero, N., & Voorhis, P. (2010). Recidivism among a white-collar sample: Does personality matter? *Australian and New Zealand Journal of Criminology, 43*, 156–174. doi:10.1375/acri.43.1.156

*Lowenkamp, C. T., & Bechtel, K. (2007). The predictive validity of the LSI-R on a sample of offenders drawn from the records of the Iowa Department of Corrections Management System. *Federal Probation, 71*, 25–29.

Lowenkamp, C. T., Holsinger, A. M., & Cohen, T. H. (2015). PCRA revisited: Testing the validity of the Federal Post Conviction Risk Assessment (PCRA). *Psychological Services, 12*, 149–157. doi:10.1037/ser0000024

*Lowenkamp, C. T., Holsinger, A. M., & Latessa, E. J. (2001). Risk/need assessment, offender classification, and the role of childhood abuse. *Criminal Justice and Behavior, 28*, 543–563. doi:10.1177/009385480102800501

Lowenkamp, C. T., Johnson, J. L., Holsinger, A. M., VanBenschoten, S. W., & Robinson, C. R. (2013). The Federal Post Conviction Risk Assessment (PCRA): A Construction and validation study. *Psychological Services, 10*, 87–96. doi:10.1037/a0030343

*Lowenkamp, C. T., & Latessa, E. J. (2004). *Validating the Level of Service Inventory–Revised in Ohio's community based correctional facilities*. Cincinnati: Center for Criminal Justice Research.

*Lowenkamp, C. T., Lemke, R., & Latessa, E. (2008). The development and validation of a pretrial screening tool. *Federal Probation, 72*, 2–9.

*Lowenkamp, C. T., Lovins, B., & Latessa, E. J. (2009). Validating the Level of Service Inventory–Revised and the Level of Service Inventory: Screening Version with a sample of probationers. *Prison Journal, 89*, 192–204.

Loza, W. (2005). *The Self-Appraisal Questionnaire (SAQ): A tool for assessing violent and non-violent recidivism*. Toronto, ON: Mental Health Systems.

Mamalian, C. A. (2011). *State of the science of pretrial risk assessment*. Washington, DC: Bureau of Justice Assistance.

*Meaden, C. (2012). *The utility of the Level of Service Inventory–Revised versus the Service Planning Instrument for women in predicting program completion in female offenders.* Master's thesis, Central Connecticut State University, New Britain, CT.

Miller, H. A. (2006a). *Manual of the Inventory of Offender Risk, Needs, and Strengths (IORNS).* Odessa, FL: Psychological Assessment Resources.

*Miller, H. A. (2006b). A dynamic assessment of offender risk, needs, and strengths in a sample of pre-release general offenders. *Behavioral Sciences and the Law, 24,* 767–782. doi:10.1002/bsl.728

Miller, J., & Maloney, C. (2013). Practitioner compliance with risk/needs assessment tools: A theoretical and empirical assessment. *Criminal Justice and Behavior, 40,* 716–736. doi:10.1177/0093854812468883

*Millson, B., Robinson, D., & Van Dieten, M. (2010). *Women offender case management model.* Wethersfield, CT: Court Support Services Division.

*Mitchell, O., & Mackenzie, D. (2006). Disconfirmation of the predictive validity of the Self-Appraisal Questionnaire in a sample of high-risk drug offenders. *Criminal Justice and Behavior, 33,* 449–466. doi:10.1177/0093854806287421

*Mitchell, O., Caudy, M., & Mackenzie, D. (2012). A reanalysis of the Self-Appraisal Questionnaire: Psychometric properties and predictive validity. *International Journal of Offender Therapy and Comparative Criminology, 20,* 1–15. doi:10.1177/0306624X12436504

Moher, D., Liberati, A., Tetzlaff, J., & Altman, D. G. (2009). Preferred reporting items for systematic reviews and meta-Analyses: The PRISMA statement. *PLoS Medicine, 6,* e1000097. doi:10.1371/journal.pmed.1000097

Monahan, J., & Skeem, J. (2014). Risk redux: The resurgence of risk assessment in criminal sanctioning. *Federal Sentencing Reporter, 26,* 158–166.

Monahan, J., & Skeem, J. (2016). Risk assessment in criminal sentencing. *Annual Review of Clinical Psychology, 12,* 489–513.

Morey, L. C. (1991). *The Personality Assessment Inventory professional manual.* Odessa, FL: Psychological Assessment Resources.

Motiuk, L. L., & Porporino, F. J. (1989). *Field test of the Community Risk/Needs Management scale: A study of offenders on caseload.* Correctional Service Canada, Research Branch.

Novaco, R. W. (1994). Anger as a risk factor for violence among the mentally disordered. In J. Monahan & H. Steadman (Eds.), *Violence and mental disorder: Developments in risk assessment* (pp. 21–59). Chicago, IL: University of Chicago Press.

Nuffield, J. (1982). *Parole decision making in Canada: Research towards decision guidelines.* Ottawa, ON: Solicitor General of Canada.

Obama, B. (2015). *President Obama Remarks on the Criminal Justice System.* July 14, 2015. Retrieved from http://www.c-span.org/video/?327099-4/president-obama-remarks-naacp

*O'Keefe, M. L., Klebe, K., & Hromas, S. (1998). *Validation of the Level of Supervision Inventory (LSI) for community-based offenders in Colorado: Phase II.* Model, CO: Department of Corrections.

Pew Center on the States (2009). *One in 31: The long reach of American corrections.* Washington, DC: The Pew Charitable Trusts.

Quinsey, V. L., Harris, G. T., Rice, M. E., & Cormier, C. A. (2006). *Violent offenders: Appraising and managing risk* (2nd ed.). Washington, DC: American Psychological Association.

Rice, M. E., & Harris, G. T. (2005). Comparing effect sizes in follow-up studies: ROC Area, Cohen's d, and r. *Law and Human Behavior, 29,* 615–620. doi:10.1007/s10979-005-6832-7

*Robuck, B. (1976). *A study of inmate outcome in Kentucky.* Unpublished doctoral dissertation, University of Kentucky, Lexington, KY.

*Rubin, M., Rocque, M., & Ethridge, W. (2010). *An analysis of probation violations and revocations in Maine probation entrants in 2005–2006.* Portland, ME: Justice Research and Statistics Association.

*Schlager, M. D. (2005). *Assessing the reliability and validity of the Level of Service Inventory–Revised (LSI-R) on a community corrections sample: Implications for corrections and parole policy.* Unpublished doctoral dissertation, Rutgers University, Newark, NJ.

Scurich, N., & Monahan, J. (2016). Evidence-based sentencing: Public openness and opposition to using gender, age, and race as risk factors for recidivism. *Law and Human Behavior, 40,* 36–41. doi:10.1037/lhb0000161

*Shaffer, D. K., Kelly, B., & Lieberman, J. D. (2010). An exemplar-based approach to risk assessment: Validating the Risk Management Systems instrument. *Criminal Justice Policy Review, 22,* 167–186. doi:10.1177/0887403410372989

*Simourd, D. (2006). *Validation of risk/needs assessments in the Pennsylvania Department of Corrections: Final report.* Hampden Township, PA: Department of Corrections.

Singh, J. P. (2013). Predictive validity performance indicators in violence risk assessment: A methodological primer. *Behavioral Sciences & the Law, 31,* 8–22. doi:10.1002/bsl.2052

Singh, J. P., Desmarais, S. L., Hurducas, C., Arbach-Lucioni, K., Condemarin, C., de Ruiter, C., . . . Otto, R. K. (2014). Use and perceived utility of structured violence risk assessment tools in 44 countries: Findings from the IRiS Project. *International Journal of Forensic Mental Health Services, 13,* 193–206. doi:10.1080/14999013.2014.922141

Singh, J. P., Desmarais, S. L., & Van Dorn, R. A. (2013). Measurement of predictive validity in studies of risk assessment instruments: A second-order systematic review. *Behavioral Sciences & the Law, 31,* 55–73. doi:10.1002/bsl.2053

Singh, J. P., Grann, M., & Fazel, S. (2011). A comparative study of risk assessment tools: A systematic review and metaregression analysis of 68 studies involving 25,980 participants. *Clinical Psychology Review, 31,* 499–513. doi:10.1016/j.cpr.2010.11.009

Skeem, J. L., Winter, E., Kennealy, P. J., Louden, J. E., & Tatar II, J. R. (2014). Offenders with mental illness have criminogenic needs, too: Toward recidivism reduction. *Law and Human Behavior, 38,* 212–224. doi:10.1037/lhb0000054

Smith, P., Cullen, F., & Latessa, E. (2009). Can 14,737 women be wrong? A meta-analysis of the LSI-R and recidivism for female offenders. *Criminology & Public Policy, 8,* 183–208. doi:10.1111/j.1745-9133.2009.00551.x

Starr, S. B. (2014). Evidence-based sentencing and the scientific rationalization of discrimination. *Stanford Law Review, 66,* 803–872.

*Tillyer, M. S., & Vose, B. (2011). Social ecology, individual risk, and recidivism: A multilevel examination of main and moderating influences. *Journal of Criminal Justice, 39,* 452–459. doi:10.1016/j.jcrimjus.2011.08.003

Tully, R. J., Chou, S., & Browne, K. D. (2013). A systematic review on the effectiveness of sex offender risk assessment tools in predicting sexual recidivism of adult male sex offenders. *Clinical Psychology Review, 33,* 287–316. doi:10.1016/j.cpr.2012.12.002

United States Parole Commission. (2003). *Rules and procedures manual.* Chevy Chase, MD: U.S. Parole Commission.

Van der Knaap, L. M., & Alberda, D. L. (2009). *De predictieve validiteit van de Recidive Inschattingsschalen (RISc) [Predictive validity of the Recidivism Risk Assessment Scales (RISc)].* Den Haag, the Netherlands: Ministerie van Justitie, WODC.

Van Dieten, M., & Robinson, D. (2007). *The Service Planning Instrument (SPIn).* Ottawa, ON: Orbis Partners.

Van Voorhis, P., Wright, E. M., Salisbury, E., & Bauman, A. (2010). Women's risk factors and their contributions to existing risk/needs assessment: The current status of gender responsive assessment. *Criminal Justice and Behavior, 34,* 261–288. doi:10.1177/0093854809357442

Viljoen, J. L., McLachlan, K., & Vincent, G. M. (2010). Assessing violence risk and psychopathy in juvenile and adult offenders: A survey of clinical practices. *Assessment, 17,* 377–395. doi:10.1177/1073191109359587

Vincent, G. M., Guy, L. S., Fusco, S. L., & Gershenson, B. G. (2012). Field reliability of the SAVRY with juvenile probation officers: Implications for training. *Law and Human Behavior, 36,* 225–236. doi:10.1037/h0093974

*Vose, B., Lowenkamp, C. T., Smith, P., & Cullen, F. T. (2009). Gender and the predictive validity of the LSI-R: A study of parolees and probationers. *Journal of Contemporary Criminal Justice, 25,* 459–471. doi:10.1177/1043986209344797

Walmsley, R. (2013). *World prison population list* (10th ed.). London, England: International Centre for Prison Studies.

Walmsley, R. (2012). *World female imprisonment list* (2nd ed.). London, England: International Centre for Prison Studies.

Walters, G. D. (1995). The Psychological Inventory of Criminal Thinking Styles Part I: Reliability and preliminary validity. *Criminal Justice and Behavior, 22,* 307–325. doi:10.1177/0093854895022003008

Walters, G. D. (2011). Predicting recidivism with the Psychological Inventory of Criminal Thinking Styles and Level of Service Inventory–Revised: Screening Version. *Law and Human Behavior, 35,* 211–220. doi:10.1007/s10979-010-9231-7

Walters, G. D. (2012). Criminal thinking and recidivism: Meta-analytic evidence on the predictive and incremental validity of the Psychological Inventory of Criminal Thinking Styles (PICTS). *Aggression and Violent Behavior, 17,* 272–278. doi:10.1016/j.avb.2012.02.010

Webster, C. D., Douglas, K. S., Eaves, D., & Hart, S. D. (1997). *HCR-20: Assessing risk for violence* (Version 2). Vancouver, Canada: Mental Health, Law, & Policy Institute, Simon Fraser University.

*Wright, E. M., Van Voorhis, P., Bauman, A., & Salisbury, E. (2007). *Gender-responsive risk/needs assessment: Final report.* St Paul, MN: Department of Corrections.

*Yacus, G. M. (1998). *Validation of the risk and needs assessment used in the classification for parole and probation of Virginia's adult criminal offenders.* Unpublished doctoral dissertation, Old Dominion University, Norfolk, VA.

Yang, M., Wong, S. P., & Coid, J. (2010). The efficacy of violence prediction: A meta-analytic comparison of nine risk assessment tools. *Psychological Bulletin, 136,* 740–767. doi:10.1037/a0020473

Supplemental Table

Benchmarks Across Indices of Predictive Validity

	Indices of Predictive Validity				
Benchmarks	Cohen's *d*	Correlation (r_{pb})	Area Under the Curve (AUC)	Odds Ratio (OR)	Somer's *d*
Poor	< .20	< .10	< .55	< 1.50	< .10
Fair	.20–.49	.10–.23	.55–.63	1.50–2.99	.10–.19
Good	.50–.79	.24–.36	.64–.71	3.00–4.99	.20–.29
Excellent	≥ .80	.37–1.00	.71–1.00	≥ 5.00	.30–1.00

Notes: Benchmarks were anchored to Cohen's *d* (1988) and based upon the calculations of Rice and Harris (2005) for AUC values and Chen, Cohen, and Chen (2010) for the odds ratios.

Part II

Risk/Needs Assessment in North America

2

The CAIS/JAIS Approach to Assessment

Christopher Baird

Introduction

Recent literature typically lists three primary objectives for correctional risk assessments: accurate identification of high-risk cases so agencies can target resources to cases most at risk of reoffending; identification of criminogenic needs; and identification of services and supervision strategies that reflect the motivations, learning style, capacities, and circumstances of each offender. The latter objective is commonly referred to as "responsivity."

Virtually all risk assessment models attempt to accurately triage offenders into low-, moderate-, and high-risk groups and do so with varying degrees of success. However, most standard approaches to risk assessment do not necessarily identify needs that are truly criminogenic for each individual; nor do they adequately address responsivity.

Over a four-year period (2006–2010), the National Council on Crime and Delinquency (NCCD) evaluated existing assessment protocols and selected components that could be blended to create a system that effectively addressed the three objectives listed above. The first system, Correctional Assessment and Intervention System™ (CAIS), was developed for adult offenders followed by the development of a similar model for juveniles (Juvenile Assessment and Intervention System™ [JAIS]). Though nearly identical in format and purpose, the juvenile and adult models differ significantly in content.

This chapter describes this assessment approach in detail including information describing how the system was developed, and provides data on the validity of the risk instruments integrated into CAIS™ and JAIS™, the validity and reliability of the Case Management Classification (CMC) component of CAIS, and results of evaluations conducted to date. Data from agencies currently using CAIS and/or JAIS, as well as recent innovations to both systems are also presented. Finally, additional research needed to further strengthen the system is discussed.

History of Development

CAIS and JAIS can both be traced to the original Wisconsin Case Classification and Staff Deployment Project (1975–1980). This project recognized that effective case management requires four interrelated components: risk assessment; needs assessment; a case planning strategy that responds to risk, needs, offender characteristics, and proclivities; and a means for assigning resources to cases based on these assessments. Four research principles drove the development of the Wisconsin system: validity, reliability, equity, and utility. To help ensure both face validity and practicality, eight probation and parole officers were assigned, half time for

Handbook of Recidivism Risk/Needs Assessment Tools, First Edition. Edited by Jay P. Singh, Daryl G. Kroner, J. Stephen Wormith, Sarah L. Desmarais, and Zachary Hamilton.
© 2018 John Wiley & Sons, Ltd. Published 2018 by John Wiley & Sons, Ltd.

three years, to the development effort. With support from the National Institute of Corrections (NIC), the Wisconsin system became a national model (known as the NIC Model Probation and Parole Management System), implemented in hundreds of county probation and parole agencies and nearly every state-administered agency in the United States. By 2004, it was, by far, the most widely used assessment system in the nation (Flores, Travis, & Latessa, 2004).

The Wisconsin system introduced three specific innovations to correctional assessments. The first two were (1) the introduction of a standardized needs assessment intended to enhance reliability among staff members and provide a basis for case planning, and (2) a reassessment system to address changes in risk and need profiles over time. Though these innovations represented important improvements to the assessment methodology, the most sophisticated innovation was the development of a case management component, originally known as CMC. The purpose of CMC was to provide clinical insight to every case entering probation or parole and help officers develop effective case plans incorporating supervision strategies, treatment programs, and responses to behaviors that best facilitate successful rehabilitation and community safety. In essence, CMC addressed "responsivity" long before the term was added to corrections' lexicon. In the mid-1980s, a juvenile assessment model was developed, based on the same framework and principles as the adult system.

In 2007, after an exhaustive three-year review of existing assessment protocols, NCCD determined that the NIC model required updating, but still represented the most comprehensive approach to assessment available to corrections. The organization then undertook an effort to update the original model, automating the system and introducing the following enhancements:

1) Computerized scoring: All components are automatically scored and a report recommending specific strategies and programs is instantaneously produced upon completion of the assessment.
2) Updated actuarial risk instruments were embedded in both the adult and juvenile systems. Moreover, if an agency had a well-validated instrument already in use, both CAIS and JAIS provide the flexibility needed to replace the NCCD risk tool with the agency's risk assessment instrument.
3) Gender specificity in CAIS/JAIS report: Outputs generated by CAIS/JAIS link the risk level and identified needs with gender-specific programs and approaches likely to produce positive results. Recommendations are produced for community supervision, institutions, and school personnel. These recommendations were developed by the director of the NCCD Center for Women and Girls.
4) A reassessment module that includes risk and needs reassessments and integrates these assessments with CMC and Strategies for Juvenile Supervision (SJS) recommendations to produce case plan revisions based on progress, emerging needs, or changes in the risk level of the offender.
5) Cross-referencing of recommendations: In a small percentage of cases (about 3%), scores for two different strategy groups are within 3 points. For these cases, the report lists primary and alternative strategies and programs in the case plan. If one approach does not provide the desired results, workers can turn to an alternative plan.
6) A state-of-the-art aggregate data-reporting package for planning, evaluation, budgeting, and tracking purposes.

Because recommendations produced by CAIS and JAIS are comprehensive, the system can be used in jails, prisons, and juvenile facilities, as well as with offenders on probation and parole. This allows for a continuum of care where all components of the justice system share goals and objectives for each offender regardless of where the offender is initially placed.

The following diagram illustrates how cases are processed using the CAIS/JAIS approach to assessment:

CAIS/JAIS Interview Completed at Admission

⇩

Risk Level Assigned

⇩

Needs Integrated into Supervision Plan Recommendations

⇩

Both Juvenile and Adult Reassessments are Completed Every Six Months

⇩

Supervision Plan Revised Based on Reassessment

Development and Validation of Risk Assessment

The original Wisconsin risk assessment instrument was constructed on a sample of 250 randomly selected cases and subsequently validated using a cohort of first 4,231 classified with the instrument. Validity was measured by the degree of discrimination attained in revocation rates for offenders assigned to different risk levels. These rates were: 2% for low-risk cases; 12.8% for medium-risk cases and 32.6 for high-risk cases. Table 2.1 presents an even greater breakdown of revocations by score level from the original validation study (Baird, Heinz, & Bemus, 1979).

As the above description of enhancements made to the original Wisconsin system indicates, risk assessment in CAIS/JAIS varies among jurisdictions using the model. All, however, follow a specific set of principles. First, the initial risk instrument must be a validated actuarial tool. Ideally, it would be a tool developed and validated for the population of the agency where it is implemented. Second, if no such instrument is available, NCCD provides recommended risk assessments (one for adults, another for juveniles) that have been validated in

Table 2.1 Initial Wisconsin Validation Results. Revocation Rates by Risk Scores, Two-Year Follow-Up.

Initial Risk Score	Cases Assessed	Cases Revoked	Revocation Rate
0–3	543	5	0.9%
4–7	1,243	28	2.5%
8–9	492	28	5.7%
10–11	387	38	9.8%
12–14	432	54	12.5%
15–19	498	78	15.7%
20–24	362	94	26.0%
25–29	252	94	37.3%
30 and above	141	60	42.6%
Total	**4,231**	**479**	**11.3%**

other agencies. These tools are composed of both static and dynamic risk factors. Regardless of whether the agency starts with these instruments or uses a risk instrument developed for their population, the CAIS and JAIS systems are designed to collect all data needed to validate (and revise if necessary) each tool for each participating jurisdiction. This reflects the original NIC recommendation that all agencies that adopt the Wisconsin risk assessment instrument conduct validation studies as soon as sufficient data are available to support the effort (NIC, 1981). This allows each site to make needed revisions to items, item weights, and cutoff scores to ensure optimal classification results. For example, drug laws vary among states and are enforced differently in different jurisdictions. Hence, the relationship between drug usage and recidivism may vary as well. Requiring each agency using a risk instrument to conduct periodic validations and make necessary changes helps ensure the tool represents current laws, policies, local populations and practices, optimizing validity in each jurisdiction. JAIS/CAIS risk validations delineate all analyses by race and gender. If results indicate differences in the way the system treats different groups of cases, revisions are made to risk instruments to ensure that equity is preserved.

The recommended NCCD risk instrument for adults is a slight modification of the original Wisconsin scale that has been validated in several jurisdictions. Factors contained on the recommended adult risk assessment instrument are:

- Employment
- Address changes in the last year
- Offender's *pattern* of *associates*
- Age at first *arrest* (adult or juvenile)
- Number of prior offenses
- Has offender ever been convicted (or adjudicated)?
- Number of prior jail sentences
- Number of prior periods of probation or parole supervision (including juvenile)
- Has offender ever had a probation or parole revoked?
- Percentage of criminal behavior related to alcohol abuse
- Percentage of criminal behavior related to other drug use.

A large number of validations have been completed by agencies using the risk model. The most recent validations were completed in Travis County, Texas (Fabelo, Nagy, & Prins, 2011) and in Wisconsin (Eisenberg, Bryl, & Fabelo 2009). The Wisconsin validation found the system still worked well 34 years after it was introduced, but some minor revisions improved its performance. Results of a risk validation conducted in Nevada are generally representative of results obtained in other agencies. Nevada Probation and Parole adopted the Wisconsin Risk Assessment in the mid-1980s and conducted two separate validations over the next 12 years. The second validation was initiated in 1997 using a randomly selected sample of 1,268 cases, stratified by region. Although the original Wisconsin tool effectively separated cases into low-, moderate-, and high-risk categories, small changes to item weights and cutoff scores, coupled with the deletion of one item significantly improved scale validity. Results of the Nevada validation are presented in Table 2.2 (Wagner, Quigley, Ehrlich, & Baird, 1998).

The recommended risk assessment tool for young people in the juvenile justice system was developed for the Office of Juvenile Justice and Delinquency Prevention's (OJJDP) Graduated Sanctions Program, using data from validations conducted in 14 separate jurisdictions (Wiebush, 2003). Those jurisdictions represented every section of the United States, including state agencies in Arizona, Maryland, Michigan, Missouri, New Mexico, North Carolina, Oklahoma, Rhode Island, and Virginia. Wiebush selected only those items that appeared on

Table 2.2 Comparison of Validation Results. Nevada Department of Probation and Parole Risk Assessment Instruments.

Risk Level	Nevada Validation		Nevada Revised	
	N	Rate of Recidivism	N	Rate of Recidivism
Low	286 (23%)	9%	229 (23%)	8%
Moderate	433 (34%)	24%	596 (47%)	22%
High	549 (43%)	45%	433 (35%)	51%

a majority of the tools reviewed and exhibited strong correlations with recidivism. The items contained on the initial risk scale are listed below:

- Number of schools in the past two years (include normal transitions)
- Peer relationships
- Youth's substance use
- Age of earliest arrest or referral to court or court services
- Number of arrests or referrals to court for criminal (non-status) offenses (include current)
- Number of arrests, referrals to court, or court services for drug offenses (include current)
- Number of court referrals for violent/assaultive offenses
- Total number of court-ordered out-of-home placements.

Results from a recent validation study of the risk tool for boys (a separate instrument is used for girls in this jurisdiction), conducted in Solano County, California, are presented in Table 2.3. This instrument clearly classified males effectively across all major racial/ethnic groups represented. (Baird et al., 2013). AUCs ranged from .65 to .68 for each racial/ethnic group tested.

Table 2.3 Solano County Probation Department. JSC Risk Assessment Instrument. Recidivism by Risk Level for Boys. Twelve Month Follow-up.

Risk Level	All Cases		Hispanic/Latinos		Whites		Black/African Americans	
	Percent at Level	Adjudication	Percent at Level	Adjudication	Percent at Level	Adjudication	Percent at Level	Adjudication
Low	15%[*]	18.8%	13%	25.0%	21%	20.9%	11%	13.6%
Moderate	43%	47.9%	43%	51.0%	40%	37.0%	44%	53.1%
High	43%	64.4%	43%	65.4%	39%	61.5%	44%	64.0%
Base Rate		50.7%		53.3%		43.1%		53.6%
Sample Size		880		240		202		394

*It should be noted that a much higher percentage of cases entering probation score at the low-risk level. Unless these youth have been adjudicated for an assaultive offense, they are screened out of probation and not included in the agency's database. Therefore, no follow-up information was available on these cases. The rate of recidivism for low-risk cases is undoubtedly lower than what is reported here.

NCCD recommends that agencies using the CAIS/JAIS systems use gender-specific risk tools developed for women and girls in the justice system. This is important because (1) women and girls generally recidivate at far lower levels than males, and (2) females usually comprise less than 20% of any correctional population. Therefore, risk assessment instruments developed on a combined population of males and females may fail to identify factors related to female recidivism and result in substantial inequities for women and girls. Often, these instruments will classify women and girls to higher risk levels than actual outcomes indicate is appropriate (i.e., "high risk" women recidivate at a lower rate than men classified as moderate risk). Carefully constructed gender-specific risk assessment tools can help eliminate these inequities. The correct tool is automatically integrated into the full CAIS/ JAIS protocol when the gender of each case is entered into the system.

NCCD currently has data on over 70,000 risk assessments from agencies using the recommended risk models. Table 2.4 breaks down placement at each risk level by gender.

Both the adult and juvenile risk assessments have been tested for inter-rater reliability and equity as well, meeting criteria for each measure established by NCCD. NCCD recently conducted a comprehensive evaluation of seven different risk instruments used in juvenile justice and found the risk instrument embedded in JAIS was the most reliable of the tools tested (Baird et al., 2013). Workers agreed on the risk level assigned to each case in the study 92% of the time (270 risk ratings). This study reported an Intraclass correlation (ICC) of .90 for risk levels assigned and .92 for risk scores provided by each rater, far surpassing levels of inter-rater reliability found for most other risk instruments tested in this study. The adult and juvenile risk assessment instruments recommended by NCCD are in the public domain and can be freely adopted by agencies not interested in the full CAIS or JAIS models. If desired, training and implementation assistance are available from NCCD (http://www.nccdglobal.org).

Development of CAIS/JAIS Needs Assessment Instruments

NCCD has long maintained that independent needs assessment is an essential component of any effective assessment model. Many models combine risk and need assessments, referring to needs contained in these systems as "dynamic risk factors" or "criminogenic needs." While there is no question that certain needs are correlated with recidivism and are, therefore, risk factors as well, addressing other needs may well be more important to the success of individual offenders. A general and, at best, modest correlation with recidivism does not mean the need is related to the criminal behavior of an individual offender. Thus, labelling needs as criminogenic, based on simple correlations with recidivism, implies a claim of causality that far exceeds what can be legitimately concluded from risk assessment.

Furthermore, assessing only those factors that correlate with recidivism often results in failure to assess needs that may be truly related to the criminal behavior of individual offenders.

Table 2.4 NCCD Initial Risk Instruments. Distribution by Gender.

Risk Level	Men	Women	Boys	Girls
Low	18.1%	22.2%	23.4%	21.6%
Moderate	43.5%	43.4%	48.2%	52.8%
High	38.4%	34.4%	28.3%	26.1%

In essence, the practice of focusing only on those needs that correlate with recidivism is a misguided effort to merge risk assessment—which uses group data to inform fundamental case decisions—with case planning, which must be based on issues and circumstances specific to each case.

There are three primary objectives of CAIS and JAIS needs assessment. The first is to ensure that a core set of potential needs is assessed for every case. The second is to add consistency in need identification and severity ratings. This is accomplished by adding definitions to guide both identification and ratings of severity. The final objective is to combine needs assessment with CMC/SJS results to focus service plans on those needs that are crucial to address to enhance the potential for success in the community.

These instruments closely align with the original Wisconsin needs assessment tool, which was subjected to rigorous inter-rater reliability testing, using structured interviews conducted with 10 cases, augmented by case files. Ratings of each need factor were completed by approximately 50 probation/parole officers. Agreement on the existence of a specific need exceeded 80% for all but one factor on the needs assessment instrument (NIC, 1981).

Needs included on the original Wisconsin instrument are presented below. One measure of reliability, percentage agreement among raters, is provided for each factor (Baird, Heinz, & Bemus, 1979).

- Academic/Vocational Skills   .88
- Employment   .90
- Financial Management   .93
- Family Relationships   .86
- Peer Relationships   .89
- Emotional Stability   .79
- Alcohol Usage   .94
- Drug Usage   .91
- Cognitive Ability   .79
- Health   .89
- Sexual Behavior   .84

The CAIS/JAIS needs assessments are also gender-specific, available in the public domain, and can be adopted freely by any justice agency.

Development, Synopsis, and Evaluation of CMC/SJS

While simple actuarial risk assessments and independent needs assessments are essential elements of CAIS and JAIS, it is the inclusion of the CMC and SJS case management systems that separates CAIS and JAIS from other justice assessment models. The following discussion describes: (a) the assessment process; (b) development of CMC and SJS; (c) a synopsis of CMC/SJS supervision strategies; and (d) results of evaluations conducted to date.

CAIS and JAIS each use a comprehensive structured interview to obtain information needed to assign each offender to the appropriate supervision strategy group. The interview takes approximately 45 minutes to complete and immediately produces a comprehensive report that includes the individual's risk level and principal needs to address, recommends a supervision strategy and treatment programs, and notes any special issues identified during the interview. In California, JAIS provides workers with a Title IV-E case plan in a format that allows the worker to modify the report if appropriate. CAIS and JAIS reports are designed to provide workers with information that will increase each person's chance of success; protect the community; improve institutional adjustment and behavior; and provide guidance for developing case plans tailored to the characteristics, circumstances, capabilities, and learning style of each offender. A sample report is presented in Appendix at the end of this book.

It is important to note that while the interview provides much of the information needed to complete all elements of the assessment, workers are also trained to rely on prior records and case files to validate information obtained from each interview and to ensure the accuracy of information collected. As noted below, data on reliability was integrated into the scoring systems of both the CMC and SJS model components.

Historically, turning information gathered during assessments into effective case plans relied solely on the clinical skill of a case manager or supervising officer. However, over the past 50 years attempts have been undertaken to systematize the process to ensure that assessment data are interpreted accurately and case plans incorporate services and strategies most likely to produce positive outcomes. The most elaborate of these endeavors was the I-Level system developed for the California Youth authority by Marguerite Warren and her colleagues (Warren, 1976). Though promising, the I-Level system required extensive training and ultimately proved too expensive and time-consuming when increases in correctional populations severely strained available resources.

Development of the I-Level system, as well as the subsequent development of CAIS and JAIS, demonstrates that creation of an assessment model that addresses "responsivity" is a complex undertaking, requiring far more analysis than that needed to create risk and needs assessments. In essence, responsivity requires a system that provides a clinical consultation for every case assessed. Development of CMC and SJS each took three to four years of data analysis and system design. This process is described below.

A team of three psychologists and several probation and parole officers developed the original CMC and SJS components of CAIS and JAIS (Lerner, Arling, & Baird, 1986). The first step was to design an intake interview to provide a detailed description of each offender's prior system involvement, characteristics, current circumstances, needs, and social and intellectual capacities. This information would then serve as the basis for determining how best to supervise and treat each offender to maximize the potential for success.

As offenders were admitted to probation or released to parole, each was interviewed by one of the project psychologists who then developed a comprehensive case plan that included specific recommendations for working with the offender in the community. Each interview was audiotaped and sent to the two other project psychologists who independently developed their own case plans. All recommendations included explicit predictions of attitudes, problems, and behaviors that officers would likely encounter; the clinician's judgment on what factors were driving each offender's criminal behavior; and specific recommendations on services, programs, and supervision approaches that would help the offender succeed. In total, 250 cases (750 independent evaluations) were used to construct CMC.

After recommendations were independently developed for each case, team members met to discuss similarities and differences and to agree, as a group, on the best approach to supervision. Over time, five basic supervision strategies emerged based on substantial similarities in both the characteristics of offenders and recommended supervision approaches. To enhance consistency among interviewers, a scoring guide was developed providing guidelines for interpreting answers to each question in the interview. Finally, a supervision guide was created that included services, programs, and supervision strategies the clinicians thought would produce positive outcomes for each offender group.

At this point in the development process, all classifications were based on the collective clinical judgment of the development team. The next step was to determine if a scoring system could be developed that would reliably place offenders in the same category selected by the clinicians. The development team determined that scoring should be based not only on a factor's ability to discriminate between offenders in each grouping, but also on the consistency (reliability) of ratings among team members. As a result, the scoring system developed (based on 256 calculations) placed nearly 99% of offenders in the study cohort in the same supervision group selected by the clinicians. Because the scoring system is based on measures of both validity and inter-rater reliability, it has proved to be especially robust over time. Criteria used for weighting factors are presented in Table 2.5 (NIC, 2003).

SJS development (1983–87) was identical to that used for CMC. JAIS produces recommendations for four different offender groups.

Synopsis of CMC Supervision Strategies

Although there are extremely important differences in recommendations the system provides (supervision strategies, programs, and responses to violations, etc.) for adults and juveniles, key descriptors of CAIS and JAIS case types and recommended strategies are similar. Brief synopses of each supervision strategy are provided below.

Selective Intervention (SI)

This group is characterized by a prosocial value system and a stable lifestyle. The offense history is usually limited, with the current offense often the first committed. Criminal conduct is generally the result of an isolated stressful event or situation or a specific psychological issue. Those with a psychological issue are placed in a treatment subgroup (SI-T).

SI cases usually present the fewest supervision problems and require the least amount of officer time. They generally have strong insight and respond well to reality-oriented counseling. They are usually honest and adhere to reporting requirements.

SI-T offenders, however, often require long-term treatment to deal with one specific issue (e.g., serious neurosis, chemical abuse, etc.). Caseworkers must confront any denial expressed by SI-T cases and insist that they get the treatment needed. Failure to provide needed treatment may well result in continued serious offending.

SI cases are sometimes involved in violent offenses. The Selective Intervention label is not meant to imply that supervision is not required, but that efforts should focus on a specific problem that is likely a primary cause of offending or delinquent behavior.

Table 2.5 Criteria to Establish Item Weight

Item Weight	Item Validity*	Item Reliability**
± 3	$P < .001$	.90 +
± 2	$P < .01$	.80 +
± 1	$P < .05$	.70 +

*Represents the significance level attained in discriminating one group from all others (t test for proportions).

**Represents percentage agreement among raters. There were 250 cases rated by 3–5 psychologists for a total of 843 ratings.

When placed in institutions, SI inmates often experience excessive anxiety. Depression may occur, especially during the early stages and may include suicidal thoughts and extreme swings from self-blame to denial of all responsibility. They may develop a perceived need for protection or acceptance which can result in exploitation by more criminally oriented or sophisticated peers.

Casework/Control (CC)

This group is characterized by chronic instability that is often the product of chaotic and abusive childhoods. This instability is frequently manifested in chemical abuse, serious emotional problems, frequent changes in employment and residence, and attachments to others who are equally unstable. While these cases typically have adequate vocational skills, success is often blocked by emotional and chemical problems, poor self-esteem, self-defeating behavior, and negative personal relationships.

In an institution, CC cases often have problems with peers and staff alike. Problems with authority and impulsivity often result in institutional misconduct. As for criminal behavior found in this group, misconduct may range from trivial to serious. During periods of stress, self-mutilation or suicide attempts may occur.

The goal is to "even out" the highs and lows this group experiences, ensuring they attend needed treatment programs, monitoring closely for attendance, participation, and respective behavior changes in their daily lives. As such, this group requires substantial resources and consumes significant officer time. They are difficult to work with as they frequently sabotage efforts to assist them.

When follow-up data were collected on the CMC construction cohort, developers found that this group frequently absconded when they finally seemed to be making progress. The team hypothesized that these cases are used to failure and potential success can produce substantial anxiety.

Environmental Structure (ES)

These offenders are characterized by a general lack of social and vocational skills. They are easily influenced by more sophisticated individuals and often commit crimes due to their association with more criminally oriented peers. Intellectual deficits are also frequently observed in these cases, which further contribute to the lack of social, vocational, and survival skills. Their crimes are generally impulsive, unsophisticated, and often motivated by the desire to be accepted by others. To gain the favor of associates, they can be convinced to undertake acts of violence. Such crimes, however, are rarely planned or committed due to malice. It is much more common that their criminal roles are determined by more sophisticated peers.

In institutions, ES inmates are susceptible to manipulation and exploitation. They have great difficulty differentiating between positive and negative influences. They are often not accepted as equals in housing units, and they are used and manipulated by others. For this group, even short-term incarceration should be the absolute last resort and, if incarcerated, decisions regarding housing and job placement are critical to their well-being.

Because ES offenders lack insight, counseling and therapy must avoid abstraction and generalization. Development of social skills should be stressed as well as assertiveness and constructive use of leisure time. Intellectual and vocational testing is essential to avoid establishment of unrealistic goals. In some instances, sheltered living and work situations are necessary.

Limit Setting (LS)

LS offenders are characterized by a criminal orientation and a lack of commitment to societal values. They have little interest in applying their skills or talents to socially acceptable endeavors.

Their criminal behavior is generally motivated by money, excitement, and power. Criminal histories can be lengthy, marked by numerous felonies and violent or aggressive offenses. They usually experience a fair degree of comfort in institutional settings and know how to manipulate the environment. Hence, LS inmates often dominate the more desirable jobs and program placements. They often emerge in leadership roles within the inmate power structure. Therefore, impressionable or vulnerable inmates (such as ES inmates) should be protected from this group. ES and LS inmates should never share housing units.

Public protection and officer safety are often important concerns in community supervision. All rules should be detailed in advance and consistently enforced. Failure to do so will be seen as weakness and rule-violating behavior will likely increase until directly confronted. Whenever possible, attempts should be made to foster interest in legal means to meet financial, power, and excitement needs.

NCCD has collected data on over 70,000 CAIS/JAIS classifications. Table 2.6 presents results by gender for both adults and juveniles. Females are more likely to classify as CC cases while the proportion of males falling into the LS group is more than double the percentage of females classified LS. It is important to note that over half of all juveniles classify as SI and most are low risk, indicating they could move through the system quickly and most are unlikely to recidivate.

As expected, there is a strong correlation between risk and CMC classifications. Over half of all LS and CC cases score high risk while only 5% of SI cases score at the high-risk level. Table 2.7 presents the percentage of cases found at each risk level, delineated by gender and CMC category.

CAIS and JAIS training is offered by NCCD. If the entire model is adopted, classroom training is conducted over a three-day period. Trainers then review and provide feedback on the

Table 2.6 CMC/SJS Distribution by Gender

	N	CC	ES	LS	SI-I	SI-T
Men	41,053	33%	7%	21%	10%	28%
Women	9,297	47%	5%	8%	10%	30%
Boys	16,007	12%	17%	19%	53%	–
Girls	5,656	25%	9%	9%	57%	–

Table 2.7 Risk Levels by CMC Categories

Risk Level	CC	ES	LS	SI-I	SI-T
Men					
Low	3.3%	8.8%	1.0%	53.4%	36.5%
Moderate	42.7%	52.0%	39.0%	41.0%	46.9%
High	54.0%	39.2%	60.0%	5.6%	16.6%
Women					
Low	5.3%	10.0%	0.7%	62.9%	39.7%
Moderate	45.3%	53.6%	40.5%	32.8%	40.1%
High	49.4%	36.4%	58.8%	4.3%	20.2%

first two assessments conducted by staff. Agencies can also simply adopt the risk and need scales at no cost. In this case, NCCD recommends a one-day training session for all staff.

CMC Evaluation Results

Several state agencies, including probation and parole agencies in Wisconsin, South Carolina, Texas Parole, and the Community Control Program in Florida, have evaluated the impact of CMC on recidivism. The National Institute of Justice also funded an evaluation of CMC used in a prison setting in the state of Washington. In addition, Travis County, Texas, Probation undertook an evaluation of CMC (called Strategies for Case Supervision or SCS in Texas) in 2006. Results from the largest and most recent of these studies are presented below.

In 1998, Florida evaluated the impact of CMC on offenders placed in its Community Control Program. Established as an alternative to prison, the program was used for approximately 11,000 offenders a year whose sentencing guideline scores fell in a range that recommended incarceration. The program emphasized control: caseloads were limited to 25 per officer, frequent contact with offenders was required, and additional controls such as electronic monitoring were often utilized. Other than CMC, there were no differences in supervision requirements or services provided to cases in the experimental and comparison groups. During the study period, about half of all Community Control admissions (n = 55,000) were placed with officers who had been trained in CMC. The remaining admissions comprised the comparison group. Although placement was not explicitly randomized, researchers found no significant differences in cases assigned to each group. Four of the five admission groups were tracked for two years. The final cohort was tracked for 12 months (Leininger, 1998).

Results of the Florida study are presented in Figure 2.1. In every annual cohort, offenders supervised under CMC guidelines had significantly higher rates of success. On average, CMC produced a 16% reduction in recidivism (a 26% relative decline in the recidivism rate).

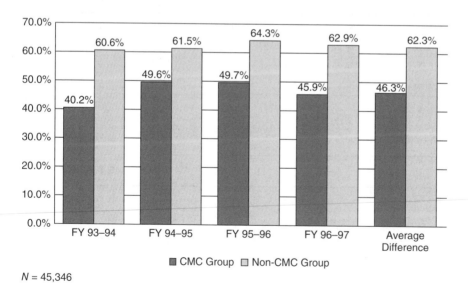

N = 45,346

Figure 2.1 Evaluation results: Florida reconviction rates, Community Control Program.

Table 2.8 Texas Board of Pardon and Parole. Percent Pre-Revocation at One Year.

Case Type	High Risk	Moderate Risk	Low Risk	Total
CMC	24.7% (58/235)	16.9% (103/608)	12.6% (42/333)	17.3% (203/1,176)
No CMC	32.1% (95/296)	25.3% (187/740)	13.3% (45/339)	23.8% (327/1,375)
Total	**28.8% (153/531)**	**21.5% (290/1,348)**	**13.0% (87/672)**	**20.8% (530/2,551)**

Quite obviously, significant savings are possible when CMC is combined with a structured alternative to incarceration and applied to a large number of cases.

The Texas Parole study was similar to that conducted in Florida. Offenders released on parole were assigned to either officers trained in CMC or to caseloads where officers had not yet been trained. The study group was comprised of all cases ($n = 2,551$) released over a two-month period in 1986; 1,176 were supervised by officers trained in CMC, while 1,375 cases made up the comparison group. Researchers determined there were no significant differences in the overall profiles of the two groups. Recidivism was defined as issuance of a pre-revocation warrant within one year of release. While no difference was found for low-risk cases assigned to the two groups, moderate- and high-risk offenders supervised under CMC guidelines had significantly better outcomes. When the high- and moderate-risk groups were combined, the relative decline in recidivism was 31.5%. Overall results are presented in Table 2.8 (Eisenberg & Markley, 1987).

In 2011, the Council of State Governments Justice Center released a report highlighting the achievements of the Travis County, Texas, Adult Probation Department (Fabelo, Nagy, & Prins, 2011). Their report *A Ten Step Guide to Transforming Probation Departments to Reduce Recidivism* promoted a core component of the Travis County program, CMC, or as it is known in Texas, SCS. The Travis County approach shared SCS and risk results with judges in a structured format to encourage increased use of community-based options to incarceration. This approach resulted in a 20% reduction in felony probation revocations in 2010 when compared to the year preceding implementation. In addition, the percentage of felony probationers revoked for administrative reasons fell from 54% to 36%.

Combined, the six evaluations of CMC indicate the system can have a substantial impact on the success of offenders in the community. The system has proven robust enough to work well over time and across programs with different policies and approaches to supervision. Finally, while evaluations have not been completed on CMC's juvenile counterpart (SJS/JAIS), a large proportion of admissions to Florida's Community Control Program were very young, high-risk offenders. This, coupled with the fact that CAIS and JAIS are identical in purpose, design, and method of development represents considerable promise that similar results are possible in juvenile justice.

Current Issues and Future Directions

The CAIS and JAIS systems provide a comprehensive approach to assessment. Further, both CAIS and JAIS contain components that have, at different times, been recommended by NIC and the oldest criminal justice research organization in the United States, NCCD. The risk instruments recommended (assuming an agency has no tool validated on their population) are simple, straightforward, and have proven valid and reliable. The needs assessments are well anchored, comprehensive, and reliable. When integrated with CMC and SJS recommendations, they provide the basis for effective case planning, identifying programs and supervision strategies that correspond to the circumstances, needs, and learning style of each individual. Further, the automated features of the system add efficiency, producing recommended case plans both at initial assessment and reassessment. Real-time aggregate data is available to every worker, supervisor, and manager, greatly enhancing management oversight and the potential for maintaining program fidelity.

There is, however, need for continuing and additional research. The most pressing research need is for a comprehensive study of the impact of the SJS component on outcomes for juveniles. Although its adult counterpart (CMC) has been the subject of several evaluations, none has yet been completed for SJS. Few agencies using JAIS have the resources required to complete such a study, but as more agencies adopt the system, such funding may become available. Existing databases are now available to support such an evaluation.

Additional research on implementation and system fidelity is also needed. This author's 40 years of experience with implementing assessment systems in agencies throughout the United States, Canada, Australia, and other countries indicate that reassessment is often completely overlooked or conducted only when a major issue arises. Even when managers are provided with automated systems that track compliance with reassessment schedules, probation and parole officers frequently fail to comply with reassessment requirements. This seriously compromises the degree of structure the system is designed to offer agencies and places serious limitations on data needed to improve training, implementation, and model components. The need for management oversight to ensure fidelity to system design should be emphasized as systems cannot be improved unless their limitations are recognized.

References

Baird, C., Heinz, R., & Bemus, B. (1979). *The Wisconsin case classification/staff deployment project: a two-year follow-up report.* Madison, WI: Division of Corrections.

Baird, C., Johnson, K., Healy, T., Bogie, A., Wicke Dankert, E., & Scharenbroch, C. (2013). *A comparison of risk assessment instruments in juvenile justice.* Madison, WI: National Council on Crime and Delinquency.

Eisenberg, M., Bryl, J., & Fabelo, T. (2009). *Validation of the Wisconsin Department of Corrections risk assessment instrument.* New York, NY: Council of State Governments Justice Center

Eisenberg, M., & Markley, G. (1987). *Something works in community supervision.* Federal Probation, 51 (4).

Fabelo, T., Nagy, G., & Prins, S. (2011). *A ten-step guide to transforming probation departments to reduce recidivism.* New York, NY: Council of State Governments Justice Center.

Flores, A. W., Travis, L. F., & Latessa, E. J. (2004). *Case classification for juvenile corrections: An assessment of the Youth Level of Service/Case Management Inventory (YLS/CMI).* Washington, DC: US Department of Justice.

Leininger, K. (1998). *Effectiveness of case management classification.* Tampa, FL: Florida Department of Corrections Research and Analysis.

Lerner, K., Arling, G., & Baird, C. (1986). Client management classification: Strategies for case supervision. *Crime and Delinquency, 32,* 254–271. doi:10.1177/0011128786032003002

National Institute of Corrections. (1981). *The Model Probation and Parole Management Program.* Washington, DC: Author.

National Institute of Corrections. (2003). *Classification in probation and parole: A model systems approach-supplemental report: The Client Management Classification system.* Retrieved from http://nicic.gov/Library/000936

Warren, M. Q. (1976). *Interventions with juvenile delinquents.* p. 172–204 in M.K. Rosenbaum (ed) Pursuing Justice for the Child, Chicago, University of Chicago Press.

Wagner, D., Quigley, P., Ehrlich, J., & Baird, C. (1998). *Nevada Probation Risk Assessment Findings.* Madison, WI: National Council on Crime and Delinquency.

Wiebush, R. (2003). *Graduated sanctions for juvenile offenders: A program model and planning guide.* National Council of Juvenile and Family Court Judges.

3

Correctional Offender Management Profiles for Alternative Sanctions (COMPAS)

Tim Brennan and William Dieterich

Introduction

The name COMPAS stands for "Correctional Offender Management Profiles for Alternative Sanctions" indicating that its core values involve alternatives to mass incarceration, accurate risk assessment, public safety, institutional safety, fairness and racial equity in criminal justice decision support, and enhancing community-based rehabilitative alternatives for offenders. The risk assessment components include both static and dynamic risk factors and well-validated risk and need factors to guide correctional interventions and decrease the likelihood of re-offending. Multiple evaluations of COMPAS by different research teams have confirmed its predictive validity and generalizability across several states; diverse justice agencies; and across a range of racial, gender, and offense groups. COMPAS has also been shown by independent research teams to effectively predict recidivism of Black and White offenders with equal accuracy with no evidence of race bias, as discussed later in this chapter.

COMPAS was designed as an automated web-based software package that integrates risk and needs assessment to support criminal justice decision-makers at multiple decision-making junctures in criminal justice. It supports decisions involving risk, offender management, treatment and case planning, early release decisions, parole and reentry planning, and post-release supervision. Agencies using COMPAS include pretrial release units, jails, prisons, probation and parole agencies, and treatment providers. Most recently it is being carefully introduced into courts—not to determine sanctions, but to provide background risk/needs information to support the widely used Risk-Need-Responsivity (RNR) principles to enhance crime-reduction and rehabilitation components of sentencing to support probation agents in preparing pre-sentence investigation reports.

Purposes of COMPAS

The major purposes of the COMPAS risk/need instrument are as follows:

Predictive Risk Assessment

COMPAS uses accurate, well-validated, and race-neutral actuarial predictive methods for several criminal justice risk outcomes, including violent recidivism, general recidivism, failure to appear (FTA) for court, failure for technical violation/non-compliance, absconding, disciplinary behaviors during incarceration, and other outcomes of use to agencies.

Handbook of Recidivism Risk/Needs Assessment Tools, First Edition. Edited by Jay P. Singh, Daryl G. Kroner,
J. Stephen Wormith, Sarah L. Desmarais, and Zachary Hamilton.
© 2018 John Wiley & Sons, Ltd. Published 2018 by John Wiley & Sons, Ltd.

Explanatory and Needs Assessment

COMPAS provides standardized and normed measures for all of the major risk, need, and explanatory factors to help criminal justice decision-makers to better understand offenders, develop case formulations, and to guide their use of the RNR principles for placement, rehabilitation, and treatment targeting for offenders.

Avoiding the Various Disconnects between Assessment, Treatment, and Outcomes

The web-based design of COMPAS and its integrated database achieves seamless connections between causal theories of crime, risk/needs assessment, treatment goals, treatments provided, and monitoring of short and long-term outcomes. Such connectivity can provide a foundation for evidence-based decision-making.

Different versions for Different Organizational Purposes and Target Populations

Different versions of COMPAS are customized for male and female offenders, youth offenders, internal prison classifications, and reentry versions.

Methodological Goals

Design goals of COMPAS include comprehensive theory-guided selection of risk and need factors, transparency of its risk assessment methods, generalizability across regions and justice agencies, user friendliness/efficiency, racial fairness and equity, and state-of-the-art quantitative methods, with periodic revisions/upgrades to keep pace with advances in criminal justice and criminology.

Background and History of Development

COMPAS was first developed in 1998 and has been regularly revised over the years as the knowledge base of criminology has grown and as correctional practices evolve. In a review of the state of the art in correctional assessment, Andrews, Bonta, and Wormith (2006) identified COMPAS as an example of the emerging fourth-generation (4G) approach to correctional assessment. When COMPAS was initially designed, the LSI-R represented the state of the art of the then current third generation (3G) risk/needs assessments in the 1990s (Andrews, Bonta, & Wormith, 2006). Of particular merit was the LSI incorporation of theory-guided assessment based on social learning. At that time, a prevailing weakness was that most risk and need assessments were virtually devoid of guidance from causal theories of crime (Brennan, 1987; Sechrest, 1987). Using LSI and other 3G instruments as a developmental context, multiple design goals were adopted for COMPAS partly on the basis of the history of offender classification, current explanatory theories of crime, and by relying on several major reviews of risk assessment at that time. COMPAS can perhaps be best understood by clarifying its design goals and features. These design goals are now discussed.

Incorporate Theoretical Guidance in Selecting Relevant Scales to Achieve a Comprehensive Coverage of Explanatory Factors

This goal concerns the interface from theory to assessment. The theoretical design (content validity) of COMPAS was extended beyond social learning theory to include core factors from several other main theories of crime—Strain theory, Control theory, Routine Activities theory,

General Theory of Crime, and others (Cullen & Agnew, 2003; Lykken, 1995; Palmer, 1992; Sampson & Laub, 2005).

Incorporate Empirical Guidance from Meta-analytic Research on Predictive Factors

The research-to-practice design of COMPAS was also guided by meta-analytic research to identify the strongest predictive factors for recidivism. Thus, the "Central Eight" risk factors identified by meta-analytic studies (Gendreau, Goggin, & Little, 1996) were all included in COMPAS: (1) History of antisocial behavior, (2) Antisocial personality, (3) Antisocial cognition, (4) Antisocial associates, (5) Family factors, (6) Educational/Vocational problems, (7) Leisure/recreation, and (8) Substance abuse. These are further discussed later in content validity.

Incorporate the Strength/Resiliency Perspective

The strength-based approach is included in COMPAS as a natural extension of its goal of comprehensive assessment (Andrews, Bonta, & Wormith, 2006; Ward, 2015). These address strength and resiliency factors such as job and educational skills, successful employment, adequacy of finances, safe and stable housing, family bonds, social and emotional support, and non-criminal parents and friends.

Incorporate Gender-Responsive Risk and Need Factors

Female-specific factors were generally missing from most prior 3G risk/needs assessments. Thus, when Van Voorhis and colleagues developed valid gender-responsive assessment instruments these were built into COMPAS (Van Voorhis, Bauman, Wright, & Salisbury, 2009). These have been critical in developing the Women's Pathways model that is now implemented as an Internal Classification system in the Massachusetts Women's Prisons (Brennan, Breitenbach, Dieterich, Salisbury, & Van Voorhis, 2012; Brennan, Oliver, & Dieterich, 2014; Oliver, Brennan, & Dieterich, 2014).

Dynamic vs. Static Items in COMPAS Risk Assessments

COMPAS includes both static and dynamic (changeable) risk factors. In fact, most of its explanatory and need factors are changeable such as: antisocial attitudes, associates/peers, rates of antisocial behavior, personality problems, school or work histories, leisure/recreational problems, and substance use.

Built-In Data Validity Tests and Error-Checking

In designing COMPAS assessment two latent tests of data validity were introduced to identify cases and responses where there is a suspicion of lying, sabotage, or incoherent responses. These are embedded within the self-report section, as follows: (1) a defensiveness or "impression management" test to assess whether a subject is distorting responses by "faking good," and (2) a test of incoherence/random responding to detect offenders who may sabotage their interviews or provide incoherent responses (Brennan & Oliver, 2002). In each case an automated alarm is triggered to alert staff of such problems (Brennan, Dieterich, & Ehret, 2009).

Flexible Access to External "In-Depth" Diagnostic Assessments

Agencies often wish to automate "special purpose" in-depth assessments for specific target populations, e.g., sex offenders, drunk drivers, domestic violence cases; or special assessments of complex factors such as antisocial attitudes, antisocial personality, and so on. COMPAS software allows rapid incorporation of such external assessment tools, provided that permission is granted from the author of the tool. Examples include the NIJ mental health screener and DVSI-R domestic assault screen (Williams & Grant, 2006).

Advanced Analytical Methods for Risk Prediction

COMPAS from its inception moved beyond traditional Burgess additive scaling to incorporate contemporary data analytic and machine learning (ML) methods for both predictive risk models and for its explanatory/treatment offender classification methods. Specifically for risk prediction models, logistic regression, Lasso (least absolute shrinkage and selection operator) regression, and survival analysis were used for variable selection and weighting. From this developmental work, the final COMPAS risk models for general recidivism and violent recidivism were finalized and are documented in Brennan, Dieterich, and Ehret (2009). To develop an "Internal Prison Classification" to guide treatment and management of incarcerated offenders bootstrapped K-means methods were used. To correctly assign new intake detainees to this explanatory classification, Random Forests (RF) and Support Vector Machines (SVM) were tested for accuracy of assignment, with RF finally chosen to operationalize the classification software (Breitenbach, Dieterich, & Brennan, 2009; Brennan et al., 2008; Oliver, Brennan, & Dieterich, 2014).

Multiple Dependent Criterion Variables

COMPAS goes beyond a single "general" recidivism risk outcome to include several criterion risk outcomes that are critical for different agencies at different decision-stages and for different target populations e.g., general recidivism, violent recidivism, technical failures, pretrial failures, absconding, disciplinary problems while incarcerated (Brennan et al., 2009).

Systematic Re-validation and Calibration to Accommodate Offender Population Changes

For large client agencies periodic re-validation, re-norming, and calibration studies have been requested and conducted. Thus, COMPAS norming and calibration procedures are periodically tested based on newer samples. This has not typically required major changes to the current risk models, but has involved minor adjustments to cut points. However, progressively larger samples have served to solidify the national norms and norms for major institutions, e.g., prison, jail, and community-based offender populations.

Ease of Use and Efficiency

Practical efficiency is paramount for large criminal justice agencies. This goal particularly distinguishes risk assessments developed for academic/research purposes from those developed for applied working agencies (Fishman & Neigher, 1987). A variety of practical goals require attention to designing user-friendly and efficient software that produces succinct case reports focused on the decision-relevant risk/needs data. For example, the final risk models for general recidivism and violent recidivism use only a small subset of the risk factors, while avoiding the full set of needs and explanatory factors for decisions where a comprehensive assessment is not immediately needed (Brennan et al., 2009).

Scalability—Agency Control Over Data Needs and Staff Workloads
for Specific Processing Decisions

COMPAS software allows agencies to select/suppress any scales to customize the selected assessment factors at each particular decision stage to match staff workload capacities and decision responsibilities. Pretrial Services, for example, may select only the Pretrial Release Risk Scale and its own preferred mix of needs scales for their decisions. Probation may select Violent Risk and General Recidivism Risk Scales and any other need scales seen as essential for their decisions. These selections have no impact on the basic risk models since these are cordoned off and uninfluenced by such scale in/out selections.

Integrated Database and Seamless Links from Risk/Needs Assessment
to Case Management, Treatment Goals, Treatments Provided, and Outcomes

COMPAS is built on an integrated database that seamlessly links criminal histories, current offense data, offender risk/needs, treatment goals, sentencing decisions, treatments/programs given, and outcomes monitoring. This integration addresses perennial complaints of "disconnects" between risk/needs assessment, treatment, and outcomes (Wormith, 2001).

Generalizability of Predictive Accuracy Across Regions, Agencies,
and Racial/Gender Categories

Generalizability of a risk scale can be claimed if a risk assessment instrument maintains its predictive validity across diverse regions, in different criminal justice institutions, and for major offender categories (e.g., race, gender, prisons, probation, etc.). Generalizability is required for any nationally distributed instrument. It partly rests on standardized data collection, standardized training, use of universally validated risk and need factors, effective implementation, and highly reliable scales. The basic Core COMPAS risk models have been tested for predictive validity across diverse regions, on different criminal justice populations, gender and race groups, and also evaluated by independent research teams. They have consistently achieved good risk accuracies (Brennan et al., 2009; Farabee, Zhang, Roberts, & Yang, 2010; Flores, Bechtel, & Lowenkamp, 2016; Lansing, 2012; Mann, Gulick, Blomberg, Bales, & Piquero, 2012). AUC values for the diverse offender populations are typically close to, or higher than .70 demonstrating accuracy and generalizability.

Versions of COMPAS

While the main Core COMPAS risk models are the primary focus of this chapter, several specific versions of COMPAS needs and explanatory scales have been developed for criminal justice target populations that are critical at different stages of a criminal career, are located in different criminal justice agencies, and may have distinct patterns of risks and needs. These alternate versions are discussed next.

Youth COMPAS

This targets youth aged 11 through 18 who have had an initial contact with the justice system. A theory-guided approach was again used to select key explanatory and predictive scales that are highly relevant for youth. The design goal was to assure a sufficiently comprehensive assessment to support staff in case interpretation, to identify treatment goals, and to achieve a deeper understanding of youth. Its 32 scales address family, school, peer relations, attitudes, personality, leisure activities, and community. The system includes risk assessments as well as an explanatory treatment-oriented youth classification. This explanatory classification uses a person-centered ML pattern-seeking approach for both boys and girls separately and has been replicated in several different states (Brennan, 2008; Brennan et al., 2008; Brennan & Breitenbach, 2009).

Reentry COMPAS

The target population for this version involves longer term incarcerated detainees, particularly those incarcerated for two or more years, primarily in prisons. Its design goals involve both risk assessment and an explanatory treatment classification for internal management, housing placements, rehabilitation programs, and reentry planning. While Core COMPAS is driven by current and prior street life and current crimes, it became obvious that after about two or more years of incarceration certain criminogenic needs (e.g., peer relations, vocational skills/ resources, family support) could undergo substantial changes. Additionally, reentry COMPAS has access to data that was not available at the beginning of a sentence (e.g., disciplinary history, prison adjustment, program attendance/performance, updated educational/vocational skills). Thus, an updated perspective was required for reentry assessments for additional factors that may influence effective reentry.

Women's COMPAS

The target population of this version is incarcerated women. This version uses the Reentry COMPAS gender-neutral scales, but adds the gender-responsive test instruments of Van Voorhis et al. (2009). These include trauma, self-efficacy, mental health, relationships issues, safety, parenting, and other factors critical for women. It offers a highly informative coverage to support relevant needs assessment, case interpretation, treatment planning, and data for the internal classification of women detainees to guide management of women detainees. The internal women's classification used a "person-centered" holistic approach for its development. Detailed descriptions of Women's COMPAS are provided in several publications and national conference papers (Brennan et al., 2012; Kilawee-Corsini, Pelletier, Zachary, & Brennan, 2016; Oliver, Brennan, & Dieterich, 2014).

The COMPAS system has several additional design features and procedures that may contribute to a full description of its functionality.

Norming or Standardization Samples

For implementations in new agencies COMPAS typically uses a large norming (standardization) representative sample of the agencies' target population. These allow the development of norm-referenced decile scores and cutting points to indicate whether a case is high or low compared to an appropriately defined norming sample. Representative samples are typically achieved by random sampling from the selected agency target population. With most medium-sized agencies, norming samples of approximately 700–900 cases have been used. Smaller agencies can initially use previously established national norms that have been compiled from the cumulative corpus of COMPAS studies nationwide. Locally specific norm scoring can be subsequently developed, if desired, when the local jurisdiction sample sizes become sufficiently large to support these procedures. Normative scores are then used to provide a variety of transformation scores (e.g., standard scores, deciles, quantiles, and z-scores). However, a surprising number of agencies prefer the traditional labels of low, medium, and high risk.

Given the nationwide range of COMPAS user agencies, very large samples have been compiled, over several years, to establish composite national normative population data sets for specific criminal justice sub-populations. Such national norms have been developed for the following eight criminal justice target populations to fit different institutions: (1) Male prison/parole, (2) Male jail, (3) Male probation, (4) Male national composite, (5) Female prison/parole, (6) Female jail, (7) Female probation, and (8) Female national composite. The overall male and female composites were generated from a stratified sampling approach based on published national proportions of offenders in jails, prison/parole, and probation agencies. Separate norms were published for adult male and female offenders in generating these national composite norms.

Settings for COMPAS Assessments (Pretrial, Community Corrections, Prison/Jail)

From its inception, COMPAS procedures were developed in real-life correctional agency settings—initially in jails, pretrial agencies and probation and subsequently in prison and parole contexts, each with their appropriate target populations. Most agencies have several decision stages where the COMPAS assessment is most appropriately placed (e.g., pre-sentence release assessments, initial jail classification, and prison intake). The COMPAS data entry interface allows agencies a flexible configuration procedure to specify the exact mix of information needs and scales for each decision juncture of an agency. Northpointe staff often partner with client agencies to map their case flow processes and select specific decision points to optimally select the needed information content of the assessment.

Web-based Implementation of Assessments and Subsequent Treatment and Outcome Data

COMPAS is designed as a Web-based integrated system to achieve substantial efficiencies in data collection, data integration, and linking of data across the major decision junctures in the justice system. This integration allows user agencies to track cases from intake to case closure and thus to support sequential case management, monitoring, short and long-term data feedback and to support subsequent evaluation research and evidence-based decision-making.

Predictive and Needs/Explanatory Scales

COMPAS distinguishes between risk and needs scales designed to identify and measure specific explanatory factors, needs, and intervention targets to inform case plans. The two principal risk-predictive models that are the main focus of this chapter are now discussed.

Model 1—COMPAS General Recidivism Risk scale. This is a linear equation initially derived from a Lasso regression model (Tibshirani, 1996) in a sample of pre-sentence investigation and probation intake cases in 2002 in New York State. Detailed descriptions of these models are given in Brennan and Oliver (2002), and Brennan et al. (2009). The primary factors making up this scale involved age, prior criminal history, criminal associates, drug involvement, and early indicators of juvenile delinquency problems. All of these selected risk factors are well validated predictors of recidivism (Desmarais & Singh 2013; Gendreau et al., 1996). The model was trained to predict an outcome of any new offense arrest within two years of intake assessment. Scale items were selected through diagnostic modeling strategies initially using Lasso regression and logistic regression. Updates to this scale are periodically developed to further improve predictive accuracy.

Model 2—COMPAS Violent Recidivism Risk scale. This equation is derived from a regression model developed in 2006 in a sample of pre-sentence investigation and probation intake cases. It was initially trained to predict violent offenses (misdemeanor and felony) within two years of intake. The scale inputs include history of violence, history of non-compliance,vocational/ educational problems, the person's age at intake, and the person's age at first arrest. The strong association of these factors with future violence has been established in previous research (Gendreau et al., 1996).

Additional Risk Models for Other Criminal Justice Criterion Outcomes

Several other outcome risk models have been developed to predict absconding, failure to appear for court (FTA), community failure/technical violations not involving a new arrest, return to prison, and others—as needed by client agencies.

Measures of Predictive Accuracy

The AUC is typically used to assess accuracy in COMPAS risk validation studies since it is the most widely used measure of predictive accuracy. However, we also report failure probabilities, odds ratios, and hazard ratios, and other measures of predictive accuracy in technical reports for client agencies. COMPAS risk scales generally achieve predictive accuracy in a modest to strong range depending on specific age, gender, racial groups, offense categories, and across different geographical areas. AUC values typically range from .68 to .77, with most exceeding .70. Thus, COMPAS risk scales generally match or exceed the AUC values of competitive instruments (Brennan et al., 2009; Flores et al., 2016; Lansing, 2012).

Independent Validation Studies by External Researchers, from Diverse Geographical Areas

Repeated validation studies have been conducted for COMPAS risk assessment models over the past several years in multiple jurisdictions, diverse gender and racial groups, and diverse justice agencies. These studies result from several client agencies conducting local validation studies (e.g., state agencies in New York, Florida, California, and Michigan) and using independent research teams. These independent studies have repeatedly confirmed the good predictive accuracy of COMPAS risk models (Brennan et al., 2009; Dieterich, Oliver, & Brennan, 2014a; Farabee et al., 2010; Flores et al., 2016; Lansing, 2012; Mann et al., 2012).

Follow-up Data and Time Frames

Follow-up data for predictive validation studies are typically obtained from state and/or county criminal justice databases (e.g., new arrests, new convictions, return to prison, offender disciplinary reports from jail or prison, FTA data from pretrial or court data). Follow-up time periods have ranged from a one-year outcome, to more extended two- or three-year and up to five-year follow-up. These typically require careful coordination with local criminal justice research departments to obtain outcome variables, match cases, and apply database modifications to ensure anonymity of cases.

Internal Classification for Jails/Prisons for Offender Management and Responsivity

Internal Classifications (IC) have been developed for the COMPAS system to guide prison staff in differential treatments of diverse offender categories to address responsivity issues regarding offender management, housing, case planning, preparing offenders for reentry, and post-release planning. Traditionally internal classifications were designed to identify treatment relevant offender groups that have highly differentiated needs to guide internal detainee management (Brennan, 1987; Palmer, 1992; Van Voorhis, 1994; Warren, 1971). These internal classifications transcend the limited information content of external security classifications and go beyond the "one size fits all" strategy. Most prior internal classifications suffered from multiple flaws as noted in the pessimistic national evaluations of existing internal classifications (Hardyman, Austin, Alexander, Johnson, & Tulloch, 2002). However, over the last decade substantial advances have occurred in theoretical design, content validity, reliability, and statistical stability of internal classifications (Brennan et al., 2014; Harris & Jones 1999). These advances are exemplified in COMPAS by the Women's Pathway program in Massachusetts Women's Prison that applies differential internal management and treatment approaches for several diverse categories of women detainees (Brennan, 2012; Kilawee-Corsini et al., 2016; Oliver, Brennan, & Dieterich, 2014).

Theoretical Foundations of COMPAS

A major design goal of COMPAS was to base it on a strong theoretical foundation. At the time of its initial development, the leading 3G system was the LSI-R exemplifying a theory-guided approach relying mainly on social learning theory. However, since there is evidence of multiple heterogeneous pathways to crime (Brennan & Breitenbach, 2009; Cullen & Agnew, 2003; Lykken, 1995) the strategy in COMPAS was to go beyond social learning to include a broader coverage of major theoretical approaches to match the heterogeneity of the offender population. Thus, COMPAS assesses core variables from social learning theory, strain theory, control/bonding theory, routine activities theory, social disorganization, and the General Theory of Crime. These theories and their key factors in COMPAS are now briefly discussed.

Social Learning Theory

This emphasizes modeling of behavior and social learning from close peers and local community and the acquisition attitudes, motives, and skills. Key factors include: antisocial peers, antisocial attitudes, and antisocial or high crime neighborhoods (Lykken, 1995).

The General Theory of Crime

This theory integrates elements of antisocial personality (e.g., impulsivity, anger), antisocial unstable families and inadequate parenting with a high-risk opportunity lifestyle as basic causes of criminal behavior (Gottfredson & Hirschi, 1990).

Strain Theory/Social Marginalization

This emphasizes social marginalization, inadequate social roles, low social/human capital and poor resources to cope with such strains. Key factors include school failure, job failure, blocked social aspirations, few positive social roles, social isolation, and antisocial attitudes (Agnew, 1992).

Routine Activities Theory

This identifies a high-risk unstructured lifestyle as an important situational precipitator of crime. The key factors include boredom/restlessness, few prosocial leisure activities, unemployment/not in school, antisocial peers, and substance abuse (Cohen & Felson, 1979).

Social Disorganization/Sub-cultural Theories

This emphasizes the social and physical environment including high crime neighborhoods, poverty, and sub-cultural norms that differ from mainstream norms as important criminogenic factors for crime. Current perspectives are described in the *Code of the Street* (Anderson, 2000) and include factors such as unstable neighborhoods, poor housing, single parent families, unemployment, transience, poverty, gangs, and easy drug accessibility.

Control/Restraint Theories

This theory emphasizes the strength or weakness of various social bonds to family, school, beliefs, church, etc., that may restrain people from antisocial behaviors. Key factors include family bonds, parenthood, marital bonds, prosocial beliefs/attitudes, prosocial engagement bonds (Hirschi, 1969; Agnew & Cullen, 2003).

Data Collection and Interviewing

COMPAS uses a multimodal approach with three data gathering components: an official records section, an interview section, and a self-report section.

Official Records/File Review

This data ideally is collected before conducting an interview. Source documents include state and national criminal histories, institutional behavior reports, police reports, and in some cases the pre-sentence investigation reports etc. This component covers about one third of the overall data.

Interview Section

Semi-structured interviewing is typically used for this component. Training includes use of basic Motivational Interviewing (MI) skills, including open-ended questions, role-play exercises, active listening skills (ALS), paraphrasing, reflections, probing, and skills to guide the conversation through the various substantive domains of the instrument. Training also involves clarifying the meanings of all COMPAS questions to ensure common understandings. Training strategies also include how to deal with difficult interview situations and to minimize suspicion, resistance, or anxiety during the interview. The software also provides interviewers with immediate access to all question definitions, by including hyperlinks or "Tool Tips" giving direct access to written definitions and explanations of each question. To obtain such definitions the interviewer simply scrolls over the question on the assessment screen to quickly access a dropdown written definition of the question. Two hidden data validation tests (Lie/Faking good and Coherence tests) are embedded in the questionnaire. At the end of an interview these produce automated alerts to the interviewer to check and verify any instances of random incoherent responding as well as defensiveness and out-of-range responses.

Standard interviewing can also be used, as needed, for reading-impaired respondents. For such cases staff simply read each successive question aloud from the questionnaire and enter the person's responses. Staff interviewers are instructed to clarify the meanings of any questions if asked, or where they suspect the respondent has not understood the question.

Self-Report Paper and Pencil Section

This component largely focuses on life history, family, education, attitudes, and other personal areas. This section also contains several defensiveness scale items to detect "faking good" responses to questions. Staff may provide assistance to clarify interpretation of questions and to ensure a private protected environment.

Scoring Guidelines

Scoring guidelines are based on large norming sample distributions for each local site to establish cut points for decile levels, to compute probability scores, or simply to provide the traditional low, medium, and high designations. A surprising number of agencies prefer these simple nominal labels. For some small agencies, national norms may initially be used until sufficiently large numbers of cases have been locally collected to develop stable normative scores. High, medium, and low labels are set using decile score intervals that are imposed on the normative sample distributions, as follows: low (1–4), medium (5–7), and high (8–10). With the completion of calibration studies and large norming samples, some agencies prefer probability scores rather than deciles. Selecting high, medium, and low segments typically requires discussion with local administrators and policymakers to determine cutting points. Northpointe can also provide more technical approaches to cutting point thresholds and decision criteria (Dieterich, Oliver, & Brennan, 2014b). Such procedures for cutting points and local decision-making rules are quite independent of the actual risk model since the collected set of risk factors and weights are unchanged by these decision rules.

Administrator Qualifications and Training Modules

Basic 2-day Training

All interviewers attend a two-day COMPAS training session, with updates and retraining as requested by agency administrators. To date, interviewers have largely consisted of experienced correctional officers or probation/parole officers of criminal justice agencies that have implemented COMPAS. Additionally, the basic training sessions can be augmented by additional training for local supervisors that focuses on quality assurance and supervisory roles. The basic training modules focus on topics such as: MI interviewing techniques, preliminary collection of criminal histories and case file data, the logic and validation of actuarial risk assessment, strengths/weaknesses of risk assessment, links to the RNR principles, understanding the criminological theories that underlie COMPAS, case interpretation skills, dealing with difficult or anxious respondents, the pros/cons of discretionary overrides, and the requirements of supervisory review and appropriate documentation of overrides. The software also continually monitors override counts, the presence of supervisory review, and documentation of reasons for overrides.

Software Training

Software training is a separate module that is included in both basic and train-the-trainer workshops. It addresses how to use, navigate, and follow the different screen modules of the COMPAS software. All training materials are included in a basic COMPAS User Guidance Manual that is provided to all trainees and supervisors.

Train-the-Trainer Workshops

These include all materials in the basic two-day training. However, selected sections are covered in greater depth, particularly the tools for interpreting the offender profile data, linking needs to treatment goals, detailed explanations of the causal theories of crime embedded within COMPAS, and skills for synthesizing data into case formulations. Supervisory skills emphasize quality control, error detection, use of discretionary overrides, positive feedback to staff, and the importance of regular "case review meetings" where staff can discuss difficult or interesting cases, resolve ambiguities, and consider the use of such cases for ongoing learning opportunities.

Anomaly or Error Detection

As noted earlier, two automated data validation tests are embedded within COMPAS assessment software. These are a "faking good" test and an incoherence/random responding test. Such validation procedures have been used in several well-known psychometric tests, e.g., MMPI and MCMI. They are used to alert interviewers to erroneous, anomalous, or inconsistent offender responses to questions. At the end of an assessment interview, all suspicious responses are automatically flagged by the software and provided to the interviewer. Interviewers are instructed to review/discuss all problematic responses and make revisions on the basis of additional probing to clarify the flagged responses. Technical details are available in Brennan and Oliver (2002).

Coding Integrity Checks

Missing values and out-of-range values are automatically identified and the interview cannot be closed until such responses are properly reviewed and corrected.

Reliability Research

Internal Consistency Reliability

Internal consistency of each COMPAS subscale is initially established by traditional item analysis, followed by factor analysis for scale refinement of each specific subscale and to establish the factorial validity of each subscale. Cronbach's alpha coefficient is used to assess levels of internal consistency of all COMPAS subscales. By convention, alphas of .70 and above indicate acceptable internal consistency (Nunnally & Bernstein, 1994).

Table 3.1 provides summary statistics and alpha coefficients for the Core COMPAS subscales in a sample of 15,315 inmates assessed from January 2010 through January 2012 by the Michigan Department of Corrections (MDOC). The results show that most COMPAS scales meet the .70 criterion for internal consistency. Similar results are found in other jurisdictions.

The few subscales in Table 3.1 with lower alphas refer to index measures or to higher order factors that were not designed to achieve high internal consistency since index terms can contain items not expected to be highly inter-correlated. For example, Violence History (.53) and Current Violence (.52) are both index measures consisting of diverse offense types that do not necessarily correlate with each other. Similarly, Family Crime (.62) is an index of diverse problems of different family members. In contrast, Social Adjustment (.54) and Criminal Opportunity (.66) are both based on higher order factor analysis of the total set of subscales

Table 3.1 Summary Statistics and Alpha Coefficients for COMPAS Core Scales in a Prison Intake Sample from the Michigan Department of Corrections (*n* = 15.315)

	Items	Min	Max	Mean	SD	Alpha
Criminal Involvement	4	0.00	19.00	8.82	4.66	c.75
Noncompliance History	5	0.00	21.00	4.49	4.23	.65
Violence History	9	0.00	16.00	2.13	2.37	.52
Current Violence	7	7.00	13.00	8.21	1.28	.53
Criminal Associates	7	7.00	22.00	9.75	2.66	.71
Substance Abuse	10	10.00	20.00	12.81	2.40	.76
Financial Problems	5	5.00	15.00	8.21	2.34	.70
VocEd Problems	11	11.00	30.00	19.60	3.89	.71
Family Crime	6	6.00	12.00	7.57	1.50	.62
Social Environment	6	6.00	12.00	7.54	1.82	.81
Leisure	5	5.00	17.00	7.86	3.52	.86
Residential Instability	10	9.00	30.00	13.26	3.70	.71
Social Adjustment	15	12.00	37.00	20.23	3.44	.54
Socialization Failure	13	7.00	32.00	12.10	3.76	.69
Criminal Opportunity	14	13.00	39.00	21.23	4.45	.66
Social Isolation	8	8.00	40.00	16.90	4.85	.83
Criminal Thinking	10	10.00	45.00	20.73	4.91	.80
Criminal Personality	13	13.00	58.00	31.84	5.71	.70

and thus involve several different source factors from these two domains. Cronbach's alpha is less applicable for either indexes or higher order scales, given the explicit multidimensionality of these measures.

Test-Retest Reliability

COMPAS scales have been found to have good test-retest reliability. Farabee et al. (2010) reported that the test-retest reliability of COMPAS was in the excellent range. In their independent study these researchers compared the test-retest reliability of COMPAS Core scales to those of the LSI-R subscales. The test-retest reliability for the COMPAS scales produced correlations ranging from .70 to 1.00, with an average correlation above .80, compared to the average test-retest reliability for the LSI-R scales of .64. Thus, COMPAS had higher test-retest reliability than the LSI.

Inter-rater Reliability

Desmarais and Singh (2013) noted that inter-rater reliability is "rare" among current risk assessment instruments. This is particularly the case when risk instruments are being used in an operational context of crowded and over-worked criminal justice agencies—as opposed to research studies. Difficulties can involve staff reluctance due to high workloads, staff turnover, untrained staff entering the project, and logistical difficulties in arranging for multiple interviewers to assess the same case, particularly when caseloads are high. However, regarding COMPAS two IRR studies are currently underway in two state agencies. These are planned to examine inter-rater reliability at the item, scale, and risk level categories.

Several additional approaches are used in COMPAS to upgrade the reliability of all COMPAS data and scales, as follows:

On-Screen Hyperlinks to Give Staff Immediate Access to Question Definitions

Reliability is also enhanced when users have a clear understanding of each specific question. As noted earlier all question definitions in the COMPAS assessment instruments have hyperlinks embedded in each assessment screen, so that staff users—during an assessment—can immediately access a question's definition.

Systematic Identification, Removal, or Revision of Problematic Questions

Staff training and ongoing quality control during the early pilot testing and development of COMPAS involved an ongoing dialogue between COMPAS staff and agency users to identify any ambiguous questions or problems in how staff understood or interpreted questions. Once ambiguous questions were identified they were either dropped or revised until staff users had clear common understandings of all questions. Such revisions, as expected, gradually diminished so that the data items and scale structures have been stable over the last few years. However, if user agencies suggest any valid and useful change, the merits and impact of such changes are carefully examined and revised as needed. For example, Michigan DOC, for fairness concerns, requested that convictions rather than arrests be used in the predictive models of COMPAS. Revised models were tested showing that this switch to convictions had virtually no impact on levels of predictive accuracy with virtually identical AUC levels. Notwithstanding this finding, the revised model using convictions was made available for Michigan.

Using Machine Learning (ML) Classifiers to Achieve High Reliability of Prison Classification Assignments

Over the past two years, Northpointe has pilot tested and incorporated ML classifiers (Random Forests, Support Vector Machines) into its internal prison/jail classifications to reliably assign new cases to their appropriate offender category. This classification task requires complex feature matching between each new case and the prison's internal classification system. Accurate assignment is critical since such assignments have been an Achilles heel in prior internal institutional assignments. In pilot tests these procedures achieved impressive kappa coefficients in the range of the .80 and above. This is exemplified in the Women's Pathways project in the Massachusetts Women's Prison (Kilawee-Corsini et al., 2016; Oliver, Brennan, & Dieterich, 2014)

Latent Factor Structure of the Overall COMPAS Assessment Domain

Factor analytic studies have been applied to the full set of COMPAS explanatory and need scales to clarify the meanings and higher order factor structure underlying these basic COMPAS scales. This differs from the narrower within-scale factor analysis studies that were used to clarify the specific dimensionality and central meaning of each subscale and their highest loading items

(Brennan & Oliver, 2002). This inter-scale analysis was used to clarify the basic dimensionality and links to theoretical structures underlying the full set of COMPAS subscales. The Scree Plots suggested an eight basic dimensional structure. These eight factors were interpretable and captured 73% of the variance of the total set of scales as described below.

1. Early Starter, High Violence Risks with Very Low Social Capital

This factor dimension is defined by younger offenders, early onset of serious and violent delinquency, high-risk lifestyles, high violence risk, and poor educational vocational resources, but, as yet, with low adult criminal histories.

2. Extent of Criminal Involvement

This dimension reflects the history and extent of criminal involvement. It matches a general criminal involvement factor identified in several prior meta-analytic studies as a critical predictive risk factor.

3. Social Marginalization

This dimension is defined by poverty, poor educational/vocational resources, low social support, and unstable/poor housing. It appears to be a core dimension in strain theory and social exclusion.

4. Violence

This factor is defined by current violent felonies, history of violence, and high risk of future violence.

5. Antisocial Personality and Attitudes

This dimension fuses antisocial personality and antisocial attitudes with an additional strong loading on antisocial families. It is highly reminiscent of the core dimensions of the General Theory of Crime (Gottfredson & Hirschi, 1990).

6. Socialization and Social Learning in Antisocial Environments

This is a social process dimension defined by early onset, high crime families, high-risk peers, and extensive criminal histories. It reflects a conjunction of factors related to a sub-cultural context and social learning (Lykken, 1995).

7. Transience, Unstable Residence, Drugs, and Poor Social Adjustment

This dimension is strongly connected to transience, substance abuse, conflicted social adjustment, and high risk of FTA.

8. Antisocial High-Risk Lifestyle

This is defined by low prosocial opportunities, high-risk lifestyle and high opportunities for antisocial behavior, and antisocial peers. It reflects a core dimension of routine activities theory.

Criterion Validity: Predictive and Concurrent Validity

Predictive Validity of COMPAS Has Been Replicated in Multiple Jurisdictions, Multiple Agencies, and by Different Research Teams

The predictive validity of the COMPAS General Recidivism Risk Scale (GRRS) and Violent Recidivism Risk Scale (VRRS) have been validated in diverse geographical areas, diverse criminal justice agencies, and diverse gender and race categories. Table 3.2 provides the AUC results from studies conducted in the Michigan Department of Corrections (MDOC), New York State Office of Probation and Correctional Alternatives (OCPA), California Department of Corrections and Rehabilitation (CDCR), and Broward County Sheriff's Department. For details, see the publications by the respective research teams (Brennan et al., 2009; Dieterich, Brennan, & Oliver, 2011; Dieterich, Oliver, & Brennan, 2011; Farabee et al., 2010; Flores et al., 2016; Lansing, 2012). Regarding benchmarks for predictive accuracy Rice and Harris (1995) have suggested that AUC scores greater than .56, .64, and .71, respectively, correspond to "small," "medium," and "large" effect sizes. This table indicates that a majority of predictive scores for COMPAS instruments in these various studies fall in the large effect size range.

Predictive Validity Across Gender and Racial Groups (Criterion Related Validity)

Turning to gender and racial groups several outcomes studies have examined the predictive validity and equity of the COMPAS risk scales for such groups. Brennan et al. (2009) found that the COMPAS General Recidivism Risk Scale performed equally well for Black and White males at predicting arrest outcomes in a probation sample (*n* = 2,328). The AUCs for any arrest within two years were comparable at .67 for Black men and .69 for White men. For felony arrest the AUCs were .73 for Black males and .71 for White males.

In a more political context Angwin, Larson, Mattu, and Kirchner (2016) of the investigative journalism group ProPublica claimed that the COMPAS risk scales were biased against African Americans in a sample of defendants in Broward County, Florida, and additionally claimed that

Table 3.2 AUC Results from Six Studies of the Predictive Validity of the COMPAS General Recidivism Risk and Violent Recidivism Risk Scales

Study	N	Year	Any Arrest	Felony	Person	TechViol.	Prison Return
NY Probation[a]	(*n* = 2,328)	2009	.680	.700	.710		
NY Probation[b]	(*n* = 13,993)	2012	.710				
MDOC Reentry[c]	(*n* = 25,347)	2011		.710	.700	.690	.720
MDOC Probation[d]	(*n* = 21,101)	2011		.670	.740	.710	
CDCR Reentry[e]	(*n* = 25,009)	2010	.700		.650		
Broward Jail[f]	(*n* = 6,172)	2016	.710		.710		

a) Brennan et al. (2009).
b) Lansing (2012).
c) Dieterich, Brennan, and Oliver (2011).
d) Dieterich, Oliver, and Brennan (2011).
e) Farabee et al. (2010).
f) Flores et al. (2016).

all risk assessment systems in criminal justice were biased against Blacks. However, subsequent analyses of the same Broward County data by independent researchers (Flores et al., 2016) and by Northpointe researchers (Dieterich, Mendoza, & Brennan, 2016) refuted the findings of Angwin et al. (2016) and identified serious flaws in their methods. Both rejoinder studies found that the COMPAS General Recidivism Risk Scale and Violent Recidivism Risk Scale performed with equivalent accuracy for Black and White defendants. Flores et al. (2016) found that the COMPAS models for General Recidivism Risk Scale and Violent Recidivism Risk Scale were good predictors for both any arrests and violent arrests, and predicted equally well for Black and White defendants. Flores et al. obtained the following AUCs for the General Recidivism Risk Scale decile score predicting any arrest within two years: .70 for Blacks, .69 for Whites, and .71 in the sample overall. For the Violent Recidivism Risk Scale (decile score) for predicting any violent arrest within two years, Flores et al. obtained AUCs of .70 for Blacks, .68 for Whites, and .71 in the sample overall. In another analysis of the Broward County data, Dieterich et al. (2016), Table 3.3 reported similar AUC results to those of Flores et al., with both studies again rejecting the ProPublica claims.

A further independent study of the predictive accuracy of COMPAS by Farabee et al. (2010) examined findings for 23,653 men and women, and White, Black, and Hispanic racial groups in the California Department of Corrections and Rehabilitation. This large sample of prisoners had been released on parole, and the study had a two-year follow-up. Table 3.4 displays AUCS for the "any arrest" outcome study reported by Farabee et al. (2010). These results also confirm that AUCS are highly similar for men, women, White, Black, and Hispanic groups. Again, most AUC values are in the .70 range and thus comparable to other well-established risk instruments.

These various results taken together indicate that the predictive validity of the General Recidivism Risk Scale is good overall and closely equivalent for men and women, and for White, Black, and Hispanic offenders.

Table 3.5 displays AUCS for a similar study in the Michigan Department of Corrections (MDOC) on a very large reentry sample. The outcome was any arrest within three years following release from prison into the community. As in the previous analysis, the results are provided for the entire sample (All) and for the men, women, White, Black, and Hispanic groups.

Table 3.3 AUC results for the General Recidivism Risk Scale (GRRS) Decile Scores and Violent Recidivism Risk Scale (VRRS) Decile Scores by Dieterich et al. (2016) on the Same Data used by ProPublica

Sample	*n*	Nfail	Base rate	AUC	Lower 95% CI	Upper 95% CI
GRRS						
White	2,103	822	.39	.69	.67	.72
Black	3,175	1,661	.52	.70	.69	.72
All	6,172	2,809	.46	.71	.70	.72
VRRS						
White	1,459	174	.12	.68	.64	.73
Black	1,918	404	.21	.71	.68	.74
ALL	4,020	652	.16	.72	.70	.74

Table 3.4 AUCS for the General Recidivism Risk Scale for a California Prison Sample. The AUCs Are Calculated Separately for the Different Subgroups Defined by Gender and Ethnicity/Race

	N	Nfail	AUC	Lower 95% CI	Upper 95% CI
Men	21,015	14,819	.71	.70	.71
Women	2,638	1,595	.69	.67	.71
White	7,268	4,683	.70	.69	.71
Black	6,447	4,813	.69	.67	.70
Hispanic	8,514	5,980	.71	.70	.72
All	23,653	16,414	.70	.70	.71

Table 3.5 AUCS for the General Recidivism Risk Scale and "Any Arrest" Outcome for a Michigan Reentry Sample. AUCs are Calculated Separately for Different Gender and Ethnicity/Race Subgroups

	N	Nfail	AUC	Lower 95% CI	Upper 95% CI
Men	13,439	5,427	.73	.72	.74
Women	961	341	.74	.71	.77
White	7,177	2,807	.75	.74	.76
Black	6,571	2,720	.71	.69	.72
Hispanic	289	89	.78	.73	.84
All	14,400	5,768	.73	.72	.74

The AUCs in Table 3.5 vary from .71 (Black) to .78 (Hispanic). It may be noted that the effective sample size for the Hispanic group is relatively small, which resulted in a broader 95% confidence interval. The AUCs for men (.73) and women (.74) are similar. The AUCs for White (.75) and Black (.71) do differ slightly but both values are reasonably high and in the "large" range.

Content Validity—Coverage of Relevant Factors

Content validity is a key design feature of any RNA and indicates whether a risk instrument includes a comprehensive coverage of relevant factors or a narrow, oversimplified coverage. Risk assessment instruments that narrowly focus on risk alone—typical of second generation instruments—often shorten an instrument to very few variables, ranging from four or five up to perhaps 15 items, that are mostly static criminal history items. This results in a brief efficient risk assessment, although the deficit of such instruments is that they are largely incapable of guiding treatment, internal management, reentry planning, or for guiding RNR principles. COMPAS attempts to meet this need for a brief risk assessment instrument by offering short, highly focused risk models. However, for its needs assessment it expands the content validity by assessing a comprehensive range of explanatory needs and treatment factors as listed in Table 3.6. This provides a broad explanatory profile of each offender to case managers if all scales are selected. This comprehensive coverage is also used for the internal classifications for both male and female prison detainees that aim to guide internal offender management and to

Table 3.6 Concurrent Correlations between COMPAS Subscales and Criminal History Features

COMPAS Scale	Age at First	Prior Arrests	Parole Returns	Prior Prisons	Assault Tickets
Criminal Associates	−.28	.23	.17	.17	.19
Substance Abuse	−.07	.22	.14	.15	.06
Financial Problems	−.07	.08	.06	.05	.04
VocEd Problems	−.24	.16	.13	.11	.15
Family Crime	−.22	.10	.04	.02	.07
Social Environment	−.16	.10	.11	.13	.13
Leisure	−.13	.04	.02	.00	.05
Residential Instability	−.09	.10	.11	.09	.11
Social Adjustment	−.27	.22	.13	.11	.15
Social Isolation	−.02	.08	.07	.06	.07
Criminal Thinking	−.13	.06	.03	.02	.10
Criminal Personality	−.24	.15	.11	.09	.16

With $n = 25{,}773$, a correlation of .013 is significant at $p < .05$ (2-tailed).

fully support the RNR principles. As noted earlier the two strategies used to achieve a broad comprehensive content validity for COMPAS, are as follows.

Meta-analytic Selection

Meta-analytic research has identified a handful of the most powerful predictive factors for criminal behavior (Andrews, Bonta, & Wormith, 2006). These include: antisocial cognition, antisocial companions, antisocial personality, history of criminal involvement, substance abuse, employment problems, school/education problems, and leisure/recreation. These key factors, often known as the "big eight," are all included in the COMPAS assessment (Table 3.6).

Theory-based Selection

A second broad approach is to select the core factors from several major criminological theories for inclusion into the COMPAS assessment. These theories include: control theories (social isolation, leisure/recreation, unemployment); Strain theory (educational/vocational failure, poverty); Routine Activities theory (antisocial opportunities/lifestyle); and others. However, we acknowledge the lack of true experimental research studies that have definitively demonstrated causal links between all such factors and criminal recidivism (Monahan & Skeem, 2014).

Predictive Validity of Specific COMPAS Subscales

Several prospective studies have examined the predictive correlations of the more specific COMPAS subscales for future arrest and related outcome variables. Again, these studies have been conducted in diverse states, such as New York, Michigan, California, and others (Brennan et al., 2009; Dieterich, Brennan, & Oliver, 2011; Lansing, 2012). For example, Farabee et al. (2010) used a California sample of 23,635 soon-to-be-released inmates that were followed for two years post release from prison to examine the predictive validity of the various needs and explanatory subscales (Table 3.6). Validity coefficients included point biserial correlations, AUCs, and odds ratios (OR). As expected, the overall General Risk scale had the strongest association with a new arrest with an AUC of .70, and an OR of 3.31. Several COMPAS subscales had OR values that were meaningfully and significantly linked to recidivism. For example, the criminal associates subscale alone had an AUC of .60 and an OR of 1.09, indicating that for every one-unit increase in the criminal associates raw score the odds of recidivism increase by 9%. Other subscales with encouraging OR values include poverty (8%), vocational/education problems (11%), early socialization problems (13%), and family crime (11%). Importantly, these results are highly similar to prior LSI studies for subscale predictive accuracy levels (Barnoski & Aos, 2003).

Calibration

The default cutting-point scheme in COMPAS uses a norm-referenced approach that converts the raw risk scores to specific ranges of decile scores for use as input to policy-guided decision rules for cut points. Calibration, as noted earlier involves assessing the correspondence between the predicted probabilities from a predictive model and the actual observed probabilities in the population of interest. An alternative scheme is also available in COMPAS that converts the risk scale scores into predicted probabilities. We note that when working with predicted probabilities, certain issues require close attention. If the intent is to convert the risk scale scores to predicted probabilities and take these probabilities at face value to guide policy and practice, then the predicted probabilities must be carefully calibrated to the specific population and event of interest. If there is good correspondence between the predicted and observed probabilities, the predictions are regarded as reliable. Model calibration thus requires that a well-designed outcome study, with sufficient sample size, is conducted. Additionally, Northpointe researchers have developed more specialized calibration approaches for absolute risk in the presence of competing events. A detailed example of this calibration approach in a prison reentry sample is found in Dieterich, Oliver, and Brennan (2014b).

Discrimination and Dispersion

The performance of a risk scale depends on more than calibration. The risk scale should also have the ability to discriminate effectively between recidivists and non-recidivists. As noted elsewhere, the area under the receiver operating characteristic curve (AUC) is typically used to measure discrimination ability. For binary outcomes, such as those in logistic regression models, the AUC can be interpreted as the probability that a randomly selected recidivist will have a higher risk score than a randomly selected non-recidivist. However, in addition to good discrimination ability, a risk scale should also achieve good dispersion when offender groups are segmented into risk levels. This means that the risk levels should effectively separate an agency offender population into groups that have distinctly different recidivism rates. This feature of the risk levels can be evaluated using measures such as the Dispersion Index for Risk (DIFR). The DIFR is a weighted composite log odds of the difference between the base rate of failure in the overall sample and the base rates of failure in the different risk levels (Silver, Smith, & Banks, 2000).

Flores et al. (2016) examined the discrimination and dispersion of the COMPAS General Recidivism Risk Scale and Violent Recidivism Risk Scale in the Broward County, Florida pretrial sample. They found good discriminative ability and good dispersion for both of these COMPAS risk scales. For violent recidivism, failure rates were 11%, 26%, and 45% respectively for low, medium, and high groups, with a DIFR value of .63 and an AUC of .71, and other results indicating broadly similar discrimination and dispersion for White and Black groups. This study also noted that these findings were very similar to discrimination and dispersion findings for other well-validated risk assessment instruments (Flores et al., 2016). It should be noted that the DIFR is a base rate-dependent measure that generally should not be compared across study samples.

Construct Validity—Factorial, Concurrent, and Criterion Validity

Construct validity pertains to whether a scale measures what it is supposed to measure, and whether it correlates in expected ways with the criterion outcomes (e.g., recidivism) and with other theoretically related scales. However, before dealing with such correlations, a first critical issue for construct validity is to establish whether a scale measures one construct, with a *clear* meaning, and is uni-dimensional in contrast to having ambiguous meanings with mixed facets and is potentially multi-dimensional. Factorial validity addresses these two questions. This test was applied to all COMPAS subscales as a first step in establishing their construct validities (Brennan & Oliver, 2002). Few other risk assessment scales in criminal justice have paid attention to factorial validity and uni-dimensionality at the subscale level (Via, Dezember, & Taxman, 2017).

Factorial Validity of COMPAS Subscales

Factor analysis was applied to the item sets of each separate COMPAS subscale to clarify whether it was uni-dimensional and to identify its core meaning (using principal components with oblimin rotation). The results confirmed that each subscale met the requirements of a single dimension. In each analysis the first eigenvalue typically accounted for two to three times the variance of the second eigenvalue, indicating a highly dominant central/first dimension. Second, the item loading patterns were large for the first component and small or mixed for the second component again indicating a single dominant and clear meaning of each factor. The few items that showed mixed and ambiguous loadings on the first and second component were dropped from the final subscales. Finally, we note that the eigenvalues for the second component were mostly less than one indicating a weak second component. These results confirm that each COMPAS subscale was uni-dimensional with a clear central meaning (Brennan & Oliver, 2002).

Construct and Convergent Validity

Construct validity of a scale is cumulatively established by observing significant correlations between a scale (e.g., drug abuse) and other scales that measure the same or theoretically similar constructs (e.g., Substance Abuse Subtle Screening Inventory [SASSI]). This is also often referred to as convergent validity. A useful demonstration of convergent validity for several Core COMPAS subscales is shown in a study that examined correlations between the LSI-R subscales with COMPAS subscales (Farabee et al., 2010). The LSI is considered the gold standard of correctional risk and need assessment. It has several scales that are analogous to similar scales in COMPAS (although using different items and different names). The Farabee study found highly significant correlations between several matched pairs of LSI-R and COMPAS Core scales. The correlations between these pairs of constructs from LSI-R and COMPAS include: Criminal Involvement (.64); Vocation/Education (.51); Criminal Associates (.48); Substance Abuse (.53); Financial problems (.49); and Residential Stability (.57). For other pairs where the correlations were lower it was clear that the subscales were assessing different facets of the same construct (e.g., the COMPAS Leisure scale has a stronger focus on absence of prosocial activities and was more clearly theoretically based on Hirschi's concept of "low engagement bonds" (Andrews & Bonta, 2006; Hirschi, 1969). Below we note several additional findings that contribute cumulative evidence for construct validity of COMPAS subscales.

Substance Abuse

The COMPAS Core substance abuse measure was found to correlate positively ($r = .44$) with the SASSI in a study for the Michigan Department of Corrections.

COMPAS Subscale Correlates with Official Criminal Behaviors and Age of Onset

Developmental and life course criminology asserts several hypotheses that early onset of delinquency should correlate with more serious delinquency, lower achievement, social adjustment problems, criminal personality, criminal attitudes, and vocational educational problems (Moffitt, 1993). Table 3.6 shows correlations between COMPAS Core subscales with several criminal history indicators obtained from official records from the Wisconsin Division of Adult Community Corrections. The sample consisted of 25,773 Core COMPAS assessments conducted between 2012 and 2013. Most of these correlations are in line with theoretical expectations. Offenders with earlier age at first arrest have significant correlations with key COMPAS subscales including: Criminal Associates ($r = -.28$), Family Crime ($r = -.22$), Vocational/Educational Problems ($r = -.24$), and Social Environment ($r = -.16$) (Farrington, Jolliffe, Loeber, Stouthamer-Loeber, & Kalb, 2001).

Criminal Attitudes and Criminal Personality Scales

Table 3.6 also shows that Age at First Arrest correlates negatively with Criminal Attitudes ($r = -.13$) and with Criminal Personality ($r = -.24$) again comporting with developmental theory asserting that offenders with early onset are more likely to have high scores on antisocial personality measures. These observed relationships between COMPAS subscales and criminal history indicators recur in the California, Michigan, and Wisconsin DOC samples adding to the cumulative evidence of construct validity of these subscales, and paralleling the relationships between risk factors and serious and violent trajectories found in developmental criminological research (Herrenkohl et al., 2000; Tolan & Gorman-Smith, 1998).

Implementation Research

User Satisfaction

Strong indicators of user commitment and satisfaction are shown when an agency institutionalizes a risk/needs assessment system into its policy and procedures, maintains systematic training, successfully conducts independent predictive validations, and maintains use of the same system for over 10 years, up to the present. These features have been true for COMPAS in several major state DOC systems including Michigan, New York, California, Wyoming, and others. A further indicator of such satisfaction is indicated when a criminal justice agency initially incorporates COMPAS only on a limited basis and then steadily expands its use across the total agency to a broader range of target populations. This has also occurred with several client agencies.

Impact Evaluation and Cost/Benefit Analyses of COMPAS

Another key question for any risk and need assessment is whether it achieves tangible benefits for an agency in terms of impact on critical operations and policy goals. These issues of real impact were central in a large-scale evaluation study for the Broward County Sheriff's office. This large agency funded the Florida State University's Center for Criminology and Public Policy Research to conduct an evaluation project to assist with policy and planning for the sheriff's office. The main goals were to implement risk assessment to decrease pretrial stays, reduce the jail population, reduce runaway costs, test the predictive accuracy of COMPAS, and conduct a detailed cost-benefit analysis (Mann et al., 2012). The three more specific roles of COMPAS risk assessment (introduced in May 2008) were (1) to assist the First Appearance Judge with release decisions, (2) to determine appropriate supervision levels for increased use of community placements, and (3) to identify needs of offenders to improve case management purposes.

The Mann et al. report concluded that ". . . one indication of the impact of changes in policies and practices was the closure of one jail in October 2009. Deferring the construction of a new jail and closing another has saved taxpayers millions of dollars." More specifically the authors also noted that ". . . the expansion of pretrial in 2008 appears to have contributed to a decrease of more than 1,000 incarcerated individuals by 2010. Furthermore, the average length of stay in jail was reduced to 26.79 days." They noted the impact of COMPAS in increasing the efficiency and accuracy in making pretrial release and community placement recommendations. As a result, the Sheriff's Office reduced pretrial jail stays by implementing the risk assessment tool and by linking this to a continuum of jail alternatives such as day reporting, probation, drug court, pretrial services, and others. Detailed cost/benefit tables estimated that the savings were in the hundreds of millions of dollars.

Current Issues and Future Directions

Currently, offender classification and risk assessment appear to be on the threshold of major advances in several fronts. The ongoing development plans for COMPAS are progressing in all of these areas:

1. Data Analytic Advances

Powerful new methods are emerging for both predictive forecasting and non-linear Machine Learning (ML) that are already equaling, or in some cases exceeding, the traditional stalwart of multiple regression. While not yet ready to replace the current two Core COMPAS regression models for general risk assessment and violent risk assessment we have already incorporated Random Forest, Support Vector Machines, and other ML methods for both offender risk prediction and classification (Breitenbach et al., 2009; Brennan & Oliver, 2013; Oliver, Brennan, & Dieterich, 2014). For example, ML methods in COMPAS software are central to the Women's Pathways Prison Internal Classification in the Massachusetts Department of Corrections (Kilawee-Corsini et al., 2016).

2. Advances in Automated Data Collection Procedures

This important development is often discussed under the rubric of "big data" and promises to dramatically expand the ease of use, scope, and volume of criminal justice data. This potential torrent of data will prompt the need for new data compression and multivariate methods to expand our analytical capacity to integrate and synthesize hundreds of potential risk factors. In this regard, we have explored the use of Lasso as well as other ML methods that are adept at handling very large numbers of potential predictor variables, and other ML techniques for high dimensional data (Brennan & Oliver, 2013; Oliver, Brennan, & Dieterich, 2014).

3. Diverse Pathways to Crime and New Internal Classifications for Prisons

Current research is consistently establishing that there are multiple pathways to crime and heterogeneous kinds of offenders, so that a "one size fits all" approach seriously compromises all attempts to understand, manage, and treat offenders. For example, with the arrival of gender-responsive assessment instruments for women, we have seen a substantial enrichment of risk assessment and classification for diverse categories of women offenders. The women's pathways and classification project has moved rapidly from pure research (Brennan et al., 2012) into the applied area and is now routinely used in Massachusetts Women's Prison and has been strongly endorsed by prison staff and treatment providers at the 2016 Congress of Corrections (Kilawee-Corsini et al., 2016). The same argument applies to the heterogeneity of male offenders.

4. Advances in Decision Analytic Methods for Setting Cut Points in Risk Assessment Scales

Innovations in the use of decision-analytic methods for setting cut points for policy decisions have recently been incorporated into the design of COMPAS. These explore technical innovations occurring in related disciplines (e.g., medical decision-making) for possible use in correctional practice. For example, the typical approach is to create several risk levels (low, medium, high) by imposing cutting points on the continuous calibrated predicted probability scores for each risk scale. However, a broader approach is to evaluate multiple criteria at each threshold to better guide the location of the cuts in forming risk levels. Such criteria might include calibrated predicted probability of recidivism; false positive fraction; true positive fraction; predictive values; selection ratios; and others. Such criteria can be systematically presented as columns in a decision table and this table can be supplemented with utility functions and decision curves (Vickers & Elkin, 2006). We have much to learn about the ways in which classification statistics can be established, particularly in the presence of "competing events" that are so common in criminal justice populations. An example of such an application in a reentry sample is found in Dieterich, Oliver and Brennan (2014b).

References

Agnew, R. A. (1992). Foundation for a general strain theory of crime. *Criminology, 30*, 84–87.

Anderson, E. (2000). *Code of the street: Decency, violence, and the moral life of the inner city.* New York, NY: Norton and Company.

Andrews, D., & Bonta, J. (2006). *The psychology of criminal conduct.* Cincinnati, OH: Mathew Bender and Company.

Andrews, D. A., Bonta, J., & Wormith, J. S. (2006). The recent past and near future of risk and/or needs assessment. *Crime and Delinquency, 52*(1), 7–27.

Angwin, J., Larson, J., Mattu, S., & Kirchner, L. (2016). *Machine bias* (May). ProPublica.

Barnoski, R., & Aos, S. (2003). Washington's offender accountability act: An analysis of the Department of Corrections' risk assessment (Document No. 03-12-1202). Technical Report, Washington State Institute for Public Policy, Olympia, WA.

Breitenbach, M., Dieterich, W., & Brennan, T. (2009). Creating risk-scores in very imbalanced datasets. In Y. S. Koh and N. Rountree (Eds.), *Rare association rule mining and knowledge discovery: Technologies for infrequent and critical event detection* (pp. 231–254). Hershey, PA: IGI Global.

Brennan, T. (1987). Classification: An overview of selected methodological issues. In D. M. Gottfredson and M. Tonry (Eds.), *Prediction and classification: Criminal justice decision making* (pp. 201–248). Chicago, IL: University of Chicago Press.

Brennan, T. (2008). Explanatory diversity among female delinquents: Examining taxonomic heterogeneity. In R. T. Zaplin (Ed.), *Female offenders: Critical perspectives and effective interventions*. Sudbury, MA: Jones and Bartlett Publishers.

Brennan, T. (2012). Introducing multi-axial classification for criminal justice agencies: Design, purposes, and benefits. *International Association for Correctional and Forensic Psychology Newsletter, 44*(3) (July), 1–10.

Brennan, T., & Breitenbach, M. (2009). The taxonomic challenge to general theories of delinquency: Linking taxonomy development to delinquency theory. In O. Sahin and J. Maier (Eds.), *Delinquency: Causes, reduction and prevention* (pp. 1–38). Hauppauge, NY: Nova Science.

Brennan, T., Breitenbach, M., & Dieterich, W. (2008). Towards an explanatory taxonomy of adolescent delinquents: Identifying several social psychological profiles. *Journal of Quantitative Criminology, 24*, 179–203.

Brennan, T., Breitenbach, M., Dieterich, W., Salisbury, E. J., & Van Voorhis, P. (2012). Women's pathways to serious and habitual crime: A person-centered analysis incorporating gender responsive factors. *Criminal Justice and Behavior, 39*, 1481–1508.

Brennan, T., Dieterich, W., & Ehret, B. (2009). Evaluating the predictive validity of the COMPAS risk and needs assessment system. *Criminal Justice and Behavior, 36*, 21–40.

Brennan, T., & Oliver, W. L. (2002). Evaluation of reliability and predictive validity of the COMPAS scales. Technical Report, Northpointe Institute for Public Management, Traverse City, MI.

Brennan, T., & Oliver, W. L. (2013). The emergence of machine learning techniques in criminology. *Criminology and Public Policy, 12*, 551–562.

Brennan, T., Oliver, W. L., & Dieterich, W. (2014). A new internal classification for prisons. Paper presented at the American Society of Criminology Annual Meeting, San Francisco, CA.

Cohen, L. E., & Felson, M. (1979). Social change and crime rate trends: A routine activity approach. *American Sociological Review, 44*, 588–608.

Cullen, F. T., & R. Agnew (2003). *Criminological theory: Past to present* (2nd ed.). Los Angeles, CA: Roxbury Publishing.

Desmarais, S. L., & J. P. Singh (2013). Instruments for assessing recidivism risk: A review of validation studies conducted in the U.S. Technical Report, Council of State Governments Justice Center, New York.

Dieterich, W., Brennan, T., & Oliver, W. L. (2011). Predictive validity of the COMPAS Core risk scales: A probation outcomes study conducted for the Michigan Department of Corrections. Technical Report, Northpointe Inc., Traverse City, MI.

Dieterich, W., Mendoza, C., & Brennan, T. (2016). COMPAS Risk Scales: Demonstrating accuracy equity and predictive parity: Performance of the COMPAS risk scales in Broward County. Technical Report, Northpointe Inc., Traverse City, MI.

Dieterich, W., Oliver, W. L., & Brennan, T. (2011). Predictive validity of the Reentry COMPAS risk scales: An outcomes study with extended follow-up conducted for the Michigan Department of Corrections. Technical Report, Northpointe Inc., Traverse City, MI.

Dieterich, W., Oliver, W. L., & Brennan, T. (2014a). Predictive validity of the COMPAS reentry risk scales: An outcomes study conducted for the Michigan Department of Corrections: Updated results on an expanded release sample. Technical Report, Northpointe Inc., Traverse City, MI.

Dieterich, W., Oliver, W. L., & Brennan, T. (2014b). Setting decision cut points for the new VFO and Non-VFO COMPAS Core risk scales: A research report on the use of predicted probabilities in the COMPAS Core application. Technical Report, Northpointe Inc., Traverse City, MI.

Farabee, D., Zhang, S., Roberts, R. E., & Yang, J. (2010). COMPAS validation study: Final report. Technical Report, UCLA Integrated Substance Abuse Programs.

Farrington, D. P., Jolliffe, D., Loeber, R., Stouthamer-Loeber, M., & Kalb, L. M. (2001). The concentration of offenders in families, and family criminality in the prediction of boys' delinquency. *Journal of Adolescence, 24*, 579–596.

Fishman, D.B., & Neigher, W.D. (1987). Technological assessment: Tapping a third culture for decision-focused psychological measurement. In D.R. Peterson and D.B. Fishman (Eds.), *Assessment for Decision* (pp. 44–76). Rutgers University Press.

Flores, A. W., Bechtel, K., & Lowenkamp, C. (2016). False positives, false negatives, and false analyses: A rejoinder to machine bias: There's software used across the country to predict future criminals. And it's biased against blacks. *Federal Probation,* September.

Gendreau, P., Goggin, C., & Little, T. (1996). A meta-analysis of the predictors of adult off ender recidivism: What works! *Criminology, 34*, 575–607.

Gottfredson, M. R., & Hirschi, T. (1990). *A general theory of crime.* Stanford, CA: Stanford University Press.

Hardyman, P. L., Austin, J., Alexander, J., Johnson, K. D., & Tulloch, O. C. (2002). Internal prison classification systems: Case studies in their development and implementation. Washington, DC: US Department of Justice, National Institute of Corrections.

Harris, P., & Jones, P. R. (1999). Differentiating delinquent youths for program planning and evaluation. *Criminal Justice & Behavior, 26*(4), 403–434.

Herrenkohl, T. I., Maguin, E., Hill, K. G., Hawkins, J. D., Abbott, R. D., & Catalano, R. F. (2000). Developmental risk factors for youth violence. *Journal of Adolescent Health, 26*, 176–186.

Hirschi, T. (1969). *Causes of delinquency.* Berkeley, CA: University of California Press.

Kilawee-Corsini, C., Pelletier, K., Zachary, J., & Brennan, T. (2016). Pathways to change: A blueprint for developing successful gender-specific trauma-informed correctional programs. Paper presented at the American Correctional Association 146th Congress of Correction, Boston, MA.

Lansing, S. (2012). New York State COMPAS-Probation risk and needs assessment study: Evaluating predictive accuracy. New York State Division of Criminal Justice Services, Office of Justice Research and Performance, Albany, New York.

Lykken, D. T. (1995). *The antisocial personalities.* Hillsdale, NJ: L. Erlbaum.

Mann, K., Gulick, K., Blomberg, T., Bales, W., and Piquero, A. (2012). Broward County's jail population management. *American Jails,* January, 14–19.

Moffitt, T. E. (1993). Adolescence-limited and life-course persistent antisocial behavior: A developmental taxonomy. *Psychological Review, 100*, 674–701.

Monahan, J., & Skeem, J. (2014). Risk redux: The resurgence of risk assessment in criminal sanctioning. *Federal Sentencing Reporter, 26*, 158–166.

Nunnally, J. C., & Bernstein, I. H. 1994. *Psychometric theory* (3rd ed.). New York, NY: McGraw-Hill.

Oliver, W. L., Brennan, T., and Dieterich, W. (2014). Women's reentry pilot study: Massachusetts Department of Correction. Technical Report, Northpointe Inc., Traverse City, MI.

Oliver, W. L., Dieterich, W., & Brennan, T. (2014). Predicting recidivism with machine learning algorithms: A comparison of models. ACA Annual Conference, Washington, DC.

Palmer, T. (1992). *The re-emergence of correctional intervention*. Newbury Park, CA: Sage.

Rice M. E., & Harris, G. T. (1995). Violent recidivism: Assessing predictive validity. *Journal of Consulting and Clinical Psychology, 63*(5), 737–748.

Sampson, R. J., & Laub, J. H. (2005). A life course view of the development of crime. *Annals of the American Academy of Political and Social Science, 602*, 12–45.

Sechrest, L. (1987). Classification for treatment. In D. M. Gottfredson and M. Tonry (Eds.), *Prediction and Classification: Criminal Justice Decision Making* (pp. 293–322). Chicago, IL: Chicago University Press.

Silver, E., Smith, W. R., & Banks, S. (2000). Constructing actuarial devices for predicting recidivism: A comparison of methods. *Criminal Justice and Behavior, 27*, 733–764.

Tibshirani, R. (1996). Regression shrinkage and selection via the lasso. *Journal of the Royal Statistical Society, 58*, 267–288.

Tolan, P. H., & Gorman-Smith, D. (1998). Development of serious and violent offending careers. In R. Loeber and D. P. Farrington (Eds.), *Serious and violent juvenile offenders: Risk factors and successful interventions* (pp. 68–85). Thousand Oaks, CA: Sage.

Van Voorhis, P. (1994). *Psychological classification of the adult male prison inmate*. Albany, NY: State University of New York Press.

Van Voorhis, P., Bauman, A., Wright, E. M., & Salisbury, E. J. (2009). Implementing the Women's Risk/Needs Assessments (WRNAs): Early lessons from the field. *Women, Girls, & Criminal Justice, 10*, 81–82, 89–91.

Via, B., Dezember, A., & Taxman, F. S. (2017). Exploring how to measure criminogenic needs: Five instruments and no real answers. In F. S. Taxman (Eds.), *Handbook on risk and need assessment: Theory and Practice* (pp. 312–330). New York, NY: Routledge.

Vickers, A. J., & Elkin, E. B. (2006). Decision curve analysis: A novel method for evaluating prediction. *Medical Decision Making, 26*, 565–574.

Ward, T. (2015). Detection of dynamic risk factors and correctional practice. *Criminology and Public Policy, 14*(1), 105–111.

Warren, M. Q. (1971). Classification of offenders as an aid to efficient management and effective treatment. *Journal of Criminal Law, Criminology, and Police Science, 62*, 239–258.

Williams, K. R., & Grant, S. R. (2006). Empirically examining the risk of intimate partner violence: The Revised Domestic Violence Screening Instrument (DVSI-R). *Public Health Reports, 121*, 400–408.

Wormith, J. S. (2001). Assessing offender assessment: Contributing to effective correctional treatment. *ICCA Journal on Community Corrections*, July, 12–18.

4

The Federal Post-Conviction Risk Assessment Instrument: A Tool for Predicting Recidivism for Offenders on Federal Supervision

Thomas H. Cohen, Christopher T. Lowenkamp, and Charles Robinson

Introduction

The United States federal supervision system has undergone a substantial structural and conceptual transformation since 2002 involving the movement of this system to an outcome-based approach focusing on crime reduction (Alexander & VanBenschoten, 2008; IBM Strategic Assessment, 2004). Established in 1925 by the Federal Probation Act, the U.S. Courts were provided with jurisdiction to appoint federal probation officers for the purpose of supervising offenders sentenced to probation or paroled from federal prison or military installations (Cohen & VanBenschoten, 2014; U.S. Courts, 2014). The Sentencing Reform Act of 1984 ended federal parole and resulted in officers becoming responsible for supervising offenders either through a term of supervised released or straight probation (Johnson, Lowenkamp, VanBenschoten, & Robinson, 2011). Supervised release refers to the supervision of offenders by federal probation officers for a period of about two to three years after completion of their prison sentences within the Federal Bureau of Prisons (BOP), while probation-only sentences means that the offender was sentenced directly to federal supervision without the imposition of an incarceration term.[1] There were nearly 138,000 offenders on federal supervision during fiscal year 2016 of which 86% were serving a term of supervised release with the remaining 13% receiving probation-only sentences (Decision Support Systems, 2016).

For most of its existence, the federal supervision system was primarily focused on the outputs of monitoring offender behavior and reporting offender non-compliance (Alexander & VanBenschoten, 2008; Johnson et al., 2011). This monitoring focused approach began to change in the early 2000s as advances in social science research, in conjunction with the need to employ resources more efficiently, lead to major changes in the role of federal probation officers. While federal probation officers are still required to monitor offender behavior and report non-compliance, reductions in future criminal behavior has become a major component and goal of the federal probation system (Alexander & Vanbenschoten, 2008; Johnson et al., 2011; Hughes, 2008; VanBenschoten, 2008).

The movement towards an outcome-based system focusing on recidivism reduction commenced around 2004 when the federal supervision system underwent a broad-based strategic assessment conducted by a team of private consultants (IBM Strategic Assessment, 2004). One of the assessment's primary recommendations was that the federal supervision system

---

1 For more information about supervised release terms, see 18 USC § 3583 and for more information about probation sentences, see 18 USC § 3561.

Handbook of Recidivism Risk/Needs Assessment Tools, First Edition. Edited by Jay P. Singh, Daryl G. Kroner, J. Stephen Wormith, Sarah L. Desmarais, and Zachary Hamilton.
© 2018 John Wiley & Sons, Ltd. Published 2018 by John Wiley & Sons, Ltd.

"become a results-driven organization with a comprehensive outcome measurement system" (Alexander & VanBenschoten, 2008, pp. 1–2). After this strategic assessment, a working group within the U.S. Courts generated a series of policies and procedures providing a foundation for changing the system of federal post-conviction supervision (Cohen & VanBenschoten, 2014; VanBenschoten, 2008). This paradigmatic shift towards an outcome-based system focused on recidivism reduction resulted in the three major principles of community corrections becoming the guiding tenets of the federal supervision system (Andrews & Bonta, 2010; Gendreau, Little, & Goggin, 1996; Kennedy & Serin, 1997; Latessa & Lovins, 2010). These include the principle that officers work most intensively with high-risk offenders (the risk principle), focus on the criminogenic needs of higher risk offenders (need principle), and match treatment modalities with the ability and learning styles of offenders (responsivity principle) (Andrews, Bonta, & Hoge, 1990; Andrews & Bonta, 2010; AOUSC, 2011; Lowenkamp, Johnson, VanBenschoten, Robinson, & Holsinger, 2013; Van Voorhis & Brown, 1996).

The U.S. federal supervision system's embrace of the risk-need-responsivity model (hereinafter referred to as the RNR model) as a method for supervising offenders with the goal of reducing recidivism and protecting the general community necessitated that the system implement and embrace a fourth generation risk assessment instrument capable of ascertaining the risk of an offender reoffending and identifying criminogenic factors that, if changed, could reduce the likelihood of recidivism (Andrews & Bonta, 1998; Johnson et al., 2011; Lowenkamp et al., 2013). In order to accomplish these objectives, this instrument would have to measure the presence of both static (e.g., characteristics that do not change over time such as criminal history) and dynamic (e.g., characteristics amenable to change such as substance abuse problems) risk factors that would allow for the prediction of offenders most likely to commit new crimes and for the identification of factors that would be amenable to change from community corrections interventions. It would also have the capacity to evaluate whether any responsivity issues (e.g., treatment barriers) including low intelligence, mental health disorders, transportation difficulties, or child care issues hindered treatment (AOUSC, 2011). The development and deployment of the federal Post Conviction Risk Assessment (PCRA) instrument signifies one of the primary efforts to integrate all elements of the RNR model into the U.S. federal supervision system (Cohen & VanBenschoten, 2014; Johnson et al., 2011; Lowenkamp et al., 2013; Lowenkamp, Holsinger, & Cohen, 2015).

The PCRA is a fourth generation actuarial assessment tool developed for the federal supervision system. Basically, this tool is used operationally by federal probation officers to assess an offender's likelihood of recidivism, ascertain dynamic criminogenic needs that could be changed through treatment/monitoring interventions, and identify potential barriers (i.e., responsivity issues) to treatment. Moreover, the PCRA integrates this information about risk, criminogenic needs, and responsivity factors into the federal supervision system's case management system that allows for effective case planning and offender management. An overview of the PCRA risk assessment tool will be provided in this chapter. Initially, for background purposes, it will provide an overview of the historical development of risk assessment tools and then discuss the use of these tools in the federal supervision system. Next, it will describe the development, validation, and implementation of the PCRA, detail the PCRA's administration and scoring mechanisms, and discuss the ways in which this instrument was deployed in the federal supervision system. The chapter will then highlight key research work that has currently been completed using this risk assessment tool. The chapter will conclude by discussing future developments for the PCRA; these primarily include upcoming major changes taking place with this instrument through implementation of a new violence trailer.

Overview of Risk Assessment Tools

The assessment of offender risk has evolved over time from decisions based on clinical judgment to ones grounded on actuarial risk tools. For much of the twentieth century, probation officers would gather information about an offender through a series of unstructured interviews and documentation reviews and then apply their best judgment to assess offender risk (Andrews & Bonta, 2010; Bonta, 1996; Connolly, 2003; Lowenkamp et al., 2013; Van Voohis & Brown, 1996). This method of assessing risk began to change in the 1970s with the emergence of second generation risk assessment techniques utilizing actuarial approaches.[2] These second generation instruments relied almost exclusively on unchangeable or static risk factors (e.g., criminal history) and hence were unable to assess whether offenders were improving or worsening during their supervision periods (Lowenkamp et al., 2013). Addressing this limitation led to the development of third generation actuarial devices capable of both measuring an offender's static criminogenic factors and tracking an offender's dynamic criminogenic characteristics (e.g., low self-control, antisocial personality, antisocial values, criminal peers, substance abuse, dysfunctional family, and employment and/or educational problems) that when changed had the potential to reduce the likelihood of recidivism (Taxman, Shepardson, & Byrne, 2004).

The past several years have witnessed the introduction of fourth generation risk assessment instruments. In addition to including both static and dynamic predictors, this most recent iteration of these actuarial devices incorporates the responsivity principle by allowing officers to deliver interventions that are most "suited to the learning styles and abilities" of supervised offenders (AOUSC, 2011, p. 3). Specifically, officers can use these devices to tailor interventions geared towards an offender's particular circumstances by assessing whether a variety of factors including an offender's reading and cognitive capacities, intelligence levels, or residential, transportation, or child care issues might hinder the effective dissemination of treatment (Bonta & Andrews, 2007; Bonta & Wormith, 2007; Johnson et al., 2011; Lowenkamp et al., 2013). In addition, fourth generation risk instruments seamlessly integrate an offender's criminogenic needs and responsivity factors into a probation or community correction's case management system allowing for the more efficient implementation of a treatment or intervention regime (Andrews et al., 1990).

History of Actuarial Instruments in the Federal Probation System

Actuarial risk tools have a long history of being used in the federal supervision system (Eaglin & Lombard, 1982; Ohlin, 1951; Tibbits, 1931). An attempt to measure the extent to which actuarial risk tools were being utilized by federal probation officers was first conducted by the Administrative Office of the U.S. Courts (AOUSC) and Federal Judicial Center (FJC) in the 1970s (AOUSC, 2011; Eaglin & Lombard, 1982). Both the AOUSC and FJC surveys found that a variety of risk assessment tools were being utilized by officers throughout the federal districts and that these instruments were primarily being used to inform officers about the amount of time, resources, and effort that should be allocated to offenders at different risk levels (AOUSC, 2011; Eaglin & Lombard, 1982).

---

2 It should be noted that some of the earliest actuarial risk assessment tools were utilized in the 1920s for paroled offenders (see Andrews & Bonta, 2010; Burgess, 1928).

Another survey conducted by the FJC in 1982, found over 24 risk assessment instruments in use for offenders on federal probation or parole and assessed the validity of four of these tools in terms of their predictive accuracy.[3] Generally, all instruments assessed measured various static factors associated with recidivism risk including an offender's criminal history, age, employment status, educational attainment, residential stability, and substance abuse issues (AOUSC, 2011). The FJC study recommended that the instrument used by the District of Columbia should be adopted and implemented nationally because its performance was superior to the other studied tools in assessing an offender's risk of recidivism. After further testing and modifications, the AOUSC implemented this tool on a national basis in the federal probation system and renamed it the Risk Prediction Scale 80 (RPS-80) (AOUSC, 2011).[4]

The FJC began developing a new risk assessment tool for the federal supervision system in the early 1990s in response to growing concerns by the Judicial Conference Committee on Criminal Law that the risk assessment instruments being used at that time (i.e., RPS-80 for probation supervision and SFS for parole supervision) were diminishing in predicative accuracy (AOUSC, 2011). This tool, named the Risk Prediction Index or RPI for short, was generated from a construction sample of 2,651 offenders and was built through an analysis of the relationship between several predictive factors[5] and the recidivism outcomes of arrests for any criminal offenses or revocations from supervision (Lombard & Hooper, 1998). The tool was further field tested on a verification sample of 278 offenders in 11 districts and found to be more highly correlated with recidivism outcomes compared to the RPS-80 and SFS (AOUSC, 2011). The RPI was approved for national use by the Judicial Conference in 1997 and the Federal Probation and Pretrial Services Office (PPSO)[6] began requiring that it be scored on all offenders placed on federal post-conviction supervision or probation during that year (AOUSC, 2011).

While the RPI represented an improvement in risk prediction for the federal supervision system there were several limitations to this tool that eventually led to the search for alternative risk assessment devices (AOUSC, 2011; VanBenschoten, 2008). These limitations included the fact that the RPI was a second generation risk instrument that relied on static predictors to determine offender risk; moreover, no efforts had been made to integrate the RPI into the case management system utilized by federal probation officers (AOUSC, 2011; Johnson et al., 2011; Lowenkamp et al., 2013). Given the RPI's static structure and the existence of its scoring process outside the case management system, this instrument could not be used to identify the dynamic criminogenic needs that were amenable to change nor could it be used to assist officers in the development of case supervision plans (AOUSC, 2011; VanBenschoten, 2008). These issues led PPSO to opt for a newer generation of risk tools that would have the capacity to measure and detect changes in risk over time, identify criminogenic risk factors, and integrate risk information generated from the risk tool into an offender's supervision plans (Andrews & Bonta, 2010; AOUSC, 2011; VanBenschoten, 2008).

---

3 These tools included the California BE61A (modified) developed by the State of California, the Revised Oregon Model developed by the U.S. Probation Office for the District of Oregon, the U.S. Parole Commission Salient Factor Score (SFS), and the U.S.D.C 75 Scale developed by the U.S. Probation Office for the District of Columbia (AOUSC, 2011; Eaglin & Lombard, 1982).

4 The SFS continued to be used for federal parolees.

5 The predictive factors found to be correlated with recidivism outcomes and included on the RPI are age at start of supervision, number of prior arrests, use of weapon in instant offense, employment status, history of alcohol and drug abuse, prior history of absconding from supervision, attainment of college degree, and family relations (Eaglin, Gilbert, Hooper, & Lombard, 1997).

6 PPSO refers to the Federal Probation and Pretrial Services Office within the Administrative Office of the U.S. Courts.

PPSO decided to develop its own actuarial risk assessment instrument after considering whether to purchase any of the commercially available risk tools currently in use by various non-federal entities (AOUSC, 2011). This investigation process involved meeting with developers of several risk assessment tools including the Level of Service/Case Management System (LS/CMI), the Correctional Offender Management Profiling for Alternative Sanctions (COMPAS), and the Risk Management Systems (RMS) and pilot testing some of these instruments in several federal districts (AOUSC, 2011). After evaluating these instruments and seeking advice from a panel of governmental and academic experts, PPSO concluded that its preference would be in creating an in-house risk assessment tool rather than buying a commercially available product. Considerations that went into this decision included the costs associated with implementing any commercially available risk tool,[7] the fact that these commercial products were developed and normed on a population of offenders outside the federal supervision system, the potentiality for being able to modify an in-house risk tool for the purpose of improving risk prediction and conducting ongoing research, and the fact that many existing risk tools did not measure an offender's criminal attitudes or thinking, an element shown by the research to be strongly predictive of criminal behavior (Andrews & Bonta, 2010; AOUSC, 2011). These issues resulted in PPSO developing and deploying the PCRA assessment tool.

Development and Implementation of the Federal Post Conviction Risk Assessment Instrument

The development of the PCRA is fairly well documented (see AOUSC, 2011; Johnson et al., 2011; and Lowenkamp et al., 2013). In summary, the PCRA was developed based on a sample of 185,297 offenders that were released to federal supervision between October 1, 2004 and August 13, 2009. Due to missing data the final sample size included 103,071 unique offenders. These offenders were split into construction (N = 51,428) and validation (N = 51,643) groups. The data used to construct and validate the PCRA included data from the offenders initial case plan period only. A second validation sample was created by using data from subsequent case plan periods (193,586) (Lowenkamp et al., 2013).

A fairly traditional approach was used to develop the PCRA. Multivariate models were used to select the final items to be included on the PCRA. Weights for those items were determined based on the magnitude of the bivariate relationship between the selected factors and re-arrest. This method was chosen due to its transparency and, to date, there is little research indicating the superiority of more complex weighting structures over dichotomous coding risk factors (see Gottfredson & Gottfredson, 1979; Gottfredson & Snyder, 2005; Harcourt, 2007; Silver, Smith, & Banks, 2000). Once the final scoring algorithm was determined, a composite score was calculated for each case in the analysis. Cutoff scores parsing the offenders into four risk categories of low, low/moderate, moderate, and high were developed using visual inspection of the data. Although the data cutoffs were fairly evident, alternative cutoffs were tested with confirmation of best fit as determined through the use of chi-square analysis (Lowenkamp et al., 2013).

After development, federal probation officers were trained to score the PCRA using a face-to-face regional training model. More than 1,000 officers were trained through several

---

7 The costs associated with purchasing and maintaining the support networks for these instruments, including the fact that many of these commercial products charge for each assessment, further justified the decision to build an in-house assessment tool.

multiday regional training sessions held in North Carolina, the District of Columbia, Utah, and Michigan. The training sessions included a review of the principles of effective classification, an introduction to the PCRA scoring rules, and opportunities to practice scoring each domain of the PCRA independently and with the full instrument. The installation of the instrument also required trained officers to pass an initial certification exam intended to measure the officer's ability to apply the PCRA scoring rules as intended. Passing the initial certification allowed the officer to access the instrument for use on existing and new federal probation clients. The deployment of the PCRA also included an ongoing certification process intended to measure an officer's continued ability to apply the scoring rules as intended.

Administration and Scoring of the PCRA

The PCRA is administered through the scoring of two sections. The first section is scored by probation officers (i.e., officer assessment), while offenders under supervision are responsible for completing the other section (i.e., offender assessment). The scoring processes for both the officer and offender sections of the PCRA are subsequently detailed in what follows.

Officer Section of the PCRA

At present, there are 15 scored factors on the PCRA that measure an offender's risk characteristics on the following domains: criminal history, education/employment, substance abuse, social networks, and cognitions (e.g., supervision attitudes). The criminal history domain contains six factors that measure the number of prior felony and misdemeanor arrests, prior violent offense activity, prior varied (e.g., more than one offense type) offending pattern, prior revocations for new criminal behavior while under supervision, prior institutional adjustment while incarcerated, and offender's age at the time of supervision. The education/employment domain includes three factors officers use to assess an offender's educational attainment, current employment status, and work history over the past 12 months. In regards to the substance abuse domain, officers score offenders on two factors that measure whether an offender has a current alcohol or drug problem. The social network domain includes three factors that measure an offender's marital status, presence of an unstable family situation, and the lack of any positive prosocial support networks. Lastly, cognitions scores an offender on one factor that assesses an offender's attitude towards supervision and change (AOUSC, 2011).

Officers are responsible for scoring each of the 15 PCRA risk categories by interviewing offenders, reviewing relevant documents, and examining the pre-sentence reports at the beginning of the supervision period. The PCRA scoring process uses a Burgess approach where each of the 15 scored factors is assigned a value of one if present and zero if absent. The exceptions include number of prior arrests (3 potential points) and age at intake (2 potential points).[8] In theory, offenders can receive a combined PCRA score ranging from 0 to 18 and these continuous scores translate into the following four risk categories: low (0–5), low/moderate (6–9), moderate (10–12), or high (13 or above). As previously discussed, these risk categories were developed by visually inspecting the data and supplementing this approach

---

8 Assigning scores ranging from zero to three may seem counterintuitive to current trends that involve the development of weighted risk assessments; however, there is significant evidence to support the argument that this method still outperforms clinical approaches and is more robust across time and sample variations (Gottfredson & Snyder, 2005; McEwan, Mullen, & Mackenzie, 2009).

with cluster analysis. Although the data cutoffs were fairly evident, alternative cutoffs were tested with confirmation of best fit as determined by chi-square analysis and produced results showing that the categories explicated above provided the most effective categories assessing offender risk (Lowenkamp et al., 2013). The risk categories inform officers about an offender's probability of reoffending and provide guidance on the intensity of supervision that should be imposed on a particular offender (AOUSC, 2011; Johnson et al., 2011; Lowenkamp et al., 2013).

The Officer Section of the PCRA also contains 15 additional factors that are rated but not currently scored by the officer. These rated but non-scored factors were included in the instrument because other empirical research, and officer input, suggested that they should be correlated with offender recidivism activity and assist officers in their case management efforts; however, at the time of instrument deployment, the Federal Probation and Pretrial Services system did not have the data to substantively assess whether these factors contributed to the PCRA's risk prediction accuracy outside the scored factors (AOUSC, 2011).[9] When the PCRA was initially implemented, it was decided to empirically explore whether these non-scored factors would eventually be incorporated into the instrument's scoring mechanism by testing whether they contributed to risk prediction above that of the scored factors (Lowenkamp et al., 2013). Subsequent research showed that most of these non-scored factors did not contribute to the PCRA's risk prediction effectiveness and hence were removed from the instrument. The decision to remove many of the non-scored predictors provided the context for implementing a trailer capable of assessing the probability of an offender being involved in a catastrophically violent crime (Serin, Lowenkamp, Johnson, & Trevino, 2016).

Lastly, the Officer Section of the PCRA has a responsivity section measuring the presence of barriers to successful intervention and treatment (Cohen & Whetzel, 2014). These included queries on whether low intelligence, physical handicaps, reading and writing limitations, mental health issues, lack of any desire to change, homelessness, transportation issues, language, ethnic or cultural barriers, history of abuse/neglect, or interpersonal anxiety were serious enough to impede treatment (AOUSC, 2011). While these responsivity factors are not integrated into the risk score, they are provided as output on an officer's case management screen so that officers can understand and address any barriers or obstacles that might impede an offender's treatment regime (Cohen & Whetzel, 2014).

Handling Scoring Omissions and Missing Data

It is important to note that a prorated scoring system is used to handle scoring omissions or missing data in the Officer Section of the PCRA. The prorated system works by adjusting the raw scores upwards to account for up to five missing predictor items. Based on statistical analysis, it was determined that the PCRA scores continued to maintain validity when the score was based on 10 or more items. PCRA assessments with over five missing items are considered invalid. Even though the PCRA score was considered valid with up to five items missing, an adjustment table was created to prorate a score for the missing items. This proration was developed from multivariate models predicting the actual full 15-item PCRA score with the PCRA score minus the randomly selected missing factors. A proration method is used to account for missing scores because this process is considered more accurate than assuming that missing items are rated as zero, which potentially underestimates risk, or rating them at the maximum score, which potentially overestimates risk.

---

9 See AOUSC (2011) for a summary of the non-scored factors.

Offender Section of the PCRA

The Offender Section of the PCRA is used to inform officers about an offender's criminogenic thinking styles; however, at present, information from this section is not included in the risk prediction score. Rather, this section measures an offender's criminal thinking styles through a self-administered questionnaire which is based heavily upon the Psychological Inventory of Criminal Thinking Styles (PICTS). Developed using data from a population of offenders serving in the Federal Bureau of Prisons, the PICTS is used to assess an offender's criminal thinking patterns (Walters, 2013, 2012; Walters, Hagman, & Cohn, 2011). In theory, officers can use information generated from this assessment to better understand whether an offender manifests any elevated adverse criminogenic thinking characteristics and construct interventions tailored to address these forms of negative thinking.

The Offender Section of the PCRA works through officers administering an 80-item questionnaire to the offender that attempts to gauge whether they possess eight thinking styles associated with the support and maintenance of criminal activity (Walters, 2012, 2013). These criminal thinking styles include mollification, cutoff, entitlement, power orientation, sentimentality, super-optimism, cognitive indolence, and discontinuity (Walters, 2013).[10] Most importantly, the PICTS sums the eight above-described criminal thinking styles into a "general criminal thinking" score, which is used to identify offenders with elevated criminal thinking at the highest and most general level. Several studies have shown that the general criminal thinking score is the most "reliable, stable, and valid measure on the PICTS and is often the PICTS indicator used to predict institutional adjustment and recidivism" (Walters, 2013, p. 42).

In addition to these criminal thinking styles, the PICTS generates scores that are translatable into scales which can be used to assess scorer validity, higher order criminal thinking, and several factor and content indices. The validity scales includes a confusion-revised and defensiveness-revised score that essentially provides information on whether the offender's scores represented a valid assessment of their criminal thinking (Walters, 2013). The higher order scales include measures of an offender's proactive or reactive criminal thinking. An elevated proactive criminal thinking score means that the offender is goal directed, focused, and engages in thinking that is "devious, calculated, and scheming" (Walters, 2013, p. 43). Conversely, an elevated reactive score implies that the offender is impulsive and hot-blooded and engages in thinking that is "hostile, impetuous, and emotional" (Walters, 2013, p. 43). Lastly, the content and factor scale indices assess an offender's thinking in regards to problem avoidance, infrequency, self-assertion/deception, denial of harm, fear of change, and current and historical criminal thinking (Walters, 2013).[11]

Information from the Offender Section of the PCRA is extracted into the PCRA cognitions domain and then is used to provide officers with information on whether the offender has elevated general criminal thinking, proactive criminal thinking, reactive criminal thinking, and/or any of the following criminal thinking styles of mollification, cutoff, entitlement, power orientation, sentimentality, super-optimism, cognitive indolence, and discontinuity.

Highlighting Addressable Criminogenic Needs

Once the Officer and Offender Sections of the PCRA have been completed, the case management system for Federal Probation produces a standardized output summary sheet providing

---

10 For exact definitions of these specific criminal thinking styles see AOUSC (2011) and Walters (2013). For information about the validity and reliability of the PICTS as a means of measuring criminal thinking see Walters (2013) and Walters et al. (2011).
11 See Walters (2013) for definitions of these factor and content scales.

information on the offender's overall risk classification, criminogenic needs, and responsivity factors (AOUSC, 2011). To reiterate, the risk classification scheme provides information on whether the offender should be designated into the recidivism risk categories of low, low/ moderate, moderate, or high risk. Criminogenic needs highlights whether the offender evidences any crime-driving factors (i.e., education/employment, substance abuse, social-networks, and criminal thinking cognitions) that should could be addressable during an offender's supervision term. Hierarchical rules driven by both theory and research are used by the PCRA to rank these needs by the following orders of importance: criminal thinking, social networks, substance abuse, and job placement or educational attainment (Andrews & Bonta, 2010; Andrews, Bonta, & Hoge, 1990; Cohen & VanBenschoten, 2008; Gendreau, Little, & Goggin, 1996). The decision to employ this ranking method was driven by theories emphasizing the necessity of focusing on those needs that were empirically shown to be strongly correlated with criminal conduct such as criminal thinking over other criminogenic drivers including education or employment that, while correlated with crime, generally have a weaker relationship with this outcome (Andrews & Bonta, 2010). Hence, if the assessment indicates that an offender has criminal thinking, social network, and substance abuse-related issues, it encourages officers to tailor interventions aimed at addressing criminal thinking and social networks first before substance abuse. Lastly, the output page provides officers with information on the presence of any responsivity factors (e.g., treatment barriers) that should be addressed for the purpose of ensuring the efficacy of an offender's treatment regime (AOUSC, 2011).

The Role of Supervision Overrides in the PCRA's Risk Assessment Mechanism

After completing the Officer and Offender Sections of the PCRA and reviewing the offender's overall risk classification, criminogenic needs, criminal thinking characteristics, and responsivity factors, judicial policy allows officers the option of departing from the PCRA's risk classification scheme by placing an offender into a different risk level than that originally assigned (Guide to Judicial Policy, 2014). For instance, offenders classified in the low-risk category by the PCRA could be overridden to a higher risk level for supervision purposes should the officer feel that, in their professional judgment, the PCRA score underrepresents his/her risk to reoffend. This component of the risk classification process is referred to as professional discretion or supervision override. Professional overrides, hence, allow federal probation officers discretion to depart from the actuarial score when the totality of an offender's characteristics suggests that the offender be supervised at levels that diverge from the original risk classification. According to judicial policy, officers should rarely use overrides and if necessary, they should occur for policy-related reasons if the offender meets the following specified criteria: sex offender, persistently violent, mental health, or serious youthful offender. Officers deciding to initiate overrides outside these policy-related criteria must provide a rationale for doing so; these non-policy overrides are labeled discretionary overrides (Guide to Judicial Policy, 2014).

The PCRA Assessment and Reassessment Policy

According to judicial policy, officers should commence the PCRA assessment process as soon as the local office is advised of a prisoner's upcoming release to federal supervision. Policy mandates that all initial PCRA assessments should be completed within 30 days of the start of an offender's term of supervised release. For those offenders sentenced to probation or who are received onto federal supervision without at least 45 days of advance notification, the plan is due no later than 60 days after the supervision or probation term begins (Guide to Judicial Policy, 2014). In regards to PCRA reassessments, policy requires officers to conduct the second PCRA assessment within six months after the initial assessment. Officers are then required to conduct the third PCRA reassessment 12 months after the second assessment with subsequent assessments occurring at 12-month intervals until the offender's supervision term is completed (Guide to Judicial Policy, 2014). It should be noted that policy also allows officers to conduct reassessments outside the six- and 12-month time intervals if the offender manifests significant improvements or non-compliance with their supervision regime. Lastly, officers are not required, but can at their discretion, conduct reassessments for offenders placed into the lowest risk category by the PCRA (Guide to Judicial Policy, 2014).

Overview of Research Using the PCRA

Since the development and deployment of the PCRA, there have been multiple research studies conducted using this instrument. This research encompasses a wide range of topical areas including efforts at revalidating the PCRA's predictive validity, investigating the PCRA's dynamic risk characteristics, examining the PCRA for race and gender bias, evaluating the predictive value of the PICTS criminal thinking styles, and researching the PCRA's usefulness in understanding special federal offender populations such as sex offenders. In addition, the PCRA has provided a foundation for other research topics involving the federal supervision system including the utilization of supervision overrides, the implementation of the low-risk supervision policy, and the exploration of long-term recidivism patterns. This section of the PCRA chapter will summarize key findings from these studies in order to provide the reader with an understanding of the depth and breadth of research conducted using this risk tool.

Revalidation of the PCRA's Predictive Validity

There have been two major efforts aimed at revalidating the PCRA's predictive validity (Lowenkamp et al., 2015; Luallen, Radakrishnan, & Rhodes, 2016). The first study conducted by Lowenkamp et al. (2015) used assessments completed by U.S. probation officers on 113,281 offenders during the course of supervision to assess the PCRA's validity in predicting re-arrest for any new criminal conduct and re-arrest for violent offenses at six, 12, 18, and 24-month intervals.[12] Overall, this research showed the PCRA being a valid predictor for both re-arrests involving any offenses or violent offenses. For example, results from Table 4.1 show offenders classified in the low-risk category having a 12-month re-arrest rate (any) of 4%, followed by low/moderate at 12%, moderate at 23%, and high at 35% (Lowenkamp et al., 2015). These results were in the anticipated direction (i.e., higher failure rates with each increasing risk categorization). In addition, the revalidation study showed PCRA categorizations significantly differentiating between the likelihood of re-arrests for violence (Lowenkamp et al., 2015). The 12-month violence re-arrest rates (see Table 4.2) for each PCRA categorization were 1% (low), 2% (low/moderate), 6% (moderate), and 10% (high). Moreover, these findings were supported by the area under the receiver operating characteristic curve (AUC–ROC) values which ranged between .70 and .77 depending on the subsample, outcome being predicted, and follow-up time.

The second PCRA revalidation study was conducted by a team of outside researchers at Abt Associates (Luallen et al., 2016). In findings mirroring those reported by

---

12 The study also explored whether the PCRA manifested any potential for race/gender bias; however, these findings were superseded by other studies focusing specifically on the PCRA and race/gender (Skeem & Lowenkamp, 2016; Skeem, Monahan, & Lowenkamp, 2016).

Table 4.1 Post Conviction Risk Assessment Failure Rates for Any Arrest, by Offender Follow-Up Period

	Offender Follow-Up Period						
	6 Months – Any Arrest		12 Months – Any Arrest		18 Months – Any Arrest		24 Months – Any Arrest	
PCRA Category	N	Failure Rate	N	Failure Rate	N	Failure Rate	N	Failure Rate
Low	47,693	2%	36,290	4%	24,383	6%	11,745	7%
Low-Moderate	44,342	6%	32,747	12%	21,190	16%	9,985	20%
Moderate	16,706	13%	12,002	23%	7,654	31%	3,695	36%
High	4,540	22%	3,267	35%	2,046	44%	955	51%
Total	113,281	6%	84,306	11%	55,273	15%	26,380	18%
AUC-ROC		.73		.73		.74		.73
r		.20		.26		.30		.32

Note: Reprinted from Lowenkamp, C. T., Holsinger, A. M., & Cohen, T. H. (2015). PCRA revisited: Testing the validity of the Federal Post Conviction Risk Assessment (PCRA). *Psychological Services, 12*(2), 149–157.

Table 4.2 Post Conviction Risk Assessment Failure Rates for Violent Arrests, by Offender Follow-Up Period

	Offender Follow-Up Period						
	6 Months – Violent Arrest		12 Months – Violent Arrest		18 Months – Violent Arrest		24 Months – Violent Arrest	
PCRA Category	N	Failure Rate	N	Failure Rate	N	Failure Rate	N	Failure Rate
Low	47,693	0%	36,290	1%	24,383	1%	11,745	1%
Low-Moderate	44,342	1%	32,747	2%	21,190	4%	9,985	4%
Moderate	16,706	3%	12,002	6%	7,654	8%	3,695	10%
High	4,540	6%	3,267	10%	2,046	13%	955	17%
Total	113,281	1%	84,306	2%	55,273	3%	26,380	4%
AUC-ROC		0.77		0.76		0.76		0.76
R		0.11		0.14		0.17		0.19

Note: Reprinted from Lowenkamp, C. T., Holsinger, A. M., & Cohen, T. H. (2015). PCRA revisited: Testing the validity of the Federal Post Conviction Risk Assessment (PCRA). *Psychological Services, 12*(2), 149–157.

Lowenkamp et al. (2015), this study found that the PCRA, as currently designed, was an effective tool for classifying offenders and that this instrument achieved a level of predictive validity comparable with other instruments such as the LSI-R. For example, Luallen et al. (2016) noted that the PCRA generated AUC-ROC scores for a 12-month follow-up period that fell between .73 and .74 values. In addition to these findings, Luallen et al. (2016) explored the PCRA's predictive effectiveness by the type of recidivism offense. Overall, these researchers found that the strength of the PCRA's classification scheme varied by the type of recidivism offense committed. Specifically, the PCRA performed well in predicting commonly occurring offenses including drug, violent and property offenses, but was found to be less effective in predicting rarer offenses, such as immigration or public order crimes (Luallen et al., 2016).

Investigating the PCRA's Dynamic Characteristics

The next set of studies explored the PCRA's capacity to measure changes in an offender's recidivism risk characteristics over time and investigated whether changes in risk were correlated with recidivism outcomes. Cohen and VanBenschoten's (2014) study examined which of the dynamic criminogenic factors of offenders measured by the PCRA were changing for the better or worse between assessments. The study tracked a population of 21,152 offenders placed on federal supervision from May 2010 through October 2013 who had at least two PCRA assessments during this time. Results showed that many of the higher (e.g., high or moderate) risk offenders improved by moving to a lower risk classification category by their next assessment. For example, Figure 4.1 shows that nearly half (47%) of offenders initially classified as high risk and about a third (32%) of offenders initially classified as moderate risk were reclassified into a lower risk category by their second assessment (see Figure 4.1). Moreover, most offenders placed into the lower risk categories of low/moderate or low risk manifested few changes in their risk classifications between assessments (Cohen & VanBenschoten, 2014).

Cohen and VanBenschoten (2014) also investigated which of the dynamic PCRA risk domains were most amenable to change between assessments. In general, they found that offender's employment and substance abuse-related risk factors were most likely to decrease by the second assessment. Specifically, Table 4.3 shows the PCRA risk factors measuring employment status, work history, current drug problem, and current alcohol problem decreasing the most for high- and moderate-risk offenders. Conversely, the risk factors assessing educational status, social networks, and cognitions manifested fewer changes by the second assessment for these higher risk offenders (Cohen & VanBenschoten, 2014).

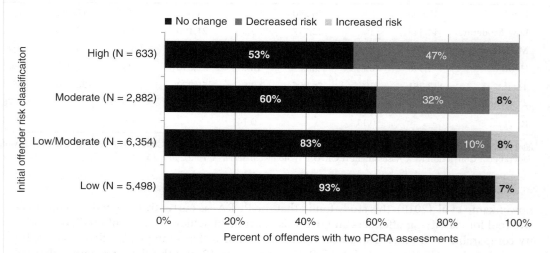

Figure 4.1 Changes in risk classification for offenders placed on federal supervision with at least two Post Conviction Risk Assessment (PCRA) evaluations.
Note: Reprinted from "Does the Risk of Recidivism for Supervised Offenders Improve Over Time? Examining Changes in The Dynamic Risk Characteristics for Offenders under Federal Supervision" by Cohen, T.H. & VanBenschoten, S.W., 2014. *Federal Probation, 78(2)*, 41-56.

Table 4.3 Changes in Individual Post Conviction Risk Assessment (PCRA) Characteristics for Offenders Placed on Federal Supervision between their First and Second Assessments

Scored Dynamic PCRA Characteristics	High Risk			Moderate Risk		
	1st PCRA	2nd PCRA	Percent Change	1st PCRA	2nd PCRA	Percent Change
Education & employment						
Less than high school or has only GED	86%	83%	-2%	73%	71%	-2%
Currently unemployed	79%	49%	-30%	63%	39%	-23%
Recent unstable work history	87%	66%	-21%	65%	50%	-15%
Drugs & alcohol						
Current alcohol problem	44%	29%	-15%	18%	13%	-5%
Current drug problem	67%	45%	-23%	37%	30%	-8%
Social networks						
Single, divorced, separated	96%	93%	-3%	92%	90%	-2%
Unstable family situation	57%	50%	-8%	30%	29%	-2%
No positive pro-social support	64%	54%	-10%	30%	26%	-4%
Cognitions						
Lacks motivation to change	42%	34%	-8%	15%	18%	2%
Number of offenders with at least 2 PCRAs	633	633		2,882	2,882	

Note: Includes high and moderate risk offenders with at least two PCRA assessments.
Reprinted from Cohen, T. H. & VanBenschoten, S. W. (2014). Does the risk of recidivism for supervised offenders improve over time? Examining changes in the dynamic risk characteristics for offenders under federal supervision. *Federal Probation,* 78(2), 41–56.

Cohen, Lowenkamp, and VanBenschoten (2016a) followed up their PCRA change work with another study exploring the relationship between changes in an offender's risk characteristics and recidivism outcomes. This study tracked a population of 64,716 offenders placed on federal supervision who received at least two PCRA assessments. In findings similar to that of Cohen and VanBenschoten (2014), the study found that nearly two-fifths of high and a third of moderate risk offenders were reassessed into lower risk levels by their next assessment. Among those offenders moving to a lower risk level, most of these changes occurred because an offender attained employment or demonstrated improvement in the substance abuse risk domain (Cohen, Lowenkamp, & VanBenschoten, 2016b). Most importantly, changes in offender risk were associated with changes in re-arrest rates. Specifically, high, moderate, and low/moderate-risk offenders with decreases in either their risk classifications or overall PCRA scores had lower recidivism rates compared to their counterparts whose risk levels or scores either remained unchanged or increased, while increases in offender risk were associated with higher rates of re-arrests.

The relationship between change in risk and recidivism outcomes are highlighted in Figure 4.2. Figure 4.2 shows the relationship between the 12-month re-arrest rate after the

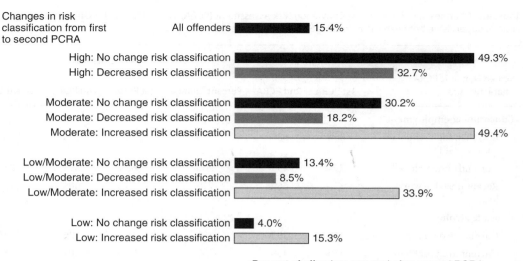

Changes in risk classification from first to second PCRA

All offenders — 15.4%

High: No change risk classification — 49.3%
High: Decreased risk classification — 32.7%

Moderate: No change risk classification — 30.2%
Moderate: Decreased risk classification — 18.2%
Moderate: Increased risk classification — 49.4%

Low/Moderate: No change risk classification — 13.4%
Low/Moderate: Decreased risk classification — 8.5%
Low/Moderate: Increased risk classification — 33.9%

Low: No change risk classification — 4.0%
Low: Increased risk classification — 15.3%

Percent of offenders arrested after second PCRA

Figure 4.2 Relationship between changes in PCRA categories and offender arrest outcomes, by initial risk classification (reprinted from journal).
Note: Figure tracks a subset of offenders followed for at least one year after their second PCRA. Changes represent re-classification of offenders into different risk categories.
Reprinted from Cohen, T. H., Lowenkamp, C. L., & VanBenschoten, S. W. (2016). Examining changes in offender risk characteristics and recidivism outcomes: A research summary. *Federal Probation, 80*(2), 57–65.

second PCRA for offenders whose risk classifications increased, decreased, or remained unchanged between assessments. In an interesting pattern that emerges when reviewing the re-arrest rates of offenders whose classification changed between assessments, high-risk offenders reclassified as moderate risk had a re-arrest rate (33%) that was closer to that of moderate risk offenders who demonstrated no change between time 1 and time 2 (30%) than to those high-risk offenders with no change in risk (49%). In addition, moderate-risk offenders whose risk classification increased from time 1 to time 2 had a re-arrest rate (49%) that was essentially identical to the re-arrest rate of high-risk offenders that experienced no change in risk between assessment periods (49%). This trend was seen, to varying degrees, across all risk categories (Cohen et al., 2016b).

This study also generated crucial evidence in support of the low-risk principle. Specifically, offenders in the lowest risk category saw no recidivism reduction if they had a decrease in either their overall PCRA score or in any of their risk domains. Figure 4.3, for example, shows the relationship between changes in the raw PCRA risk scores and recidivism outcomes. Reductions in the risk score for low and low/moderate-risk offenders were not consistently associated with appreciable reductions in arrest rates. This was especially the case for low-risk offenders, whose arrest rates were essentially the same regardless of whether the overall PCRA score decreased by 1, 2, or 3 or more points. This key finding is consistent with the risk principle and provides evidence that probation officers should be cautious about allocating resources and services to low-risk offenders who do not seem to benefit from efforts aimed at reducing their criminal risk factors (Cohen, Lowenkamp, & VanBenschoten, 2016a; Cohen et al., 2016b).

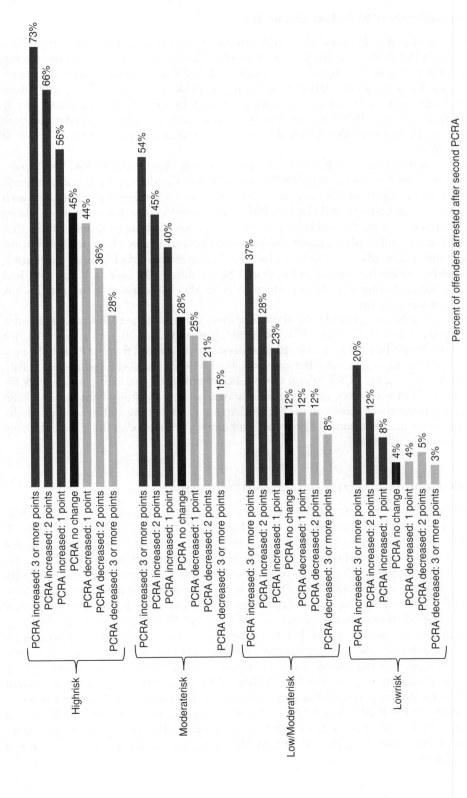

Figure 4.3 Relationship between changes in PCRA raw scores and offender arrest outcomes, by initial risk classification.
Note: Reprinted from Cohen, T. H., Lowenkamp, C. L., & VanBenschoten, S. W. (2016). Examining changes in offender risk characteristics and recidivism outcomes: A research summary. *Federal Probation, 80*(2), 57–65.

Studies Investigating the PCRA for Race/Gender Bias

Recent studies by Skeem and Lowenkamp (2016) and Skeem, Monahan, and Lowenkamp (2016) have investigated the PCRA for potential race/gender biases. The Skeem and Lowenkamp research empirically tested the predictive accuracy of the PCRA across offender race categories. Specifically, it examined the relationships among race, risk assessment (PCRA), and future re-arrests using a sample of 34,794 federal offenders. While the study found that Black offenders obtained higher average PCRA scores than White offenders, most of the racial differences in the PCRA scores (about 69%) were attributable to the criminal history domain (Skeem & Lowenkamp, 2016).

Importantly, results showed no evidence of race-based test bias for the PCRA. The instrument strongly predicted re-arrests for both Black and White offenders across the instrument's risk levels. In order to conceptualize any racial differences in the form of the relation between the PCRA and re-arrest, Skeem and Lowenkamp (2016) estimated the predicted probabilities of any re-arrest based on moderated regression models, grouped those probabilities together for each PCRA score, and displayed those grouped probabilities by race. These predicted probabilities show the likelihood of re-arrest for Black and White offenders being much more similar than dissimilar in form (i.e., elevation and shape). Stated differently, a given PCRA score had essentially the same meaning—i.e., same probability of recidivism—across the two race groups (Skeem & Lowenkamp, 2016).

Skeem et al. (2016) also empirically tested the predictive fairness of the PCRA across offender gender categories. When the PCRA was constructed, gender was omitted as a potential risk factor. Based on a study population of 14,310 offenders, results showed that the PCRA strongly predicted arrests for both genders—but overestimated a women's likelihood of recidivism. In other words, for a given PCRA score, the predicted probability of arrest was higher for women than men. In regards to score differences across gender, the study found that women obtained slightly lower mean scores on the PCRA than men and that this difference was wholly attributable to men's greater criminal history, a factor already embedded in the U.S. Sentencing Guidelines (Skeem et al., 2016).

Evaluating the Predictive Value of the PICTS Criminal Thinking Styles

The PCRA research has also encompassed studies examining the predictive value of information generated from the Offender Section of the PCRA (Walters & Cohen, 2016; Walters & Lowenkamp, 2016). To reiterate, the Offender Section of the PCRA is based primarily on the PICTS and is used to assess whether an offender has any elevated styles of criminal thinking measured by this tool (e.g., general, reactive, or proactive forms of criminal thinking). The study by Walters and Lowenkamp (2016) sought to determine whether the PICTS predicted general recidivism in a sample of 81,881 male and 14,519 female offenders on federal probation or supervised release. Results showed that the PICTS General Criminal Thinking, Proactive, and Reactive scores and all but the super-optimism criminal thinking style scale predicted recidivism in follow-ups of six or more months, 12 or more months, and 24 or more months with effect sizes in the low/moderate to medium range (Walters & Lowenkamp, 2016). This study also demonstrated that the PICTS General Criminal Thinking score contributed significantly to recidivism prediction in both males and females above and beyond the information provided by the PCRA. Results from this study are suggestive that the PICTS might serve as a useful informational guide to other risk assessment devices in providing comprehensive information about an offender's criminal thinking styles and proclivities (Walters & Lowenkamp, 2016).

Another study by Walters and Cohen (2016) examined whether an increase in criminal thinking predicted a heightened risk for recidivism in a sample of offenders under federal supervision. Using a one-year change on the General Criminal Thinking (GCT) score of the PICTS, the effect of an increased GCT score on subsequent recidivism was tested in 35,147 male and 5,254 female federal probationers and supervised releases. The results revealed that a rise in GCT was an incrementally valid predictor of time until first re-arrest in both men and women after controlling for age, criminal history, and race/ethnicity and predicted the presence of a subsequent re-arrest during a one-year follow-up in men regardless of initial GCT score. Although these effect sizes were relatively small, they were still statistically significant and, hence, support the assumption that criminal thought process, as measured by the PICTS GCT score, is a dynamic risk predictor (Walters & Cohen, 2016).

The PCRA and Special Offender Populations

A couple of recently published studies have delved into using the PCRA for the purpose of informing the system about the risk characteristics and recidivism outcomes of special offender populations. Recently, Cohen and Spidell (2016) used the PCRA to examine the risk characteristics of 7,416 male sex offenders placed on post-conviction supervision for the following offenses: child pornography, transporting minors for illegal sexual activities, sexual assault, and violation of the Sex Offender Registration and Notification Act (SORNA). It also compared the risk levels between sex and non-sex offenders. As shown in Figure 4.4, sex offenders, with the exception of those convicted of sexual assault and SORNA laws, had lower risk levels than the non-sex offender population. For example, 12% of the sex offenders with PCRA assessments were classified as either moderate or high risk; in comparison, 26% of the non-sex offenders

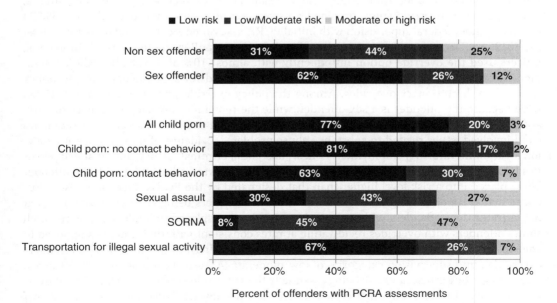

Figure 4.4 Post Conviction Risk Assessment (PCRA) risk categories for federal sex offenders by instant conviction offense.
Note: Reprinted from Cohen, T. H., & Spidell, M. C. (2016). How dangerous are they? an analysis of sex offenders under federal post-conviction supervision. *Federal Probation, 80*(2), 21–32.

were grouped into the moderate or high-risk categories. Child pornography offenders were especially likely to be considered low risk with nearly all (97%) of these offenders initially being assessed in the low or low/moderate-risk categories. Among offenders convicted of non-child pornography offenses, almost half the SORNA (47%) and about a quarter of those convicted of sexual assault (27%) were classified moderate or high risk by the PCRA (Cohen & Spidell, 2016).

Similar to the PCRA analysis, the recidivism patterns also varied across the conviction types. Offenders convicted of child pornography exhibited lower general and violent re-arrest rates and supervision revocations compared to offenders convicted of SORNA or sexual assault. The recidivism activity for the SORNA offenders was particularly high, with about two-fifths of these offenders being rearrested within the three-year follow-up period.

This study also explored the PCRA's effectiveness at predicting subsequent recidivism for federal sex offenders on post-conviction supervision. AUC-ROC score analysis showed that the PCRA accurately predicted recidivism involving arrests for any felony or misdemeanor offenses (AUC-ROC = .72), violent offenses (AUC-ROC = .79), and supervision revocations (AUC-ROC = .77) for the federal sex offender population. However, the PCRA was less predicative when the instrument was used to assess the likelihood of sexual recidivism (AUC-ROC = .63). This finding, however, was not too surprising because the PCRA was never constructed to predict sexual recidivism nor was it designed to measure sexual deviance (Cohen & Spidell, 2016).

Studies Using the PCRA to Investigate Supervision Overrides, Implementation of the Low-Risk Policy, the Presence of Responsivity Issues, and Convergence of Long-Term Recidivism Rates Across Risk Levels

In addition, PPSO staff have used the PCRA as a basis for other research topics including an examination of supervision overrides, an investigation of responsivity issues, an exploration of the low-risk supervision policy, and an examination of long-term recidivism patterns. The supervision override study provided an overview of professional overrides for 58,524 offenders under federal supervision with initial PCRA assessments conducted between August 31, 2012 and December 30, 2013 (Cohen, Pendergast, & VanBenschoten, 2016c). In general, officers used the override option infrequently with almost 10% of the 58,500 PCRA assessments in the study population being overridden. Two-thirds of adjustments involved policy rather than discretionary overrides. Among the policy overrides, nearly three-fourths (72%) were because the offender is a sex offender, while the remainder involved rationales for persistently violent behavior or severe mental illness. The most common discretionary rationales cited involved issues related to substance abuse problems, evidence of non-compliant behavior, location monitoring, employment issues, substantial criminal history, and financial penalties (Cohen et al., 2016c). Almost all overrides were an upward adjustment with the offender being placed into a risk level higher than that designated by the PCRA. Overrides also influenced actual supervision practices with overridden offenders being contacted by officers at higher rates than offenders without overrides. Lastly, as displayed in Table 4.4, this research shows offenders with overrides recidivating at rates consistent with their initial as opposed to adjusted risk levels. For example, Table 4.4 shows the recidivism rates for low-risk offenders overridden into supervision categories of low/moderate (4% arrest rate), moderate (5% arrest rate), or high (4% arrest rate) risk being essentially the same as low-risk offenders without overrides (4% arrest rate). Similar patterns of offenders with upward overrides also held for low/moderate and moderate-risk offenders (Cohen et al., 2016c).

Another study relied on the PCRA to examine the presence of responsivity factors (e.g., treatment barriers) for nearly 20,000 federally supervised offenders with an initial PCRA assessment between November 1, 2013, and March 30, 2014 (Cohen & Whetzel, 2014). Overall, this

Table 4.4 Twelve-Month Arrest Rates for Federal Offenders With Overrides, by Initial Risk and Adjusted Supervision Levels

| Initial Risk Levels | Adjusted Supervision Levels | | | | | | | |
| | Low | | Low/Moderate | | Moderate | | High | |
	Number	% Arrested	Number	% Arrested	Number	% Arrested	Number	% Arrested
Low	**17,881**	**4.0%**	928	3.6%	358	4.8%	1,272	4.2%
Low/Moderate	62	6.5%	**21,593**	**10.9%**	787	12.6%	1,157	10.8%
Moderate	6	—	20	10.0%	**10,197**	**21.0%**	907	21.0%
High	0	—	1	—	5	—	**3,350**	**32.0%**

Note: Bold font denotes that no supervision override occurred.
Percentages show arrest rates within 12 months of first PCRA assessment.
— Not enough cases to produced statistically reliable estimates.
Reprinted from Cohen, T. H., Pendergast, B., & VanBenschoten, S. W. (2016). Examining overrides of risk classifications for offenders on federal supervision. *Federal Probation, 80*(1), 12–21.

study found that 28% of these offenders had a responsivity problem that hindered an offender's success on supervision. Issues involving the ability to obtain adequate transportation and problems associated with mental health were the most common treatment barriers. In general, offenders classified on the higher end of the risk continuum were more likely to face barriers of inadequate transportation, disinterest in program participation, mental health, and residential issues compared to their lower risk counterparts. Lastly, the percentage of offenders with a responsivity factor varied widely from a high of 57% to a low of 10% across the federal judicial districts.

Another PCRA-related study provided a preliminary analysis on the implications of the low-risk policy for the federal supervision system (Cohen, Cook, & Lowenkamp, 2016d). This study examined the relationship between the low-risk policy and officer/offender contact patterns, explored whether the recidivism rates for low-risk offenders had changed after enactment of this policy, and analyzed whether the collection of court-imposed financial penalties differed after the low-risk policy took effect. In general, it showed that low-= and low/moderate-risk offenders in the post-policy group had fewer officer/offender contacts compared to their pre-policy counterparts (Cohen et al., 2016d). Importantly, the policy of supervising low-risk offenders less intensively has not compromised community safety. Post-policy low-risk offenders were no more likely to recidivate compared to their pre-policy counterparts. For the most part, federal probation officers continued to successfully monitor the collection of court-owed fines despite the fact that less time and resources were being expended on the low-risk population. Restitution payments, however, did decrease noticeably under the low-risk policy (Cohen et al., 2016d).

Lastly, Flores, Holsinger, Lowenkamp, and Cohen (2017), used the PCRA to examine whether offender recidivism rates begin to converge across risk categories over time and ascertain the predictive validity between multivariate models using fixed (logistic regression and AUC-ROC) and variable (Cox regression and Harrell's C) follow-up approaches. Using a sample of 27,156 offenders and a 10-year follow-up, results showed that the risk of recidivism declined as a function of time offense-free for all but low-risk offenders, and that the recidivism risk probability for high, moderate, and low/moderate offender risk converged at about seven years (Flores et al., 2017). In addition, this study demonstrated few substantive differences in prediction between the Cox and logistic regression analyses, along with their related Harrell's C and AUC-ROC validity estimates.

In summary, this research highlights several key findings about the PCRA risk tool. Specifically, these studies show that the PCRA is highly effective in classifying offenders into different risk categories and predicting their probability of recidivism and that this tool is dynamic, meaning it can measure change in an offender's recidivism risk characteristics over time and that change in risk is correlated with re-arrest outcomes. Moreover, this research has shown that the PCRA is race neutral in terms of recidivism prediction and that the predictive value of this instrument can be enhanced by using information gleaned from the PICTS criminal thinking styles component of this instrument. In addition to these major findings, other research has demonstrated the PCRA's importance in understanding special offender populations, supervision overrides, the low-risk supervision policy, and long-term recidivism patterns.

PCRA 2.0 and the Future of the PCRA

The original PCRA predicted general recidivism based on scored factors related to criminal history, social networks, education/employment, drug and alcohol use, and cognitions. Overrides occurred for offenders with persistently violent histories because the PCRA did not properly assess an offender's propensity towards violence. In recognition of this limitation, PCRA 2.0 was created, which incorporates a violence risk assessment. PCRA 2.0 allows for better accuracy in identifying individuals at an elevated risk for committing a violent act based on a combination of static risk factors and current PICTS scales (Serin et al., 2016).[13] Now that officers can for the first time empirically assess an offender's likelihood of committing a violent offense during supervision, PCRA 2.0 should result in better decision-making in the case planning and risk management process, mitigation of the risk of harm to the community, and enhancement of officer safety.

By identifying offenders with a proclivity to commit violent criminal acts, PCRA 2.0 encourages the utilization of more intense monitoring practices for these problematic individuals. In other words, the higher the risk an individual presents according to PCRA 2.0, the more intense the monitoring practices. Intensive monitoring techniques may include, but are not limited to, increased field contacts, collateral contacts, drug testing, computer monitoring, and third party risk assessment. Policy and procedures requiring more supervision contacts with higher risk individuals may also be implemented. Frequency alone, however, is not enough to deter future crime; therefore each contact must be purpose driven and viewed as an opportunity to mitigate risk. In order to make contacts more purposeful, officers should routinely review the individual factors that led the individual to become more at risk to violently reoffend (Serin et al., 2016).

Evidence suggests that the effectiveness of correctional interventions is enhanced when officers match proper monitoring strategies, restrictions, and interventions (Andrews &

---

13 The static risk factors in the violence trailer include current violent arrest, plans violence, age at first arrest, history of stalking, history of treatment non-compliance, gang membership, ever used weapon, current domestic violence charge, prior domestic violence arrests, and ever victimized stranger. The PICTS scales in the violence trailer include power orientation, entitlement, denial of harm, and self-assertion/deception (see Serin et al., 2016).

Bonta, 2010; Landenberger & Lipsey, 2005; Lowenkamp & Latessa, 2005; Lowenkamp, Latessa, & Holsinger, 2006). Therefore, the multi-level assessment integrated into PCRA 2.0 should make case planning more individualized, allow officers to better recognize offenders who are at a higher risk of re-arrest for a violent offense, and assist in meeting supervision objectives.

Conclusion

This chapter provided an overview of the PCRA risk tool utilized in the federal supervision system by discussing the history of assessments in the federal supervision system, highlighting the development, validation, and implementation of the PCRA, detailing its administration and scoring mechanisms, and providing a generalized overview of the research work that has been conducting using this tool. With the development and deployment of the PCRA, the federal supervision system for the first time possesses a dynamic actuarial tool capable of assessing an offender's risk of recidivism and measuring changes in these recidivism risk characteristics over time. While the PCRA represents a substantial advancement in the adoption of RNR principles into the federal supervision system, improvements and advances are continually being incorporated into this instrument. With the upcoming integration of a violence trailer, the launching of PCRA 2.0 represents a major effort aimed at enhancing this instrument's capabilities at predicting violence. Most importantly, the violence trailer will provide officers with a tool for identifying potentially violent offenders and hence serve as a mechanism for protecting the community. In sum, the PCRA's predictive efficacy, its ability to measure change in risk, its capacity to inform research on federal supervision, along with its enhanced abilities at predicting violence, all combine to make this instrument one of the foundational tools for the supervision of federal offenders.

References

Administrative Office of the U.S. Courts (AOUSC) (2011). *An overview of the federal post conviction risk assessment.* Washington, DC: Administrative Office of the U.S. Courts.

Alexander, M., & VanBenschoten, S. W. (2008). The evolution of supervision in the federal probation system. *Federal Probation, 72*(2), 15–21.

Andrews, D. A., Bonta, J., & Hoge, R. D. (1990). Classification for effective rehabilitation: Rediscovering psychology. *Criminal Justice and Behavior, 17*, 19–52.

Andrews, D., & Bonta, J. (1998). *The psychology of criminal conduct* (2nd ed.). Cincinnati, OH: Anderson Publishing.

Andrews, D., & Bonta, J. (2010). *The psychology of criminal conduct* (5th ed.). Cincinnati, OH: Anderson Publishing.

Bonta, J. (1996). Risk-needs assessment and treatment. In A. T. Harland (Ed.), *Choosing correctional options that work: defining the demand and evaluating the supply* (pp. 18–32). Thousand Oaks, CA: Sage.

Bonta, J., & Andrews, D.A. (2007). *Risk-Need-Responsivity Model for offender assessment and rehabilitation.* Ottawa, ON: Public Safety Canada.

Bonta, J., & Wormith, S. (2007). Risk and need assessment. In G. McIvor & P. Raynor (Eds.), *Developments in social work with offenders* (pp. 131–152) London, England: Jessica Kingsley.

Burgess, E. W. (1928). Factors determining success or failure on parole. In A. Bruce, E. Burgess, & A. Harno (Eds.), *Prediction and classification: Criminal justice decision making.* Chicago, IL: University of Chicago.

Cohen, T. H., Cook, D., & Lowenkamp, C. T. (2016d). The supervision of low risk offenders: How the low-risk policy has changed federal supervision practices without compromising community safety. *Federal Probation, 80*(1), 3–11.

Cohen, T. H., Lowenkamp, C. T., & VanBenschoten, S. (2016a). Does change in risk matter?: Examining whether change in offender risk characteristics influence recidivism outcomes. *Criminology and Public Policy, 15*(2), 263–296.

Cohen, T. H., Lowenkamp, C. T., & VanBenschoten, S. (2016b). Examining changes in offender risk characteristics and recidivism outcomes. *Federal Probation, 80*(2), 57–65.

Cohen, T. H., Pendergast, B. & VanBenschoten, S. (2016c). Examining overrides of risk classifications for offenders on federal supervision. *Federal Probation, 80*(1), 12–21.

Cohen, T. H., & Spidell, M. (2016). How dangerous are they?: An analysis of sex offenders under federal post-conviction supervision. *Federal Probation, 80*(2), 21–32.

Cohen, T. H., & VanBenschoten, S. W. (2014). Does the risk of recidivism for supervised offenders improve over time?: Examining changes in the dynamic risk characteristics for offenders under federal supervision. *Federal Probation, 78*(2), 41–52.

Cohen, T. H., & Whetzel, J. (2014). The neglected "R"—Responsivity and the federal offender. *Federal Probation, 78*(2), 11–18.

Connolly, M. (2003). *A critical examination of actuarial offender-based prediction assessments: guidance for the next generation of assessments.* Washington, DC: U.S. Department of Justice, National Institute of Justice.

Decision Support Systems, Report # 1009 (2016). *Post-Conviction Risk Assessment instrument and supervision levels national metrics.* Internal report retrieved from http://www.uscourts.gov

Eaglin, J., Gilbert, S., Hooper, L., & Lombard, P. (1997). *RPI Profiles: Descriptive information about offenders by their RPI scores.* Washington, DC: Federal Judicial Center.

Eaglin, J., & Lombard, P. (1982). *A validation and comparative evaluation of four predictive devices for classifying federal probation caseloads.* Washington, DC: Federal Judicial Center.

Flores, T., Holsinger, A., Lowenkamp, C. T., & Cohen, T. H. (2017). Time-free effects in predicting recidivism using both fixed and variable follow-up periods: Do different methods produce different results. *Criminal Justice and Behavior, 44*(1), 121–137.

Gendreau, P., Little, T., & Goggin, C. (1996). A meta-analysis of the predictors of adult offender recidivism: What works! *Criminology, 34*(4), 575–607.

Gottfredson, D., & Snyder, H. (2005). *The mathematics of risk classification: Changing data into valid instruments for juvenile courts.* Washington, DC: U.S. Department of Justice, Office of Juvenile Justice and Delinquency Prevention.

Gottfredson, S. D., & Gottfredson, D. M. (1979). Screening for risk: A comparison of methods. *Criminal Justice and Behavior, 7*(3), 315–330.

Guide to Judiciary Policy. (2014). *Guide to judiciary policy: Volume 8, probation and pretrial services.* Washington, DC: Administrative Office of the U.S. Courts.

Harcourt, B. (2007). *Against prediction.* Chicago, IL: University of Chicago Press.

Hughes, J. (2008). Results-based management in federal probation and pretrial services. *Federal Probation, 72*(2), 4–14.

IBM Strategic Assessment. (2004). *Strategic assessment: Federal Probation and Pretrial Services System,* Washington, DC.

Johnson, J. L., Lowenkamp, C. T., VanBenschoten, S. W., & Robinson, C. R. (2011). The construction and validation of the federal Post-Conviction Risk Assessment (PCRA). *Federal Probation, 75*(2), 16–29.

Kennedy, S., & Serin, R. (1997). Treatment responsivity: Contributing to effective correctional programming. *ICCA Journal, pp.* 46–52.

Latessa, E. J., & Lovins, B. (2010). The role of offender risk assessment: A policy maker guide. *Victims and Offenders, 5*(3), 203–219.

Landenberger, N. A., & Lipsey, M. W. (2005). The positive effects of cognitive behavioral programs for offenders: A meta-analysis of factors associated with effective treatment. *Journal of Experimental Criminology, 1*, 451–476.

Lombard, P., & Hooper, L. (1998). *RPI FAQs Bulletin.* Washington, DC: Federal Judicial Center.

Lowenkamp, C. T., Holsinger, A., & Cohen, T. H. (2015). PCRA revisited: Testing the validity of the Federal Post-Conviction Risk Assessment (PCRA). *Psychological Services, 12*(2), 149–157.

Lowenkamp, C. T., Johnson, J., VanBenschoten, S., Robinson, C., & Holsinger, A. (2013). The Federal Post-Conviction Risk Assessment (PCRA): A construction and validation study. *Psychological Services, 10*(1), 87–96.

Lowenkamp, C. T., & Latessa, E. J. (2005). Increasing the effectiveness of correctional programming through the risk principle: Identifying offenders for residential placement. *Criminology & Public Policy, 4*, 263–290.

Lowenkamp, C. T., Latessa, E. J., & Holsinger, A. M. (2006). The risk principle in action: What have we learned from 13,676 offenders and 97 correctional programs? *Crime & Delinquency, 52*, 77–93.

Luallen, J., Radakrishnan, S., & Rhodes, W. (2016). The predictive validity of the Post-Conviction Risk Assessment among federal offenders. *Criminal Justice and Behavior, 43*(9), 1173–1189.

McEwan, T. E., Mullen, P. E., & MacKenzie, R. (2009). A study of the predictors of persistence in stalking situations. *Law and Human Behavior, 33*, 149–158.

Ohlin, L. (1951). *Selection for Parole.* New York, NY: Russell Sage Foundation.

Serin, R., Lowenkamp, C. T., Johnson, J., & Trevino, P. (2016). Using a multi-level risk assessment to inform case planning and risk management: Implications for officers. *Federal Probation, 80*(2), 10–15.

Silver, E., Smith, W. R., & Banks, S. (2000). Constructing actuarial devices for predicting recidivism: A comparison of methods. *Criminal Justice and Behavior, 27*(6), 733–764.

Skeem, J., & Lowenkamp, C. T. (2016). Risk, race, and recidivism: Predictive bias and disparate impact. *Criminology, 54*(4), 680–712.

Skeem, J., Monahan, J., & Lowenkamp, C.T. (2016). Gender, risk assessment, and sanctioning: The cost of treating women like men. *Law and Human Behavior, 40*(5), 580–593.

Taxman, F., Shepardson, E., & Byrne, J. (2004). *Tools of the trade: A guide to incorporating science into practice.* Washington, DC: U.S. Department of Justice, National Institute of Corrections.

Tibbits, C. (1931). Success and failure on parole can be predicted. *Journal of Criminal Law & Criminology, 22*, 11–50.

United States Courts. (2014). *History of federal probation and pretrial services.* Retrieved from http://www.uscourts.gov/FederalCourts/ProbationPretrialServices/History.aspx

VanBenschoten, S. W. (2008). Risk/Needs assessment: Is this the best we can do. *Federal Probation, 72*(2), 38–42.

Van Voorhis, P., & Brown, K. (1996). *Risk classification in the 1990s.* Washington, DC: U.S. Department of Justice, National Institute of Corrections.

Walters, G. (2012). Criminal thinking and recidivism: Meta-analytic evidence on the predictive and incremental validity of the Psychological Inventory of Criminal Thinking Styles (PICTS). *Aggression and Violent Behavior, 17*, 272–278.

Walters, G. (2013). *The Psychological Inventory of Criminal Thinking Styles (PICTS).* Allentown, PA: Center for Lifestyle Studies.

Walters, G., & Cohen, T. H. (2016). Criminal thought process as a dynamic risk factor: Variable- and person-oriented approaches to recidivism prediction. *Law and Human Behavior, 40*(4), 411–419.

Walters, G., Hagman, B., & Cohn, W. (2011). Towards a hierarchical model of criminal thinking: Evidence from item response theory and confirmatory factor analysis. *Psychological Assessment, 23*(4), 925–936.

Walters, G., & Lowenkamp, C. T. (2016). Predicting recidivism with the Psychological Inventory of Criminal Thinking Styles (PICTS) in community-supervised male and female federal offenders. *Psychological Assessment, 28*(6), 652–659.

5

The Inventory of Offender Risk, Needs, and Strengths (IORNS)

Holly A. Miller

The Inventory of Offender Risk, Needs, and Strengths (IORNS) is a 130-item self-report measure that is intended to assess static risk, dynamic risk/need, and protective strength factors as they relate to general, violent, and sexual offending behavior. Each of the items is brief, is answered by endorsing as either true or false, and written at the third-grade reading level. The IORNS consists of four indices, eight scales, 14 subscales, and two validity scales. The indices of the IORNS include the Overall Risk Index (ORI), Static Risk Index (SRI), and the Protective Strength Index (PSI), with each serving to provide a summary of the offender's overall functioning or level of risk/need in each of these areas. The ORI is a composite score of all three of the index scores (static, dynamic, and protective) and provides an overall estimate of risk level and treatment needs compared to an offender of the same age and gender. The SRI consists of 12 items that are historical (or unchangeable) that have been found to be related to offending behavior and recidivism. The DNI consists of 79 items, which target specific areas of risk that are related to offending behavior and can be targeted in treatment and management for change. The PSI includes 26 items reflecting factors that have been found to promote resiliency and relate to desistance from offending behavior (see Table 5.1).

The indices of DNI and PSI consist of several scales and subscales that reflect the individual constructs identified as significant to risk assessment and treatment/management focus. The DNI consists of six scales including Criminal Orientation, Psychopathy, Intra/Interpersonal Problems, Alcohol/Drug Problems, Aggression, and Negative Social Influence (see Table 5.1). Higher scores on the DNI and the scales indicate higher dynamic risk and levels of treatment need. In order to provide additional interpretive value and information for treatment, several of the scales were analyzed for content clusters and developed into subscales. With the exception of the ADP and ENV scales, all other dynamic need scales include subscale information. The CRO scale is comprised of the Procriminal Attitudes (PCA) and Irresponsibility (IRR) subscales, and Manipulativeness (MAN), Impulsivity (IMP), and Angry Detachment (AND) subscales were identified for the Psychopathy scale. The IIP scale consists of Esteem Problems (EST) and Relational Problems (REL) subscales to help to determine if the offender's issues stem more from how they feel about themselves or how they relate to others (or both). The AGG scale is comprised of the Aggressive Behaviors (ABX) and Hostility (HOS) subscales, and the NSI consists of the Negative Friends (NFR) and Negative Family (NFA) subscales. Within the PSI, the PER scale is comprised of the Cognitive/Behavioral Regulation (CBR), Anger Regulation (ANR), and Education/Training (EDT) for employment subscales. Increasing subscale scores for the protective strength scales indicate higher levels that may serve the offender in the desistance of criminal/violent behavior.

Handbook of Recidivism Risk/Needs Assessment Tools, First Edition. Edited by Jay P. Singh, Daryl G. Kroner, J. Stephen Wormith, Sarah L. Desmarais, and Zachary Hamilton.
© 2018 John Wiley & Sons, Ltd. Published 2018 by John Wiley & Sons, Ltd.

Table 5.1 IORNS Index and Scale Descriptions

Index/Scale	Description
Overall Risk Index (ORI)	Composite score of the SRI, DNI, and PSI for a global estimate of risk and treatment/management need
Static Risk Index (SRI)	Historical, unchangeable items related to offending behavior
Dynamic Need Index (DNI)	Changeable factors related to offending behavior
Criminal Orientation (CRO)	Positive attitudes towards criminal behavior; denial of responsibility; disregard for others
Psychopathy (PPY)	Manipulation of others; impulsivity; detachment from emotion
Intra/Interpersonal Problems (IIP)	Feelings of personal and interpersonal inadequacy
Alcohol/Drug Problems (ADP)	Alcohol and drug-use-related problems
Aggression (AGG)	Hostility, anger, and physical aggression toward others
Negative Social Influence (NSI)	Support network involved with alcohol/drug and/or criminal behavior
Protective Strength Index (PSI)	Changeable factors related to the desistance of offending behavior
Personal Resources (PER)	Factors related to protection from criminal behaviors and desistance from crime
Environmental Resources (ENV)	Prosocial support from family and friends
Validity Scales	
Inconsistent Response Style (IRS)	Answering related pairs of items inconsistently
Favorable Impression (FIM)	Denial of commonly endorsed transgressions

The IORNS includes two validity scales that assess the response style and consistency of answers. The Inconsistent Response Style (IRS) scale is comprised of a series of closely related item pairs. If several of these item pairs are not answered consistently, the respondent may not have been attending appropriately to the measure or had trouble reading the items. The Favorable Impression (FIM) scale (see Table 5.1) assesses whether the individual may be attempting to portray themselves in a favorable manner. The validity scales are particularly important to assess the accuracy of the results since the IORNS is a self-report measure.

Although the IORNS includes assessment of risk/need variables that have been previously found to predict criminal, violent, and sexual assaulting behaviors, and has shown predictive utility for recidivism in a few studies (see below), the driving force in the IORNS development was the assessment of risk factors in order to identify and track these variables for specific focus in the treatment and management of offenders. The measure was not developed to be an actuarial tool. Thus, the development studies and initial examinations of the IORNS do not include predictive utility estimates for various outcomes.

Rationale and Development of the IORNS

With the large number of offenders incarcerated, on parole or probation, in mandated treatment programs, and on the sex offender registries, there is an increasing need to identify offenders who are at risk of behaving violently, reoffending sexually, or who are at risk for continued general recidivism. Relevant criminal justice contexts include: (a) parole hearings, (b) inmate classifications, (c) sexually violent predator evaluations, (d) probation risk assignment, and

(e) treatment need and progress evaluations. Although the assessment of future risk of reoffense is the primary purpose of several of these evaluations, risk assessment has important utility for the treatment and management of offenders. It is argued that risk assessment, or identifying factors that are related to criminal and violent behavior, serves several important purposes (e.g., Harris & Rice, 1997; Jackson & Guyton, 2008; Miller, 2006a; Serin, Chadwick, & Lloyd, 2016). First, risk assessment is utilized to examine the risk of recidivism. Identifying risk factors and criminogenic needs that can be targeted to help rehabilitate and/or manage an offender is a second important purpose. Third, risk assessments can also help identify factors related to desistance of criminal behavior that may also help effectively treat offenders.

Although researchers examining the IORNS have provided some predictive evidence for the measure, the IORNS was developed to provide treatment providers and supervision officers with an efficient tool for the assessment of variables related to criminal behavior and desistance from crime for treatment and management purposes. The IORNS was developed to provide an efficient measure of risk and protective factors to be targeted and continually assessed for change. Identifying important risk and strength variables allows for the most effective treatment and management of offenders. The rationale for the IORNS development stemmed from expressed needs and frustrations of both treatment providers and supervising officers within the criminal justice system, where evidence-based programing is becoming the norm. Specifically, treatment providers working with offenders (both within and outside of a prison environment) voiced frustration related to the limitations and time commitments of existing measures and a desire for a comprehensive and validated method of assessing and monitoring change in variables related to recidivism. They voiced a need for a measure that would allow them to determine what factors were most important for treatment focus for individual offenders, and for the ability to evaluate program effectiveness in a quantitative manner. A second need voiced by treatment providers, researchers, and criminal justice personnel was the need of a tool that would assess all three areas of factors related to reoffense: static risk, dynamic need, and protective factors. Third, criminal justice personnel reported a need for an efficient measure of risk and need that does not require extensive training and extensive inter-rater reliability practice. These concerns and frustrations were heard consistently over several correctional and offender treatment-related conferences and risk assessment workshops.

In an attempt to meet these voiced needs in risk assessment, the overall goal of the IORNS was established: a self-report risk assessment measure that identifies as many of the variables related to criminal and violent behavior as possible, and allows for the assessment of change in these variables through time, management, or treatment. Development of the IORNS as a self-report measure provides economical advantage over a person-administered assessment in that extensive experience and training are not necessary for the reliable administration and scoring. Previous research has indicated the effectiveness of self-report measures in the predictions of criminal and violent behavior (Loza & Green, 2003; Loza, Neo, Shahinfar, & Loza-Fanous, 2005; Motiuk, Motiuk, & Bonta, 1992).

In order to develop a comprehensive measure that assessed relevant constructs related to recidivism and the desistence from criminal behavior, Miller (2006) identified all variables that were found to consistently relate to these outcomes for item development. Constructs were chosen based on their relationship strength with recidivism, desistence, or protective outcomes with general, violent, and sexual offending behavior. When the IORNS was developed the literature for static and dynamic risk/need variables was vast. Although research examining protective strengths in adult offenders was quite limited at that time (somewhat improved currently), researchers were beginning to recognize the importance of including protective factors in the assessment of offender risk (Rogers, 2000; Shedrick, 1999; Stouthamer-Loeber, Wei, Loeber, & Masten, 2004).

Construction of the IORNS' items followed several guidelines. First, efforts were made to reduce potential influence of response style (both negative and positive). Items were written to be as normative as possible with several keyed in opposite directions. Efforts were made to keep the reading level around the third grade given the lower educational attainment levels for many offender populations. In an effort to fulfill the goal of developing a comprehensive risk/ need assessment tool, Miller (2006b) ensured that a broad array of constructs related to offending behavior and desistance from crime were represented in the initial item development. All constructs that exhibited relatively consistent evidence of a relationship to such behaviors were included as possible IORNS constructs. Furthermore, constructs that exhibited minor differences in the predictive accuracy based on offender type were also included to ensure adequate construct representation across offense types. For example, the construct of self-esteem has been more closely related to sexual recidivism than general recidivism, but was included in the construct list (Thornton, Beech, & Marshall, 2004).

The IORNS development process progressed from constructs, to written items, and to item and factor analysis for final item selection. The IORNS originated with 201 items written to represent several constructs related to criminal, violent, and sexual offending behavior identified in the literature. Table 5.2 provides a list of the constructs utilized to develop items and the IORNS Professional Manual (Miller, 2006b) reports the empirical support for each construct.

To select the best functioning items from the initial item pool, the 201 items were administered to 526 male and female adults representing college students, general offenders, and sexual offenders. From the initial list, 174 items were retained for the second phase of item selection. These items were given to additional 115 imprisoned or probated general and sexual offenders and combined with the original sample for factor analysis. Principal Axis (PA) factor analysis with Promax (oblique) rotation was conducted on the static, dynamic, and protective strength items. The results indicated that a single factor of static risk, six factors representing dynamic risk/need, and two factors representing protective strengths indicated the best fitting model. From this analysis, a total of 44 items that did not load highly on one of the factors were deleted.

Table 5.2 Static, Dynamic, and Protective Constructs for Initial IORNS Item Development

Static and Protective Constructs	Dynamic Constructs
Static	
Age at first crime	Procriminal attitudes
Early conduct problems	Irresponsibility
Previous violent behavior	Negative social influence
Stranger victims	Impulsivity
Previous revocation of parole/probation	Antisocial/Psychopathy
	Disregard for others
Protective	Alcohol/drug problems
Family/Social Support	Low self-esteem
Education/Training for employment	Intimacy problems
Social participation/connection	Low treatment compliance
Effective problems solving/Self-regulation	Hostility/Aggression

The final static factor, called the SRI, consists of 12 items. The DNI is comprised of 79 items within those six factors. The PSI includes 26 items within two factors.

A separate PA factor analysis was conducted on the 79 dynamic risk/need items based on theoretical consideration of dynamic factors structurally independent from static risk and protective strength factors. Results of this analysis confirmed that the dynamic risk/needs were best represented by six factors (scales) including Criminal Orientation, Psychopathy, Intra/Interpersonal Problems, Alcohol/Drug Problems, Aggression, and Negative Social Influence. Another PA was completed on the 26 items representing protective strengths. Results indicated that a two-factor solution was the best fitting model: Personal Resources and Environmental Resources.

Second-order factor analyses were completed because of the a priori theoretical identification of constructs related to risks and strengths where each dynamic and protective factor scale was analyzed to determine the presence of increased specificity through sub-factors (now called subscales). PA factor analysis with Promax rotation was conducted separately on each of the six dynamic factors/scales and the two protective strength factors/scales. Results indicated several subscales for the majority of IORNS factors/scales. Table 5.3 presents the subscales identified.

The items for the IORNS' validity scales were chosen by item-total correlations, factor loadings, and item-pair relationships. For the Favorable Impression Scale (FIM), 13 items were chosen that best reflected the denial of minor transgressions shared by virtually all people (e.g., "I have taken my frustration out on other people") by item-total correlations and factor loadings. Once the final items had been chosen for all of the IORNS scales, item-pair correlations were examined

Table 5.3 Overview of the IORNS Subscales

Scale/Subscale	Items
Criminal Orientation (CRO)	
Procriminal Attitudes (PCA)	10
Irresponsibility (IRR)	9
Psychopathy (PPY)	
Manipulativeness (MAN)	8
Impulsivity (IMP)	7
Angry Detachment (AND)	7
Intra/Interpersonal Problems (IIP)	
Esteem Problems (EST)	7
Relational Problems (REL)	6
Aggression (AGG)	
Hostility (HOS)	4
Aggressive Behaviors (ABX)	7
Negative Social Influence (NSI)	
Negative Friends (NFR)	4
Negative Family (NFA)	3
Personal Resources (PER)	
Cognitive/Behavioral Regulation (CBR)	9
Anger Regulation (ANR)	5
Education/Training (EDT)	5

for the construction of a scale to assess response inconsistency, or the degree to which respondents answer similar items inconsistently. Ten item pairs were chosen to create the Inconsistent Response Scale (IRS) based on high ($r > .45$) item intercorrelations and similar item content.

Standardization

For any assessment measure of risk, needs, and strengths, normative comparisons are essential. In practice, examiners will be asked to make decisions for an offender based on how his or her scores compare to others. The use of offender populations in risk assessment research supports such comparisons (Miller, 2006b). As such, the male and female IORNS offender samples should primarily be utilized for normative comparison purposes. In some circumstances, however, an examiner may wish to compare an examinee's scores to the general or community population. For example, if an examiner is making a recommendation for release, she may wish to compare the offender's protective strength scores to a community sample. If a researcher is examining risk and/or protective strengths in a community or college sample, he or she may want to compare scores to community members and offender populations. For these reasons, the IORNS has normative samples for offender and community comparisons.

The normative offender group ($N = 482$) for comparisons is comprised of five separate offender samples including general male incarcerated and probated offenders, male sexual imprisoned and probated offenders, and general incarcerated female offenders. Strengths of these samples for comparisons include: (a) representation of both genders, (b) composition of different offender types, and (c) an overrepresentation of racial/ethnic minorities (more closely relating to actual offender compositions in most states). The normative community adult group represents a similar distribution of adults across the United States based on age, gender, and race. Participants in the normative community sample were recruited from multiple geographic regions and in a variety of settings. For a specific breakdown of each sample, please see the Professional Manual (Miller, 2006b). Based on examination of the distributions of the IORNS index and scale scores, age and gender normative groupings within the offender and community samples are provided in six different combinations (e.g., male offenders 18–29 years old, female community 30–39 years old).

For each normative group, the means, standard deviations, skewness, kurtosis, and cumulative frequency distributions were calculated for the IORNS index and scale scores. Because most of the constructs assessing risk, needs, and strengths are not normally distributed, non-normalized T scores were chosen. Additionally, a regression-based continuous norming process was followed with the IORNS data because of the relatively small sample sizes for some of the age and gender groupings. Given limited raw score ranges and concomitant attenuated internal consistency, T scores were not used for subscale score scaling purposes. Instead, cumulative frequencies for each subscale were inspected for adequate distribution of raw scores across various percentile cutoff points. These cut points were used to determine if comparative scores were lower, average, or higher than the normative distribution scores (Miller, 2006b).

Reliability

The reliability of the IORNS has been tested in several ways. First, the development samples and additional research samples after the IORNS development have examined the internal consistency of the measure. Miller (2006b) presents coefficient alpha results for each of the normative offender and community samples. The internal consistency is reported to be satisfactory for each of the indices and scales on the IORNS, ranging from .74 to .90 in the offender normative group, and from .60 to .90 in the community normative group (Miller, 2006b). Additional research has reported similar internal consistency scores for the IORNS indices and scales. Miller (2006a), in a sample of 162 general male offenders, reported coefficient alphas ranging from .66 to .91 and Miller (2015) reported similar ranges (.78 to .92) with a sample of 110 male sexual offenders. Because the IORNS index scores consist of composites of the scores from their relative scales, composite reliabilities for each index were calculated using the traditional composite formula suggested by Guilford (1954) and Nunnally and Bernstein (1994). Composite reliabilities for the IORNS index scores range from .79 to .92 in the normative offender and community samples (Miller, 2006b).

Two measures of reliability were provided in a sample of 314 general male and female offenders that were serving two years or less in a state jail (most were drug and property offenders; Bergeron & Miller, 2013). The McDonald's wh (McDonald, 1999), which is the reliability estimate recommended by Revelle and Zinbarg (2009), and the glb, which are recommended by Sijtsma (2009) as better alternatives to the Cronbach's alpha. Bergeron and Miller (2013) report strong reliability scores for each assessment over the dynamic needs and protective strength scales, with wh scores ranging from .81 to .93 and glb scores ranging from .80 to .93 at the first administration of the IORNS in their study. Reliability scores for both of these estimates were lower, but similar in the second administration of the IORNS in the sample (Bergeron & Miller, 2013).

IORNS test-retest stability was examined during the development of the measure (Miller, 2006b) in a sample of male and female undergraduates tested 21 days apart. The IORNS demonstrated good test-retest reliability with the Index scores ranging from .68 to .86, scales ranging between .65 to .84, and subscales ranging from .42 (IRR) to .89 (ABX).

Validity

Evidence of IORNS validity has been demonstrated by: (a) item content, (b) the convergence and divergence of IORNS scores with other measures of risk, need, protective strength, personality, and psychopathy, (c) internal structure, and (d) predictive relationships. As described previously, the item content of the IORNS was developed after careful review of the literature and writing an outline of important constructs related to general, violent, and sexual criminal behavior and the desistance from crime. During the development stages of the IORNS, these constructs were qualitatively reviewed by several experts in the fields of risk assessment, offender treatment, and offender monitoring to identify possible missing or inappropriate constructs. Expert review did not identify any inappropriate or missing constructs (Miller, 2006b).

Construct Validity

The construct validity of the IORNS was examined closely in the development of the IORNS and has since been examined with additional samples of offenders. Participants in the various offender samples during IORNS development were administered subsets of concurrent measures as a means of evaluating the relationships between the IORNS and other assessments related to offender recidivism and desistance. In the sample of male incarcerated general offenders, the IORNS index, scale scores, and subscale scores were significantly related to criminal history variables, times previously in jail or prison, the Level of Service Inventory–Revised (LSI-R; Andrews & Bonta, 1995) scales, related scales on the Personality Assessment Inventory (PAI; Morey, 1991) such as the Antisocial Features scale ($r = .57$ with IORNS Overall Risk

Index) and Drug Problems scale ($r = .67$ with IORNS Alcohol/Drug Problems), the Substance Abuse Subtle Screening Inventory-3 (SASSI-3; Miller, Roberts, Brooks, & Lazowski, 1997), and the State Trait Anxiety Inventory (STAI; Spielberger, 1983) where total anxiety levels were significantly (negatively) related to protective factors on the IORNS.

In the developmental sample of incarcerated sexual offenders, the IORNS was significantly related to the overall scores and several of the scales on the Sexual Offender Needs Assessment Rating Scale (SONAR; Hanson & Harris, 2001). For example, the SONAR Stable Total score was significantly correlated with the ($r = .49$) Overall Risk Index (ORI) and the Protective Strength Index (PSI; $r = -.35$) on the IORNS. Construct validity with the sample of sexual offenders also was demonstrated by relationships between several of the IORNS indices, scales, and subscales with the Personality Assessment Inventory (PAI; Morey, 1991), the Psychopathy Checklist-Revised (PCL-R; Hare, 1991), and the Psychopathic Personality Inventory–Revised (PPI-R; Lilienfeld & Widows, 2005). Specifically, the Dynamic Needs Index (DNI) and the Psychopathy (PPY) scale of the IORNS were correlated with the Antisocial Features (ANT) of the PAI at .59 and .52, respectively. The Static Risk Index (SRI) of the IORNS was correlated with the PCL-R Factor 2 score at .70 and the PPY scale of the IORNS was significantly related ($r = .73$) to the Machievellian Egocentricity (ME) scale of the PPI-R. Further construct validity with sexual offenders was presented with the developmental sample of probated sexual offenders (see Miller, 2006b).

Construct validity has also been examined with samples of female offenders. In a sample of 99 incarcerated female general offenders, numerous significant relationships were found between the IORNS indices, scales, and subscales with reported history variables. The ORI correlated highly with previous nonviolent arrests ($r = .50$), number of previous times in prison ($r = .41$), and past physical abuse ($r = .47$). Other notable relationships include significant associations between the IORNS DNI and a history of physical and sexual abuse ($r = .42$ and .31, respectively), several alcohol/drug-related variables and the DNI ($r = .41$ to .51), and the ADP, PPY, and NSI scales of the IORNS ($r = .30$ to .65). The IORNS indices, scales, and subscales were also found to significantly relate to several of the PAI constructs reflecting pathological personality functioning. The ORI was highly correlated with several of the personality indicators: The ORI related to the PAI BOR ($r = .71$), AGG ($r = .67$), and the DRG ($r = .65$). Significant relationships were found between the Static Risk Index (SRI) of the IORNS and the AGG, ANT, and DRG scales of the PAI ($r = .52$ to .54), indicating that, similar to male offenders, the IONRS SRI is highly related to constructs that have been consistently associated with antisocial, aggressive, and drug-related problems. The Dynamic Needs Index (DNI) was significantly associated with severe personality pathology, with the highest correlations found with the Borderline Features, Schizophrenia, Aggression, and Paranoia scales ($r = .76$ to .80). Other notable relationships were found between the IORNS AGG scale and the subscales with PAI AGG scale ($r = .76$ to .84) and between the Environmental Resources (ENV) protective scale on the IORNS and the Nonsupport (NON) scale of the PAI ($r = -.84$).

Additional construct validity of the IORNS ORI has been demonstrated in large samples of male and female offenders. In the developmental samples, male and female offenders were split into high and low (quartiles) groups of overall risk and compared on several variables indicating that delineation of the ORI score is meaningful. For both male and female offenders who scored in the top 25% of the ORI score distribution demonstrated a significantly greater number of previous arrests, incarcerations, and violent crimes compared to the male and female offenders in the bottom 75% of the ORI distribution. In a sample of 162 general male offenders, Miller (2006a) split the sample by a cut raw score of 62 on the ORI, corresponding with the 75th percentile in the sample. Independent t tests were utilized to compare offenders scoring in the top 25% of the ORI score distribution to male offenders in the lower 75%

on several validity variables. Results indicated that the offenders scoring in the top 25% of the Overall Risk Index were significantly higher on variables of criminal history, risk as measured by the LSI-R, personality pathology as measured by the PAI (BOR, ANT, AGG), psychopathy constructs, depression, and anxiety. These data provide further evidence that the ORI of the IORNS provides meaningful distinctions for risk and treatment need.

Internal Structure

The internal structure of the IORNS has also been examined as a form of validity evidence. Within the developmental samples of the IORNS, the indices, scales, and subscales all correlated in expected directions (Miller, 2006b). Additionally, factorial validity analyses indicated loadings for dynamic risk in male offenders ranging between .42 and .82 and .34 to .86 for female offenders. For the protective strength factor, female and male offenders had factors loadings of .73 and .84, respectively. Bergeron and Miller (2013) utilized a sample of male and female offenders (N = 314) to assess the stability of the IORNS structure over time, as well as the ability of the IORNS to track change in treatment. The authors reported further evidence of the stable factor structure of the IORNS DNI and PSI scales; factor loadings and intercepts of items did not change over time.

Predictive Validity

Predictive validity of the IORNS has been examined in general and sexual offenders. In a sample of 162 general male offenders, Miller (2006a) examined initial predictive validity by obtaining recidivism data 15 months after the IORNS assessment and release of the participants from prison. In this study, all offenders were released into a halfway house and recidivism was defined as any violations that returned the offender back to prison. Recidivism "offenses" ranged from breaking curfew (technical violation) to committing a new criminal charge. Because infractions were common for the offenders (the majority of the sample was returned to prison at least once during the study), the results compared offenders who had two or more infractions/new charges to offenders who did not violate or had one violation since release. Offenders who were sent back to prison two or more times scored significantly higher on the Overall Risk Index (ORI) and the Dynamic Needs Index (DNI) indices of the IORNS. These offenders also scored significantly lower on the Protective Strength Index (PSI), indicating that they have fewer protective factors than the offenders who did not recidivate or who only violated one time. In the analyses of the IORNS scales, Miller (2006a) reported that the offenders who were higher violators had significantly increased scores on the scales of Psychopathy, Criminal Orientation, and the Alcohol/Drug Problems. This group also scored significantly higher on the subscales of Manipulativeness, Impulsivity, and Irresponsibility. The offenders who did not reoffend scored significantly higher on the protective strength scales and subscales of Personal Resources and Cognitive/Behavioral Regulation. Because the majority of the recidivism type in this study were technical violations and not new criminal offenses, and the two could not be differentiated, other predictive statistics were not conducted.

In a study that focused on protective strengths, Miller (2015) examined the relationship between protective factors and risk with recidivism in a sample of 110 male incarcerated sexual offenders. Over a fixed recidivism time of six years, 6%, 10%, and 27% of the sample recidivated sexually, violently (not including sexual), and generally once released. Because of the low base rate of sexual and violent recidivism, AUC values were computed (see Table 5.4). The AUC values related to the predictive validity of the ORI, SRI, DNI, and PSI indicated that the SRI was only predictive of general recidivism, whereas the DNI was a significant predictor for violent

Table 5.4 Areas Under the Curve for Sexual, Violent, and General Recidivism for IORNS Indices in a Sample of Known Sexual Offenders

Index	AUC	SE	Significance	95% CI
Sexual recidivism				
SRI	.58	.14	.55	[.32, .85]
DNI	.77	.07	.05	[.63, .90]
PSI	.86	.05	.02	[.73, .92]
ORI	.83	.05	.01	[.75, .91]
Violent recidivism				
SRI	.60	.08	.35	[.45, .75]
DNI	.74	.08	.02	[.57, .90]
PSI	.72	.09	.04	[.54, .89]
ORI	.70	.09	.05	[.54, .83]
General recidivism				
SRI	.71	.07	.00	[.57, .85]
DNI	.71	.06	.00	[.56, .83]
PSI	.67	.07	.02	[.54, .80]
ORI	.77	.06	.00	[.66, .89]

Note: AUC = area under the curve; SE = standard error; CI = confidence interval; SRI = Static Risk Index; DNI = Dynamic Need Index; PSI = Protective Strength Index; ORI = Overall Risk Index.

and general recidivism for this sample of sexual offenders. The PSI was a significant predictor for sexual, violent, and general recidivism. The Overall Risk Index (ORI), which takes into account static, dynamic, and protective strengths, significantly predicted sexual and general recidivism.

Tracking Change through Treatment

As the intended purpose of the IORNS is to enable comprehensive risk, need, and protective factor assessment for the purposes of treatment and management of offenders, the ability of the measure to track potential change is paramount. With the exception of a few studies (Labrecque, Smith, Lovins, & Latessa, 2014; Olver & Wong, 2009; Olver, Wong, Nicholaichuk, & Gordon, 2007; Raynor, 2007; Schlager & Pacheco, 2011; Vose, Smith, & Cullen, 2013), many dynamic risk and need assessments have assumed that these variables change through treatment instead of providing evidence of the measure/variables being effectively tracked through time and/or treatment. Less frequent even, is the assessment of measure stability over administrations, whether the measurement properties of the risk assessment remain invariant across administration times. Without measurement stability, it is impossible to determine if score changes are due to error or actual change over time or through treatment. Initial examination of the IORNS' ability to track changes through treatment was presented during the developmental years of the tool (Bergeron, Miller, Tsang, & Clark, 2010; Miller, Davis, Torres, Palac, & Engman, 2006). Miller et al. (2006) tracked a sample of sexual offenders through a prison-based treatment program. The authors administered the IORNS at the beginning, middle, and end of treatment and over an 18-month period. Overall results indicated no significant changes in the SRI over treatment, as expected with historical risk factors, and significant decreases in the DNI between the beginning and end of treatment times. Additionally, the PSI scores significantly increased through treatment.

Bergeron et al. (2010) investigated the IORNS indices and scale scores across two treatment administrations with a large sample ($N = 1,203$) of general male and female offenders. The authors first examined the factor structure for stability over the two assessments and found reasonably well-fitting models at both administration points. Additionally, the authors reported significant decreases in DNI scales and significant increases in PSI scales through administrations. However, without measurement stability assessment of the IORNS across administration points, it can only be assumed that these changes are due to effective treatment. In order to provide stability assessment of the factors measured by the IORNS, Bergeron and Miller (2013) examined whether indices assessed by the IORNS that are expected to change through treatment success, actually changed due to intervention versus measurement error across administrations.

With a sample of 314 male and female offenders, Bergeron and Miller (2013) examined pre- and post-treatment administrations of the IORNS over a four-month period of intense pre-release programing. As the SRI and its items are not expected to vary or change over time or treatment, the scales on the DNI and PSI were examined over the two administrations. Results indicated that the measurement properties of the DNI and PSI scales were invariant over time; the models suggested that none of the DNI or PSI factor loadings displayed evidence of significant variance in factor loadings across administrations. Subsequent latent difference score model results suggested that the scales of the DNI decreased and scores of the PSI scales increased over the assessment periods, measuring potential effectiveness of the offender release program (Bergeron & Miller, 2013). This study was the first to present evidence of invariance of any risk assessment measure at different points in treatment, indicating that the IORNS is effective at tracking changes of variables related to risk through treatment and the examiner can be assured that the change is in fact due to positive treatment effects rather than measurement error.

Case Illustration

To help illustrate the utility of the IORNS in the treatment process, the following case study is presented. Because the IORNS was developed to provide focused treatment and continued assessment of several static, dynamic, and protective strength factors related to offending behavior, the IORNS is given at the beginning of the treatment process to aid in the identification of risk variables important to a particular offender. An initial IORNS assessment can also be compared to additional IORNS results at any stage in treatment and when the offender is considered treatment complete. The following case study provides an example of how the IORNS can be utilized to prepare initial treatment goals for an offender. The IORNS is often utilized as part of an evaluation that includes a clinical interview and other assessment tools.

Mr. B is a 25-year-old White male who is serving a probated sentence of 10 years for sexual assault of a child. His community supervision officer referred him for sexual offender treatment as part of his probation requirements. This evaluation serves as his intake assessment and will determine if he is appropriate for group treatment, and if appropriate, his initial goals and focus for treatment. The following information is provided by a clinical interview, the Static-99R, and the administration of the Personality Assessment Inventory (PAI; Morey, 1991) and the IORNS (Miller, 2006b).

Mr. B reports that he has lived with his mother in a small town for his entire life and has no contact with his biological father. He states that his parents separated when he was three years old and knows very little about him. Mr. B reports that he has one younger brother who is 16 years old and that they get along "for the most part." He states that his mother's boyfriend of nine years also lives with them. He reports that he has an uncle that has been arrested numerous times, but reports no other family members having criminal histories or abusing substances. Mr. B claims that he has no history of being abused physically, emotionally, or sexually. He states that he had a four-year relationship, with the mother of his child, when he was in high school. Mr. B reports that he has a seven-year-old daughter who lives with her mother. He states that he has had his current girlfriend (who is 20 years old) for the last five months.

Mr. B reports that he did well in school, mostly A and B grades and played for the football team. He had plans on attending college but states that this "charge has made that very difficult." He has worked at many fast food restaurants over the last several years and claims that he has never been fired from a job and gets along well with supervisors and co-workers.

Mr. B states that he has never received treatment for mental health or substance abuse issues. He reports that he felt depressed after he was charged with this offense, but has never felt suicidal or taken any medications for mood or sleep problems. He denies any history of alcohol or drug abuse.

Mr. B reports that he learned about sex through his friends at school and that his mother discussed safe sex and the use of condoms. He states that he has had approximately 20 sexual partners, several being "one night stands." He denies use of prostitutes, public masturbation, or any sexual behavior that would cause him problems. Mr. B reports that he has used pornography, but not on a consistent basis. His pornography content is reported to be "all adult normal stuff." He states that his sexual behavior has never gotten him into trouble until this offense. He reports that he met his 13-year-old victim through a friend and they started texting and spending some time together. He states that she started kissing him and that they engaged in fondling and he penetrated her vagina with his finger. Mr. B reports that she wanted to have sex, but they did not have intercourse. He states that she told him that she was 17 years old and that he was "tricked into this mess." He says he feels betrayed and is angry with the victim. The police report and victim statement is much different. The victim reported that she and Mr. B began consensual kissing and when he attempted to have sex with her she told him no, but he did not stop.

During the evaluation, Mr. B was cooperative, alert, well groomed, and rapport was easily established. He seemed to have above average intellectual functioning and read consent forms easily and quickly. He demonstrated little responsibility for his offending behavior and blamed the victim. The assessment protocol for Mr. B included the Personality Assessment Inventory (Morey, 1991), the Inventory of Offender Risk, Needs, and Strengths (IORNS), the Static-99R, and two measures of cognitions related to sexual behavior with others and victim consequences. On the Static-99R, Mr. B scored a 1, placing him in the low-risk level to recidivate sexually. His PAI validity results indicated he answered the items in a defensive manner, attempting to portray himself as relatively free from common shortcomings to which most people admit (PIM $T = 67$). Other PAI validity indicators were in the normal range. Although Mr. B answered the PAI in a defensive manner, and his results are likely an underestimate of his current psychological functioning, he did elevate a couple of the clinical scales. He obtained elevations on the Borderline Features and Nonsupport scales.

The IORNS was given to Mr. B to assess level of risk and treatment need compared to male offenders his age. Similar to the PAI response style, Mr. B answered the IORNS items in a defensive manner. In fact, his Favorable Impression Scale was scored at the 98th percentile compared to male offenders his age. His Overall Risk Index (ORI) was scored at the 5th percentile. However, his risk and treatment need assessment is likely an underestimate of his actual risk/need. Despite the extreme defensiveness in response style, Mr. B elevated two of the dynamic risk/needs scales. His score on the Criminal Orientation (CRO) scale was at the 81st percentile compared to male offenders his age. The subscales of the CRO indicate that he reported high levels of procriminal attitudes and irresponsibility. Mr. B also elevated the Intra/Interpersonal Problems scale, indicating significant difficulties with his self-esteem and relationships with others. On the protective strength scales, Mr. B reported average levels of personal and environmental resources (at the 42nd and 45th percentiles, respectively) and high levels of education or training for employment.

IORNS summary sheet scores

Index/Scale	Raw Score	T Score	%ile
Static Risk Index (SRI)	1	34	9
Criminal Orientation (CRO)	3	54	81
Psychopathy (PPY)	1	37	14
Intra/Interpersonal Problems (IIP)	2	52	75
Alcohol/Drug Problems (ADP)	0	33	16
Aggression (AGG)	1	38	20
Negative Social Influence (NSI)	0	33	7
Dynamic Need Index (DNI)	7	35	8
Personal Resources (PER)	17	51	42
Environmental Resources (ENV)	7	51	45
Protective Strength Index (PSI)	24	54	57
Favorable Impression (FIM)	11	72	98

On the measures of thinking, Mr. B reported a few cognitive distortions as they related to adults having sexual contact with children. He also reported little victim empathy or understanding of how his offense could have impacted the victim. He strongly disagreed that he hurt the victim in any way or that he exploited or took advantage of her. He agreed with the statement "It was the victim's fault that it happened."

Overall results indicate that Mr. B was not completely honest and open when responding to interview questions or when answering items on the psychopathology, risk, and cognitive measures. His personality, psychopathology, and risk/need profiles are consistent with someone who is not admitting to even minor flaws that most people admit to. Despite this defensive responding he still elevated scales that indicate specific areas for treatment focus and concern, such as irresponsibility, esteem issues, and relationship problems. His offense version is very different than the police report and victim statement. The results of his interview and testing indicate that he is appropriate for, and should begin, sexual offender treatment and work on specific areas to decrease the likelihood of further offending behavior. It is recommended that Mr. B focus on the following initial treatment goals:

1) Report all symptoms or difficulties in order to target all treatment needs
2) Take responsibility for the offending behavior
3) Examine possible contributing factors of self-esteem and relationship issues, and irresponsibility to his offending behavior

4) Acknowledge and disclose possible victim impact
5) Work towards understanding all of the contributing factors to the offense.

Utility and Future Directions of the IORNS

The case illustration highlights the intended purpose and utility of the IORNS. The IORNS assessment helps to identify important risk, need, and protective strength factors that are related to offending behavior. The IORNS administration at the beginning of treatment helps to identify several variables for treatment target and continued assessment. As previous reviewers of the IORNS have indicated (e.g., DeClue, 2007), the IORNS adds utility to decision-making within treatment and supervision programs. Treatment providers and evaluators can utilize the scores from the IORNS to form hypotheses about an offender's problem areas, needs, and progress in treatment.

If an evaluator desires to utilize the IORNS for predictive purposes, further research is warranted to examine the predictive utility of the IORNS with different offender types and outcomes, especially in relationship with change scores. Research has informed that the IORNS can track change through treatment and/or time, but the level of change required to reduce risk has yet to be examined. As it stands, little predictive evidence has been accumulated for the IORNS. In fact, DeClue (2007), in his review of the IORNS for use in sexually violent predator (SVP) assessments, states that the IORNS could add utility to decision-making in sexual offender treatment programs by assessing and tracking important variables related to offending, but the IORNS should not be utilized for risk prediction. This advice remains valid until significant predictive validity research is conducted.

Since the IORNS was developed to serve as a tool to assess risk, need, and protective factors in the treatment and management of offenders, and it is currently being utilized for such purposes, future research is warranted to examine whether specific treatment modalities can effectively change corresponding IORNS scores. For example, if a treatment program focuses on changing cognitive distortions, examining whether the IORNS subscale of Procriminal Attitudes effectively tracks changes through treatment could be very informative for the client, treatment provider, and program evaluator.

References

Andrews, D. A., & Bonta, J. L. (1995). *Level of Service Inventory–Revised* (LSI-R). North Tonawanda, NY: Multi-Health Systems.

Bergeron, C. L., & Miller, H. A. (2013). Tracking change through treatment with the Inventory of Offender Risk, Needs, and Strengths. *Psychological Assessment, 25*, 979–990.

Bergeron, C. L., Miller, H. A., Tsang, S., & Clark, A. (March 2010). *Tracking changes and consistency of IORNS factor structure through treatment*. Poster presentation at the meeting of the American Psychology-Law Society, Vancouver, BC, Canada.

DeClue, G. (2007). Review of the Inventory of Offender Risks, Needs, and Strengths (IORNS). *The Journal of Psychiatry & Law, 35*, 51–60.

Guilford, J. P. (1954). *Psychometric methods*. New York, NY: McGraw-Hill.

Hanson, R. K., & Harris, A. J. R. (2001). A structured approach to evaluating change among sexual offenders. *Sexual Abuse: A Journal of Research and Treatment, 13*, 105–122.

Hare, R. D. (1991). *The Hare Psychopathy Checklist-Revised.* Toronto, ON, Canada: Multi-Health Systems.

Harris, G. T., & Rice, M. E. (1997). Risk appraisal and management of violent behavior. *Psychiatric Services, 48,* 1168–1176.

Jackson, R. L., & Guyton, M. R. (2008). Violence risk assessment (pp. 153–181). In R. Jackson (Ed.), *Learning forensic assessment.* New York, NY: Routledge/Taylor & Francis Group.

Labrecque, R. M., Smith, P., Lovins, B. K., & Latessa, E. J. (2014). The importance of reassessment: How changes in the LSI-R risk score can improve the prediction of recidivism. *Journal of Offender Rehabilitation, 53,* 116–128.

Lilienfeld, S., & Widows, M. R. (2005). *(PPI-R) professional manual.* Lutz, FL: Psychological Assessment Resources.

Loza, W., & Green, K. (2003). The Self-Appraisal Questionnaire: A self-report measure for predicting recidivism versus clinician-administered measures: A 5-year follow-up study. *Journal of Interpersonal Violence, 18,* 781–797.

Loza, W., Neo, L. H., Shahinfar, A., & Loza-Fanous, A. (2005). Cross-validation of the Self-Appraisal Questionnaire: A tool for assessing violent and nonviolent recidivism with female offenders. *International Journal of Offender Therapy and Comparative Criminology, 49,* 547–560.

McDonald, R. P. (1999). *Test theory: A unified treatment.* Mahwah, NJ: L. Erlbaum.

Miller, H. A. (2006a). A dynamic assessment of offender risk, needs, and strengths in a sample of pre-release general offenders. *Behavioral Sciences and the Law, 24,* 767–782.

Miller, H. A. (2006b). *Inventory of Offender Risk, Needs, and Strengths (IORNS): Professional Manual.* Odessa, FL: Psychological Assessment Resources.

Miller, H. A. (2015). Protective strengths, risk, and recidivism in a sample of known sexual offenders. *Sexual Abuse: A Journal of Research and Treatment, 27,* 34–50.

Miller, H. A., Davis, K., Torres, A., Palac, C. A., & Engman, G. (September 2006). Assessing risk, treatment need, and strengths in a sample of sexual offenders. Paper presented at the Association for the Treatment of Sexual Abusers (ATSA) Annual Conference, Chicago, IL.

Miller, F. G., Roberts, J., Brooks, M. K., & Lazowski, L. E. (1997). *SASSI-3 user's guide.* Bloomington, IN: Baugh Enterprises.

Morey, L. C. (1991). *The Personality Assessment Inventory professional manual.* Odessa, FL: Psychological Assessment Resources.

Motiuk, M., Motiuk, L., & Bonta, J. (1992). A comparison between self-report and interview-based inventories in offender classification. *Criminal Justice and Behavior, 19,* 143–159.

Nunnally, J. D., & Bernstein, I. H. (1994). *Psychometric theory* (3rd ed.). New York, NY: McGraw-Hill.

Olver, M. E., & Wong, S. C. P. (2009). Therapeutic responses of psychopathic sexual offenders: Treatment attrition, therapeutic change, and long term recidivism. *Journal of Consulting and Clinical Psychology, 77,* 328–336.

Olver, M. E., Wong, S. C. P., Nicholaichuk, T., & Gordon, A. (2007). The validity and reliability of the Violence Risk Scale—Sexual Offender Version: Assessment sex offender risk and evaluating therapeutic change. *Psychological Assessment, 19,* 318–329.

Raynor, P. (2007). Risk and need assessment in British probation: The contribution of LSI-R. *Psychology, Crime, & Law, 13,* 125–138.

Revelle, W., & Zinbarg, R. E. (2009). Coefficients alpha, beta, omega, and the glb: Comments on Sijtsma. *Psychometrika, 74,* 107–120.

Rogers, R. (2000). The uncritical acceptance of risk assessment in forensic practice. *Law and Human Behavior, 24,* 595–605.

Schlager, M. D., & Pacheco, D. (2011). An examination of changes in LSI-R scores over time: Making the case for needs-based case management. *Criminal Justice and Behavior, 38,* 541–553.

Serin, R. C., Chadwick, N., & Lloyd, C. D. (2016). Dynamic risk and protective factors. *Psychology, Crime & Law, 22,* 151–170.

Shedrick, C. (1999). Practitioner review: The assessment and management of risk in adolescents. *Journal of Child Psychology and Psychiatry, 40,* 507–518.

Sijtsma, K. (2009). On the use, the misuse, and the very limited usefulness of Cronbach's alpha. *Psychometrika, 74,* 107–120.

Spielberger, C. D. (1983). *Manual for the State-Trait Anxiety Inventory.* Redwood City, CA: MindGarden.

Stouthamer-Loeber, M., Wei, E., Loeber, R., & Masten, A. S. (2004). Desistance from persistent serious delinquency in the transition to adulthood. *Development and Psychopathology, 16,* 897–918.

Thornton, D., Beech, A., & Marshall, W. L. (2004). Pretreatment self-esteem and posttreatment sexual recidivism. *International Journal of Offender Therapy and Comparative Criminology, 48,* 587–599.

Vose, B., Smith, P., & Cullen, F. (2013). Predictive validity and the impact of change in total LSI-R score on recidivism. *Criminal Justice and Behavior, 40,* 1383–1396.

6

The Level of Service (LS) Instruments

J. Stephen Wormith and James Bonta

The Level of Service (LS) refers to a collection of offender risk/need assessment instruments that have evolved from its initial version more than 25 years ago. All versions share a number of essential common features. However, theory, research, and practice have helped to shape subsequent iterations with various modifications and innovations. In addition, some adaptations have been made to accommodate the legal and social/cultural contexts of the international community. For example, the legal age of a youth in conflict with the law will vary from country to country as will levels of educational attainment. As we will point out later, these modifications have not significantly diminished the predictive validity of the instruments.

The LS instruments are fundamentally a quantitative tool, consisting of both static risk and dynamic (criminogenic) need items, all of which are scored in a dichotomous, 0-1 format. Items were selected for a combination of theoretical and empirical reasons (discussed below) that apply across demographic characteristics, such as age, gender, race, and ethnicity. However, there are overlapping youth (ages 12 to 18) and adult (ages 16 years and older) versions that accommodate developmental differences between adolescent and adult offenders. This chapter focuses exclusively on adult versions, noting only that the most popular and current youth version is the Youth Level of Service/Case Management Inventory (YLS/CMI; Hoge & Andrews, 2002). The LS instruments adhere to an interview-based data collection protocol, although assessors are encouraged to use multiple sources of information, such as collateral contacts (e.g., family, previous case managers) and file documents (e.g., criminal records, presentence reports, and clinical assessments) to score their items.

Applications of the LS are many and varied. The LS instruments were originally designed for sentenced offenders in prison and in the community on probation or parole, although increasingly they are being used in pre-sentence circumstances to inform the court about the suitability of community supervision and the accused's treatment needs. They may be used to determine the level of institutional security, judicial sentencing conditions of probation, the amount of supervision in the community, whether to release an offender on parole and if so to where (halfway house or community) and under what conditions, and appropriate referral to treatment or programming for criminogenic needs. Although they were never designed, nor should they be used, to assist in the conviction process, the LS instruments may be used to assist in making bail or other pre-conviction decisions. The instruments must be administered by a trained assessor. With a combination of both static and dynamic items, they are designed to predict recidivism and other antisocial behavior, such as institutional misconduct or breach of supervision, over both the short (less than six months) and long (more than two years) term.

Handbook of Recidivism Risk/Needs Assessment Tools, First Edition. Edited by Jay P. Singh, Daryl G. Kroner, J. Stephen Wormith, Sarah L. Desmarais, and Zachary Hamilton.
© 2018 John Wiley & Sons, Ltd. Published 2018 by John Wiley & Sons, Ltd.

The Origins and Evolution of the Level of Service (LS) Instruments

In the late 1970s, the late Don Andrews (Wormith, 2011, 2017) was working with staff in the Ottawa (Canada) probation offices in an effort to structure decisions around offender risk. Regular meetings were held between probation officers led by the area chief probation officer Jerry Kiessling. Also in attendance at many of these meetings was James Bonta. The early meetings were brainstorming sessions where probation officers offered what they thought were the important characteristics of their clients and their situations that were relevant to successful community supervision. The very first product was a 30-page document that described over a hundred factors that may be relevant to assessing offender risk (for example, being male was a scored risk factor). Recognizing that this lengthy assessment process would be unwieldy for probation officers to use on a regular basis, subsequent meetings focused on reducing the number of items to make a more relevant and user-friendly assessment instrument.

The result was the 59-item, fourth version of the Level of Supervision Inventory (LSI-IV). It is noteworthy that the word "supervision" in the title of the instrument was replaced with "service" in 1995 to better reflect the treatment aspect of the instrument. The vast majority of the items were the same as in the LSI-R with one notable exception—there were two risk items relating to age (under 18 years of age and under 20). Bonta and Motiuk (1982) reported on the predictive validity of the LSI with respect to post-program recidivism. They administered the LSI-IV to 112 inmates placed in correctional halfway houses who were then followed up for one year after their release from prison. Drawing upon the province's correctional database they found LSI-IV total scores to predict reincarceration ($r = .41$).

Andrews continued developing the LSI-IV leading to LSI-V and eventually to LSI-VI, the precursor to the LSI-R. During these transitions, a few criminal history items were added (e.g., three or more present offences) and other items were dropped (e.g., marital status) for a total of 58 items. More importantly, age and gender were not part of LSI-VI as they were viewed as ageist and sexist. Further, analyses showed that removing these items did not affect the assignment of supervision levels. In his first report, Andrews (1982) reported on program outcomes for 561 probationers who were assessed with the LSI-VI and found total scores to predict early terminations of probation supervisions and new convictions while on probation ($r = .46$). In a second report (Andrews & Robinson, 1984) the probationers from the 1982 study were followed for an average of 2.2 years after their probation term ended and data from a new sample of 97 probationers were presented. For the extended follow-up sample, LSI-VI total scores continued to predict reconvictions as it did for the validation sample.

Soon after publication of the LSI second report by Andrews and Robinson (1984) the community branch of the correctional services in Ontario implemented the LSI across the province. The institutional branch was much slower in adopting the LSI despite the growing evidence supporting its use with inmates (e.g., Bonta & Motiuk, 1987, 1990, 1992). Eventually the LSI became the classification instrument for institutions (1996).

In 1993, Andrews and Bonta began work on developing the LSI-R. The LSI-VI was reduced to 54 items in the LSI-R by deleting the subcomponent on probation and parole conditions (four items) which did not add to the predictive validity of the instrument. This left 10 subcomponents with the Criminal History and Education/Employment subcomponents having the most items and Leisure/Recreation having the least (two items). The Level of Service Inventory–Revised (LSI-R) was published in 1995 by Andrews and Bonta along with a scoring guide that included detailed instructions for interviewing and scoring and that summarized the research evidence on the LSI-R to that date.

As adoptions of the LSI-R grew, it became apparent that some high-volume jurisdictions needed a screening instrument to triage their cases. Consequently, the eight-item LSI-R

Screening version (LSI-R: SV) was published (Andrews & Bonta, 1998). Two principles guided the creation of the LSI-R: SV. The first was that the items selected from the LSI-R must demonstrate the ability to predict recidivism. The second was that the majority of the items must be dynamic to remind the user that the instrument is designed to inform treatment decisions. Guidelines were also provided as to when to consider administering the full LSI-R (scores three to five) and when it is mandatory (scores six to eight).

The development of the Level of Service/Case Management Inventory (LS/CMI; Andrews, Bonta, & Wormith, 2004) grew out of research conducted in the Canadian provinces of Ontario and Manitoba. In 1994, the correctional services in Ontario undertook a major review of the LSI. Front-line users from both community and institutional corrections along with senior managers were consulted. The review led to a major revision to the LSI called the Level of Service Inventory—Ontario Revision (LSI-OR; Andrews, Bonta, & Wormith, 1995). There were three major changes made. First, the subcomponents measuring general risk/need factors were re-arranged to bring them into alignment with the Central Eight risk/need factors (discussed in the next section). This meant creating a new subcomponent called Antisocial Pattern and moving Financial Problems, Accommodations, and Emotional/Personal into an entirely new section, Other Client Issues, and/or subsuming them under Antisocial Pattern.

The second major change was the creation of new sections that assessed specific risk/need factors (e.g., sexual and violent risk factors), prison experience, and responsivity factors. Although the new sections yielded scores, without supportive evidence as to their predictive validity, scores on these sections were not used to make classification decisions. The third change was the addition of an assessment of strengths or protective factors. This was a feature that users and managers asked for specifically during the consultation process. Thus, for each of the eight risk/need components, staff had an opportunity to provide a structured assessment of possible strength. The LSI-OR's section structure is identical to Sections 1 through 8 of the LS/CMI with minor changes at the item level. What was missing in the LSI-OR was case management planning sections that were subsequently added in the release of the LS/CMI.

Bonta and his colleagues (Bonta, Rugge, Scott, Bourgon, & Yessine, 2008; Bonta, Rugge, Sedo, & Coles, 2004) reported on research that closely examined the supervision practices of Manitoba probation officers with their clients. One of the surprising findings was that after completing a risk/need assessment the probation officers made little use of the information in case planning and supervising their clients. The assessment was duly filed and forgotten. Therefore, in developing the LS/CMI, particular attention was given to including case management planning and monitoring (Sections 9 and 10) into the *same* assessment form. This addition was designed to make it difficult for correctional staff to ignore the link between assessment and intervention. The LS/CMI was published in 2004 and by integrating case management with assessment, it became a fourth generation instrument (Andrews, Bonta, & Wormith, 2010). Given that some correctional agencies already had a case management system in place and did not need a full LS/CMI, the LS/RNR, which does not include the case management portion (Sections 9 and 10 of the LS/CMI), was published four years later (Andrews, Bonta, & Wormith, 2008).

The Theoretical Underpinnings of the LS

The LS instruments are based on a General Personality and Cognitive Social Learning theory (GPCSL; Bonta & Andrews, 2017). The GPCSL perspective views criminal behavior as having multiple causes with eight major domains of influence referred to as the Central Eight risk/ need factors (see Table 6.1). There are also individual differences among the Central Eight.

Some offenders, for example, will have a lengthy criminal history and difficulties in the areas of education/employment, substance abuse, and procriminal associates and others only in the domains of family/marital and procriminal attitudes. These differences may also be apparent within the individual over time. For example, a person may only engage in crime when intoxicated and in the presence of procriminal others. In GPCSL, analysis of the individual is paramount and there is no simple explanation for criminal behavior (i.e., crime is not simply a lack of poor self-control, being impoverished, socially marginalized, etc.).

There are a few things to note in Table 6.1. First, the Central Eight risk/need factors are ordered to mirror the subcomponents of Section 1 of the LS/CMI and LS/RNR. That is, the two risk/need assessment instruments are congruent with GPCSL. When the LSI-R was developed, GPCSL theory had not matured fully to articulate the Central Eight. The Emotional/Personal subcomponent of the LSI-R was overly concerned with general feelings of emotional distress and psychotic illness and less so with antisocial personality features as measured under Antisocial Pattern. The second observation of the Central Eight is that all the risk/need factors except for Criminal History are dynamic, criminogenic needs. They are aspects of the offender and his/her situation that are amenable to change through planned treatment interventions. Finally, inherent in the Central Eight and the general rehabilitative stance of GPCSL is the value assigned to strengths in theory and in the LS/CMI and LS/RNR. By building on strengths, the offender's risk to reoffend is diminished.

Criminal history plays a large role in theory and assessment. A lengthy criminal history, in the language of behavioral psychology, reflects a history of many rewards and few punishments for procriminal behavior, and also few rewards and many punishments for prosocial behavior (the "social learning" in GPCSL). When criminal behavior is highly varied (e.g., crimes are both violent and non-violent, occurs in the community and in prisons) it indicates that the reward/punishment contingencies for criminal conduct are stable across settings. In the LS instruments

Table 6.1 The Central Eight Risk/Need Factors and the Assessment of Strengths in a General Personality and Cognitive Social Learning Theory

---

Criminal History. The number and variety of criminal activities.
Strength: Criminal behavior is rare or absent.

Education/Employment. Low levels of performance and satisfactions.
Strength: Strong attachments to students/co-workers/teachers/bosses and high levels of performance and satisfaction.

Family/Marital. Poor quality marital and family relationships and the direction of influence are procriminal.
Strength: Positive relationships with prosocial family members; for youth positive parental monitoring and supervision.

Leisure/Recreation. Low levels of involvement and satisfactions in prosocial leisure activities.
Strength: High levels of involvement and satisfactions in prosocial leisure activities.

Companions. Includes both association with procriminal others and relative isolation from prosocial others.
Strength: Close and frequent association with prosocial others; no association with criminal others.

Alcohol/Drug Problem. Problems with alcohol and/or other drugs.
Strengths: No evidence of substance abuse, has negative attitudes toward substance abuse.

Procriminal Attitude/Orientation. Attitudes, values, and thoughts favorable to crime.
Strength: Rejects procriminal attitudes; endorses prosocial attitudes.

Antisocial Pattern. Impulsive, risky sensation-seeking, hostile, emotionally callous.
Strength: Good problem-solving and self-control.

Adapted from Bonta and Andrews (2017)

(except for the LSI-R: SV), there are 10 items in the Criminal History subcomponent reflecting the significant weight given to measuring criminal behavior over time and settings.

GPCSL is a *general* theory of criminal conduct and posits that the Central Eight is applicable across gender, age, and race. This is a contentious issue as some scholars question why risk factors specific to social class, racial minorities, and women do not play a more prominent role in the LS instruments. From a GPCSL perspective poverty, race, gender, and age are potential responsivity factors and they are acknowledged in the Responsivity Considerations section of the LS/CMI and LS/RNR. Age is addressed by the development of the YLS/CMI (Hoge & Andrews, 2002). With respect to specific risk factors for racial minorities and women, the extant research evidence demonstrates that the Central Eight remain relevant (the research is discussed in the validity section).

GPCSL theory states that behavior, criminal or not, is learned and maintained in adherence to the principles of social learning theory. Behavior that is reinforced will be repeated, behavior that is punished will be suppressed, and we learn from observing others. These are overly simplistic statements but they get at the gist of social learning theory. A more comprehensive description of the principles of learning can be found elsewhere (Bonta & Andrews, 2017).

The learning and maintenance of behavior is a function of the rewards and punishments associated with criminal and prosocial behavior. Moreover, the sources of the rewards and costs can be found in the social domains of education/employment, family/marital, leisure/recreation, companions, and in the social context of alcohol/drug use. For these reasons, GPCSL encourages assessing multiple domains and not just a few. Even at the item level, one can see the influence of the GPCSL perspective. Take, for example, the items in the Companions subcomponent of the LSI-R, LS/CMI, and LS/RNR. We have "some criminal acquaintances" indicating an opportunity to observe criminal behavior and be rewarded for crime and "some criminal *friends*" (italics added) where the influence of rewards for crime are greater. Then we add the items assessing the absence of prosocial companions who can model and reward prosocial behavior and punish criminal behavior. Taken together one can see the role of observational learning and rewards and punishment in the learning and maintenance of behavior. Similar analyses can be made with the other subcomponents (e.g., education/employment) and their items (e.g., being unemployed isolates one from prosocial others and activities). No other offender risk/need assessment instrument has such a theoretical foundation.

Administration

Scoring the LS instruments

Each version of the LS includes its own scoring manual with detailed instructions for each item. Rather than allow for prorating of missing items, assessors are encouraged to score each item. If an item cannot be scored for lack of information, administrators are directed to leave the item blank. This is tantamount to giving the client the benefit of the doubt and not scoring the item as being present. In other words, to score a "1," evidence must exist to indicate that the item is present. Most versions of the LS allow for up to four missing/unscored items. However, experience has demonstrated that this rarely occurs.

In addition to the dichotomous scoring of all LS items (absent = 0, present = 1), special attention was given to the dynamic items in LSI-VI and continued in subsequent versions. In order to reflect more nuanced differences between offenders (and changes over time), a number of dynamic items (e.g., 13 of 43 items in LS/CMI) are first scored on a four-point scale that is measured in the *positive* direction (very unsatisfactory with a clear need for improvement = 0 to satisfactory with no need for improvement = 3). Ratings are then collapsed into problematic (1) and not problematic (0) for tallying the total risk/need score. This was done for a couple of reasons. First, it was designed to facilitate accurate scoring along what essentially were continuous variables, some of which could change over a short period of time (e.g., participation/performance at school or work) and consequently subject to criticism for their potential lack of reliability. As a general rebuttal to naysaying academics, practitioners, and administrators who complain about including dynamic items in offender risk assessment, we have routinely referred to Gendreau, Little, and Goggin's (1996) meta-analysis, in which dynamic items had at least as high a predictive validity (mean $r = .15$) as static items (mean $r = .12$), across 482 and 536 correlations, respectively.

Second, the four-point scale was designed to reflect positive or negative change over time that may not be sufficient to change the overall rating of an offender on a specific item (from risk to no risk, or vice versa). For example, an offender's performance at work can be dismal. He or she is often late for work, works very slowly, takes long breaks, and is on the verge of being fired. An active intervention by the probation officer (PO) convinces the client to make a more concerted effort and the client's on-the-job behavior and productivity improve, but still lag behind the quality of his or her coworkers. Noting this change in performance, the PO changes the rating from a 0 to a 1, acknowledging and rewarding the offender for a move in the right direction. But the client is not "out of the woods" yet and so the item is still scored as a risk. At the other end of the scale, an offender's performance at work has been exemplary. The quality of his or her work has been excellent, he or she has always been on time, and volunteered for overtime whenever it was offered. However, the PO has noticed that the offender's enthusiasm for his employment has waned recently, he seldom accepts an opportunity to work overtime, and he has become less punctual. Consequently, the PO has changed his rating from a 3 to a 2. In other words, the offender's score is "relatively satisfactory" and is not scored as a risk. However, the PO is sending a message that some decrement in the client's work performance has been noticed. In this manner, these 0 to 3 ratings convey relevant case management information to staff and the offender.

Training

Earlier, we described the Manitoba probation study that found probation officers did not use the results of their risk/need assessment to inform case management to the best of their ability. This highlighted the need to introduce a more formal and structured approach to case management leading to the development of the LS/CMI. However, the findings also revealed a need to pay close attention to the integrity of risk/need assessments. In general, two steps must be taken to ensure that the LS instruments are implemented as intended. First, users need to be carefully trained, and second, continuous monitoring must occur to ensure fidelity.

Often lip service is paid to providing good training, but is not always practiced. The training curriculum needs to be meaningful and understandable to the participants, there must be sufficient supervised practice with the instrument, and the trainer must be credible. Comprehensibility and practice are basic pedagogical tenets. The personal skills and knowledge of the trainer are also very important. The trainer must be able to convey his/her knowledge effectively to the audience and to establish rapport with trainees in order to motivate them to listen and try new skills. The authors and publisher of the LS instruments have developed criteria of competence not only for the front-end user but also for trainers. Table 6.2 provides an overview of the steps required for a candidate to become a master trainer in the LS/CMI.

LS/CMI master trainers are the highest level of trainers who are certified to train not only within their organization (like LS/CMI trainers) but also outside their agency both nationally and internationally. Thus, they meet all trainer requirements (e.g., successfully pass a LS knowledge test). Furthermore, master trainers must meet additional standards of competency that require, for example, a theory test and a review of a video of them delivering elements of

Table 6.2 LS/CMI Master Trainer Requirements

Required Qualifications:	a) Post graduate university degree b) Background/experience in forensic psychology, correctional settings, or training and development c) Met all trainer requirements d) MHS/author approved
Preferred Qualifications:	Experience delivering workshops
Training:	3–5 days of trainer training
Previous Experience:	Minimum of 20 LS/CMI administrations
Content Test:	Minimum passing grade of 85%
Rating Test:	Minimum passing grade of 85%
Theory Test:	The minimum passing grade is 85%.
Video Submission:	Submit a video conducting 2 modules of a User training session (one didactic and one interactive component).
Audit:	Authors, MHS, or Authorized Certifier have the right to audit Train-the-Trainer programs for quality assurance purposes.

an actual training seminar. Finally, a standardized curriculum developed by MHS in collaboration with the authors is provided for all trainers to follow. The standards are high but they are necessary to ensure the best training possible for new users.

Studies of the LS have found that the predictive validities (r) vary from the low teens to the high forties. This variability points to the importance of high-quality training, careful implementation, and ongoing monitoring. As described, considerable effort is made to address the issue of training. Since training is provided by highly qualified individuals, relatively little of the source of variation in predictive validities can be attributed to the quality of training (although staff resistance to something new may play an independent role). A more important potential source of variation occurs *after* training where the responsibility for implementation and quality control rests with the agency rather than the authors or publishers of the LS.

Bonta and Andrews (2017) describe what they label as "organizational inattention to the integrity of assessment" (p. 245). It is important to monitor staff scoring the LS and making use of it in the way the instrument was intended (i.e., case planning and treatment services). Not surprisingly, one of the big culprits is the failure to provide sufficient resources to the training (e.g., "can the training be done in one day?") and implementation (e.g., assigning staff to monitor the proper use of the instrument). Even after careful training, steps must be taken to ensure that levels of competency are maintained. For example, the state of Colorado invested resources to monitor staff scoring of the LSI-R post-training. In a review of a sample of 133 LSI-R records across the state, they found that 13% had errors (Bonta, Bogue, Crowley, & Motiuk, 2001). Most of the errors were addition mistakes, but others were more serious, with misunderstandings of the interpretation and scoring of items. The state addressed this problem by providing refresher training sessions.

Another important factor that should be considered is the monitoring of the professional override in the LS instruments (discussed in more detail later). Typically, the research shows that overrides lower the predictive accuracy of LS assessments (Guay & Parent, 2017; Wormith, Hogg, & Guzzo, 2012). The User Manuals for the LS instruments suggest caution when using an override and to do so only with justification. Therefore, both training and monitoring the use of the LS should be sensitive to overrides. Excessive use of overrides (over 5% of cases) should be quickly addressed and corrected otherwise the value of the assessment is compromised. Finally, monitoring should ensure that the instrument is used in adherence to the function of the LS assessment. For example, low-risk offenders should be diverted to the least restrictive alternative and treatment services matched to clients' assessed criminogenic needs. In sum, the quality of training and ongoing monitoring of its use is essential to the fidelity of the LS assessment.

Reliability

Assessments completed using the LS instruments have been submitted to various kinds of reliability analysis. The most commonly assessed type of reliability has been internal consistency. Item-total reliability, inter-subsection reliability, and subsection-total reliability are versions of internal consistency. Summaries of these statistics, along with standard errors of measurement, are reported in detail in the LS manuals (Andrews & Bonta, 1995; Andrews et al., 2004). The most widely used measure of internal consistency is Cronbach's (1951) alpha, which is a measure of the average inter-item relationship. Table 6.3 summarizes alpha coefficients on the LSI-R total score and the 10 domain scores from 14 independent data sets. Table 6.4 summarizes alpha coefficients on the LS/CMI and its eight domains from 12 independent data sets.

Table 6.3 Internal Consistency as Measured by Cronbach's Alpha for the Total Score and Subsection Scores of LSI-R

Study	Total	CH	E/E	Fin	F/M	Acc	L/R	Co	A/DP	E/P	A/O
1	.82	.75	.74	.75	.74	.74	.74	.73	.75	.74	.76
2	.64	.62	.74	.07	.29	.06	.35	.45	.68	.38	.47
3	.71	.64	.67	.69	.67	.70	.67	.68	.71	.69	.71
4	.77	.68	.68	.71	.71	.71	.72	.70	.72	.73	.72
5	.79	.84	.81	.46	.52	.78	.67	.62	.86	.70	.66
6	.90	.83	.74	.36	.49	.54	.65	.69	.84	.69	.57
7	.90	.82	.56	.55	.28	.38	.59	.78	.80	.70	.45
8	.94	.81	.81	.53	.59	.61	.70	.59	.84	.69	.70
9	.84	.64	.82	.31	.55	.34	.69	.79	.67	.71	.98
10	.86	.74	.75	.43	.52	.44	.66	.70	.70	.70	.80
11	.88	.72	.80	.23	.49	.53	.60	.81	.81	.72	.68
12	.93	.84	.78	.39	.56	.63	.73	.46	.85	.58	.72
13	.89	.82	.79	.02	.24	.36	n.a.	.75	.82	.45	.60
14	.92	.88	.75	.17	.36	.66	-.07	.52	.91	.73	.20
Average	.84	.76	.75	.41	.50	.53	.59	.66	.78	.66	.64

Total = Total LSI-R; CH = Criminal History; E/E = Education/Employment; Fin = Financial; F/M = Family/Marital; Acc = Accommodation; L/R = Leisure/ Recreation; Co = Companions; A/DP = Alcohol/ Drug Problem; E/P = Emotional/Personal; A/O = Attitudes/Orientation; n.a. = not available.
1 = Bonta, Motiuk, & Ker (1985); 2 = Andrews et al. (1984); 3 = Bonta & Motiuk (1985); 4 = Bonta & Motiuk (1986a); 5 = Wadel et al., (1991); 6 = Faulkner, Andrews, Wadel, & Hawkins (1992); 7 = Stevenson & Wormith (1987); 8 = Hollin, Palmer & Clark (2003); 9 = Flores, Lowenkamp, & Latessa (undated); 10 = Lowenkamp & Latessa (undated); 11 = Holsinger, Lowenkamp, & Latessa (undated); 12 = Palmer & Hollin (2007); 13 = Rettinger (1998); 14 = Folsom & Atkinson (2007).
Extended from Andrews, Bonta, & Wormith (2010)

Table 6.4 Internal Consistency as Measured by Cronbach's Alpha for the Total Score and Subsection Scores of LS/CMI

Study	Total	CH	E/E	F/M	L/R	Co	A/DP	PA/O	ASP
1	.89	.76	.87	.48	.71	.84	.46	.80	.67
2	.88	.74	.82	.39	.50	.51	.47	.78	.65
3	n.a.	.81	.82	.24	n.a.	.83	.81	.60	.60
4	.91	.80	.79	.32	.56	.67	.78	.47	.50
5	.87	.64	.78	.45	.46	.70	.78	.35	.48
6	.92	.86	.84	.39	.49	.63	.82	.62	.54
7	.90	.70	.75	.57	.67	.72	.84	.82	.51
8	.88	.78	.73	.69	.86	.77	.76	.76	.76
9	.86	.65	.76	.35	.45	.61	.87	.45	.43
10	n.a.	.73	.85	.52	.71	.62	.83	.67	.52
11	.92	.87	.84	.39	.43	.63	.84	.60	.51
12[*]	.92	.83	.85	.58	.36	.60	.77	.73	.55
Average	.90	.76	.81	.45	.56	.68	.75	.64	.56

[*]Coefficients are expressed as Kuder-Richardson 20 (KR-20).
Total = Total LS/CMI; CH = Criminal History; E/E = Education/Employment; F/M = Family/Marital; L/R = Leisure/ Recreation; Co = Companions; A/DP = Alcohol/Drug Problem; PA/O = Procriminal Attitudes/Orientation; ASP = Antisocial Pattern; n.a. = not available.
1 = Andrews (inmates; 1995); 2 = Andrews (probationers; 1995); 3 = Rettinger (1998); 4 = Girard (1999); 5 = Rowe (1999); 6 = Andrews, Bonta, & Wormith (Ontario; 2004); 7 = Andrews, Bonta, & Wormith (US; 2004); 8 = Nowicka-Sroga (2004); 9 = Simourd (2004); 10 = Mills, Jones, & Kroner (2005); 11 = Hogg, (2011) and Wormith & Hogg (2011); 12 = Guay (2016).
Extended from Andrews, Bonta, & Wormith (2010)

Alpha coefficients from the 54-item LSI-R produced a mean alpha on the total score of .84, while the 43-item LS/CMI produced a mean alpha on the total score of .90. Alphas on domain scores were routinely lower on both versions, although some domains had consistently higher alphas on both versions of the LS than other domains. For example, criminal history generated an average alpha of .76 on the LSI-R and the LS/CMI, education/employment generated a mean alpha of .75 on the LSI-R and .81 on the LS/CMI, and alcohol/drug problem generates a mean alpha of .78 on the LSI-R and .75 on the LS/CMI. On the other hand, average alphas on the LSI-R and LS/CMI, respectively, were .50 and .45 for family/marital, .59 and .56 for leisure/ recreation, .66 and .68 for companions, and 64 and .64 for criminal attitudes. These domains were typically shorter (for example, leisure/recreation has only two items) than the previous domains (e.g., criminal history has 10 items). Domains that were excluded in the LS/CMI also tended to have lower alphas in the LSI-R (finance .41, accommodation, .43, and emotional/ personal .66). Before proceeding, a word of caution is suggested about measures of internal consistency, particularly the interpretation of alpha, in risk assessment scales.

To begin, Sijtsma (2009) has noted that alpha is, at best, a measure of internal consistency, and not even a good one at that. This is the case, in part, because alpha is affected by the number of items and is not a measure of scale reliability per se, as the term is traditionally known. In particular, it does not contain any information about the internal structure of the scale and, being based on a single administration of the instrument, it does not convey any information about the accuracy of the single administration of the instrument (Sijtsma, 2009). Moreover, its limited value applies particularly to measures of offender risk. In fact, high alphas may be counterproductive to the development of a good offender risk assessment scale (Baird, 2009). Duwe and Rocque (2017) adhered to this viewpoint in their development and modification of risk assessment tools for Minnesota. They adopted the strategy that assembling a wide array of risk items that contribute to antisocial behavior, but were not strongly related to each other, would generate a more robust risk assessment scheme than using items that all tap into the same construct. Hence, we are not overly concerned about modest alphas for the LS domains.

Inter-rater reliability and test-retest reliability has also been assessed, although the later is confounded by the dynamic nature of LS assessments and its impact on test-retest reliability with increasing time intervals. In our view, inter-rater reliability, the capacity for two assessors to generate the same score when the assessment is conducted at the same time, is more critical. Regretfully, this kind of reliability check has not been conducted often in the field, largely because of the added cost to the correctional agency. However, in a research context, based on file reviews only, Stewart (2011) produced inter-class correlations (ICCs) of .977 for the LSI-R and .940 for the LS/CMI. However, rater agreement was both lower and varied across the various domains. Criminal history, education/employment, and substance abuse all had ICCs greater than .90 on both the LSI-R and the LS/CMI. Lower ICCs on the LSI-R and LS/CMI, respectively, were found on family/marital (ICC = .846 and .846), associates (ICC = .768 and .602), and leisure/recreation (ICC = .701 and .479). The lowest ICCs were found on criminal attitudes (ICC = .408 and .341). ICCs on domains unique to LSI-R were .746 for financial, .963 for accommodation, and .546 for personal emotional. The ICC for the antisocial pattern domain of the LS/CMI was .820.

Stewart's (2011) analysis of item reliability is also instructive. Items with ICCs below .30 included the following: suspended or expelled at least once (.13 from education/employment LSI-R and LS/CMI); ever fired (.35 from education/employment domain in LSI-R); three or more address changes in the last year (.28 from accommodation domain in LSI-R); reliance on social assistance (.36 from financial domain in LSI-R); mental health treatment – present (.20 from emotional/personal in LSI-R); psychological assessment indicated (.38 from emotional/personal domain in LSI-R); and poor attitude towards sentence/offense (.33 from criminal attitude domain in LS/CMI). It is noteworthy that five of the seven items in this analysis were excluded in the LS/CMI.

Finally, in an examination of what approximates parallel forms reliability of the LS, two studies examined scores on both the LSI-R and LS/CMI on their respective participants. Rowe (1996) found a correlation of .96 between the total scores of the LSI-R and the LS/CMI on 340 incarcerated male offenders, while Stewart (2011) found a correlation of .86 on 101 incarcerated female offenders.

Validity

As is the case with reliability, there are various types and means of assessing scale validity. Studies of concurrent validity examine similarities between scales that purport to measure the same construct or serve the same function, such as the prediction of offender recidivism. In fact, the selection of LSI-R items and domains was driven partly by their relationship with alternative measures of similar constructs, including self-report scales from the MMPI. These "multi-method" correlations of common constructs varied from .27 for the criminal attitude domain (Andrews, Kiessling, Mickus, & Robinson, 1986) to .67 for the emotional/personal domain (Bonta & Motiuk, 1985).

Elsewhere, Rowe (1999) examined the correlation between the LS/CMI total and domain scores with two popular earlier instruments, the Salient Factor Score (SFS; Hoffman, Stone-Meierhoefer, & Beck, 1978), which was used in federal jurisdictions throughout the USA, and the Statistical Information on Recidivism (SIR: Nuffield, 1982), which was used at the time throughout the Canadian federal corrections agency. The LS/CMI total score correlated .57 with the SIR scale and .44 with the SFS. Interestingly, the criminal history domain correlated more highly with these earlier instruments, .69 and .62, respectively, than the total LS/CMI score. Conversely, the other seven domains correlated with the SIR scale from .12 (leisure/recreation) to .49 (antisocial pattern), and with the SFS from .08 (leisure/recreation) to .34 (alcohol/drug problem).

These findings provide an interesting, instructive, and not surprising pattern. The SIR scale and the SFS are static, second generation instruments (Andrews, Bonta, & Wormith, 2006); hence their highest correlations were with the criminal history domain of the LS/CMI. Since the LS/CMI total score is the sum of scores on the static criminal history domain plus the seven other criminogenic need domains, most of which had low to moderate correlations with the SIR and SFS, it is both theoretically and mathematically reasonable to find that the correlation between the LS/CMI total score and the SIR and SFS scales was lower than when the LS/CMI criminal history domain was correlated with them. In fact, such an outcome is desirable if one takes the position that risk factors for offender recidivism are both multiple and diverse (Andrews et al., 2004). This is the same underlying reason that very high internal consistency, as measured by alpha, is not necessarily a desired psychometric property of offender risk instruments.

Factor analytic studies have also reflected the multidimensionality to the LS instruments. In the first factor analysis, Andrews, Bonta, Motiuk, & Robinson (1984) examined LSI-R assessments and found a two-factor solution for inmates and a three-factor solution for probationers. However, the first factor in both solutions had significant factor loadings from all of the LSI-R domains, leaving the authors to conclude that the LSI-R captures an underlying construct of "generalized trouble" and measures a "propensity to engage in crime." Although Palmer and Hollin (2007) reported a one-factor solution; two-factor (Bonta & Motiuk, 1986a; Hollin, Palmer & Clark, 2003; Loza & Simourd, 1994; Simourd & Malcolm, 1998) and three-factor solutions (Bonta & Motiuk, 1986b, Stevenson & Wormith, 1987) have been more common with the LSI-R. Taking a different approach, Guay's (2016) analysis of domain scores from a sample of 3,682 offenders from the Canadian province of Quebec, used a French translation of the LS/CMI and found a single factor. This finding suggested that, although different in content, the Central Eight domains have a common feature of criminality.

Predictive validity, however, remains one of the major criteria for evaluating offender risk assessment instruments. Over the last 35 years, assessments completed using the LS instruments have been submitted to three kinds of predictive validity studies that include the following: (1) single studies that assessed the predictive validity of a given LS instrument on a single, defined sample of offenders or multiple offender groups; (2) studies that compare the predictive validity of a given LS instrument to other risk assessment instruments that were administered to a common sample of offenders; and (3) meta-analyses that examine multiple predictive validity studies of a given LS instrument by itself, of the LS instrument in comparison to other instruments that are applied to the same samples of offenders, and of the LS instrument in comparison to other instruments that are applied to different samples of offenders. Our concentration is on the meta-analyses as they provide a convenient and accurate means of summarizing what are now hundreds of predictive validity analyses.

At least six meta-analytic and multiple-sample studies have focused exclusively on adult versions of the LS instruments (Andrews et al., 2011; Andrews et al., 2012; Desmarais, Johnson, &

Singh, 2016; Olver, Stockdale, & Wormith, 2014; Smith, Cullen, & Latessa, 2009; Wilson & Gutierrez, 2014). These studies were conducted, in part, to assess the predictive validity of LS instruments across various demographic moderators. In addition, three meta-analyses have been conducted on youth versions of LS (Schwalbe, 2007; Schwalbe, 2008; Olver, Stockdale, & Wormith, 2009). At least five meta-analyses (Campbell, French, & Gendreau, 2009; Gendreau et al., 1996; Gendreau, Goggin, & Smith, 2002; Singh, Grann, & Fazel, 2011; Yang, Wong, & Coid, 2010) have compared the LS to other popular risk assessment instruments. However, with the exception of the Gendreau studies, only violent, as opposed to general recidivism was considered as an outcome. Moreover, most of the studies included in these meta-analyses did not apply multiple instruments to a common sample. Rather, comparisons were made pooling studies from many different offender populations, which makes comparisons between instruments problematic.

Between-study comparisons of predictive validity have included a variety of instruments. The PCL-R (Hare, 2003) has most commonly been compared to the LS instruments. Gendreau et al.'s (2002) meta-analysis favored the LS instruments both overall (general recidivism: $r = .37$, $k = 33$, vs. $r = .23$, $k = 30$; violent recidivism: $r = .26$, $k = 16$, vs. $r = .21$, $k = 26$) and when limited to the few within-studies comparisons that have been conducted (general recidivism: $r = .37$ vs. $r = .26$, $k = 6$; violent recidivism: $r = .24$, vs. $r = .22$, $k = 5$), thus setting off a spirited debate (Hempill & Hare, 2004). Gendreau et al. (1996) reported that the predictive validity of assessments completed using the LS instruments was similar to those completed using the Wisconsin Risk/Need instrument (Baird, Heinz, & Bemus, 1979; $r = .32$) and modestly superior to those completed using the SFS (.26) and MMPI-based scales (.21).

Other meta-analyses have focused on violence risk prediction. Campbell and her colleagues (2009) examined the predictive validity of LS and PCL-R assessments with mean correlations of $r = .25$ ($k = 19$) and $r = .24$ ($k = 24$), respectively, as well as with HCR-20 (Webster, Douglas, Eaves, & Hart, 1997; .25, $k = 11$), SIR (Nuffield, 1982; $r = .24$, $k = 17$), and VRAG (Harris, Rice, & Quinsey, 1993; $r = .27$, $k = 14$) assessments. Yang, Wong, and Coid (2010) also examined the predictive validity of assessments completed using nine instruments from 28 original studies. In addition to the Area under the curve (AUC) for LSI-R assessments of .65 ($k = 3$), they reported AUCs for PCL-R (.65, $k = 16$), OGRS (Copas & Marshall, 1998; .71, $k = 2$), RM2000V (Thornton, 2007; .70, $k = 3$), VRAG (.68; $k = 17$), HCR-20 (.71, $k = 16$), SIR (.68, $k = 3$), and VRS (Wong & Gordon, 2006; .65, $k = 4$) assessments, all of which translated into "medium" effect sizes (Cohen, 1988). Consequently, they concluded, "If prediction of violence is the only criterion for the selection of a risk assessment tool, then the tools included in the present study are essentially interchangeable" (p. 759).

Finally, Singh and his colleagues (2011) examined the predictive validity of assessments using nine instruments, including sexual offender scales, on violent or sexual recidivism from 68 studies in 88 independent samples. They reported that "an instrument used to identify adults at risk for general offending, the Level of Service Inventory—Revised (LSI-R), and a personality scale commonly used for the purposes of risk assessment, the Psychopathy Checklist—Revised (PCL-R), produced the lowest" (p. 499) predictive validities as measured by median AUCs (.67, $k = 3$, and .66, $k = 10$, respectively). They reported that other instruments received AUCs as follows: SVR-20 (Boer, Hart, Kropp, & Webster, 1997; .78, $k = 3$), SORAG (Quinsey, Harris, Rice, & Cormier, 1998; .75, $k = 6$), VRAG (.74, $k = 10$), SAVRY (Borum, Bartel, & Forth, 2002; .71; $k = 8$), HCR-20 (.70, $k = 80$, SARA (Kropp & Hart, 2000; .70, $k = 1$), and Static-99 (Hanson & Thornton, 1999; .70, $k = 12$) and concluded that "there are substantial differences between the predictive validity of these tools" (p. 509).

Recently, we have questioned the comparability of these findings (Williams, Wormith, Bonta, & Sitarenios, 2017). Specifically, we argue that Singh et al. (2011) conducted an "apples-to-oranges" comparison with studies differing in terms of the purpose of the respective instruments, the types of offenders to which they were applied, and the definition and means by which recidivism was operationally defined. Second, they dichotomized the prediction instruments in what might be described as an arbitrary manner with unknown, possibly different impacts of predictive validity across instruments. Third, they elected to use one, albeit popular, means of measuring predictive validity (i.e., AUCs), while our reanalysis, using their calculations of positive predictive power PPV), for illustrative purposes, placed the LSI-R fourth of the nine scales, although all had overlapping confidence intervals, supporting Yang et al.'s (2010) conclusion noted above. Finally, they ignore practical reasons for selecting a risk instrument in spite of the fact that their collection included very different kinds of instruments, namely, static, dynamic, and structured professional judgment (SPJ) approaches.

The most complete LS meta-analysis to date was conducted by Olver and his colleagues (2014), and generated effect sizes from 128 studies and 151 independent samples from a total of 137,931 offenders. Mean effect sizes were calculated for LS total and domain scores on both general and violent recidivism. Gender, ethnicity, geographic region, and LS version were assessed as moderators of effect size. The overall weighted mean correlations between the LS total score and general recidivism was .29 (random effects, 95% confidence interval = .27 to .31; k = 124) and violent recidivism was .23 (random effects, 95% confidence interval = .19 to .27; k = 39). The predictive validity of domain scores for general and violent recidivism are presented in Table 6.5. The number of effect sizes was considerably fewer for violent recidivism (k = 5 to 19) than for general recidivism (k = 10 to 55). The number of effect sizes by domain

Table 6.5 Predictive Validity Estimates of LS Total Score and Domains on General, Violent and Sexual Recidivism

LS Scale	General Recidivism r (95% CI) k	Violent Recidivism r (96% CI) k
Total score	.29 (.27–.31) 124	.23 (.19–.27) 39
Criminal History	.28 (.25–.32) 55	.21 (.16–.27) 18
Education/Employment	.24 (.21–.27) 55	.20 (.15–.24) 19
Family/Marital	.14 (.12–.16) 54	.11 (.09–.14) 19
Financial[a]	.12 (.09–.15) 29	.09 (.01–.18) 5
Accommodation[a]	.14 (.11–.16) 30	.15 (.04–.25) 5
Companions	.22 (.19–.25) 58	.17 (.11–.22) 19
Leisure/Recreation	.16 (.13–.19) 53	.12 (.08–.16) 19
Alcohol/Drug Problem	.20 (.16–.23) 54	.13 (.09–.18) 19
Personal/Emotional[a]	.14 (.10–.18) 45	.17 (.09–.25) 12
Antisocial Pattern[b]	.31 (.26–.35) 10	.23 (.22–.24) 7
Procriminal Attitude	.19 (.16–.22) 55	.18 (.14–.21) 19

All weighted random effect sizes (r) are significant (i.e., 95% CI does not include 0). Dashes denote insufficient k (<2) to compute effect sizes. Prediction of sexual recidivism is among sexual offenders only while the prediction of general and violent recidivism is across all offender groups.
a) LSI and LSI-R only.
b) LS/CMI only.
CI = confidence interval.
Adapted from Olver, Stockdale, & Wormith (2014) Tables 3 and 4.

varied as some domains were in all versions of the LS (e.g., education/employment), while others (e.g., antisocial pattern) were not. Although individual domains tended to predict general recidivism better than violent recidivism (e.g., antisocial pattern: .31 for general recidivism and .23 for violent recidivism), other domains predicted types of recidivism equally well (e.g., criminal attitudes: .19 for general recidivism and .18 for violent recidivism). These means included 30 coefficients on general recidivism and 13 on violent recidivism that were derived from youth versions of the LS.

The large number of studies also allowed Olver and his colleagues (2014) to examine differences in effect size across various moderators including jurisdiction/country, and version of the LS, as well as gender, race, and ethnicity, which are discussed in the subsequent Current Issues section. Weighted mean effect sizes for LS total scores on general and violent recidivism are presented in Table 6.6. The findings were generally comparable to previous meta-analyses that also examined these moderators (Andrews et al., 2011; Andrews et al., 2012). It should be noted that some coefficients are limited to studies that make comparisons on the same samples (within study), while others are based on all coefficients that apply to the specific moderator category. In our view, the former coefficients provide a more accurate statistic for comparison across moderator attributes as they are derived from the same set of offender populations.

A marked difference was found across jurisdictions or nations. Predictive validity of general recidivism was significantly higher in Canada than outside North America, which, in turn, was significantly higher than in the USA. A similar pattern, although not quite as extreme, was found for the prediction of violent recidivism.

Substantial differences in the prediction of general recidivism were found for different versions of the LS instruments, ranging from .42 for the LSI-OR and LS/CMI to .25 for the LSI-R. At first blush, these differences are surprising, given the similarity between versions of the LS instruments. However, further examination revealed that these comparisons were confounded by the moderator, jurisdiction/country, as more than 65% of the LSI-R studies were American, while less than 15% were Canadian, while the majority of LS-OR and LS/CMI studies were Canadian.

Although the jurisdiction/country variable probably accounts for most of the variation in predictive validity across versions of the LS instruments, there is no simple explanation for the substantial variation in predictive validity across jurisdictions/nations. Various possibilities have been considered. One is that the sheer size of the American offender population in its many jurisdictions across the country is so large that the quality of data collection suffers. However, the predictive validities found in US jurisdictions with even the most thorough training, implementation, and quality assurance that are equal or superior to any in Canada (e.g., Haas, Davidson, & Wormith, 2014) remain relatively low (Orsini, Haas, & Spence, 2015).

Such findings have led us to consider, not the quality or accuracy of the assessment, but the quality and accuracy of the outcome measure, recidivism. With its complex criminal justice system, consisting of federal institutions, 50 state systems, and countless counties, each with varying degrees of independence, one wonders about two possibilities. One pertains to the consistency with which criminal behaviors are punished across the country and the second concerns the capacity of researchers to measure recidivism accurately across multiple juridictions' data sets. It should also be noted that different effect sizes by jurisdiction are not limited to LS studies. The Yang et al. meta-analysis (2011) revealed that effect sizes in Canada were significantly greater that in the US across eight instruments, including the LS.

Since Olver et al.'s (2014) meta-analysis, subsequent predictive validity studies continue to emerge from around the world. These studies have examined the predictive validity among special offender groups, including driving while impaired offenders (Pilon, Jewell, &

Table 6.6 Predictive Validity Estimates of Level of Service Total Score for General and Violent Recidivism by Gender, Ethnicity, and Jurisdiction

Categories within Moderator Variables	General Recidivism r (95% CI) k	Violent Recidivism r (95% CI) k
Gender (all studies)		
Male	.30 (.27–.34) 80	.24 (.20–.27) 30
Female	.31 (.26–.35) 45	.26 (.20–.32) 12
Gender (within studies)		
Male	.29 (.24–.34) 31	.29 (.21–.35) 6
Female	.29 (.24–.35) 31	.25 (.22–.27) 6
Ethnicity (all studies)		
Ethnic minority	.27 (.22–.32) 36	.24 (.17–.31) 6
Non-minority	.29 (.23–.34) 24	.23 (.10–.35) 5
Ethnicity (within studies)		
Ethnic minority	.29 (.23–.34) 29	.24 (.17–.31) 6
Non-minority	.28 (.23–.34) 23	.21 (.06–.34) 4
Jurisdiction (all studies)		
Canada	.38 (.35–.41) 51	.26 (.23–.29) 28
United States	.20 (.18–.23) 52	.12 (.11–.13) 7
Outside North America	.30 (.28–.33) 19	.20 (.14–.26) 4
Version of LS (all studies)		
LSI	.32 (.27–.37) 20	.21 (.15–.28) 2
LSI-R	.25 (.22–.28) 55	.23 (.16–.28) 14
LSI-SV	.27 (.20–.33) 4	-
LSI-SR	.38 (.27–.48) 5	.28 (.15–.40) 2
LSI-OR, LS/CMI	.42 (.38–.47) 12	.27 (.22–.32) 11

Note: All weighted random effect sizes (*r*) are significant (i.e., 95% CI does not include 0). Dashes denote insufficient *k* (<2) to compute effect sizes. The *k*s for ethnic minority is higher than for non-minority in within-study comparisons because *k*s were provided for more than one ethnic minority in some studies and individual effect sizes were computed for each minority group. LSI-OR = Level of Service Inventory–Ontario Revision; LSI-SV = Level of Service Inventory–Screening Version; LSI-SR = Level of Service–Self-Report; LSI-R = Level of Service Inventory–Revised. CI = confidence interval.
Adapted from Olver, Stockdale, & Wormith (2014) Tables 5, 7, 8, 9, and 12.

Wormith, 2015) and child pornography offenders (Pilon, 2016), where, understandably, LS assessments do not perform as they do with more general measures of outcome, nor as well as specialty assessments that are designed for specific types of antisocial behavior. Although one area where LS assessments have performed very well is in the prediction of sexual offenders' general recidivism, quite well in their prediction of violent recidivism, and modestly well in the prediction of their sexual recidivism (Wormith et al., 2012). LS research has also continued with gender, racial, and ethnic minority groups as discussed later. Moreover, Guay (2016) found that assessments completed using a French translation of the LS/CMI had comparable reliability and validity as those completed using the original English version. Similarly, translations into a country's native language have demonstrated the reliability and predictive validity of the LSI-R in Guangzhou, China (Zhang & Liu, 2015) and Punjab, Pakistan (Bhutta & Wormith, 2016).

Current Issues, Concerns, and Future Directions

Questions about possible kinds of bias, particularly racial and gender bias, in the LS instruments have resulted in an ongoing debate amongst clinicians, administrators, and researchers for a couple of decades. These concerns have also spawned a considerable amount of research, including the previously reviewed meta-analyses. The fact that the origins of the LS came from White males raises a legitimate concern (Hannah-Moffat, 2009) and has led to gender-specific, or gender-responsive items and supplements (Van Voorhis, Wright, Salisbury, & Bauman, 2010). One of the features of structured risk assessment is to avoid, or at least minimize, the kinds of biases practiced, often unknowingly, by clinicians (Garb, 1997; Garb, Lilienfeld, & Fowler, 2016), so we take these questions seriously.

Concerning gender, in their early meta-analysis of studies from 1986 to 1999, Gendreau and his colleagues (2002) cited mean correlations of .45 (k = 10) for females and .33 (k = 18) for males. However, after reviewing 11 LSI-R studies, Holtfreter and Cupp (2007) concluded that LSI-R assessments perform moderately well for females who are economically motivated for crime and for the prediction of more serious reoffending, but application to women whose lives were affected by "gendered circumstances" (p. 377) is problematic.

Then, Smith et al. (2009) examined 16 studies on which within-study comparisons across gender were possible. They found an average (fixed-effects) correlation of .27 for women compared to an average correlation of .26 for men. Andrews and colleagues (2012) examined five of their own data sets on which they were also able to make within-study comparisons of LS/CMI assessments' predictive validity on male and female offenders (including young offenders) on recidivism. They found that the total LS score effect size was superior for female offenders (.53 vs. .39) and effect sizes were higher for women across all of the Central Eight domains. This was particularly the case for substance abuse, which accounted for almost all of the overall difference between males and females.

Finally, Olver et al.'s meta-analysis (2014) generated comparable effect sizes, .29 from females and .29 for males on general recidivism over 31 samples, but slightly higher for males (.29) than females (.25) for violent recidivism from six studies (Table 6.6). Therefore, our current position is that, although the LS assessment tools are applicable to and valid for both male and female offenders, there may be some differences in how the LS instruments work in terms of predicting violent recidivism and in how some domains, particularly substance abuse, might apply differentially according to gender.

Concerning race and ethnicity, most of the individual studies have focused on Indigenous offenders in Canada and Black and Hispanic offenders in the US. Again, the research is best summarized in Olver et al.'s (2014) meta-analysis (Table 6.6). They found mean effect sizes (random effects) of .30 for Aboriginal (k =13), .32 for Asian (k = 4), .30 for Black (k = 9), and .21 for Hispanics (k = 6) across a wide range of, often, independent studies for general recidivism. However, these findings were confounded by country as Aboriginal samples routinely came from Canada where the overall effect size was .38, while Black and Hispanic samples came from the US, where the overall effect size was .20. When within-studies comparisons were made, the mean effect size (random effect) on general recidivism was .28 for non-minorities ($k = 23$) and .29 for minorities ($k = 29$; some studies had multiple ethnic groups). Nonetheless, concerns continue to abound about the inequality of the LS instruments for minorities, not just in terms of predicting recidivism, but also possible differences in the LS domains (Schlager & Simourd, 2007) and in predicting institutional misconduct (Chenane, Brennan, Steiner, & Ellison, 2015). Other recent individual studies (Wormith, Hogg, & Guzzo, 2015) and meta-analyses (Gutierrez, Wilson, Rugge, & Bonta, 2013; Wilson & Gutierrez, 2014) continue to support the use of the LS instruments and their domains with Aboriginal offenders. However, some of the Central Eight domains (criminal history, alcohol/drug, and antisocial pattern) appear to be less predictive for Aboriginal offenders.

The relevance of change in risk, in relation to intervention as well as outcome, is another topic of interest with the LS instruments, as it is on other risk/need assessment instruments (e.g., Cohen, Lowenkamp, & VanBenschoten, 2016; Flores, 2016; Latessa, 2016; Vose, 2016). Dynamic predictive validity (i.e., changes in the dynamic factors predict outcomes) was found in early LS research with probationers (Andrews & Robinson, 1984) and prisoners (Motiuk, Bonta, & Andrews, 1990). This research demonstrated that more recent, proximal predictions were more accurate than earlier predictions as well as that changes in risk coincided with corresponding changes in recidivism (i.e., offenders, whose risk increased recidivated at a higher rate than those whose risk remained the same or decreased, and vice versa). These findings have been replicated numerous times in studies in the US and the UK (Miles & Raynor, 2004; Raynor, 2007; Schlager & Pacheco, 2011; Vose, Lowenkamp, Smith, & Cullen, 2009; Vose, Smith, & Cullen, 2013).

Examining a group of offenders who had already recidivated, Labrecque, Smith, Lovins, and Latessa (2014) demonstrated that the more recent (current) LSI-Rs were more predictive of subsequent recidivism than LSI-Rs from a previous admission. They also found that change in four domains on the LSI-R, specifically, criminal history leisure/recreation, antisocial associates, and antisocial attitudes were significantly associated with subsequent arrest. Taking quite a different strategy, Day, Wilson, Bodwin, and Monson (2017) examined multi-wave LSI-OR data to determine how changes on each domain from one admission to the next were related to changes on the total score (minus that particular domain). Although numerous patterns were found, changes on the Procriminal Attitude/Orientation, Criminal History, and Leisure/ Recreation subscales preceded quicker rates of change on the total risk score over time. This suggests that these domains may be key to overall change in risk and therefore might wisely be prioritized for intervention with the exception possibly of criminal history because of its static nature during any one sentence.

Use of professional overrides was one of the four original principles coined in the Risk-Need-Responsivity (RNR) model of offender assessment and intervention (Andrews, Bonta, & Hoge, 1990). The concept of a professional override can be traced back to Meehl's (1954) observation that sometimes a single, otherwise unconsidered factor, such as a client's broken leg, may have overarching impact on any actuarial prediction, for example, a prediction as to whether a person with a broken leg will attend a specific movie (Salanger, 2005). As the LS/ CMI is a RNR-based assessment instrument, it not surprising that the LS/CMI also allows for professional overrides, which permits an adjustment of risk based on an organizational policy, such as "all sexual offenders must be considered high risk." Other risk assessment instruments, such as the Correctional Offender Management Profiling for Alternative Sanctions (COMPAS; Brennan, Dieterich, & Oliver, 2004) also include a professional override in conjunction with aggravating and mitigating factors, as do a couple of sexual offender risk assessment instruments, the MnSOST-R (Gore, 2007) and the Static-99 (Hanson, Harris, Scott, & Helmus, 2007).

However, the application of the override principle to the prediction of offender recidivism has not been encouraging. In a large study of the LS/CMI in the province of Quebec, Canada, Guay and Parent (2017) found when the override was used (less than 7% of cases) it was most likely to be used to *decrease* the risk level (61% of all 237 override decisions). This resulted in decreased predictive validity. Similarly, Wormith, Hogg, and Guzzo (2012) revealed that the use of a professional override also reduced the predictive validity of the LS assessments and did so most dramatically for sexual offenders by over-predicting their likelihood of recidivism. In our view, use of the override may be permitted, but only in very special circumstances; conditions that are well defined and have an empirical support, although they do not constitute items in the LS per se. Potential candidates might be found in the list of specific risk/need factors, such as "stalking/harassment," which are listed in Section 2 of the LS/CMI.

Promoting stronger connections between LS assessment results and ongoing treatment, programming, and supervision of offenders remains an important focus of LS researchers and practitioners since Bonta et al.'s (2008) revealing analysis of probation officers' efforts with offenders generally being disharmonious with the results of their risk/needs assessment. This is not an issue only with LS instruments, but also with other tools that were specifically designed to contribute to offender intervention plans. This includes the Client Management Classification (CMC) system, which is based on the Wisconsin Risk/Need Assessment (Baird et al., 1979; Baird & Neuenfeldt, 1990), where the offender case strategy was commensurate with the CMC classification in only 26% of the cases (Harris, Gingerich, & Whittaker, 2004). In their evaluation of the national serious and violent offender re-entry initiative (SVORI) in the US, Gill and Wilson (2017) found that only half of the offender needs were addressed. Moreover, the service-need fit was related negatively to both official and self-reported recidivism.

Officials in the Netherlands have taken the crafting of the assessment-intervention link one step further with their probationers. The Recidive Inschattings Schalen (Recidivism Assessment Scales, RISc), is based on the English and Welsh Offender Assessment System (Home Office, 2002) and was modified from a third generation into a fourth generation risk/needs assessment. When Bosker and Witteman (2016) introduced a structured case management decision-making process to their RISc, they found a better match between criminogenic needs and goals, and between risk of recidivism and intensity of the plan. High-quality plans also translated to high-quality offender supervision indicating that structured decision support to a risk/need assessment can improve case management plans and contribute to the quality of probation practice. These sorts of findings lead us to the case management portion of the LS/CMI, whereby the structure of the LS/CMI guides case managers in the use of the risk/need portion of the assessment in the planning and conducting of offender case management.

Finally, we are investigating the potential for some of the alternative scoring methods, such as machine language and decision trees, which began to emerge in the field of offender risk assessment at the turn of the century (e.g., in the MacArthur study, as reported by Steadman et al., 2000). However, it is only recently that they have been subject to widespread investigation (e.g., Berk & Bleich, 2013; Brennan & Oliver, 2013; Bushway, 2013; Rhodes, 2013;

Roth & Banks, 2000). Our preliminary efforts have demonstrated that when making a binary prediction (will or will not recidivate) conventional scoring of the LS instruments does very well at either extreme (e.g., very high risk or very low risk) but deteriorates the closer one gets to a score at which half of the offenders recidivate, in which case the accuracy is around 50%. This finding is troublesome in that a disproportionately large number of offenders score in the comparable range of LS scores (particularly when the base rate of recidivism is around 50%). It is our belief that non-linear means of combining item scores on the LS instruments may improve the hit rate (true positives plus true negatives) of assessment from 70% to up 90%. It does so by looking at combinations of scored items at a given score that are more likely to lead to recidivism than other combinations of items that generate the same score. However, this work requires further investigation and analysis to support the contention that some combination of (scored) items is particularly toxic for the prediction of recidivism.

Summary and Conclusions

The LS scales are among the most well-established offender risk/need assessment instruments in use today. With more than a million registered administrations per year (Wormith, 2011), they are also among the most extensively and widely used. We believe that their popularity comes from their general applicability to offenders in a wide range of circumstances, which, in turn, is derived from their underlying theoretical perspective on antisocial criminal behavior, the General Personality and Cognitive Social Learning theory (GPCSL; Bonta & Andrews, 2017), and their long empirical tradition of success (Olver et al., 2014). The LS instruments are not "a jack of all trades but a master of none" (Duwe & Rocque, 2016). They are as valuable in assessing the risk and criminogenic needs of high-risk offenders as they are in documenting the lack of risk and criminogenic needs of low-risk offenders, each of which has its own policy and practice implications. This latter, often overlooked, point is illustrated in the following case study, which also rebuts the concerns of critics (e.g., Laws & Ward, 2011; Ward & Marshall, 2004; Ward & Stewart, 2003) that risk assessment instruments, like the LS scales, focus only on the negative aspect of offender clients and neglect their positive attributes. A very low-risk score on any domain may indicate a strength, which assessors are invited to note as such on the LS scoring form and use this finding to develop a case management plan or treatment intervention that utilizes the discovered strength to address an outstanding criminogenic need. For example, a low-risk offender could still be at risk on a certain domain, such as substance abuse, but have very strong social support within the family, a strength, such that the case management plan would call on the family resources to assist in managing the risks associated with substance abuse.

Nothing can be taken for granted when it comes to applying offender risk assessment to practice (Bonta et al., 2008; Bosker & Witteman, 2016). We believe that another strength in the LS instruments is their evolution from third to fourth generation, extending and enhancing the third generation features, which include advising case management, referring to treatment, and planning supervision. Therefore, the case management portion of the LS/CMI provides a means for practitioners to utilize the findings of an LS assessment in their planning and daily practice with offenders. Ultimately, offender risk assessment must be held accountable for its impact on correctional agencies and their staff, in addition to its impact on offender supervision and change. Continued research and evaluation is required to determine whether the LS/CMI lives up to its case management function.

Case Study

Probation Intake Report

Name: Louise Lake

Age: 37 years old

Date: April 1, 2017

Reason for Assessment

Ms. Lake is beginning a six-month period of probation. She pleaded guilty to one count of possession of narcotics for the purpose of trafficking. The conditions of probation are minimal and entail reporting as requested by the probation officer. According to the police report, Ms. Lake was found with 7 ounces of cannabis during a police raid at a local dance club. This is Ms. Lake's first conviction as an adult. During the interview, Ms. Lake presented as a cooperative and friendly woman. She answered all questions freely and appeared frank in her discussion of the present situation.

Criminal History

Official documents show no prior criminal history. Ms. Lake stated that she has never been arrested by police either as an adult or as a juvenile. Quite the contrary, she describes herself as a law-abiding citizen and ashamed of her present encounter with the law. Ms. Lake reported that the possession offence resulted from holding the cannabis for her husband who was described as a recreational user. She denied using cannabis herself and said that the police had no choice but to arrest her because "I had possession."

Education/Employment

Ms. Lake described herself as always liking school and never experiencing any behavioral or academic difficulties. She continued with school until graduating from the local university 10 years ago. She received a degree in business and presently Ms. Lake is employed by the Best-Thing department store where she is an accountant. Her employer is aware of the present offence but her job is not in jeopardy.

Best-Thing department store has been Ms. Lake's employer since she graduated from college. Her employer describes her as an excellent worker and valued employee who is well liked by the staff. Ms. Lake reported that she enjoys her work very much and that over the years she has been given increasing responsibility, which she finds both challenging and rewarding. Her supervisor is also a close friend of the family who has been quite supportive during the court proceedings. Ms. Lake works in an office with four other employees. They appear to have a very good collegial relationship, spending coffee breaks together and playing on a company bowling team.

Family/Marital

Mr. Lake's use of cannabis has been a long-standing concern for Ms. Lake. She had never liked his use of the substance, even though it was relatively infrequent (once a month). They have argued over his use in the past and these arguments have become more frequent as their daughter has become older. Ms. Lake feels that his drug use sets a bad example for their child (although her husband has never used cannabis in their daughter's presence). The present conviction has further added to the strain between the couple but Ms. Lake denies that the situation has become so intolerable that she wishes to seek a separation. Ms. Lake commented that power/control was not a relationship issue but she noted how her legal problems were linked directly to her relationship with her husband.

Ms. Lake's parents live in the city and they visit her regularly. Ms. Lake is particularly close to her mother. They have lunch at least once a week and her aunt and uncle, who are retired, look after the daughter while Ms. Lake and her husband are at work. Only one in Ms. Lake's family has been in conflict with the law. Mr. Lake was convicted of possession of a narcotic three years ago.

Leisure/Recreation

Ms. Lake is a member of her company's bowling team as well as the local Neighbourhood Watch and Block Parents organizations. The latter two activities involve monthly meetings and the preparation of a newsletter and periodic fundraising activity. In addition to these activities, Ms. Lake belongs to a neighbourhood book-reading club and during the summer, she enjoys gardening. In the winter, she takes weekend ski lessons.

Companions

To the best of her knowledge, none of Ms. Lake's friends has been involved with the criminal justice system. In fact, she finds it difficult to imagine herself associating with anyone who has been arrested by the police. Ms. Lake reported that her two closest friends (a colleague from work and an old childhood friend) know about the present offence and are shocked by it. However, they see this event as an unusual circumstance unlikely to be repeated. Actually, one of her friends drove her to the appointment for this interview.

Alcohol/Drug Problems

Ms. Lake denies ever having a drug or alcohol problem. She has never experimented with any drugs and expressed dismay that her husband still uses cannabis. The "harder" drugs are seen as substances that can destroy a person's life and she hopes that her daughter will never be exposed to its dangers. Ms. Lake drinks socially and in moderation. She will drink a glass of wine on special occasions with her last drink taken at the retirement party for a co-worker last month. Ms. Lake's description of alcohol and drug use is collaborated by her husband and mother who were interviewed by this examiner.

Attitude/Orientation

Ms. Lake admitted that she was in possession of cannabis and feels that the officer who made the arrest, did so appropriately: "Their job is to enforce the law; in the long run it is good for everybody." She thinks a re-occurrence is unlikely: She looks forward to a more normal life, working and continuing her involvement with the family and her community. Quite prepared to accept the penalty the court deemed appropriate, she feels that the judge made a fair decision and is pleased that probation was the final decision. I explained probation to her and the possibility that there may be some restrictive conditions accompanying the probation order. Ms. Lake understood and said, "Whatever is involved, I hope that the probation officer can help me put this part of my life behind me."

Antisocial Pattern

Ms. Lake presented without a single indication of a pattern of antisocial behaviour. There were no indicators of antisocial personality, no history of antisocial behaviour, no antisocial thinking, and no pattern of generalized trouble.

Other Client Issues

No other specific risk/need indicators were present. Similarly, an exploration of financial, accommodation, health, and emotional/personal issues revealed no problematic areas.

The combined family income for Ms. Lake and her husband is $93,000. Mr. Lake works as a landscape architect. They own their own home and a three-year-old car. Ms. Lake denies any difficulties in meeting mortgage or car payments. In fact, they have been able to save money for vacation trips each year and for the future education of their eight-year-old daughter. Neither Ms. Lake nor her husband has ever been on any form of social assistance.

The Lakes' home is in a quiet and well-established neighbourhood of the city. They have lived in the same residence for the past 8 years. Ms. Lake is a member of the Block Parents Association and the block captain for Neighbourhood Watch. Last year they upgraded their kitchen and bathroom and Ms. Lake hopes that this home will be their residence for many years to come.

According to Ms. Lake's mother, Ms. Lake was always a happy and sociable child. Ms. Lake did well in school and had no medical problems. She denied ever seeing a counsellor or mental health professional and described her life as very satisfactory. Her only wish is that her husband stop using cannabis.

Summary and Recommendations

Ms. Lake impresses as a sincere mature woman who appeared to have made one mistake that she wishes to forget. The results of the LS/CMI placed her in the Very Low risk-need range. Her score was two. Offenders with similar scores showed a very low likelihood of returning to crime (1). The only area that showed a potential for treatment targeting was her relationship with her husband, their disagreements over his cannabis use, and her apparent willingness to "carry" the substance on at least one occasion.

Community Case Management Plan

I discussed marital counselling with Ms. Lake and she will explore services available at a local family service agency. That agency is known to favour short term structured marital counselling with special attention to quality and equity in interpersonal relationships. There are no problematic special responsivity considerations beyond the possibility of power/control as a women's issue. Notably, marital counselling may well build on the many strengths noted in this case. They included Criminal History, Education/Employment, Leisure Recreation, Companions, Attitudes, and Pattern. Once counselling is underway and progress confirmed by the counsellor and participants, I anticipate a favorable early closure.

Jeff Atlas

Intake Probation Officer

Case Management Discharge Summary

Name: Louise Lake
Age: 37 years
Date: Sept 29, 2017

Background

Ms. Lake received a six-month period of probation for possession of cannabis. She was assessed at intake as a Very Low risk case with a multitude of strengths. Assigned to minimal supervision she was referred to a family service agency for marital counseling. The only identified criminogenic factor was marital dissatisfaction centering on her husband's occasional use of cannabis. A favorable early case closure was expected.

Case Management

Ms. Lake and her husband made early contact with the family agency and entered structured behavioral counseling with a focus on an equitable relationship. With only four counseling contacts over four weeks, the husband committed to cease drug use and Ms. Lake committed to having no contact with the substance or with her husband during the occurrence of a lapse. With four additional contacts, the counselor and the Lakes reported to this probation officer that their counseling goals had been achieved. Family-counselor phone contacts were planned for once a month for the following three months.

Case Closure

After the first eight weeks, the case was closed with the understanding that the probation officer (or Ms. Lake or the counselor) might initiate a contact at any time up to the end of the formal six-month probation period.

Sarah Repaz

Probation and Case Management Officer

For a review of Ms Lake's LS/CMI, see Andrews, Bonta, & Wormith (2004), p. 81–94.

Source: Andrews, Bonta & Wormith (2004). *Level of Service/Case Management Inventory: An Offender Assessment System: User's Manual.* (Copyright 2004, Multi-Health Systems Inc). Reproduced with permission.

References

Andrews, D. A. (1982). *The Level of Supervision Inventory (LSI): The first follow-up.* Toronto, ON: Ontario Ministry of Correctional Services.

Andrews, D. A. (1995). The psychology of criminal conduct and effective treatment. In J. McGuire (Ed.), *What works: Reducing re-offending* (pp. 35–62). Chichester, England: John Wiley & Sons.

Andrews, D. A., & Bonta, J. (1995). *The Level of Service Inventory–Revised.* Toronto, ON: Multi-Health Systems.

Andrews, D. A., & Bonta, J. (1998). *The Level of Service Inventory–Revised: Screening Version.* Toronto, ON: Multi-Health Systems.

Andrews, D. A., Bonta, J., & Hoge, R. D. (1990). Classification for effective rehabilitation: Rediscovering psychology. *Criminal Justice and Behavior, 17*, 19–52.

Andrews, D. A., Bonta, J., Motiuk, L. L., & Robinson, D. (1984). Some psychometrics of practical risk/needs assessment. Paper presented at the Annual Meeting of the American Psychological Association, Toronto, ON.

Andrews, D. A., Bonta, J., & Wormith, J. (1995). *The Level of Service Inventory–Ontario Revision (LSI-OR).* Toronto, ON: Ontario Ministry of the Solicitor General and Correctional Services.

Andrews, D. A., Bonta, J., & Wormith, J. (2004). *The Level of Service/Case Management Inventory (LS/CMI): User's manual.* Toronto, ON: Multi-Health Systems.

Andrews, D. A., Bonta, J., & Wormith, S. J. (2006). The recent past and near future of risk and/or need assessment. *Crime & Delinquency, 52*, 7–27.

Andrews, D. A., Bonta, J., & Wormith, J. S. (2008). *The Level of Service/Risk, Need, Responsivity (LS/RNR). User's manual.* Toronto, ON. Multi-Health Systems.

Andrews, D. A., Bonta, J., & Wormith, J. S. (2010). The Level of Service (LS) assessment of adults and older adolescents. In R. K. Otto & K. Douglas (Eds.), *Handbook of violence risk assessment tools* (pp. 199–225). New York, NY: Routledge.

Andrews, D. A., Bonta, J., Wormith, S. J., Guzzo, L., Brews, A., Rettinger, J., & Rowe, R. (2011). Sources of variability in estimates of predictive validity: A specification with level of service risk and need. *Criminal Justice and Behavior, 38*, 413–432.

Andrews, D. A., Guzzo, L., Raynor, P., Rowe, R. C., Rettinger, J., Brews, A, & Wormith, J. S. (2012). Are the major risk/need factors predictive of both female and male reoffending? A test with the eight domains of the Level of Service/Case Management Inventory. *International Journal of Offender Therapy and Comparative Criminology, 56*, 113–133.

Andrews, D. A., Kiessling, J. J., Mickus, S., & Robinson, D. (1986, June). Some convergent and divergent validities of the LSI. Paper presented to the annual meeting of the Canadian Psychological Association, Winnipeg, MA.

Andrews, D. A., & Robinson, D. (1984). *The Level of Supervision Inventory: Second report.* Toronto, ON: Ontario Ministry of Correctional Services.

Baird, C. (2009). *A question of evidence: A critique of risk assessment models used in the justice system.* Madison, WI: National Council on Crime & Delinquency.

Baird, C., Heinz, R., & Bemus, B. (1979). *The Wisconsin Case Classification/Staff deployment project.* Madison, WI: Wisconsin Department of Corrections.

Baird, C., & Neuenfeldt, D. (1990). *The Client Management Classification system. NCCD, Focus, 1990,* 1–7.

Berk, R. A., & Bleich, J. (2013). Statistical procedures for forecasting criminal behavior: A comparative assessment. *Criminology & Public Policy, 12,* 513–544.

Bhutta, M. H., & Wormith, J. S. (2016). An examination of a risk/needs assessment instrument and its relation to religiosity and recidivism among probationers in a Muslim culture. *Criminal Justice and Behavior, 43,* 204–229.

Boer, D. P., Hart, S. D., Kropp, P. R., & Webster, C. D. (1997). *Manual for the Sexual Violence Risk-20. Professional guidelines for assessing risk of sexual violence.* Burnaby, BC: Simon Fraser University, Mental Health, Law, and Policy Institute.

Bonta, J., & Andrews, D. A. (2017). *The psychology of criminal conduct* (6th ed.). New York, NY: Routledge.

Bonta, J., Bogue, B., Crowley, M., & Motiuk, L. L. (2001). Implementing offender classification systems: Lessons learned. In G. A. Bernfeld, D. P. Farrington, & A. W. Leschied (Eds.), *Offender rehabilitation in practice: Implementing and evaluating effective programs* (pp. 227–245). Chichester, England: John Wiley & Sons.

Bonta, J., & Motiuk, L. L. (1982). Assessing incarcerated offenders for halfway houses. November, available from J. Bonta (Jim.Bonta@gmail.com).

Bonta, J., & Motiuk, L. L. (1985). Utilization of an interview-based classification instrument: A study of correctional half-way houses. *Criminal Justice & Behavior, 12,* 333–352.

Bonta, J., & Motiuk, L. L. (1986a, August). Use of the Level of Supervision Inventory for assessing incarcerates. Paper presented at the 94th Annual Convention of the American Psychological Association, Washington, DC.

Bonta, J., & Motiuk, L. L. (1986b). *The LSI in institutions: Toronto Jail, Hamilton-Wentworth Detention Centre, Ottawa-Carleton Detention Centre.* Report # 1. Toronto, ON: Ontario Ministry of Correctional Services.

Bonta, J., & Motiuk, L. L. (1987). The diversion of incarcerated offenders to correctional halfway houses. *Journal of Research in Crime and Delinquency, 24,* 302–323.

Bonta, J., & Motiuk, L. L. (1990). Classification to halfway houses: A quasi-experimental evaluation. *Criminology, 28,* 497–506.

Bonta, J., & Motiuk, L. L. (1992). Inmate classification. *Journal of Criminal Justice, 20,* 343–353.

Bonta, J., Motiuk, L. L., & Ker, K. (1985). *The Level of Supervision Inventory (LSI) among incarcerated offenders.* Report # 1. Toronto, ON: Ministry of Correctional Services (Ontario).

Bonta, J., Rugge, T., Scott, T., Bourgon, G., & Yessine, A. (2008). Exploring the black box of community supervision. *Journal of Offender Rehabilitation, 47,* 248–270.

Bonta, J., Rugge, T., Sedo, B., & Coles, R. (2004). *Case management in Manitoba probation* (2004-01). Ottawa, ON: Public Safety and Emergency Preparedness Canada.

Borum, R., Bartel, P., & Forth, A. (2002). *Manual for the structured assessment of violence risk in youth (SAVRY).* Tampa, FL: University of South Florida.

Bosker, J., & Witteman, C. (2016). Finding the right focus: Improving the link between risk/need assessment and case management in probation. *Psychology, Crime & Law, 22,* 221–233.

Brennan, T., Dieterich, W., & Oliver, W. (2004). *The COMPAS scales: Normative data for males and females. Community and incarcerated samples.* Traverse City, MI: Northpointe Institute for Public Management.

Brennan, T., & Oliver, W. (2013). The emergence of machine learning techniques in criminology: Implications of complexity in our data and in research questions. *Criminology & Public Policy, 12,* 551–562.

Bushway, S. D. (2013). Is there any logic to using logit: Finding the right tool for the increasingly important job of risk prediction. *Criminology & Public Policy, 12,* 563–567.

Campbell, M. A., French, S., & Gendreau, P. (2009). The prediction of violence in adult offenders: A meta-analytic comparison of instruments and methods of assessment. *Criminal Justice and Behavior, 36,* 567–590.

Chenane, J. L., Brennan, P. K., Steiner, B., & Ellison, J. M. (2015) Racial and ethnic differences in the predictive validity of the Level of Service Inventory–Revised among prison inmates. *Criminal Justice and Behavior, 42,* 286–303.

Cohen, J. (1988). *Statistical power analysis for the behavioral sciences* (2nd ed.). Hillsdale, NJ: L. Erlbaum.

Cohen, T. H., Lowenkamp, C. T., & VanBenschoten, S. W. (2016). Does change in risk matter? Examining whether changes in offender risk characteristics influence recidivism outcomes. *Criminology & Public Policy, 15,* 263–296.

Copas, J., & Marshall, P. (1998). The Offender Group Reconviction Scale: The statistical reconviction score for use by probation officers. *Journal of the Royal Statistical Society, 47C,* 159–171.

Cronbach, L. J. (1951). Coefficient alpha and the internal structure of tests. *Psychometrika, 16,* 297–334.

Day, D. M., Wilson, H. A., Bodwin, K., & Monson, C. M. (2017). Change in Level of Service Inventory–Ontario Revised (LSI-OR) risk scores over time: An examination of overall growth curves and subscale-dependent growth curves. *International Journal of Offender Therapy and Comparative Criminology, 61,* 1606–1622.

Desmarais, S. L., Johnson, K. L., & Singh, J. P. (2016). Performance of recidivism risk assessment instruments in U.S. correctional settings. *Psychological Services, 13,* 206–222.

Duwe, G., & Rocque, M. (2016). A jack of all trades but master of none? Evaluating the performance of the Level of Service Inventory–Revised (LSI-R) in the assessment of risk and need. *Corrections: Policy Practice and Research, 1,* 81–106.

Duwe, G., & Rocque, M. (2017). The effects of automating recidivism risk assessment on reliability, predictive validity, and return on investment (ROI). *Criminology & Public Policy.* Online first.

Faulkner, P., Andrews, D. A., Wadel, D., & Hawkins, J. (1992). *Evaluation of a client-services management system.* Ottawa, ON: Solicitor General Canada.

Flores, A. W. (2016). The importance of measuring offender change. *Criminology & Public Policy, 15,* 259–261.

Flores, A. W., Lowenkamp, C. T., & Latessa, E. J. (n.d.). *A profile of offenders in Coles and Cumberland Counties using the LSI-R.* Cincinnati, OH: University of Cincinnati.

Folsom, J., & Atkinson, J. L. (2007). The generalizability of the LSI and the CAT to the prediction of recidivism in female offenders. *Criminal Justice and Behavior, 34,* 1044–1056.

Garb, H. N. (1997) Race bias, social class bias, and gender bias in clinical judgment. *Clinical psychology: Science and Practice, 4,* 99–120.

Garb, H. N., Lilienfeld, S. O., & Fowler, K. A. (2016) Psychological assessment and clinical judgment. In J. E. Maddux & B. A. Winstead (eds), *Psychopathology; Foundations for a contemporary understanding* (4th ed.). New York, NY: Routledge.

Gendreau, P., Goggin, C., & Smith, P. (2002). Is the PCL-R really the "unparalleled" measure of offender risk? *Criminal Justice and Behavior, 29,* 397–426.

Gendreau, P., Little., T., & Goggin, C. (1996). A meta-analysis of the predictors of adult offender recidivism: What works! *Criminology, 34,* 575–607.

Gill, C., & Wilson, D. B. (2017). Improving the success of re-entry programs: Identifying the impact of service-need fit on recidivism. *Criminal Justice and Behavior, 44*, 336–359.

Girard, L. (1999). *The Level of Supervision Inventory–Ontario Revision: Risk/need assessment and recidivism.* Unpublished doctoral dissertation. University of Ottawa, ON, Canada.

Gore, K. S. (2007). *Adjusted actuarial assessment of sex offenders: The impact of clinical overrides on predictive accuracy.* Unpublished dissertation. Iowa State University, Ames Iowa.

Guay, J.-P. (2016). L'évaluation du risque et des besoins criminogènes à la lumière des données probantes: une étude de validation de la version française de l'Inventaire de niveau de service et de gestion des cas–LS/CMI, [French validation of the Level of Service/Case Management Inventory–LS/CMI], *European Review of Applied Psychology/Revue Européenne de Psychologie Appliquée, 66*, 199–210.

Guay, J.-P., & Parent, G. (2017). Broken leg, clinical overrides and recidivism risk: An analysis of decisions to adjust levels with the LS/CMI. *Criminal Justice and Behavior.* Online First, July 12, 2017.

Gutierrez, L., Wilson, H. A., Rugge, T., & Bonta, J. (2013). The prediction of recidivism with Aboriginal offenders: A quantitative and theoretically informed review. *Canadian Journal of Criminology and Criminal Justice, 55*, 55–99.

Haas, S. M., Davidson, L. J., & Wormith, J. S. (2014). *Ensuring fidelity of offender risk assessment in large-scale correctional settings: The Quality Assurance-Treatment Intervention Programs and Supervision Initiative (QA-TIPS).* JRSA Research and Training Webinar Series (December 14, 2014). Charleston, WV: Office of Research and Strategic Planning, Division of Justice and Community Services, State of West Virginia Department of Military Affairs and Public Safety. Retrieved from http://www.jrsa.org/webinars/index.html#qa

Hannah-Moffat, K. (2009). Gridlock or mutability: Reconsidering "gender" and risk assessment. *Criminology & Public Policy, 8*, 209–219.

Hanson, R. K., Harris, A. J. R., Scott, T.-L., & Helmus, L. (2007). *Assessing the risk of sexual offenders on community supervision: The dynamic supervision project.* 2007-05. Ottawa, ON: Public Safety Canada.

Hanson, R. K., & Thornton, D. (1999). *Static-99: Improving actuarial risk assessments for sex offenders* (User Report 99-02). Ottawa, ON: Department of the Solicitor General of Canada.

Hare, R. D. (2003). *The Hare Psychopathy Checklist-Revised* (2nd ed.). Toronto, ON: Multi-Health Systems.

Harris, G. T., Rice, M. E., & Quinsey, V. L. (1993). Violent recidivism of mentally disordered offenders: The development of a statistical prediction instrument. *Criminal Justice and Behavior, 20*, 315–335.

Harris, P. M., Gingerich R., & Whittaker, T. A. (2004). The "effectiveness" of differential supervision. *Crime & Delinquency, 50*, 235–271.

Hempill, J. F., & Hare, R. D. (2004). Some misconceptions about the Hare PCL-R and risk assessment: A reply to Gendreau, Goggin, and Smith. *Criminal Justice and Behavior, 31*, 203–243.

Hoffman, P. B., Stone-Meierhoefer, B., and Beck, J. I. (1978). Salient Factor Score and release behavior: Three validation samples. *Law and Human Behavior, 2*, 47–62.

Hoge, R. D., & Andrews, D. A. (2002). *Youth Level of Service/Case Management Inventory: User's manual.* Toronto, ON: Multi-Health Systems.

Hogg, S. M. (2011). *The Level of Service Inventory (Ontario Revision) scale validation for gender and ethnicity: Addressing reliability and predictive validity.* Unpublished master's thesis. University of Saskatchewan, Saskatoon, Canada.

Hollin, C. R., Palmer, E. J., & Clark, D. (2003). Level of Service Inventory–Revised profile of English prisoners: A needs analysis. *Criminal Justice and Behavior, 30*, 422–440.

Holsinger, A. M., Lowenkamp, C. T., & Latessa, E. J. (n.d.). Ethnicity, gender and the Level of Service Inventory–Revised. Kansas City, MO: University of Missouri – Kansas City.

Holtfreter, K., & Cupp, R. (2007). Gender and risk assessment: The empirical status of the LSI-R for women. *Journal of Contemporary Criminology, 23*, 363–382.

Home Office. (2002). *Offender Assessment System OASys: User manual.* London, England: Home Office.

Kropp, P. R., & Hart, S. D. (2000). The Spousal Assault Risk Assessment (SARA) guide: Reliability and validity in adult male offenders. *Law and Human Behavior, 24*, 101–118.

Labrecque, R., Smith, P., Lovins, B., & Latessa, E. (2014). The importance of reassessment: How changes in the LSI-R risk score can improve the prediction of recidivism. *Journal of Offender Rehabilitation, 53*, 116–126.

Latessa, E. J. (2016). Does change in risk matter? Yes, it does, and we can measure it. *Criminology & Public Policy, 15*, 297–300.

Laws, D. R., & Ward, T. (2011). *Desistance from sex offending: Alternatives to throwing away the key.* New York, NY: The Guilford Press.

Lowenkamp, C. T., & Latessa, E. J. (n.d.). *A profile of offenders in Alaska using the LSI-R.* Cincinnati, OH: University of Cincinnati.

Loza, W., & Simourd, D. J. (1994). Psychometric evaluation of the Level of Supervision Inventory (LSI) among male Canadian federal offenders. *Criminal Justice and Behavior, 21*, 468–480.

Meehl, P. E. (1954). *Clinical versus statistical prediction: A theoretical analysis and a review of the evidence.* Minneapolis, MN: University of Minnesota Press.

Miles, H., & Raynor, P. (2004). *Community Sentences in Jersey: Risk, need, and rehabilitation.* St Helier, UK: Royal Court of Jersey.

Mills, J. F., Jones, M. N., & Kroner, D. G. (2005). An examination of the generalizability of the LSI-R and VRAG probability bins. *Criminal Justice and Behavior, 32*, 565–585.

Motiuk, L. L., Bonta, J., & Andrews, D. A. (1990, June). Dynamic predictive criterion validity in offender assessment. Paper presented at the Canadian Psychological Association Annual Convention, Ottawa, ON.

Nowicka-Sroga, M. (2004). *The Level of Supervision Inventory–Ontario Revision: A recidivism follow up study within a sample of young offenders.* Unpublished doctoral dissertation. University of Ottawa, ON, Canada. April.

Nuffield, J. (1982). *Parole decision-making in Canada: Research towards decision guidelines.* Ottawa, ON, Canada: Supply and Services Canada.

Olver, M. E., Stockdale, K. C., & Wormith, J. S. (2009). Risk assessment with young offenders: A meta-analysis of three assessment measures. *Criminal Justice and Behavior, 36*, 329–353.

Olver, M. E., Stockdale, K. C., & Wormith, J. S. (2014). Thirty years of research on the level of service scales: A meta-analytic examination of predictive accuracy and sources of variability. *Psychological Assessment, 26*, 156–176.

Orsini, M., M., Haas, S. M., & Spence, D. H. (2015). *Predicting recidivism of offenders released from the West Virginia Division of Corrections: Validation of the Level of Service/Case Management Inventory.* Charleston, WV: Office of Research and Strategic Planning, Division of Justice and Community Services, State of West Virginia Department of Military Affairs and Public Safety. Retrieved from http://www.djcs.wv.gov/ORSP/SAC/Documents/JCEBP%20LSCMI%20Validation%20DOC%202015.pdf

Palmer, E. J., & Hollin, C. R. (2007). The Level of Service Inventory–Revised with English women prisoners: A needs and reconviction analysis. *Criminal Justice and Behavior, 34*, 971–984.

Pilon, A. J. M. (2016). The predictive validity of general and offense-specific risk assessment tools for child pornography offenders' reoffending. Unpublished master's thesis. University of Saskatchewan, Saskatoon, Canada. Retrieved from https://ecommons.usask.ca/bitstream/handle/10388/ETD-2016-01-2414/PILON-THESIS.pdf?sequence=3&isAllowed=y

Pilon, A. J. M., Jewell, K. M., & Wormith, J. S. (2015). *Impaired drivers and their risk of reoffending.* Report submitted to Public Safety Canada. Saskatoon: Centre for Forensic Behavioural Science & Justice Studies, University of Saskatchewan.

Quinsey, V. L., Harris, G. T., Rice, M. E., & Cormier, C. A. (1998). *Violent offenders: Appraising and managing risk.* Washington, DC: American Psychological Association.

Raynor, P. (2007). Risk and need assessment in British probation: The contribution of the LSI-R. *Psychology, Crime, & Law, 13*, 125–138.

Rettinger, J. (1998). A *recidivism follow-up study to investigate risk and need within a sample of provincially sentenced women.* Unpublished doctoral dissertation. Carleton University, Ottawa, ON, Canada. September.

Rhodes, W. (2013). Machine learning approaches as a tool for effective offender risk prediction. *Criminology and Public Policy, 12*, 507–510.

Roth, L., & Banks, S. (2000). A classification tree approach to the development of actuarial violence risk assessment tools. *Law and Human Behavior, 24*, 83–100.

Rowe, R. C. (1999). *The prediction or recidivism in a parole sample: An examination of two versions of the Level of Service Inventory.* Unpublished report. Carleton University; Ottawa, ON, Canada.

Salanger, K. (2005). Clinical, statistical, and broken-leg predictions. *Behavior and Philosophy, 33*, 91–99.

Schlager, M. D., & Pacheco, D. (2011). An examination of changes in LSI-R scores over time: Making the case for needs-based case management. *Criminal Justice and Behavior, 38*, 541–553.

Schlager, M. D., & Simourd, D. J. (2007). Validity of the Level of Service Inventory–Revised (LSI-R) among African American and Hispanic male offenders. *Criminal Justice and Behavior, 34*, 545–554.

Schwalbe, C. S. (2007). Risk assessment for juvenile offenders: A meta-analysis. *Law and Human Behavior, 31*, 449–462.

Schwalbe, C. S. (2008). A meta-analysis of juvenile justice risk assessment instruments: Predictive validity by gender. *Criminal Justice and Behavior, 35*, 1367–1381.

Sijtsma, K. (2009). On the use, the misuse, and the very limited usefulness of Cronbach's alpha. *Psychometrika, 74*, 107–120.

Simourd, D. J., & Malcolm, P. B. (1998). Reliability and validity of the Level of Service Inventory–Revised among federally incarcerated sex offenders. *Journal of Interpersonal Violence, 13*, 261–274.

Singh, J. P., Grann, M., & Fazel, S. (2011). A comparative study of violence risk assessment tools: A systematic review and metaregression analysis of 68 studies involving 25,980 participants. *Clinical Psychology Review, 31*, 499–513.

Smith, P., Cullen, F. T., & Latessa, E. J. (2009). Can 14,373 women be wrong? A meta-analysis of the LSI-R and recidivism for female offenders. *Criminology & Public Policy, 8*, 183–208.

Steadman, H., Silver, E., Monahan, J., Appelbaum, P., Robbins, P., Mulvey, E., . . . Banks, S. (2000). A classification tree approach to the development of actuarial violence risk assessment tools. *Law and Human Behavior, 24*, 83–100.

Stevenson, H. E., & Wormith, J. S. (1987). *Psychopathy and the Level of Supervision Inventory.* User Report No. 1987-25. Ottawa, ON: Solicitor General Canada.

Stewart, C. A. (2011). *Risk assessment of federal female offenders.* Unpublished dissertation, University of Saskatchewan, Saskatoon, Canada.

Thornton, D. (2007). *Scoring guide for Risk Matrix 2000.9/SVC.* Retrieved from http://www.cfcp.bham.ac.uk/Extras/SCORING%20GUIDE%20FOR%20RISK%20MATRIX%202000.9-%20SVC%20-%20(ver.%20Feb%202007).pdf

Van Voorhis, P., Wright, E. M., Salisbury, E., & Bauman, A. (2010). Women's risk factors and their contributions to existing risk/needs assessment: The current status of a gender responsive supplement. *Criminal Justice and Behavior, 37*, 261–288.

Vose, B. (2016). Risk assessment and reassessment: An evidence-based approach to offender management. *Criminology & Public Policy, 15*, 301–308.

Vose, B., Lowenkamp, C. Y., Smith, P., & Cullen, F. T. (2009). Gender and the predictive validity of the LSI-R: A study of parolees and probationers. *Journal of Contemporary Criminal Justice, 25,* 459–471.

Vose, B., Smith, P., & Cullen, F. Y. (2013). Predictive validity and the impact of change in total LSI-R score on recidivism. *Criminal Justice and Behavior, 40,* 1383–1396.

Wadel, D., Hawkins, J., Andrews, D. A., Faulkner, P., Hoge, R. D., Rettinger, L. J., & Simourd, D. (1991). Assessment, evaluation, and program development in the voluntary sector. User Report #1991-14. Ottawa, ON: Solicitor General Canada.

Ward, T., & Marshall, W. L. (2004). Good lives, aetiology and the rehabilitation of sex offenders: A bridging theory. *Journal of Sexual Aggression, 10,* 153–169. doi:10.1080/13552600412331290102

Ward, T., & Stewart, C. A. (2003). The treatment of sex offenders: Risk management and good lives. *Professional Psychology: Research and Practice, 34,* 353–360. doi:10.1037/0735-7028 .34.4.353

Webster, C. D., Douglas, K., Eaves, D., & Hart, D. (1997). *HCR-20: Assessing risk for violence* (Ver. 2). Vancouver, BC, Canada: Mental Health, Law, & Policy Institute, Simon Fraser University.

Williams, K. M., Wormith, J. S., Bonta, J., & Sitarenios, G. (2017). The use of meta-analysis to compare and select offender risk instruments: A commentary on Singh, Grann, and Fazel (2011). *International Journal of Forensic Mental Health.* Online first.

Wilson, H. A., & Gutierrez, L. (2014). Does one size fit all? A meta-analysis examining the predictive ability of the Level of Service Inventory (LSI) with Aboriginal offenders. *Criminal Justice and Behavior, 41,* 196–216.

Wong, S. C. P., & Gordon, A. (2006). The validity and reliability of the Violence Risk Scale: A treatment-friendly violence risk assessment tool. *Psychology, Public Policy, and Law, 12,* 279–309.

Wormith, J. S. (2011). The legacy of D. A. Andrews in the field of criminal justice: How theory and research can change policy and practice. *International Journal of Forensic Mental Health, 10,* 78–82.

Wormith, J. S. (2017). Andrews, Donald. In K. R. Kerley (Ed.). *The encyclopedia of corrections.* New York, NY: John Wiley & Sons.

Wormith, J. S., & Hogg, S. M. (2011). *The predictive validity of sexual offender recidivism with a general risk/needs assessment inventory.* Report to the Ministry of Community Safety and Correctional Services of Ontario. Saskatoon, Canada: Centre for Forensic Behavioural Science and Justice Studies. Retrieved from http://www.usask.ca/cfbsjs/research/pdf/research_reports/ LSI%20And%20sexual%20offenders%20FINAL.pdf

Wormith, J. S., Hogg, S. M., & Guzzo, L. (2012). The predictive validity of a general risk/needs assessment inventory on sexual offender recidivism and an exploration of the professional override. *Criminal Justice and Behavior, 39,* 1511–1538.

Wormith, J. S., Hogg, S. M., & Guzzo, L. (2015). The predictive validity of the LS/CMI with Aboriginal offenders in Canada. *Criminal Justice and Behavior, 42,* 281–508.

Yang, M., Wong, S. C. P., & Coid, J. (2010). The efficacy of violence prediction: A meta-analytic comparison of nine risk assessment instruments. *Psychological Bulletin, 136,* 740–767.

Zhang, J., & Liu, N. (2015). Reliability and validity of the Chinese version of the LSI-R with probationers. *International Journal of Offender Therapy and Comparative Criminology, 59,* 1474–1486.

7

The Ohio Risk Assessment System

Edward J. Latessa, Brian Lovins, and Jennifer Lux

Overview

In 2009, the University of Cincinnati Corrections Institute (UCCI), in collaboration with the Ohio Department of Rehabilitation and Correction (ODRC) and the Ohio Office of Criminal Justice Services (OCJS), created and validated the Ohio Risk Assessment System (ORAS)—a fourth generation actuarial risk assessment system[1] designed to help correctional agencies identify offenders' risk and criminogenic need factors.

In Ohio, community corrections refers to a system of facilities or agencies that provide residential and non-residential services to convicted offenders. The programs may receive state funds, but are based in and operated by local communities (Litteral, 2015). Community Corrections Act (CCA) programs (Harris, 1996), for example, are an important component in the continuum of sanctions available to Ohio's local courts from pretrial services and diversion programs, to probation supervision services, and diversion from prison, to supervision of offenders before and after placement in a community-based correctional facility (CBCF) or halfway house. In addition, CCA programs may provide supervision services for offenders under judicial release from prison. Supervision of these offenders in CCA programs after release from CBCFs, halfway houses, and prisons provides for a transition from a structured setting into the community (Litteral, 2015). The goal of both CCA programs and CBCFs is to reduce the number of non-dangerous offenders committed to state-level institutions and county jails (Shelton, 1992), while the goal of community residential services such as halfway houses and residential placement is to provide supervision and treatment services for offenders under probation supervision or released from state prison or participating in ODRC's Transitional Control program[2] (ODRC, 2008).

In 2002, ODRC contracted with UCCI to examine the effectiveness of Ohio's halfway houses and CBCFs at reducing recidivism. One of the key findings from the study was that reductions in recidivism varied substantially based on offenders' risk levels. The study demonstrated, more specifically, that providing intensive interventions to higher risk offenders resulted in reductions in recidivism, while, conversely, providing intensive interventions

---

1 Fourth generation risk assessments consider offenders' risk and needs, while also identifying responsivity factors and case management strategies to facilitate successful intervention (Andrews, Bonta, & Wormith, 2006).

2 Offenders participating in the Transitional Control program may be placed in a halfway house for up to the last 180 days of their sentence (ODRC, 2008).

Handbook of Recidivism Risk/Needs Assessment Tools, First Edition. Edited by Jay P. Singh, Daryl G. Kroner, J. Stephen Wormith, Sarah L. Desmarais, and Zachary Hamilton.
© 2018 John Wiley & Sons, Ltd. Published 2018 by John Wiley & Sons, Ltd.

to lower risk offenders increased recidivism (Lowenkamp & Latessa, 2002). A subsequent study of community correctional supervision programs (Lowenkamp & Latessa, 2005) and follow-up CBCF and halfway house study completed in 2010, supported these results (Latessa, Brusman-Lovins, & Smith, 2010). Agencies that provided programming and treatment to higher risk offenders tended to see reductions in recidivism, but many of those same agencies saw increases in recidivism when they provided programming and treatment to lower risk offenders.

Importantly, the 2002, 2005, and 2010 studies revealed that correctional agencies across the state of Ohio used a variety of risk assessment instruments. For example, assessment tools ranged from using "home-grown" assessment instruments to actuarial risk assessment instruments, such as the Level of Service Inventory–Revised (LSI-R), to using no risk assessment instrument at all. After consultation with ODRC, OCJS, and local jurisdictions, the decision was thus made to standardize the offender assessment process across the state by developing a non-proprietary assessment system—the ORAS.

The ORAS is unique for two reasons. First, it assesses individuals at several points in the criminal justice system, including pretrial, community supervision, prison intake, and prison reentry. Second, it promotes consistency and objectivity in the assessment of offenders' risk and needs across the state as well as throughout the criminal justice system as a whole. These characteristics lead to improved communication amongst staff and help agencies avoid duplication of information from one point in the system to another (Vera Institute of Justice, 2011).

The ORAS now consists of six instruments that span the criminal justice system: (1) Pre-Trial Assessment Tool (PAT), (2) Misdemeanor Assessment Tool (MAT), (3) Community Supervision Tool (CST), (4) Prison Intake Tool (PIT), (5) Reentry Tool (RT), and (6) Supplemental Reentry Tool (SRT).[3] There are also three screening instruments: (1) Misdemeanor Screening Tool (MST), (2) Community Supervision Screening Tool (CSST), and (3) Prison Screening Tool (PST) that are designed to allow corrections professionals to determine the likelihood of recidivism for a large offender population relatively quickly.

All of the ORAS instruments examine factors about an offender that are both static (i.e., cannot be changed) and dynamic (i.e., can be changed) in nature, regardless of which phase in the criminal justice system the instrument may be used at. Table 7.1 provides an overview of each ORAS instrument. As can be seen, the tools used during earlier phases of the criminal justice system (PAT, MAT, and CST), are to be used in a community setting, while tools used during later phases of the system (PIT, RT, and SRT) are to be used in an institutional setting. Post-conviction, as offenders move deeper into the system, the instruments include more items and are separated into distinct domains that help criminal justice agencies and offenders alike identify the offender's risk and criminogenic need factors. Altogether, the identification of risk, need, *and* responsivity factors on the CST, PIT, RT, and SRT, enables staff to work in conjunction with their clients to build an individualized case plan and track behavior change over time.

Since the development of the ORAS, the tools have been implemented in several states and local counties and agencies outside of Ohio. To-date, nearly 15 states use the ORAS statewide and over 30 agencies use or are actively planning to use the tools at the county or local level.

---

3 The MAT and SRT were not part of the original ORAS system and were added later.

Table 7.1 Summary of the Ohio Risk Assessment System (ORAS)

	Pretrial Tool	Misdemeanor Assessment Tool	Community Supervision Tool	Prison Intake Tool	Reentry Tool	Supplemental Reentry Tool
Phase	Conducted at entry into the criminal justice system	Conducted prior to probation/community supervision for misdemeanants	Conducted prior to probation/community supervision and/or during parole/post-release supervision	Conducted at intake into prison	Conducted prior to release for offenders sentenced to 4 or more years in prison	Conducted prior to release for offenders sentenced to less than 4 years in prison
Domains	• Criminal History (4 items) • Employment (1 item) • Substance Abuse (2 items) • Residential Stability (1 item)	• Criminal History (2 items) • Employment (4 items) • Substance Abuse (3 items) • Peer Associations (2 item) • Criminal Attitudes & Behavioral Patterns (1 item)	• Criminal History (6 items) • Education, Employment, & Financial Situation (6 items) • Family & Social Support (5 items) • Neighborhood Problems (2 items) • Substance Abuse (5 items) • Peer Associations (4 items) • Criminal Attitudes & Behavioral Patterns (7 items)	• Criminal History (7 items) • Education, Employment, & Financial Situation (6 items) • Family & Social Support (5 items) • Substance Abuse & Mental Health (5 items) • Criminal Attitudes & Behavioral Patterns (7 items)	• Criminal History (8 items) • Education, Employment, & Financial Situation (4 items) • Criminal Attitudes & Behavioral Patterns (7 items)	• Criminal History (8 items) • Education, Employment, & Financial Situation (7 items) • Substance Abuse & Mental Health (4 items) • Criminal Attitudes & Behavioral Patterns (12 items)
Number of Variables	7	12	35	31	19	32
Outcomes Predicted	New Arrest Failure to Appear	New Arrest	New Arrest	New Arrest	New Arrest	New Arrest
Corresponding Screening Tool	No	Yes	Yes	Yes	No	No

Theoretical Framework

One of the overall goals of the ORAS at the onset of its development and validation, was to conform to the principles of effective classification (i.e., the risk, need, responsivity, and professional discretion principles). Research over the last several years has consistently shown that correctional programs that adhere to the principles of risk, need, and responsivity are more effective in changing offender behavior, and ultimately, reducing recidivism (e.g., Andrews, Bonta, & Hoge, 1990; Dowden & Andrews, 1999a, 1999b; Lowenkamp, 2004; Lowenkamp, Latessa, & Smith, 2006; Lowenkamp, Pealer, Latessa, & Smith, 2006). In line with other fourth generation risk assessment tools, the ORAS is designed to be the engine that drives effective interventions with offenders (Latessa & Lowenkamp, 2005).

Briefly, the ORAS helps agencies meet the risk principle by identifying *who* should receive the most treatment to reduce their risk of recidivism (i.e., higher-risk offenders). In addition, it helps agencies meet the need principle by uncovering *what* specific factors should be targeted to change criminal behavior. These criminogenic needs are dynamic risk factors, such as (1) antisocial attitudes, values, and beliefs; (2) antisocial peers; (3) antisocial personality characteristics; (4) family and marital discord; (5) poor education/employment performance; (6) few pro-social leisure activities; and (7) substance abuse. The ORAS also assists correctional agencies in meeting the responsivity principle by identifying barriers to treatment that may prevent an offender from being successful on community supervision or in an institutional setting (e.g., low intelligence, physical handicap, reading and writing limitations, mental health problems, motivation, transportation, child care, language, cultural barriers, history of abuse/neglect, anxiety). In this way, the ORAS helps staff determine *how* to deliver treatment in a way that matches offenders' personalities, abilities, and motivation levels. Finally, the principle of professional discretion recognizes that staff conducting the ORAS are responsible for identifying offenders' risk, need, and responsivity factors and making decisions about supervision and treatment strategies based on this information. While these decisions may be individualized to a specific offender's needs, actuarial tools are designed to predict group behavior. As a result, the ORAS allows corrections professionals to override the assessment instruments under specific circumstances (Latessa, Lemke, Makarios, Smith, & Lowenkamp, 2010).

The Creation and Validation of the ORAS

The original ORAS study was prospective in nature and included the creation and validation of four instruments—the PAT, CST, PIT, and RT—and two screening tools—the CSST and PST. During the planning phase of the project, UCCI researchers collaborated with ODRC staff to create structured data collection instruments. The instruments were developed in accordance with the research on the correlates of crime and antisocial behavior, which together, included over 200 potential risk factors. The data collection phase involved extensive interviews with offenders from various points in Ohio's criminal justice system. Both a self-report questionnaire and semi-structured face-to-face interviews were conducted, along with official record checks. Offenders were then followed for a minimum of one year to gather recidivism data (Latessa et al., 2010).

Once all data were collected, the validation phase began. This phase involved examining all of the items originally included on the data collection sheets, determining which items from the tool were found to be related to recidivism at each particular point in the criminal justice system, and combining the items into scales so that larger scores were associated with a greater likelihood of recidivism. Point values were assigned to individual items using a modified Burgess method (Burgess, 1928). In this way, scores of 1 and 2 indicate that a risk factor is present and a score of 0 indicates that a risk factor is not present. The items were subsequently combined to create a total risk scale for each tool and cutoff scores were further determined to divide cases into different risk level categories (e.g., low, moderate, high, and very high). When appropriate, different risk level categories were created for males and females (Latessa et al., 2010).

UCCI researchers recognized that many of the existing risk assessment instruments were not designed to accurately assess offenders who were incarcerated for long periods of time. As a result, many of the typical indicators, such as current employment, peer associations, and neighborhood, were no longer valid. In this way, many states were either modifying the instruments without conducting the needed research, or were simply ignoring the factors that were irrelevant for offenders with a long-term prison sentence. The original RT was therefore designed to be used with offenders who are reentering the community after a longer stay in prison (four years or more). Subsequently, the SRT instrument was developed using data from the original ORAS study to be used with offenders who are reentering the community after a short stay in prison (less than four years).

In 2014, UCCI collaborated with ODRC and several municipal courts across Ohio to examine the validity and feasibility of conducting the CST instrument on misdemeanant offenders. While the CST was found to be valid for misdemeanor offenders, constraints around large caseloads, and the amount of time it took to conduct a CST interview ultimately created a barrier for municipal courts to implement the assessment process. As such, the MAT, and corresponding screening instrument, the MST, were created and validated for municipal court populations using misdemeanant assessment data from 2012. Both the full MAT instrument and the screener are quicker to administer than the CST, but still aid staff in making supervision and programming recommendations at the municipal court level.

Administering the ORAS

Scoring for the ORAS instruments is based on a review of relevant file information, a face-to-face interview with the client, as well as a self-report questionnaire. When necessary, collateral information is also gathered to verify that information provided during the interview is accurate and/or to fill in any missing gaps. Once all of the data from the interview, self-report, and collateral resources are gathered, the assessor consults the tool's corresponding scoring guide to determine how each item should be scored. The scoring guide provides a brief overview of the assessment tool as well as an item-by-item explanation of the scoring criteria. Overall scores are subsequently based on a summation of all of the items, with higher scores indicating a greater level of risk to reoffend. As discussed, each domain can also be examined in order to determine offenders' unique criminogenic need areas for the longer instruments that include distinct sections. These may subsequently be used to build the offender's case plan, prioritizing areas of need that may be the riskiest or most immediate. Finally, each instrument includes a section where the assessor can identify offenders' specific responsivity factors or barriers to treatment. These factors are not included directly into the risk score, but they represent those characteristics of the offender and his or her circumstances that may be relevant to case planning.

While the final score and overall risk level of an offender are to be based on the structured scoring guide discussed earlier in the chapter, the ORAS also follows the principle of professional discretion in that it recognizes that the tools may not uncover every possible scenario or identify every possible criminogenic need for a particular case (Latessa et al., 2010).

Training Requirements and Qualifications

ORAS end-user training, as well as training-for-trainers, is offered through UCCI. The Institute does not require that end-users or trainers have specific certifications, licensures, or titles/positions at their agency, as long as they attend the training and are certified to use the instruments. The end-user session (i.e., the training to certify staff to conduct the ORAS instruments) is two consecutive days on-site and may include training agency staff on all of the ORAS instruments or only those instruments that are pertinent to the tools the agency will be using. The training consists of a brief overview of the risk, need, responsivity, and override principles; an introduction to the ORAS instruments; and a review of how each item on the tools is scored, followed by several opportunities to practice instruments' scoring. At the end of the training, staff are required to take a certification test to ensure they understand how to score the tools accurately.

A five-day training-for-trainers training is also offered through UCCI for agencies seeking to build their own capacity to train end-users. For the training-for-trainers session, trainees are required to be certified end-users and need to have completed several ORAS assessments on offenders. During the first three days of the training, UCCI staff help prepare the trainers for the end-user training. The last two days are then reserved for those trainers to conduct an end-user session with observation and feedback from the UCCI staff.

Finally, UCCI, in conjunction with the University of Cincinnati Information Technology Solutions Center, has developed a web-based automated system that allows users to enter ORAS assessment data, as well as create individualized offender cases plans, summary reports, and aggregate reports at the agency level. Figure 7.1 presents an example of the results that are displayed from the automated system once an individual's assessment is completed. In this particular example, the offender's total CST assessment score is 28, indicating that he is at high risk of reoffending in the future. Even further, the figure indicates that, of the seven domains included on the tool, three areas are driving the offender's high-risk level: (1) Education, Employment and Financial Situation, (2) Peer Associations, and (3) Attitudes and Behavioral

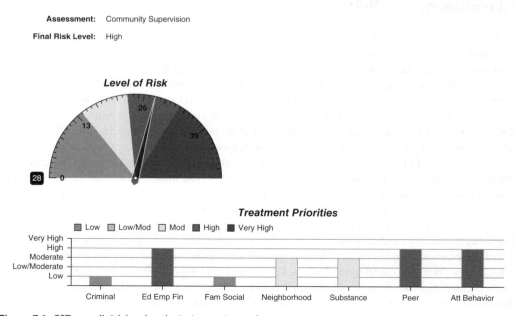

Figure 7.1 CST overall risk level and criminogenic needs.

Patterns. As such, it would be suggested that the probation officer and the offender work together to create a case plan that prioritizes and targets these areas for change through programming and intervention strategies.

The Validity of the Ohio Risk Assessment System

Ohio Validation

The initial validation of the ORAS was completed in 2009 when the instruments were created. UCCI collected data on 1,857 offenders across four stages of the criminal justice system, including pretrial, community supervision, prison intake, and reentry to the community to develop the PAT, CST, PIT, RT, and eventually, the SRT, respectively. The following subsections provide a review of the initial efforts to develop each of the ORAS instruments, as well as subsequent studies that have been conducted to revalidate some of the tools.

ORAS Pretrial Assessment Tool

The PAT was developed using a sample of 452 offenders across multiple jurisdictions in Ohio. The average time at risk for the Pretrial Tool was 11.9 months. The tool was split almost evenly by race, with 50.2% of the sample White and 46.5% African American. Gender was split approximately 75% male and 25% female.

The PAT was designed to predict new arrests, offenders' likelihood of failing to appear in court, and failure for either reason at the pretrial stage of the criminal justice system. Unlike the longer ORAS assessments which focus on assessing longer term failure, the PAT was designed to measure a shorter period of time between arrest/release from jail and final disposition. The PAT includes seven items that focus on these specific predictors of pretrial failure—three items associated with criminal history, one item measuring employment, one item measuring residential stability, and two items measuring substance abuse. Using a modified Burgess scale, raw scores on the PAT range from 0 to 9. The composite risk score subsequently translates into three risk level categories—low, moderate, and high.

Related to the predictive validity of the tool, results from the initial validation study indicate that offenders recidivated at increasingly greater rates as risk levels increased on the PAT instrument. Specifically, approximately 5% of low-risk cases were re-arrested or failed to appear, approximately 18% of moderate-risk cases were re-arrested/failed to appear, and an estimated 30% of high-risk cases were re-arrested or failed to appear. The PAT's total score was also found to be significantly correlated with outcome ($r = .22$), indicating that as total PAT scores increase, so too does an offender's likelihood to reoffend or not show up for court. Finally, the Receiver Operating Curve (ROC) Area Under the Curve (AUC) analysis yielded a value of .65.

ORAS Community Supervision Tool

One of the more widely studied tools within the ORAS suite of instruments is the CST. The CST has demonstrated its ability to predict re-arrest, with the exception of the PAT which also includes failure to appear, across multiple and diverse jurisdictions. Originally developed and validated on a sample of offenders from Ohio, the CST has been revalidated on offender samples from Indiana, Texas, and Massachusetts. The initial validation sample closely reflected Ohio's criminal justice demographics and included 672 offenders. Approximately 76% of the sample was male with an average age of about 32 years. Related to race, 70% of the sample was Caucasian, while the remaining 27% and 3% were African American and a combination of Hispanic, Asian, and Pacific Islander, respectively. The average number of months at risk was 16.9.

The CST was designed to predict new arrests and includes 35 items distributed across seven domains: (1) Criminal History, (2) Education, Employment, and (3) Financial Situation, (4) Neighborhood Problems, (5) Substance Use, (6) Peer Associations, and (7) Criminal Attitudes and Behavioral Patterns. Each domain ranges from two to seven items, with a composite score ranging between 0 to 49. The composite risk score translates into four risk levels—low, moderate, high, and very high for males and low, low/moderate, moderate, and high for females.

In addition to examining the CST's overall validity, UCCI examined its validity for gender subgroups to ensure the tool worked just as well for females as it did for males. The results indicated that each predictor was valid for both males and females; however, the overall base rate of reoffending was significantly lower for females compared to males. To offset a potential overclassification of female offenders, UCCI developed separate cutoff scores for males and females. Interestingly, UCCI found that when adjusting cutoff scores, nearly 65% of the female population fell in the low or moderate categories, while only 55% of the male sample fell in the low or moderate risk categories. These findings suggest that while predictors of recidivism are similar for males and females, the proportion of females who are at the lower end of the spectrum is higher.

When examining the predictive validity of the CST on the initial population, UCCI found incremental increases in rates of recidivism for both male and female subgroups. In particular, low-risk males recidivated at a rate of approximately 9%, moderate-risk males recidivated at a rate of approximately 34%, high-risk males recidivated at a rate of approximately 59%, and very high-risk males recidivated at a rate of approximately 69%. The correlation between males' overall risk level and recidivism was also found to be relatively strong ($r = .37$), suggesting that as offenders' CST risk levels increased, so too did their rates of recidivism. The AUC value of .71 further suggests that the CST predicts male offenders' likelihood of getting a new arrest substantially better than chance alone.

In line with the rates of failure for males, females' rates of recidivism increased as risk levels increased. Specifically, low-risk females recidivated at a rate of approximately 9%, low/moderate-risk females recidivated at a rate of approximately 22%, moderate-risk females recidivated at a rate of approximately 40%, and high-risk females recidivated at a rate of 50%.[4] Females' CST total scores were significantly and positively associated with recidivism ($r = .30$) and the AUC suggested that the instrument predicted rates of failure better than chance alone (AUC = .69) (see Figure 7.2).

When examining domain scores for the CST, findings from the initial study indicated that the strongest domains were Peer Associations ($r = .32$) and Attitudes and Behavioral Patterns ($r = .24$). The Education, Employment, and Financial Situation ($r = .22$), Criminal History ($r = .20$), and Neighborhood Problems ($r = .20$), on the other hand, demonstrated moderate correlations, while the Substance Abuse ($r = .14$) and Family and Social Support ($r = .12$) demonstrated weaker relationships.

Indiana Validation

In subsequent validation studies of the ORAS, the CST has demonstrated similar results to what was found in Ohio. In Indiana, for example, offenders recidivated at an increasingly greater rate by risk level (Latessa, Lovins, & Makarios, 2013). Specifically, low-risk males recidivated at a rate of 13%, moderate-risk males recidivated at a rate of 28%, high-risk males recidivated at a rate of 42%, and very high-risk males recidivated at a rate of 56%. The *r* value of .29 revealed

---

4 Due to the small sample size there is no "very high" category for females.

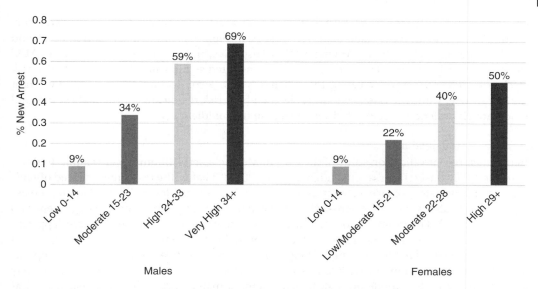

Figure 7.2 CST risk levels by recidivism for males and females. From Ohio Sample.

that the relationship between males' risk levels and recidivism was relatively strong. While the strength of the relationship between risk levels and females' rates of recidivism in Indiana was considerably weaker compared to the relationship between risk level and females' rates of recidivism in Ohio (*r* = .12 versus *r* = .30, respectively), results from Indiana still indicated that low-risk females recidivated at a lower rate, compared to their moderate-risk counterparts, who in turn recidivated at a lower rate compared to their high-risk counterparts (14%, 23%, and 26%, respectively).

Texas Validation

The validation of the CST in Texas provided an opportunity to examine the tool in greater detail due to a much larger sample size (*N* = 5,481), as well as a more diverse population (41.5% Caucasian/Non-Hispanic, 19.2% African American/Non-Hispanic, 37% Hispanic, and 1.4% inclusive of all other races) compared to previous validation studies. In addition to a racially diverse population, the Texas sample provided a diverse geographic sample with 35% of the offenders living in smaller rural counties, 25% living in medium size counties, and 40% living in larger urban counties.

Similar to previous validation studies, the CST in Texas was found to be predictive of future recidivism (Lovins & May, 2014). For both males and females, more specifically, low-risk offenders recidivated at the lowest rates, compared to low/moderate-risk offenders, who in turn recidivated at lower rates compared to high-risk offenders, and very high-risk offenders (approximately 11%, 23%, 38%, and 50%, respectively for males and approximately 8%, 20%, 31%, and 42%, respectively for females). The strength of the relationship between risk levels and recidivism was relatively strong for both gender subgroups (*r* = .29 for males and *r* = .26 for females) and AUCs suggested that the tool was predicting recidivism better than chance alone (AUC = .67 for males and .68 for females).

In addition to examining the predictive validity of the CST for males and females, the Texas study also examined the predictive validity of the tool for different racial subgroups (Caucasian/Non-Hispanics, African American/Non-Hispanics, and Hispanics). Findings suggested that the

CST was significantly correlated with outcome once again. Specifically, the tool yielded a correlation of .27 and an AUC value of .67 for Caucasian/Non-Hispanics, a correlation of .26 and an AUC value of .65 for African American/Non-Hispanics, and a correlation of .31 and an AUC value of .69 for Hispanics. The findings also demonstrated significant differences between risk levels for each subgroup, indicating that offenders who were deemed low risk recidivated at the lowest rate, while offenders who were deemed high risk recidivated at the highest rate and moderate-risk offenders recidivated somewhere in the middle.

Massachusetts Validation

In the most recent validation study of the CST in Massachusetts, findings were similar to those described previously (Latessa, Lux, Lugo, & Long, 2016). That is, the instrument placed offenders into appropriate risk level categories, as both males and females recidivated at an increasingly greater rate by risk level across the study's outcomes of interest (new arraignment and new conviction). For example, low-risk males were rearraigned at the lowest rate (approximately 21%), followed by moderate-risk males (approximately 35%) who were rearraigned at a lower rate compared to high-risk males (approximately 47%) and very high-risk males (approximately 60%). In addition, low-risk females were rearraigned at the lowest rate (approximately 21%), followed by low/moderate-risk females (approximately 32%) who were rearraigned at a lower rate compared to moderate-risk females (approximately 43%) and high-risk females (approximately 46%). Levels of risk were found to be significantly different from one another for both gender subgroups. In addition, the relationship between risk levels and new arraignment for both males and females was relatively strong and AUC values were well over 50% (i.e., chance) ($r = .25$ and AUC = .65; $r = .21$ and AUC = .63, respectively). Finally, these results held true when examining the predictive validity of the CST for Whites and non-Whites ($r = .24$ and AUC = .65; $r = .22$ and AUC = .63, respectively).

ORAS Prison Intake Tool

The PIT was developed to assist prison systems in assessing risk of offenders as they enter a secure institutional setting. While the initial study also examined predictors of institutional misconduct, the PIT's real value was in identifying those predictors at the front end of a prison stay that were still predictive as the offender returned to the community. Ultimately, the PIT provides institutions with specific measures that, if not addressed while the person is incarcerated, will lead to greater increases in recidivism. The original PIT sample was comprised of 423 offenders. Sixty-three percent were male and 54% were Caucasian. Offenders, on average, were approximately 33 years old. The average time at risk upon release was 13.3 months.

The PIT was also designed to predict new arrests and includes age of offender at the time of the assessment, plus 30 items distributed across five domains: (1) Criminal History; (2) Education, Employment, and Financial Situation; (3) Family and Social Support; (4) Substance Abuse and Mental Health; and (5) Criminal Attitudes and Behavioral Patterns. Each domain includes between five and seven items, with a total score ranging between 0 and 40. The composite risk score translates into four risk levels for males—low, moderate, high, and very high—and three risk levels for females—low, moderate, and high.

Findings from the initial validation study suggest that the tool was correlated with both male and female new arrests at .32 and .35, respectively, and predicted better than chance alone (AUC = .67 and AUC = .69, respectively). Rates of recidivism significantly increased as levels of risk increased for both gender subgroups as well. Specifically, low-risk males reoffended at a rate of approximately 17%, moderate-risk males reoffended at a rate of approximately 32%, high-risk males reoffended at a rate of approximately 58%, and very high-risk males reoffended at a rate of approximately 71%. Low-risk females reoffended at a rate of approximately 17%, moderate-risk females reoffended at a rate of approximately 33%, and high-risk females reoffended at a rate of approximately 63%. As for the specific domains, the PIT ranged from stronger correlations for the Criminal History (r = .22) and Attitudes and Behavioral Patterns (r = .21) domains, to moderate correlations for the Education, Employment, and Financial Situation (r = .19), Substance Abuse (r = .17), and Family and Social Support (r = .12) domains.

Ohio Risk Assessment System-Reentry and Supplemental Reentry Tools

The last two tools are the Reentry and Supplemental Reentry Tools. Both instruments are to be used on the back end of the system to develop a clear reentry plan for offenders as they step down from incarceration. Recall that the SRT was developed to assess those offenders who were in prison for a shorter period of time (under four years) to determine their unique reentry needs. The SRT includes age of the offender at the time of the assessment and has a total of 30 items across four domains: (1) Criminal History; (2) Education, Employment, and Social Support; (3) Substance Abuse and Mental Health; and (4) Criminal Attitudes and Behavioral Patterns. The composite score ranges between 0 and 45, translating in to low, moderate, high, and very high risk level categories based on different cutoff scores for males and females.

Findings from the initial validation study suggested that SRT risk levels were strongly associated with outcome and predicted better than chance alone for both males and females (r = .30 and AUC = .66; r = .27 and AUC = .65, respectively). Groups were significantly different from one another as well. Low-risk males reoffended at a rate of 13%, moderate-risk males reoffended at a rate of 38%, high-risk males reoffended at a rate of 51%, and very high-risk males reoffended at a rate of 63%. Similarly, low-risk females reoffended at a rate of 9%, moderate risk females reoffended at a rate of 32%, high-risk females reoffended at a rate of 45%, and very high-risk females reoffended at a rate of 75%. As for the four domains, Education, Employment, and Social Support (r = .23) and Criminal History (r = .23) were the most highly correlated areas, with Substance Abuse and Mental Health (r = .20) and Attitudes and Behavioral Problems (r = .18) falling just slightly lower.

Related to the RT assessment, initial data were also collected from the Ohio sample. Seventy-seven percent of the sample was male with nearly half being Caucasian (49%). The average time at risk was 12.8 months and the average age of the sample was 31.6 years. The RT includes age of the offender at the time of the assessment, plus 19 items across three domains: (1) Criminal History; (2) Education, Employment, and Financial Situation; and (3) Criminal Attitudes and Behavioral Patterns. The composite score ranges between 0 and 28, with cutoff scores for males translating into four categories—low, moderate, high, and very high and three categories for females—low, moderate, and high.

The RT demonstrated relatively strong correlations with recidivism (r = .36). As for the ability of the RT to predict recidivism for males and females, the RT demonstrated a moderate correlation for males (r = .30) and a strong correlation for females (r = .44). AUC values also demonstrated that the RT predicted recidivism for both gender subgroups better than chance alone (AUC = .65 and AUC = .77, respectively). Significant differences were found between risk level categories as well. Here, low-risk males and low-risk females reoffended at a lower rate, compared to their moderate-risk counterparts, who in turn reoffended at a lower rate compared to their high-risk counterparts (approximately 21%, 50%, and 64%, respectively for males and approximately 7%, 44%, and 56%, respectively for females).

In the revalidation study conducted in Indiana (Latessa et al., 2013), the RT sample was comprised of 59% male and 71% Caucasian offenders. The average time at risk was 23.6 months and the average age was 34.6 years. When examining the predictive accuracy of the RT for males and females, the findings demonstrated slightly lower correlations compared to the initial study's findings in Ohio. Specifically, male RT scores were correlated with re-arrest at .22 and females at .18. Risk level subgroups were significantly different from one another, however. For males, 29% of the low-risk group was re-arrested, while 41% of the moderate-risk group, 57% of the high-risk group, and 63% of the very high-risk group was re-arrested. For females, 15% of the low-risk group was re-arrested, while 33% of the moderate-risk group and 47% of the high-risk group was re-arrested.

As discussed, the MAT instrument was created several years after the original ORAS validation study in Ohio. This sample consisted of 1,722 offenders, approximately 76% of which were male and 86% of which were White. The average age of the MAT group was approximately 33 years. The follow-up time was just short of one year (11 months).

The MAT was designed to predict new arrests and consists of 12 items with a composite score ranging between 0 and 21. The tool includes two items related to criminal history; four items related to education, employment, and free time; three items related to substance abuse; two items related to peer associates; and one item related to antisocial attitudes. The composite risk score translates into three risk levels—low, moderate, and high for both males and females based on different cutoffs.

Results from the initial validation study of the MAT suggested that both males and females were being placed in accurate risk level groups. The tool, more specifically, indicated that low-risk males and low-risk females reoffended at the lowest rates (19% and 31%, respectively), followed by moderate-risk males and moderate-risk females (39% and 42%, respectively), followed by high-risk males and high-risk females (53% and 53%, respectively). Correlations examining the relationship between risk levels and recidivism indicated that as offenders' risk levels increased, so too did their likelihood of recidivism ($r = .23$ for males and $r = .18$ for females). AUCs also suggested that the tool was able to predict offenders' likelihood of recidivism better than chance alone (AUC = .63 for males and AUC = .60 for females).

The Reliability of the Ohio Risk Assessment System

During the recent validation study in Massachusetts, UCCI also examined the inter-rater reliability of the CST instrument (Latessa et al., 2016). Five offender vignettes were created so that trained probation officers could score the CST assessment independently based on the same information. In addition to a written narrative, participants received a filled out self-report and file review/collateral information for each scenario. Besides scoring out the assessment for each vignette, officers completed a demographics survey so that potential differences in officer characteristics could be examined.

Average inter-rater agreement overall fell just below 80%. This was likely due to the fact that there were a substantial number of individual items that produced less than 80% agreement levels. In particular, 18 items yielded rates of inter-rater reliability below 80%. Some domains appeared to have higher rates of agreement over others. In particular, the Criminal History; Education, Employment, and Financial Situation; Family and Social Support; Neighborhood Problems; and Substance Use domains produced rates of agreement at or above 80%, on average (82.2%, 86.2% 80%, 86.7%, and 85.7%, respectively). Some of the more subjective areas—Peer Associations and Criminal Attitudes and Behavioral Patterns—produced lower rates of reliability, on average (72.8% and 79.6%, respectively). Perhaps surprising, no significant differences were found when officer characteristics were examined. For example, both male and female officers yielded average CST scores of 29. In addition, both officers with little experience working for the probation department and officers with more experience working for the probation department yielded average CST scores of 29.

Implementation Research

To date there have not been any satisfaction or fidelity studies on the ORAS; however, the system has informed policy. For example, following its participation in the Justice Reinvestment Initiative, Ohio passed legislation that limited the placement of low-risk offenders in CBCFs. Further, in 2011, House Bill 86 became effective, requiring ODRC to adopt a single validated risk assessment tool to assess the likelihood of future crimes by adult offenders. The tools must be used by each municipal, county, and common pleas court when it orders an assessment for sentencing or other purposes, the probation department serving those courts, state and local correctional institutions, private correctional institutions, CBCFs, and the adult parole authority and parole board. The Bill also requires each entity to have policies that cover integrating the various tools into operations, administrative oversight, staff training, quality assurance, and data collection and data sharing. The ORAS has also been incorporated into ODRC policy and community correctional agencies business rules. The ORAS is currently used statewide (http://www.drc.ohio.gov/web/oras.htm).

Indiana has also adopted polices concerning the Indiana Risk Assessment System (IRAS) and its corresponding system for juveniles—the Indiana Youth Assessment System (IYAS). The state has established criteria for training and certification of all users and has also adopted system-wide policies for administering the tools. More specifically, the policies make it mandatory for all supervising agencies to use the IRAS and IYAS, and to also record the assessment information in the state's web-based database. The goal is to improve communication between the Indiana Department of Correction, county probation departments, problem-solving courts, and community corrections agencies, as well as the parole authority. Policy materials include a statement on the purpose of the risk assessment tools, recommended best practices, minimum statewide policies, requirements for case planning, and policies regarding reassessment. The Supreme Court also ruled in 2010 that judges may consider the results of assessments conducted by the county probation department when making sentencing decisions (*Malenchik v. State of Indiana*, 928 N.E.2D 564). This ruling, in turn, provides sentencing judges with the ability to formulate and enforce an individualized case plan for offenders. Importantly, the state has a designated Risk Assessment Task Force that was established early on in the training and implementation phase of the project that continues to oversee and monitor the use of assessments across Indiana (http://www.in.gov/judiciary/cadp/2762.htm).

Finally, in Texas, the Texas Risk Assessment System (TRAS) results have been integrated into state and local policies to ensure the utility of risk and need at every stage in the criminal justice system. Policies include, for example, partnerships with local research partners to provide ongoing analysis, monitoring, and assessment of the implementation of the tool and assessment of all offenders, including felony and misdemeanor offenders under community supervision. When the system was first implemented, over 3,000 community supervision officers were trained across the state. Today, the TRAS curriculum is included in all newly hired community supervision officer certification courses. The state is also planning to use the assessment data to assist in resource discussions, quality assurance, and funding decisions moving forward (https://www.tdcj.state.tx.us/index.html).

Use of the ORAS

In Ohio, there are approximately 4,000 trained and certified ORAS end-users from the afore-mentioned entities. The state also has a cadre of 70 trainers and six master trainers. The results from the ORAS guide the development of offender case plans, determine supervision levels, program referrals and placements, as well as types of treatment intervention. Data from ODRC indicate that, as of November 2016, the following number of ORAS assessments have been conducted:

- PAT: 46,247
- CSST: 28,398
- CST: 365,797
- PST: 122,483
- PIT: 76,247
- RT: 13,320
- SRT: 62,461

In Indiana, approximately 3,000 trained IRAS end-users have been certified across the state from various entities. The state also has 15 trainers and two master trainers. Data from the Indiana Department of Correction indicate that as of August 2016, the following number of ORAS assessments have been conducted:

- PAT: 38,200
- CSST: 185,325
- CST: 407,301
- PIT: 66,436
- RT: 11,788
- SRT: 40,957

Finally, in Texas, over 4,000 staff have been trained and certified to use the TRAS and just over 100 trainers have completed a training-for-trainers session. With the nearly 50,000 TRAS assessments completed each year, it is beneficial that the state has invested in certifying their own trainers to continue to build sustainability of the instrument internally.

Benefits of ORAS

There are several benefits to the ORAS. First, not only does the system classify offenders into risk level categories, but deeper-end instruments (i.e., those instruments used at the probation, prison intake, and reentry levels) provide case managers and other criminal justice professionals with the tools to identify and prioritize offenders' criminogenic needs. This allows agencies and facilities to effectively and efficiently allocate resources in a manner that reduces recidivism.

Second, the ORAS provides reliable assessment results at every stage of the criminal justice system, facilitating consistency in information within a local county or agency and across a state, more generally. By adopting the ORAS statewide, Ohio and others were able to bring uniformity to the assessment process so that duplication of information is reduced and communication and sharing of information is increased. The development of the web-based system is also important for keeping data consistent and improving communication, as it allows criminal justice agencies to enter ORAS assessment data in one web-based portal that can be accessed from anywhere that provides internet capabilities.

Third, the ORAS encourages states and local agencies to conform to the principles of effective classification. Specifically, the tools aid in separating offenders into risk groups based on their likelihood to reoffend, identifying dynamic risk factors that can be used to develop individualized case plans, identifying potential barriers to treatment (e.g., lack of motivation, lack of transportation, or mental illness), and providing the flexibility to use professional discretion or override under specific circumstances.

Fourth, unlike machine scored processes, the ORAS is transparent. Those conducting assessments can review the scores and clearly see which factors make up the total risk score/overall risk level. This transparency also opens the door for agencies to verify or validate the items, domains, etc. on the tools, which may lead to increased buy-in from staff and stakeholders. Latessa and Lovins (2010) explain, for example, that when staff and stakeholders trust the tools their agency is using, they are more likely to use them, and use them as intended, than when the instruments have no face validity. Evidence of tools' validity and subsequent support from staff may also help leverage the allocation of resources to particular parts of the department to create and/or expand evidence-based practices and programs (Casey, Warren, & Elek, 2011).

Finally and related to the above discussion, the ORAS is non-proprietary, meaning there is no cost associated with the use of the instruments once staff are trained and certified.[5] This also means that as jurisdictions adopt the tools, they have access to their assessment data so that they are able to conduct validation studies and modify items and cutoff scores, as dictated by research. In Texas, for example, cutoff scores on the CST were changed to ensure offenders were categorized into different risk levels based on actual observed differences in the probability of reoffending within the state. The development of the MAT in Ohio is another example of how data were used to create a shorter instrument to meet the needs of municipal courts that had high volumes of cases.

Current Issues and Future Directions

To date, the ORAS has been implemented throughout various agencies and departments across the state of Ohio, as well as several other states and local agencies. With the increasing number of staff receiving training on the instruments, and the growing number of assessments being conducted each day, UCCI are focusing their efforts on continuous quality improvement strategies and fidelity monitoring. In Ohio, for example, UCCI, in collaboration with ODRC, are conducting a revalidation and reliability study of the instruments. For the revalidation portion of the project, a random sample of assessments will be drawn from each ORAS instrument utilized by the state. This is important, as it will be the first time the instruments are validated based on ODRC assessors completing the instruments, rather than research staff who completed the assessments during the initial validation project. The reliability portion of the study will be conducted online and will include a brief questionnaire about the assessor's experiences with the ORAS system, as well as written offender vignettes that will be scored out by the participants. UCCI also has plans to validate the tools for Colorado, Connecticut, and Vermont and revalidate the tools for Indiana.

---

5 While there is no cost to use the ORAS, there is a cost for the automated version.

References

Andrews, D. A., Bonta, J., & Hoge, R. (1990). Classification for effective rehabilitation: Rediscovering psychology. *Criminal Justice & Behavior, 17*, 19–52.

Andrews, D. A., Bonta, J., & Wormith J. S. (2006). The recent past and near future of risk and/or need assessment. *Crime and Delinquency, 52*, 7–27.

Burgess, E. W. (1928). Factors determining success or failure on parole. In A. A. Bruce, J. Harno, E. W. Burgess, & J. Landesco (Eds.), *The workings of the indeterminate-sentence law and parole system in Illinois* (pp. 221–234). Springfield, IL: State Board of Parole.

Casey, P. M., Warren, R. K., & Elek, J. K. (2011). *Using offender risk and needs assessment information at sentencing: Guidance for courts from a national working group*. National Center for State Courts.

Dowden, C., & Andrews, D. A. (1999a). What works for female offenders: A meta-analytic review. *Crime and Delinquency, 45*, 438–452.

Dowden, C., & Andrews, D. A. (1999b). What works in young offender treatment: A meta-analysis. *Forum on Corrections Research, 11*, 21–24.

Harris, M. K. (1996). Key differences among Community Corrections Acts in the United States: An overview. *The Prison Journal, 76*, 192–238.

Latessa, E. J., Brusman-Lovins, L., & Smith, P. (2010). Follow-up Evaluation of Ohio's community based correctional facility and halfway house programs—outcome study. Technical Report. University of Cincinnati.

Latessa, E. J., Lemke, R., Makarios, M., Smith, P., & Lowenkamp, C. T. (2010). The creation and validation of the Ohio Risk Assessment System (ORAS). *Federal Probation, 74*, 16–22.

Latessa, E. J. & Lowenkamp, C. T. (2005). What are criminogenic needs and why are they important. *For the Record*, 15–16.

Latessa, E. J. & Lovins, B. K. (2010). The role of offender risk assessment: A policy maker guide. *Victims & Offenders, 5*, 203–219.

Latessa, E. J., Lovins, B. K., & Makarios, M. (2013). Validation of the Indiana Risk Assessment System: Final Report. Technical Report. University of Cincinnati.

Latessa, E. J., Lux, J. L., Lugo, M., & Long, J. (2016). Examining the validity and reliability of the Ohio Risk Assessment System Community Supervision Tool and Community Supervision Screening Tool. Technical Report. University of Cincinnati.

Litteral, M. (2015). The Ohio Chief Probation Officers Association (OCPOA) budget testimony FY 2016–2017. Community Corrections Act (CCA) Programs and Community Corrections, Ohio Department of Rehabilitation and Correction.

Lovins, B. K., & May, T. (2014). The Texas Risk Assessment System: Revalidating the ORAS for Texas Community Supervision. Technical Report. Texas Department of Criminal Justice-Community Justice Assistance Division.

Lowenkamp, C. T. (2004). *Correctional program integrity and treatment effectiveness: A multi-site, program-level analysis*. Unpublished doctoral dissertation, University of Cincinnati.

Lowenkamp, C. T., & Latessa E. J. (2002). Evaluation of Ohio's community based correctional facilities and halfway house programs. Technical Report. University of Cincinnati.

Lowenkamp, C. T., & Latessa E. J. (2005). Evaluation of Ohio's CCA funded programs: Final Report. University of Cincinnati.

Lowenkamp, C. T., Latessa, E. J., & Smith, P. (2006). Does correctional program quality really matter? The impact of adhering to the principles of effective interventions. *Criminology & Public Policy, 5*, 575–594.

Lowenkamp, C. T., Pealer, J., Latessa, E. J., & Smith, P. (2006). Adhering to the risk principle: Does it matter for supervision based programs? *Federal Probation, 4*, 3–8.

Malenchik v. State of Indiana 928 N.E.2D 564 (IND. 2010).

Ohio Rehabilitation and Correction (2008). *Best practices tool-kit: Community corrections and evidence-based practices*. Prepared by C. Pettway. Columbus, OH.

Shelton, M. K. (1992). *Community corrections acts for state and local partnerships. Community Corrections Association*. Rockville, MD: Mercury.

Vera Institute of Justice, Center on Sentencing and Corrections. (2011). Evidence-based practices in community supervision [Memorandum]. Delaware Justice Reinvestment Task Force.

8

Self-Appraisal Questionnaire (SAQ): A Tool for Assessing Violent and Non-Violent Recidivism

Wagdy Loza

The Self-Appraisal Questionnaire (SAQ™; Loza, 2005, Mental Health Systems [MHS]) is the first multi-dimensional self-administered questionnaire that was designed to predict violent and non-violent offender recidivism among correctional/forensic populations, and to assist with the assignment of these populations to appropriate treatment/correctional programs and different institutional security levels. The SAQ is a theoretically and empirically based instrument. It was designed to be multifaceted, covering content areas that have been demonstrated to be important for measuring criminogenic factors related to the assessment of recidivism and treatment of offenders.

Multiple studies have demonstrated the concurrent, construct, and predictive validities of the SAQ. It has also been validated in the USA, Australia, Canada, Great Britain, Singapore, South Africa, and several European countries. Samples included Caucasians, African Americans, Asians, Aboriginals, Hispanics, and offenders from other origins. The SAQ has also been validated on females, youth, and mentally ill offenders. Comparative predictive studies over two, five, and nine-year periods have demonstrated that the SAQ is at least as effective as clinician-administered, well-recognized measures. There is also evidence to indicate that the SAQ as a self-report is not affected by self-biases, lying, and/or deception. The strength of the SAQ lies in its economy, utility, ease of use, and inclusion of dynamic factors. The SAQ has been translated into different languages, among them French, Dutch, German, Polish, and Spanish. The current SAQ normative information comes from a sample of over 3,700 American adult male offenders from the states of Pennsylvania and North Carolina, as well as a Canadian sample of over 1,000 adult male offenders.

Development of the SAQ

The SAQ underwent four stages of development. First, a pool of 100 items was developed and the items were grouped into subscales based on the prediction literature. Most items were also designed to be used as targets for treatment in programs dealing with anger; substance abuse; criminal conduct; associates; and antisocial attitudes, beliefs, behaviors, and feelings. The second stage was a consultation process with several experienced correctional psychologists, case management officers, and program delivery officers. This process resulted in the reduction and modification of the item pool to 91. In the third stage of development, offenders completed the scale, and item subscale correlations and frequency of responses were calculated. Items that did not have a strong correlation with their own subscale (i.e., $r < .30$, $p > .001$) or had less than 15% or more than 85% frequency of responding were dropped. Finally, a content validity

Handbook of Recidivism Risk/Needs Assessment Tools, First Edition. Edited by Jay P. Singh, Daryl G. Kroner, J. Stephen Wormith, Sarah L. Desmarais, and Zachary Hamilton.
© 2018 John Wiley & Sons, Ltd. Published 2018 by John Wiley & Sons, Ltd.

study involving additional staff members (four psychologists and a case management officer) was completed. These judges were asked to read each item and place it in the subscale to which they felt it would most belong. Only items that achieved 75% agreement by the judges were retained. This resulted in a 72-item scale with seven subscales. Six of these subscales are used for prediction; the seventh subscale (anger) is used for assignment of offenders to treatment programs dealing with anger.

Description of the SAQ Scales

The SAQ consists of 72 items, which cover seven subscales: Criminal Tendencies (SAQCT) taps into antisocial attitudes, beliefs, behaviors, and feelings. Antisocial Personality Problems (SAQAP) covers characteristics similar to those used to diagnose Antisocial Personality Disorder (APD). Conduct Problems (SAQCP) assesses childhood behavioral problems. Criminal History (SAQCH) has been shown to be a robust predictor of future criminal acts. Alcohol/Drug abuse (SAQAD): The relationship between substance abuse and crime, including violence, is well-documented. Antisocial Associates (SAQASSO): This area has been demonstrated to be valuable in the prediction of recidivism. Anger (SAQAN) measures reaction to anger. This scale is not included in the total score of the SAQ total score because of the controversial relationship between anger and recidivism (Loza & Loza-Fanous, 1999a, 1999b). Validity subscale (SAQVAL): Items on the Validity subscale are incorporated within the other SAQ subscales, which allows one to validate the offender's truthfulness in responding to SAQ items. Examples of an item from each of these subscales include "I have carefully planned a crime before" (CT); "Since the age of 15, I have been described by others as manipulative" (AP); "I have spent time at a group home, a juvenile facility/training school/reformatory" (CP); "My criminal involvement has been getting worse" (CH); "I would not have served time if it was not for my alcohol or drug habit" (AD); and "One reason for my involvement with crime is my friends or acquaintances."

Uses of the SAQ

The SAQ can be used for the following five purposes: Prediction of post-release adjustment such as violent and non-violent recidivism, parole violations, and probability of being convicted of a new offence; prediction of institutional adjustment, and the assignment of offenders to institutional security levels; assignment of offenders to treatment programs such as substance abuse, anger management, cognitive skills, and programs dealing with antisocial attitudes, antisocial behavior, antisocial feelings, antisocial beliefs, insight, and similar types of programs; provision of information which may assist with diagnosing substance abuse, conduct problems, and antisocial personality disorder; and as a pre- and post-treatment measure to assess the effect of treatment and determine changes in offenders' attitude and attributions, particularly those related to his criminal tendencies.

Who Can Administer the SAQ?

The SAQ could be used by diverse forensic professionals such as psychologists, psychiatrists, parole officers, behavioral technologists, nurses, and other personnel trained in administering psychological tests or questionnaires. The psychiatrists and psychologists may use the

SAQ to: (a) reach diagnoses related to antisocial personality disorder, conduct disorder, and substance abuse; (b) make predictions regarding the level of risk a particular offender may pose upon release; (c) make predictions regarding institutional adjustment; (d) make suggestions regarding program participation; (e) design individualized treatment plans to deal with offenders' inappropriate responses to the SAQ's items; and (f) follow up on treatment gains. Parole and case management officers may use the SAQ to help them make decisions regarding the level of risk a particular offender may pose if released and to help determine program needs. Program delivery officers may use the SAQ to assign offenders according to their needs to appropriate programs. For example, offenders with high scores on the SAQ criminal tendencies subscale could be offered a cognitive behavior program. Similarly, offenders with high scores on the SAQ substance abuse subscale could be offered participation in substance abuse programs. Likewise, offenders with high scores on the SAQ anger subscale may be offered an anger management program. Parole officers/case managers, program officers, counsellors, can design individualized treatment plans to address offenders' inappropriate responses to the SAQ's items. Staff, regardless of their professional background, can use the SAQ as a pre and post measure to assess changes in offenders' attitudes and beliefs. Researchers can validate the SAQ on their specific population.

Although the SAQ can be administered by individuals who do not have extensive psychological training, interpreting the SAQ should be limited to psychologists, psychiatrists, behavior science technicians, and other forensic professionals who have experience with using actuarial tools and/or have a basic understanding of actuarial measures, their uses, and limitations.

Administering the SAQ

The SAQ comes in a package that consists of the questionnaire, answer sheet, scoring sheet, a profile sheet, and the manual. The person administering the SAQ, after explaining the purpose for administering the questionnaire, asks the offender to read the instructions for completing the SAQ out loud as stated in the first page of the questionnaire. The person administering the SAQ may respond to any question for clarification by the offender in a manner that does not influence the offender's response.

After the offender completes the SAQ, the person administering the SAQ checks for unanswered questions. Occasionally an offender may not be able to easily answer a question. This particular question may be explained to the offender and a response obtained. If the question does not apply to a particular offender, the answer should be "false." If the offender's response implies that both "true" and "false" may reflect his response, he/she is asked to choose the one that applies even slightly more to his/her case. If the offender still cannot choose one over the other, then it is considered as a "true" response. Ideally, no item should be left unanswered. If, however, the person administering the test is left with more than three items unanswered, he/she should be aware that this may affect the results of the particular scale that it contributes to, but not necessarily the result of the whole test. The SAQ items could be read to offenders who are illiterate and their responses entered for them on the answer sheet.

Scoring the SAQ

Individual items are scored as true (1) or false (0). After adding up the items for each subscale via the scoring sheet, the scores are then entered on the client's answer sheet. The SAQ total score is arrived at by adding up the numbers of the SAQ subscales. Completing the Validity scale of the SAQ involves verifying the accuracy of offender's responses on eight items against the offender's criminal history (i.e., FPS in Canada or FBI sheet in the USA). If no discrepancy is noted, then the SAQ is considered valid. However, if there are discrepancies between the offender's responses and the official record of his/her criminal history, the assessor should ask the offender for explanations regarding these discrepancies. If the explanation provided sounds suspicious on four or more of these items, then the offender's responses on the SAQ should be carefully considered, and the offender's responses on the rest of the items should be verified using collateral information from the official file.

Interpreting the Score of the SAQ

Based on the current research on Canadian federal offenders and American offenders, an offender is classified according to his/her score to one of four categories: low, low-moderate, high-moderate, and high risk probability for violent and non-violent recidivism. He/she may be considered for assignment to maximum, medium, or minimum security intuitions. Also, according to his/her scores of the subscales he/she may be recommended for particular programs. Professionals who prefer to report percentiles can do so by using the percentile sheet that is included the Manual (Loza, 2005).

Example of Reporting the Results of the SAQ

The SAQ is a self-report risk/need assessment tool, which helps to classify offenders to levels of risk of reoffending in a violent and non-violent manner. The SAQ also assists with the issues of institutional assignment and programming. Research results demonstrated that the SAQ is as effective at predicting recidivism as other current clinical and actuarial instruments. Research results also indicated that the SAQ is not vulnerable to deception and self-presentation biases.

It is reported that the SAQ as a self-report measure has many distinct advantages over professionally administered measures. A SAQ report might read: Mr. X's score on the SAQ placed him into the group of scores that has shown, based on the performance of other federal offenders with similar scores, to be in the low (or low/moderate or high/moderate or high-risk level) for recidivism over a two-year span. Results also indicated that he could be assigned to high (or medium or minimum security level) security institutions.

Training

Minimal training (one to two days) is required for forensic professionals to be able to administer and interpret the SAQ, particularly those who meet the criteria mentioned above in terms of qualifications for administering the SAQ. Most of the training, however, is in the areas of introduction to the SAQ, scoring, interpreting and the results, and communicating them to the referral source. Similarly, minimal training (one day) is required for non-forensic professionals. The training is focused on the area of administering the SAQ and scoring the results.

Limitations of the SAQ

The SAQ should not be used outside of its intended purposes or with offenders who are not similar to the standardization samples. Doing so will produce invalid results.

Studies Demonstrating the Psychometric Properties of the SAQ

Construct, concurrent, and predictive validity of the SAQ have been demonstrated by numerous studies. These studies also indicate that the SAQ is valid for use with diverse populations (i.e., offenders of different cultures, criminal and forensic offenders, and with male and female offenders). One of the following studies indicates that the SAQ could be used for assignment of offenders to different security levels and different rehabilitation programs.

Reliability of the SAQ

Internal consistency

Cronbach's alphas were calculated for participants from different countries and reported in Table 8.1.

Subscale/Total Correlations

In the study by Summers and Loza (2004) the correlations between SAQ total score and subscale scores ranged from .48 to .86. In Loza et al. (2004) the majority of the SAQ total scale-subscale correlations across six settings (Australia, Canada, England, N. Carolina, Pennsylvania, and Singapore) were above .70. Approximately 70% of the subscale-subscale correlations were higher than .30. In the Reyes, Gomez, & Rodriguez (2006) study there were also high total/subscale correlations. In the study by Prinsloo and Ladikos (2007) total/subscale correlations ranged from .62 to .81. All correlations were significant beyond .01.

Table 8.1 Cronbach's Alpha Reliability Coefficient

SAQ	Cronbach's Alpha							
Subscale n =	USA 3,703	CA 938	AUS 116	ENG 75	SING 520	SP-1 138	SP-2 276	SA 269
CT	.80	.79	.69	.81	.78	.72	.75	.69
AP	.53	.57	.75	.60	.72	.56	.62	.57
CP	.83	.86	.68	.89	.87	.86	.83	.82
CH	.45	.64	.75	.70	.60	.60	.66	.59
AD	.68	.75	.74	.73	.74	.82	.82	.72
Asso.	.31	.32	.76	.21	.30	.35	.35	.40
An		−.69		____	____		.69	.70
Total	.89	.91	____			.90	.92	.90

Note: USA: Participants from N. Carolina and Pennsylvania (SAQ manual, Loza, 2005); CAN = Canada (SAQ manual, Loza, 2005); AUS = Australia (Summers & Loza, 2004); Eng. = England (Evans, 2002); SING = Singapore (Loza et al., 2004); SP-1 = Spain (Reyes et al, 2006); SP-2 = Spain (Rodríguez et. al., 2016); SA = South Africa (Prinsloo & Ladikos, 2007); CT = Criminal Tendencies; AP = Antisocial Personality problems; CP = Conduct Problems; CH = Criminal History; AD = Alcohol / Drugs; Asso. = Associates; An = Anger

Test-retest reliability

In Loza, Dhaliwal, Kroner, and Loza-Fanous's (2000) study the one-week test-retest reliability coefficients were .95 for the total scale, .69 for Criminal Tendencies, .71 for Antisocial Personality Problems, .95 for Conduct Problems, .78 for Criminal History, .93 for Alcohol/Drugs, and .85 for Criminal Associates.

Construct Validity

To examine the degree to which the SAQ actually assesses the proposed constructs, each subscale was examined for its relationship with established criteria measures used to assess the same construct (Loza et al., 2000). All of the SAQ subscales that were assessed demonstrated a statistically significant relationship with the established criteria measures at P .001 (see Table 8.2). These criteria measures consisted of items and scales of the Pride in Delinquency Scale (PID; Shields & Whitehall, 1991), Criminal Sentiments Scale (CSS; Gendreau, Grant, Leipciger, & Collins, 1979), Psychopathy Checklist–Revised (PCL-R; Hare, 1991), Level of Service Inventory–Revised, (LSI-R; (LSI–R; Andrews & Bonta, 1995), and Violence Risk Appraisal Guide (VRAG; Harris, Rice, & Quinsey, 1993). The number of prior offences was tallied for each offender, and the number of offences was used to act as a construct measure for the SAQ Criminal History subscale.

Concurrent Validity

Concurrent validity of the SAQ was demonstrated by several studies as indicated in Table 8.3. These studies examined the correlations between the SAQ scores and instruments commonly used to assess risk, LSI-R, PCL-R, VRAG and the Statistical Information on Recidivism–Revised (SIR-R; Correctional Service Canada, 1997).

The second method of assessing concurrent validity involved examining the relationship between participants' SAQ scores and their offence history as measured by prior convictions. Two different assessment strategies were used. The first differentiated offenders based on their number of prior convictions. The second strategy was to differentiate offenders based

Table 8.2 Correlations Between SAQ Subscales and Criteria Measures (n = 303)

SAQ Subscales (# ITEMS)	Criteria Measures	Range of Correlations with Criteria Scales
Criminal Tendencies (27)	PID, CSS	*(.51–.58)***
Antisocial Personality Problems (5)	PCL-R	.36***
Conduct Problems (18)	PCL-R ITEM 12 PCL-R ITEM 18	*(.53–.63)***
Criminal History (6)	LSI-R's Criminal History; # of Past Offenses	*(.50–.65)***
Alcohol/Drugs (8)	Al, Dg, LS1-R (# 37, 38, 39, & 40); VRAG # 12	*(.28–.51)***
Associates (3)	LSI-R's Subscale (Companions)	.32***

Note: PID, CSS, PCL-R = Psychopathy Check List-Revised, LSI-R AL = Alcohol (Interview & file information), DG = Drug (Interview & file information), VRAG, ***p <.0001

Table 8.3 Correlations Between SAQ's Total & Subscales & PCL-R & VRAG Scales

		CT	AP	CP	CH	AD	ASSO	SAQ total
Aus.	PCL-R	.41**	.38**	.57**	.64**	.33**	.41**	.63**
	VRAG	.41**	.39**	.65**	.70**	.48**	.45**	.70**
	LSI-R	____						
Can.	PCL-R	.27**	.34**	.55**	.54**	.24**	.29**	.55**
	VRAG	.38**	.35**	.64**	.50**	.25**	.42**	.63**
	LSI-R	.27**	.39**	.52**	.55**	.52**	.31**	.59**
Eng.	PCL-R	.66**	.44**	.73**	.63**	.39*	.54**	.76**
	VRAG	____	____	____	____	____	____	____
	LSI-R	____						
USA	PCL-R	____	____	____	____	____	____	____
	VRAG	____	____	____	____	____	____	____
Sing.	LSI-R	____						____
Sing.	PCL-R	____	____	____	____	____	____	____
	VRAG	____	____	____	____	____	____	
	LSI-R	.29**	.25**	.36**	.41**	.43**	.27**	.44**
Span-2.	PCL-R	.37**	.43**	.45**	.42**	.20**	.26**	.47**
	VRAG	.44**	.47**	.57**	.57**	.54**	.43**	.65**
		.29**						

Note: USA: Participants were from N. Carolina and Pennsylvania (SAQ manual, Loza, 2005); CAN = Canada (SAQ manual, Loza, 2005); AUS = Australia (Summers & Loza, 2004); Eng. = England (Evans, 2002); SING = Singapore (Loza et al., 2004); SP-2 = Spain (Rodríguez et. al., 2016); CT = Criminal Tendencies; AP = Antisocial Personality problems; CP = Conduct Problems; CH = Criminal History; AD = Alcohol/Drugs; Asso. = Associates; PCL-R = Psychopathy Check List; VRAG = Violence Risk Appraisal Guide; **p is at least < .01

on whether or not they had a prior conviction for violence. For the first strategy, the median number of offences served as a cutoff point for two general offence groups, resulting in the low group and the high group. Participants in the high group had significantly higher SAQ subscale and total scores than the low group. For the second strategy, the SAQ scores of participants who had been convicted of at least one violent offence were placed into the violent group. Participants who had not been convicted of a violent offence comprised the non-violent group. Results showed that the scores for the SAQ total and all the scales, with the exception of the Criminal Tendencies scores, were significantly higher for the violent group (Loza et al., 2000).

The concurrent validity of the SAQ was also demonstrated in Loza et al. (2004) using the total number of offenses they had committed as a criterion. Participants from each site were divided into low and high groups. The low group included participants who were in the lowest 50% of frequencies on the total number of offenses committed, and the high included the top one half. These groups were then compared on SAQ total scores. The means for the high group were always higher than the means of the low group.

Predictive Validity

The SAQ has been examined for post-release predictive validity in two-year (Loza & Loza-Fanous, 2001), five-year (Loza & Loza-Fanous, 2003), and nine-year (Loza, MacTavish, &

Loza-Fanous, 2007) follow-up studies. The outcome criteria for the follow-up studies were similar. Looking at the two-year post-release outcome, Loza and Loza-Fanous (2000) differentiated four types of outcomes: (1) the commission of any parole violation, for example, drinking or taking non-prescribed drugs; (2) recidivism, defined as return to custody for any reason, such as suspension or revocations or a new offence; (3) the commission of a violent offence; and (4) any of the above, including convictions or negative reports from a parole supervisor. In the five-year follow-up study, outcome criteria were defined as: (1) the commission of any new offence; (2) recidivism, defined as a return to custody for any reason, such as suspension or revocation of early release; (3) the commission of a violent offence; and (4) any of the above, including negative reports from a parole supervisor. The correlations between SAQ scores and outcome for the two-year and five-year follow-up studies, and the percentage of offenders who failed in each category (i.e., the base rate) were calculated. All correlations were significant in the two-year study with the exception of Antisocial Personality Problems and Alcohol/Drug Abuse in relation to the commission of a new violent act. In the five-year study, all subscales had a significant relationship with all outcome measures. Also in the five-year study there was an increase in base rates, which would be expected given that the individuals had a longer time in which to recidivate.

In the nine-year follow-up study (Loza, MacTavish, & Loza-Fanous, 2007) the criteria measures for post-release outcome were success or failure on non-violent and violent recidivism. Results indicated significant differences between the recidivists and non-recidivists on the SAQ total and subscales scores. Furthermore, the SAQ total score and all SAQ subscale scores correlated significantly with violent and non-violent recidivism, although some subscales had weak correlations. The SAQ's accuracy in predicting post-release outcome was assessed by investigating the risk ratio for participants' failure on release. Using total SAQ scores, offenders were grouped into low, medium, and high-risk groups. Results indicated that the risk ratios for failure in the medium-risk group were 2.89 and 4.38 times higher than for those offenders in the low-risk group for recidivism and violent recidivism, respectively. Furthermore, the risk ratios for offenders failing in the high-risk group were 4.20 and 9.64 times higher than those in the low-risk group for recidivism and violent recidivism, respectively. All differences between low and medium-risk groups and low and high-risk groups were statistically significant.

To further examine the predictive validity of the SAQ, the probability of the SAQ correctly classifying offenders as either at risk or not at risk against the post-release criterion measures was also examined. Overall, the SAQ demonstrated sensitivity in the ranges of 59% for non-violent recidivism and 70% for violent recidivism and specificity in the ranges of 74% for non-violent recidivism and 62% for violent recidivism.

Another step in examining the predictive validity of the SAQ was through investigation of the SAQ's predictions of its Relative Improvement of Over Chance (RIOC; Loeber & Dishion, 1983). The RIOC was 38% for non-violent recidivism and 49% for violent recidivism. Thus the relationship between the SAQ and these outcomes is well beyond chance (i.e., 50%). Therefore, an RIOC of 38%, for example, is 38% above a 50%, or chance, rate. In Reyes, Gomez, and Rodriguez's (2006) study on Spanish offenders (2005) Relative Improvement of Over Chance (RIOC) was .75.

In the 2004 study by Summers and Loza on Australian offenders, offenders with high SAQ total scores had significantly more total number of offences, higher numbers of breaches of conditional releases, and higher numbers of violent offences. Offenders who committed violent offences scored significantly higher mean scores than those who committed non-violent offences.

In the Andreu-Rodríguez, Peña-Fernández, and Loza's (2016) study the RIOC analysis carried out on the SAQ total score revealed an AUC of .80, showing acceptable accuracy discriminating between violent and non-violent recidivist groups.

The Validity of the SAQ for Use with Female Offenders

The concurrent and predictive validities of using the SAQ were also demonstrated by utilizing 91 female offenders incarcerated in Pennsylvania and 183 incarcerated in Singapore correctional systems. There was not much difference between results obtained from this study than those obtained from male offenders (Loza, Shahinfar, & Loza-Fanous, 2005).

SAQ as a Classification Measure

The utility of the SAQ as a classification tool for offenders was investigated by Loza and Loza-Fanous (2002). Comparison measures were two other measures used by Correctional Service of Canada for classifying offenders into different institutional/security levels. Correlations demonstrate relationships between these measures and the SAQ, and that the SAQ can have utility as a classification tool.

Comparison Studies with Other Instruments

Kroner and Loza (2001) compared the predictive accuracy of the SAQ to that of the PCL-R, SIR-R, and VRAG. The SAQ demonstrated higher predictive accuracy for both general and violent recidivism, expressed in terms of violent and non-violent recidivism correlations and AUC.

In a five-year follow-up study (Loza & Green, 2003), the predictive validity of the SAQ was compared to that of SIR-R, LSI-R, PCL-R, and VRAG. Of the five assessment instruments, the SAQ had the highest correlation for general recidivism, and the second-highest correlation for violent recidivism.

In a 2007 meta-analysis, Campbell, French, and Gendreau (2009) used 88 studies from 1980 to 2006 to compare nine risk instruments and other psychological measures on their ability to predict general (primarily non-sexual) violence in adults. Column 8 of Table 8.4 indicates that SAQ came second among the nine measures in the ability to violent recidivism.

The SAQ and Deception

In their studies by Mills, Loza, & Kroner (2003) and Loza, Loza-Fanous, & Heseltine (2007) demonstrated that the SAQ is not vulnerable to deception and self-presentation biases.

Other analyses were conducted to investigate whether the SAQ is vulnerable to deception. Scores of participants who volunteered to complete the SAQ for research purposes were compared with the scores of those who completed the SAQ as part of a decision-making process. There were no significant differences between the participants who completed the SAQ as part

Table 8.4 The Prediction of Violence in Adult Offenders. A Meta-Analytic Comparison of Instruments and Methods of Assessment (Campbell, French, & Gendreau, 2009)

Measure	k	N	M_r (SD)	CI$_r$	$M_{r'}$ (SD)	CI$_{r'}$	Z^+	CI$_{z+}$
HCR-20	11	1395	.25 (.15)	.14 to .35	.25 (.13)	.16 to .34	.22	.17 to .27
LSI/LSI-R	19	4361	.25 (.08)	.21 to .28	.25 (.09)	.21 to .29	.28	.25 to .31
Adjusted[a]	18	3920	.23 (.06)	.20 to .26	.24 (.06)	.20 to .27	.25	.22 to .28
PCL/PCL-R	24	4757	.24 (.10)	.19 to .28	.24 (.10)	.20 to .28	.27	.24 to .30
Adjusted[b]	20	2862	.22 (.10)	.17 to .26	.22 (.10)	.17 to 27	.24	.20 to .28
SIR Scale	17	5618	.24 (.13)	.18 to .31	.24 (.11)	.18 to .30	.22	.19 to .25
Adjusted[c]	15	1962	.25 (.14)	.17 to .32	.24 (.12)	.18 to .31	.24	.20 to .28
VRAG	14	2082	.27 (.13)	.20 to .35	.27 (.11)	.20 to .33	.32	.28 to .36
Adjusted[d]	13	1464	.26 (.12)	.18 to .33	.26 (.10)	.19 to .32	.27	.22 to .32
Crimhistory	9	2230	.23 (.15)	.12 to .35	.22 (.14)	.12 to .33	.23	.19 to .27
LS/CMI	3	841	.37 (.09)	.14 to .59	.38 (.14)	.03 to .73	.47	.40 to .54
PCL:SV	5	641	.29 (.11)	.15 to .43	.30 (.13)	.13 to .46	.20	.12 to .28
SAQ	8	1094	.33 (.03)	.31 to .36	.33 (.05)	.29 to .38	.37	.31 to .43
SFS	5	989	.15 (.03)	.11 to .19	.15 (.05)	.09 to .21	.15	.09 to .21

Note: k = effect sizes per risk measure; N = offenders per risk measure; M_r(SD) = mean correlation coefficient and standard deviation between risk measure and misconduct; CI$_r$ = 95% confidence interval about mean correlation coefficient; $M_{r'}$ = r prime representing the M_r value adjusted for the influence of base rates; CI$_{r'}$ = 95% confidence interval about mean r'; Z^+ = r' value transformed to Fisher Z_r to approximate normality and weighted by sample size; CI$_{Z+}$ = 95% confidence interval about Z^+.
a) Q value (57.15) for LSI/LSI-R category was statistically significant. Removal of one outlier reduced Q value to non-significance.
b) Q value (48.04) for PCL-R category was statistically significant. Removal of four outliers reduced Q value to non-significance.
c) Q value (32.54) for SIR Scale category was statistically significant. Removal of two outliers reduced Q value to non-significance.
d) Q value (47.06) for VRAG category was statistically significant. Removal of one outlier reduced Q value to non-significance.
This Table was provided to W. Loza by personal communication from the second author.

of the decision-making process about their release, appeal, and/or assignment to programs versus the offenders who volunteered to complete the SAQ for research purposes. Similarly, there were no significant differences between the Canadian participants who completed the SAQ as part of the decision-making process about their release versus offenders who volunteered to complete the SAQ for research purposes. The Australian and Canadian participants who completed the SAQ for decision-making purposes had higher mean scores on the SAQ total score and the majority of the SAQ subscales than those who volunteered to complete the SAQ for research purposes (Loza et al., 2004)

Cultural Diversity Comparisons

In the study by Loza et al. (2004) results showed that there were no significant differences between the scores of the Caucasian, African American, Hispanic, and Aboriginal Australian offenders on the SAQ. These results support validity for the SAQ among culturally diverse offenders. Also, a study completed by Loza, Conley, and Warren (2004) indicated that the SAQ could be used with diverse populations (there were no significant differences between African American and Caucasian offenders on the SAQ)

Furthermore, the validation study of the use of the SAQ with female offenders (Loza et al., 2005) indicated that there were no significant differences between the responses of the African American offenders compared to Caucasian offenders on total SAQ score. Furthermore, there were no significant differences between the responses of Asian offenders from Singapore and Pennsylvania and Caucasian offenders.

Predictive Validity of the SAQ for Use with Mentally Ill Offenders

In a study by Villeneuve, Oliver, and Loza (2003), the SAQ also demonstrated satisfactory predictive validity for violent and general recidivism with a high-risk correctional psychiatric sample. In another study by Rodrigues, Seto, Ahmed, and Loza (2016) the predictive validity of the SAQ was investigated on a sample of adult male offenders with mental health problems in a correctional treatment setting in Ontario. The SAQ significantly predicted general recidivism within one year of follow-up (AUC was .74, 95% CI = [.65, .83]) and significantly predicted institutional incidents (threat, verbal aggression, or assault; AUC was .61, 95% CI = [.51–.72]).

The Validity of the SAQ for Use with Young Offenders

Hemmati (2004) validated a modified SAQ version in a sample of male/female incarcerated youth. Concurrent validity was established by correlations with three well-recognized risk/ needs assessment measures and differentiation between offender groups based number of prior convictions and a history of violence vs. no history of violence. Alphas for the SAQ scales' internal consistency, test-retest reliability were acceptable, and construct and concurrent validities were demonstrated. These findings suggest that the SAQ may be a useful risk assessment tool for youth populations.

Postgraduate Research Projects

Postgraduate research projects were completed on the SAQ. These studies included those by Reyes et al., 2006), Hemmati (2004), and Evans (2002).

Research Agenda

We encourage researchers to continue to contribute to our efforts to validate the SAQ with different types of populations and in different settings.

Conclusion

There are many advantages of using the SAQ as a self-report instrument over clinician-administered scales. The SAQ ensures maximal objectivity by employing the offenders' responses, and thereby reducing the possibility of assessor bias. It also decreases the possibility of litigation due to the offender's perception of misrepresentation by the clinician because it engages the offender more fully in the assessment process. In addition, the SAQ is more convenient and economical to use than traditional methods of risk assessment as a result of the following factors:

- Instructions provided are simple and can be given by paraprofessionals.
- Offenders provide "true" or "false" responses to the items.
- It takes approximately 15–20 minutes to complete.
- The SAQ may be administered in a group session.
- Interpreting the results is straightforward, requiring minimal professional time, and minimal training.
- There is no need for prior extensive experience or special skill in order to credibly and reliably interpret its results.
- The SAQ incorporates a large proportion of dynamic risk factors. More than 50% of the SAQ items tap into dynamic factors while some of the other well-established risk tools include minimal or no dynamic factors.
- Offenders' responses can contribute to an individualized cognitive treatment plan. For example, irrational or faulty cognition demonstrated through the endorsement of statements such as "I can fool most people if I want" or "Almost anyone would lie to save themselves from trouble" can be challenged during treatment.
- The SAQ focuses on content areas particularly related to the prediction of violent recidivism. It is the prediction of violent recidivism that is of utmost importance to clinicians, decision-makers, and the public.
- Endorsement of some of the SAQ's statements can aid clinicians in the diagnosis of antisocial personality disorder, a history of conduct disorder, and substance abuse.
- The SAQ can be used without reliance on psychiatric diagnoses or the results of other tools from previous sources.
- Nothing in the SAQ's individual items or its total score may be used to attach a negative label to the offender.

Case Study: High Risk

Reason for Referral: Intake Assessment

Mr. Smith is an 18-year-old federal offender serving a sentence of 10 years for multiple convictions of Assault, Robbery, Theft, Obstructing Justice, and Mischief. He has prior convictions for Failure to Comply with Undertaking, Obstructing Justice, and Escape. There is also a history of running away from open custody facilities. He has previously violated several probation orders. He was involved with the Children's Aid Society and the courts most of his life. As a young offender and from a very early age, he was involved in activities such as assaults, fire setting, property damage, uttering threats, and thefts. Some of his assaults involved using knives. He has a history of threatening police officers with a knife. While in custody, he attempted to injure custodial staff. Mr. Smith was administered the Self-Appraisal Questionnaire (SAQ) as part of a battery of tests for intake assessment. Initially, he was not cooperative during group testing, choosing to disregard instructions and speak with others about the item content and purpose of the assessment. Mr. Smith received a warning that he would be removed from the testing session. Then, he completed the SAQ quietly. In verifying responses to Validity Items, it was noted that Mr. Smith endorsed having a conviction for fraud but none was found on his record. He was asked about the inconsistency and said he thought he had been convicted of fraud as a youth. Mr. Smith was administered 7 subscales from the SAQ. A score of 15 out of a possible 23 indicates that he has a moderate to high degree of antisocial thoughts, feelings, and behaviors when compared to the SAQ normative sample. As a result, corrective programming for criminal tendencies should be considered. On the Antisocial Personality Problems subscale, Mr. Smith scored 4 out of a possible 5. He has already been diagnosed with several mental disorders including Antisocial Personality Disorder, Pyromania, and Attention-Deficit/Hyperactivity Disorder (ADHD). A referral to the mental health team was recommended to assess for any initial adjustment difficulties. With regards to the Conduct Problems subscale, Mr. Smith obtained a score of 17 out of 18, which indicates that he has an early history of antisocial behavior that is in the High range. This is corroborated with file information. To help Mr. Smith in learning and developing problem solving skills and prosocial behaviors, Mr. Smith will be referred to the 8-week Cognitive Skills program in order to help him learn and develop problem solving skills and prosocial behaviors. At his current age of 18, Mr. Smith has incurred 15 convictions that include serious and violent offences. His record is reflected on the Criminal History subscale score of 4 out of a possible 6. On the Alcohol and Drug Abuse subscale, Mr. Smith scored 4 out of a possible 8. This suggests that Mr. Smith has had some degree of difficulty with substances, and that these difficulties have been related to health and legal issues. Mr. Smith has stated that alcohol and/or drugs were never involved in any of his offences, and he has refused programming for substance abuse issues. However, his responses on this subscale indicate that his actions have been influenced by substance abuse. Mr. Smith will be referred for participation in the Offender Substance Abuse program after completion of the Cognitive Skills program. Mr. Smith's score on the SAQ Antisocial Associates subscale was 3 out of a possible 3. It is recommended that Mr. Smith be considered for the Visiting Volunteer program and encouraged to develop opportunities for prosocial behavior. The score of 3 out of a possible 5 on the Anger subscale places Mr. Smith in the Moderate range of Anger when compared to the normative sample. After completion of the Cognitive Skills program, he should be referred to Anger programming. Given his history and current diagnoses, Mr. Smith will also be referred to the Psychology department to be considered for individualized relaxation training sessions.

Mr. Smith's total score of 48 on the SAQ places him into the group of offenders who, based on the performance of the normative sample, are in the High probability range of committing a violent or non-violent offence within a period of approximately 2 years of their release. Ninety-nine percent of offenders in the SAQ normative sample had SAQ total scores lower than that of Mr. Smith. Mr. Smith has a history of committing general and violent offences since childhood. His SAQ subscale scores indicate programming needs on all scales. Mr. Smith requires close monitoring and a structured environment with support to complete his programming. Cognitive Skills, Substance Abuse, and Anger Management programs are appropriate for Mr. Smith. He should also be referred to the Visiting Volunteers program. Given his level of risk and institutional history, notwithstanding his programming needs, initial placement in a Maximum-security institution is recommended, with a review in 6 months.

Source: Loza, W. (2005). Self-Appraisal Questionnaire (SAQ): A Tool for Assessing Violent and Non-Violent Recidivism. Toronto, ON, Mental Health Systems (MHS).

References

Andreu-Rodríguez, J. M., Peña-Fernández, M. E., & Loza, W. (2016). Predicting risk of violence through a self-appraisal questionnaire. *The European Journal of Psychology Applied to Legal Context*, 8, 51–56.

Andrews, D. A., & Bonta, J. (1995). *Level of Service Inventory–Revised User's Manual*. Toronto, ON: Multi-Health Systems.

Campbell, M. A, French, S., & Gendreau, P. (2009). The prediction of violence in adult offenders a meta-analytic comparison of instruments and methods of assessment. *Criminal Justice and Behavior, 36*(6), 567–590.

Correctional Service Canada (1997). Statistical Information on Recidivism–Revised (SIR–R); Parole decision-making in Canada, Research towards decision guideline. Ottawa, ON: Solicitor General of Canada.

Evans, M. (2002). Reliability and concurrent validity of the Self-Appraisal Questionnaire on British offenders. Unpublished master's thesis. University of Leicester, England.

Gendreau, P., Grant, B. A., Leipciger, M., & Collins, C. (1979). Norms and recidivism rates for the MMPI and selected experimental scales on a Canadian delinquent sample. *Canadian Journal of Behavioral Science, 11*, 21–31.

Hare, R. D. (1991). Manual for the Hare Psychopathy Checklist–Revised. Toronto, ON: Multi-Health Systems.

Harris, G. T., Rice, M. E., & Quinsey, V. L. (1993). Violent recidivism of mentally disordered offenders: The development of a statistical prediction instrument. *Criminal Justice and Behavior, 20*, 315–335.

Hemmati, T. (2004). Reliability and validity of the Self-Appraisal Questionnaire in a sample of incarcerated youth. Unpublished master's thesis, Carleton University, Ottawa, ON.

Kroner, D., & Loza, W. (2001). Evidence for the efficacy of self-report in predicting violent and nonviolent criminal recidivism. *Journal of Interpersonal Violence, 16*, 168–177.

Loeber, R., & Dishion, T. (1983). Early predictors of male delinquency: A review. *Psychological Bulletin, 94*, 68–99.

Loza, W. (2005). Self-Appraisal Questionnaire (SAQ): A Tool for Assessing Violent and Non-Violent Recidivism. Toronto, ON, Mental Health Systems (MHS).

Loza, W., & Loza-Fanous, A. (1999a). Anger and prediction of violent and non-violent offenders' recidivism. *Journal of Interpersonal Violence, 14*, 1014–1029.

Loza, W., & Loza-Fanous, A. (1999b). The fallacy of reducing rape and violent recidivism by treating anger. *International Journal of Offender Therapy and Comparative Criminology, 43*, 492–502.

Loza, W., Conley, M., & Warren, B. (2004). Concurrent cross validation of the Self-Appraisal Questionnaire (SAQ): A tool for assessing violent and non-violent recidivism and institutional adjustment on a sample of North Carolina offenders. *International Journal of Offender Therapy and Comparative Criminology, 48*, 85–95.

Loza, W., Cumbleton, A., Shahinfar, A., Neo, L. H., Evans, M., Conley, M., & Summers, R. (2004). Cross validation of the Self-Appraisal Questionnaire (SAQ): An offender risk assessment measure on Australian, British, Canadian, North Carolinian, and Pennsylvanian and Singaporeans offenders. *Journal of Interpersonal Violence, 19*, 1172–1190.

Loza, W., Dhaliwal, G., Kroner, D., & Loza-Fanous, A. (2000). Reliability, construct, and concurrent validities of the Self-Appraisal Questionnaire: A tool for assessing violent and nonviolent recidivism. *Criminal Justice and Behavior, 27*, 356–374.

Loza, W., & Green, K. (2003). The Self-Appraisal Questionnaire: A self-report measure for predicting recidivism versus clinicians administered measures. A five-year follow-up study. *Journal of Interpersonal Violence, 18*, 781–797.

Loza, W., & Loza-Fanous, A. (2000). Predictive validity of the Self-Appraisal Questionnaire (SAQ): A tool for assessing violent and non-violent release failures. *Journal of Interpersonal Violence, 15*, 1183–1191.

Loza, W., & Loza-Fanous, A. (2001). The effectiveness of the Self-Appraisal Questionnaire (SAQ) in predicting offenders' post-release outcome: A comparison study. *Criminal Justice and Behavior, 28*, 105–121.

Loza, W., & Loza-Fanous, A (2002). The effectiveness of the Self-Appraisal Questionnaire (SAQ) as an offenders' Classification Measure. *Journal of Interpersonal Violence, 17*, 3–13.

Loza, W., & Loza-Fanous, A. (2003). More evidence for the validity of Self-Appraisal Questionnaire (SAQ) for predicting violent and non-violent recidivism: A five-year follow-up study. *Criminal Justice and Behavior, 30*, 709–721.

Loza, W., Loza-Fanous, A., & Heseltine, K. (2007). The myth of offenders' deception on self-report measure predicting recidivism: Example for the Self-Appraisal Questionnaire (SAQ). *Journal of Interpersonal Violence, 22*(6), 671–683.

Loza, W., MacTavish, A., & Loza-Fanous, A. (2007). A nine year follow-up study on the predictive validity of the Self-Appraisal Questionnaire (SAQ) for predicting violent and nonviolent recidivism. *Journal of Interpersonal Violence, 22*(9), 1144–1155.

Loza, W., Neo, L. H., Shahinfar, A., & Loza-Fanous, A. (2005). Cross validation of the Self-Appraisal Questionnaire: A tool for assessing violent and non-violent recidivism with female offenders. *International Journal of Offender Therapy and Comparative Criminology, 49*, 1–14.

Mills, J. F., Loza, W., & Kroner, D. G. (2003). Predictive validity despite social desirability: Evidence for the robustness of self-report among offenders. *Criminal Behaviour and Mental Health, 13*, 140–150.

Prinsloo, J. and Ladikos, A. (2007). Exploring the Application of Actuarial Criminology in Southern Africa, *Journal of Psychology in Africa, 17*(1), 83–88.

Reyes, B., Gomez, J., & Rodriguez, J. (2006). Valoración de la peligrosidad y riesgo de reincidencia en penitencairios. *Psicopatologia Clinica, legal Y Forese, 16*, 103.

Rodrigues, N., Seto, M, Ahmed, A, & Loza, W (2016). The predictive and incremental validity of two self-report risk assessment measures with adult male offenders who have mental health problems. *Criminal Justice and Behavior, 43*(5), 583–599.

Shields, I. W., & Whitehall, G. C. (1991). The Pride in Delinquency Scale. Paper presented at the eastern Ontario Correctional Psychologists' winter conference, Burritts Rapids, Canada.

Summers, R., & Loza, W. (2004). Cross Validation of the Self-Appraisal Questionnaire (SAQ): A tool for assessing violent and non-violent recidivism on Australian offenders. *Psychiatry, Psychology and Law, 11*, 254–262.

Villeneuve, D., Oliver, N., & Loza, W. (2003). Cross validation of the Self Appraisal Questionnaire with a maximum security psychiatric population. *Journal of Interpersonal Violence, 18*, 1325–1334.

9

Service Planning Instrument (SPIn)

Natalie J. Jones and David Robinson

Overview

The Service Planning Instrument (SPIn; Orbis Partners, 2003) is an assessment protocol tapping a breadth of risks, needs, and strengths among adult offender populations. The SPIn was designed to guide offender classification decisions by predicting risk of recidivism, and to identify salient criminogenic needs in order to inform case management goals. The tool is appropriate for use with male and female justice-involved clients in either community or custody settings. Two other versions of the parent SPIn tool will also be described in this article: The Service Planning Instrument for Women (SPIn-W; Orbis Partners, 2006) and the Service Planning Instrument Re-entry (SPIn Re-entry; Orbis Partners, 2013).

The SPIn-W is a special version of the protocol developed specifically to meet the needs of justice-involved females. Although the SPIn-W incorporates some specific gender-responsive content that is absent from the SPIn, the administration guidelines, structure, and general scoring protocol for both tools are analogous. It should be noted that while some criminal justice agencies have adopted SPIn-W with their female clients, most jurisdictions still administer the generic version of SPIn to both men and women. The SPIn Re-entry, in turn, is an abridged version of the larger SPIn tool that is used in re-entry settings as well as in community and custody settings. Consisting of less than half the original number of SPIn items, SPIn Re-entry shares the conventions of the larger protocol with regard to administration and goals.

Several features of the SPIn model are innovative and address important issues raised by users of criminal justice assessment tools. In particular, the incorporation of strength measures within the SPIn assessment protocol supports practitioners who adopt a strength-based paradigm in their work with correctional clients. Each of the tools features a short version, referred to as a "Pre-Screen," which provides more rapid classification of results and reduces the need for a more comprehensive needs assessment with low-risk cases. The scoring model for SPIn also disaggregates static and dynamic risk components, a feature that is particularly useful for interpretation of re-assessment results.

A structured assessment protocol, SPIn item selection was informed by both empirical and theoretical considerations. In addition, while the three variants of SPIn each yield domain and aggregate scores, these scores do not directly correspond to an empirically determined set of projected recidivism rates. Rather, estimates of recidivism rates associated with the classification scheme (i.e., low, moderate, high risk and strength) can be set in accordance with the particular needs of a jurisdiction in which the protocol is applied. Notably, meta-analytic research has indicated that such tools yield levels of accuracy that are comparable to stricter actuarial

Handbook of Recidivism Risk/Needs Assessment Tools, First Edition. Edited by Jay P. Singh, Daryl G. Kroner, J. Stephen Wormith, Sarah L. Desmarais, and Zachary Hamilton.
© 2018 John Wiley & Sons, Ltd. Published 2018 by John Wiley & Sons, Ltd.

measures, yet are arguably more flexible than the latter in that items may be included on the basis of clinical relevance (Hanson & Morton-Bourgon, 2009).

History and Development

The primary model upon which the SPIn is based is the Case Management Assessment Protocol (CMAP; Barnoski, 2003), a risk, need, and strengths juvenile assessment tool developed in Washington State by the Washington State Institute of Public Policy and the Washington Association of Juvenile Court Administrators. In 2000, Orbis Partners adapted the Youth Assessment and Screening Instrument (YASI) from the Washington model.[1] After successful implementation in several jurisdictions and with other criminal justice service providers, the YASI formed the primary template for the development of SPIn.

Serin, Chadwick, and Lloyd (2016) have remarked upon the recent trend towards the incorporation of strengths in new and revised assessment protocols. At the time SPIn was first introduced, assessment users were beginning to recognize the value of including strength scores in an effort to render assessment results more comprehensive. At the broadest level, the SPIn model defines strengths as factors that are negatively correlated with criminal justice outcomes. Moreover, strengths have the potential to attenuate the impact of risk/need factors on negative outcomes.

Strengths have traditionally been conceptualized as the absence of a criminogenic need, or the polar opposite of a criminogenic need (e.g., Harris & Rice, 2015); in either case, the typical argument for the exclusion of strengths from risk assessment protocols is the claim that they offer no new information beyond that which stems from the measurement of risks and needs. Although it is true that, in some cases, strengths do present as the opposite of a criminogenic need (e.g., good anger management skills vs. poor anger management skills), in many other instances, strengths and needs can in fact co-occur within the same content area. For example, a client can have both antisocial peers and prosocial peers, the combination of the two creating a net effect on his or her overall risk level. Many other examples can be drawn from the areas of family, employment, and social networks to illustrate that an individual can be characterized as "high need" and "high strength" within the same domain.

In sum, although strengths may be inversely correlated with risk and need factors, they can co-exist with the latter and independently contribute to the prediction of recidivism. Within the SPIn assessment model, strengths are particularly important at an aggregate level where a collection of individual strength items tends to be correlated with more positive outcomes across the continuum of risk (i.e., Jones, Brown, Robinson, & Frey, 2015). In other words, regardless of one's level of risk, criminal justice clients with higher levels of strength tend have lower recidivism rates.

In addition to supporting the inclusion of strengths in the SPIn assessment model, many criminal justice departments with large client volumes were expressing the need for a triage process that would include a more comprehensive assessment of clients who were at higher risk to recidivate. Hence, the SPIn Pre-Screen tool allows users to conduct an initial assessment to identify moderate and higher risk cases that require further attention through the administration of the Full Assessment. Another assessment issue that emerged from the field involved the desire to more clearly differentiate between static and dynamic assessment results. Anecdotally, some users argued that upon re-assessment, many clients showed little or no change because of the residual effect of static factors on overall scores. Owing to developments introduced with

---

1 Note that other versions of the original Washington model, including the Positive Achievement Change Tool (PACT; Barnoski, 2009), have been developed and introduced as well.

CMAP, YASI had addressed these issues with success and thus became an attractive protocol on which to base a more innovative assessment model for adult criminal justice populations. Overall and domain-level dynamic scores are calculated separately in order to provide greater sensitivity to assessing change on re-assessment.

Another development that was borrowed from YASI was the use of a graphic method to profile assessment results. The SPIn "wheel," depicted in Figure 9.1, is used to display a criminal justice client's assessment profile, incorporating risks, needs, and strengths into a single graphic. The wheel is used to display low (L), moderate (M), and high (H) levels of static risk (e.g., criminal history), criminogenic need, and strength.

While SPIn and its derivatives include the typical risk and need domains that are incorporated in most competing risk/need assessment devices, the development of a new assessment protocol afforded the opportunity to expand need content and update some domain terminology. As much as possible, attempts were made to group domain items around criminogenic need areas that reflected the most current foci in the field of correctional interventions. Hence, separate item clusters were used to form domains labeled Aggression and Social/Cognitive Skills, reflecting intervention streams that were developing to address anger, emotional regulation, maladaptive thinking, and interpersonal skills deficits. A domain labeled Stability was introduced to measure a series of items related to finances, accommodation, access to services, and other areas that impact success in the community. Finally, the developers of SPIn responded to calls from the field to include greater content in the area of mental health. For example, in response to growing research that linked negative outcomes to the experience of

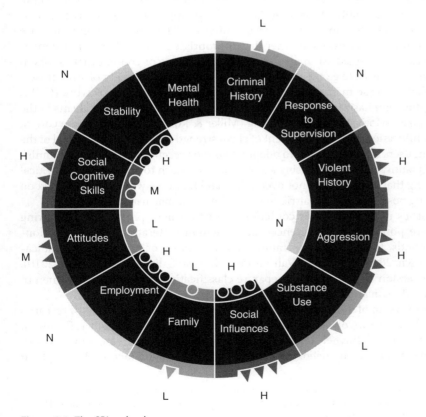

Figure 9.1 The SPIn wheel.

trauma (e.g., Anda et al., 2006), a number of SPIn items were included in the Mental Health domain to represent the experience of traumatic incidents, including physical abuse, sexual abuse, and other negative family events.

In developing SPIn, a number of steps were taken to define criminogenic need and strength content in ways that would promote greater specificity in case planning. The language used for many dynamic items (including need and strength) was chosen to suggest specific targets for behavioral change. For some domains, this involved the introduction of multiple items to represent the types of problems or behavioral targets that could present within a particular domain. For example, the Employment domain indicators tap employment motivation, vocational skill, performance, job search skills, and social adjustment on the job. Greater specificity was intended to promote better understanding of client need profiles and increase the dynamic properties of the domains. As a fourth generation assessment tool that prioritizes ongoing case management through the re-assessment and targeting of salient criminogenic needs (Andrews, Bonta, & Wormith, 2006), great attention was placed on designing the SPIn content and user interface (i.e., software) in a way that would promote clarity for developing case plans.

Theoretical Foundations

The SPIn is principally grounded in the Risk-Need-Responsivity (RNR) paradigm (Andrews & Bonta, 2010). The traditional measurement content derived from RNR via the Central Eight predictors of criminal conduct is well represented in the SPIn assessment model. The overall risk scores produced using the SPIn Pre-Screen have a direct application to the risk principle and are intended to guide decisions about service intensity. The need domain scores are employed to identify criminogenic needs in order that appropriate intervention and case management procedures can be selected. SPIn also incorporates a range of content that assists in addressing responsivity concerns (e.g., mental health, motivation, and a variety of strengths).

SPIn is also grounded in a case management model termed Collaborative Case Work (CCW; Orbis Partners, 2016) that emphasizes working collaboratively with criminal justice clients in the development of case plans. Motivational Interviewing (Miller & Rollnick, 2002) is at the core of this approach. The identification and reinforcement of client strengths is also a fundamental of the CCW model that SPIn users are encouraged to adopt when they receive training on the administration of the tool. Quantifying strengths using a systematic approach to assessment is a critical component for ensuring that strengths are not overlooked and that case workers are focused on building and reinforcing positive skills and attributes with their criminal justice clients.

SPIn also distinguishes itself from other contemporary assessment protocols by featuring a number of gender-responsive items referenced in the feminist literature such as relationship quality, family bonds, financial strain, trauma, and a number of mental health indicators (Blanchette & Brown, 2006; Daly, 1994; Van Voorhis, Wright, Salisbury, & Bauman, 2010). Notably, the primary version of SPIn features separate classification thresholds for women to safeguard against over-classification.[2]

The special women's version of SPIn, termed SPIn-W, was developed on the basis of research and field practice with justice-involved women. The gender-responsive content reflected in the main version of the tool is further augmented in SPIn-W to provide case workers with a more comprehensive profile of the needs, strengths, and responsivity factors that apply to

---

2 Determined from a preliminary recidivism study based on a six-month follow-up period, cutoffs were set in accordance with the distribution of data across risk and strength categories so as to maximize the separation of recidivism rates across low, moderate, and high categories.

justice-involved females. Gender-informed scholars argue that the genesis of female criminal conduct is grounded in early relational disruptions through abuse, neglect, or failure to bond with one or more primary caregivers. In an attempt to cope with early trauma—often inflicted by males—a young girl will engage in various survival-based coping responses that include substance abuse, fleeing the abuse by running away from home, and forging alliances with criminal male intimate partners (in which context she is often revictimized) (Belknap, 2015; Blanchette & Brown, 2006; Daly, 1994; Jones, 2017). Against a backdrop of substance abuse and mental health problems, the young female may engage in survival-based crime like theft, prostitution, and drug offenses. As such, beyond the traditional gender-neutral content featured on SPIn, SPIn-W additionally features items identified to be salient or specific to women in conflict with the law according to the gender-responsive literature; these include one's relationship with dependent children, mental health issues, quality of intimate relationships, and self-efficacy (e.g., Jones, Brown, Wanamaker, & Greiner, 2014; Salisbury & Van Voorhis, 2009).

Notably, SPIn-W also incorporates content grounded in theory and research pertaining to adverse childhood experiences (Baglivio et al., 2016; Baglivio, Wolff, & Piquero, 2015; Felitti et al., 1998; Grasso, Dierkhising, Branson, Ford, & Lee, 2016). Research has indicated that adverse childhood experiences (ACEs or ACE factors), including but not limited to multiple forms of abuse, neglect, and parental psychopathology, are catalysts for future delinquency and criminal outcomes. Consistent with the gender-responsive literature, both qualitative and quantitative data demonstrate that early relationally based trauma is more prevalent and exerts a greater criminogenic effect on females than males (Jones, Salisbury, & Kelly, 2016; National Crittenton Foundation, 2013; Rosseger et al., 2009). Accordingly, the 10 ACE indicators articulated by Felitti and colleagues (1998) have been explicitly incorporated into the recent adaptation of SPIn-W to (1) enhance predictive accuracy, and (2) inform the allocation of trauma-informed services.

Content and Measurement

As indicated, all three adaptations of the SPIn tool comprise a Pre-Screen and Full Assessment version. Containing a subset of the most highly predictive, reliable, and objectively measurable items from the Full Assessment, the Pre-Screen is used for initial triage and classification purposes. In turn, the Full Assessment is used to inform case management and service planning, primarily among moderate and high-risk cases that require more substantive intervention.[3]

The SPIn Pre-Screen is comprised of 30 items that tap risk, need, and strength components. In turn, the Full Assessment contains a total of 90 items (including the 30 from the Pre-Screen) across the following 11 domains: Criminal History, Response to Supervision, Aggression, Substance Abuse, Social Influences, Family, Employment, Attitudes, Social/Cognitive Skills, Stability, and Mental Health. Among these items, the SPIn incorporates 45 strengths (sometimes termed protective factors). Similarly constructed but with additional gender-responsive content, SPIn-W features 100 items across 11 domains. SPIn Re-entry contains a total of 39 items from the original SPIn, with 19 of these items defining the Pre-Screen. SPIn Re-entry includes all 11 domains from the larger protocol (including risk, need, and strength scores). With all three tools, a total Pre-Screen risk score is calculated based on a composite of both static risk and need (dynamic) items. The score yields a classification of low, moderate, or high risk of recidivism. Similarly, a total Pre-Screen strength score of low, moderate, or high is also produced.

---

3 Depending on resources and protocol, some jurisdictions will require completion of a Full Assessment for all clients, while others reserve Full Assessment completion for moderate to high-risk cases.

Although response options vary depending on the nature of the item, whenever possible, SPIn items are scored on Likert-type scales comprising up to five response options in order to maximize the sensitivity of the measure and enhance its capacity to quantify incremental change. In such cases, need[4] and strength typically represent opposite poles of a given construct. On the need pole, a client can be assigned a 1 (*somewhat possesses said characteristic*) or a 2 (*clearly possesses said characteristic*). On the other hand, the item might be a strength for that client, in which case he or she would be assigned a strength score of 1 or 2. A score of 0 is considered a neutral value in most item weights (see item example in Figure 9.2). Need and strength scores are generated at the aggregate level and at the domain level. Each domain may, as applicable, generate a static risk score, dynamic risk score (need score), and dynamic strength score. Domain totals are aggregated to produce the Full Assessment overall risk, need, and strength subscores, respectively. In terms of generating Pre-Screen totals, scores from individual risk/need items represented in the Pre-Screen are aggregated, as are individual strength items. On this basis, a client will have a Pre-Screen total risk score and a Pre-Screen total strength score. Although these two subscores are often combined in research contexts, they remain separate in practice. Note that only the quantitative scores yielded from the Pre-Screen are used to assess a criminal justice-involved client's risk level for classification purposes (i.e., probability of recidivism). As such, most of our validation work centers around the Pre-Screen rather than the Full Assessment.

Measurement of Strengths

The SPIn's quantitative approach to measuring a client's strengths in the spheres of personal and social resources, skills, and attitudes, stands in contrast to the methods associated with most contemporary risk assessment instruments. In the case of the Level of Service/Case Management Inventory (LS/CMI; Andrews, Bonta, & Wormith, 2004), for example, the case manager is simply asked to identify strengths (in an open-ended response format) that may be present within a given domain, without assigning a numerical score to that item.

By contrast, SPIn ascribes a quantitative score to each strength item in the battery. With this approach, it becomes possible to empirically determine whether strengths add incremental value to the prediction of recidivism and whether strengths exert a genuine buffering effect on a client's overall risk to reoffend. The SPIn assessment approach also furnishes a standardized method for re-assessing strengths over time. The calculation of SPIn strength scores also varies from the consideration of strengths on structured professional judgment tools such as the Structured Assessment of Violence Risk in Youth (SAVRY; Borum,

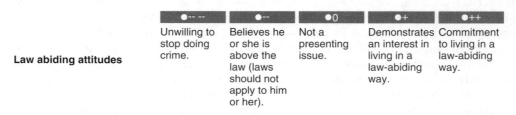

Figure 9.2 Example of a SPIn Pre-Screen item.

---

4 In describing the measures, we refer to all dynamic items or domains that are weighted to produce a positive correlation with recidivism as "need." Hence, need items or need domains represent content designed to measure criminogenic need. Generally, we use the term "risk" in reference to scores that measure static risk, or to composite scores that combine static risk and need elements to produce an overall risk of recidivism classification.

Bartel, & Forth, 2006). In the latter case, assessors assign global ratings to a series of six broad strength categories (e.g., school) that are not explicitly defined by multiple items (Lodewijks, Doreleijers, de Ruiter, & Borum, 2008).

Administration and Training

SPIn assessments are completed by case management staff, which may include probation officers, resource advocates, intervention specialists, and/or facility-based case management officers. Web-based software is used by staff to administer, score, and develop case plan goals on the basis of SPIn results. The SPIn family of tools are scored on the basis of a semi-structured interview with the client. Interview data are typically supplemented with a systematic review of collateral sources, which could include police files, correctional services records, mental health reports, substance abuse assessments, and any other relevant documentation that is available and credible.

Classroom training in the administration of SPIn assessments proceeds over a two-day period, during which time participants learn to collect file-based and interview-based information for completing the assessment. Participants practice completing the assessment based on video clips of sample interviews between case managers and justice-involved clients. Participants also learn to use the accompanying software to enter assessment data and generate SPIn results. A second two-day session is delivered to SPIn users in order to develop skills in the interpretation of SPIn results for the purpose of case planning. Normally, the second two-day session is delivered after participants have been administering the SPIn for approximately two months. The training draws heavily on Motivational Interviewing methods and provides participants with the opportunity to practice developing case plans for case studies. This four-day curriculum is also offered as a self-paced web-based e-Learning training that can normally be completed in 12 to 14 hours.

Psychometric Properties

Research Samples

The psychometric evaluations of SPIn conducted to date are primarily based on the following samples. Each is briefly described in turn.

Sample 1: SPIn Alberta custody

Access to SPIn assessment and recidivism data for an adult custody sample was granted by the Alberta Justice and Solicitor General. Intake assessments were available for a total of 752 clients from four large provincial facilities across Alberta, Canada, processed between March 2009 and May 2014 (83.5% male; $n = 628$, 16.5% female; $n = 124$). The sample was almost evenly divided between Indigenous (41.8%, $n = 314$) and non-Indigenous offenders (46.1%, $n = 347$), while 12.1% ($n = 91$) of cases were classified as "other."

Sample 2. SPIn Alberta community

SPIn assessment and outcome data were also available for 3,656 adult clients bound by community supervision across Alberta, Canada (Jones et al., 2015). The sample included 694 women and 2,962 men with a mean age at intake of 33.47 years (SD = 11.39, Range = 17.60 − 87.90). The sample was predominantly White (67.0%; $n = 2,002$ males and 446 females) and Indigenous (17.4%; $n = 460$ males and 175 females), followed by Black (Caribbean or African descent; 3.7%), Asian (2.9%), East Indian (2.5%), and other (6.6%).

Sample 3: Dismas SPIn Re-entry

Initial assessment data and preliminary (interim) outcome records were available for 4,110 clients (86.5% male and 13.5% female) served in re-entry centers under the direction of Dismas Charities across several American states. These residential clients were released by the Federal Bureau of Prisons to Dismas Charities facilities between May 2013 and May 2014. Clients' average age at assessment was 37.74 years (SD = 10.59, Range = 18 – 87), and the ethnic composition of this sample was nearly evenly divided between African American (35.3%), Caucasian (32.0%), and Hispanic (27.8%), with remaining cases falling into a "mixed/other" category (4.9%).

Sample 4: SPIn-W Connecticut community

Initial SPIn-W assessment and outcome data were available for research purposes on a sample of 274 adult female probationers processed by the State of Connecticut Judicial Branch/Court Support Services Division (CSSD) between 2007 and 2009. Part of a larger study on a case management model tailored to women, participants adhered to the following inclusion criteria: (1) at least 18 years of age at the start of their probation period, (2) had received a probation term of one year or more, (3) were not identified as a sex offender, and (4) had been classified as moderate or high risk on the basis of the Level of Service Inventory–Revised (Andrews & Bonta, 1995). The mean age of participants at intake was 34.68 years (SD = 9.24, Range = 19 – 59). In terms of ethnicity, 38.7% of women were Black, followed by White (33.6%), and Hispanic (27.7%).

Reliability Research

To date, the direct evaluation of the reliability of SPIn measures is limited to assessment of internal consistency of domains and total scores.

Internal consistency

Internal consistency levels associated with risk/need and strength subcomponents of each domain featured on the SPIn and SPIn-W Full Assessments are presented in Table 9.1 for Samples 1, 2, and 4. The majority of domains evidence acceptable reliability with Cronbach's alpha levels exceeding .70. The lower alpha levels ($\alpha < .60$) associated with remaining components are potentially attributable to a combination of issues: (1) the low number of items per domain, (2) the breadth of items subsumed under each construct (e.g., Mental Health), and (3) the potential unreliability of individual items with a low frequency of occurrence (e.g., escape from custody). In interpreting these results, it is important to note that items subsumed under each SPIn domain were simply intended to represent general content areas that were not expressly designed to reflect latent psychological constructs. Accordingly, some lower alpha values were expected and should not signal cause for concern—in fact, diversity within a domain may be an asset. At the aggregate level, respective levels of internal consistency associated with risk and strength items are in the high range at $\alpha = .85$ and $\alpha = .94$ for the SPIn custody sample, $\alpha = .86$ and $\alpha = .93$ for the SPIn community sample, and $\alpha = .86$ and $\alpha = .93$ for the SPIn-W sample.

Inter-rater reliability

Although the inter-rater reliability of the SPIn tools has yet to be measured, the construction and content of these instruments largely parallel those of the youth version of the assessment protocol (YASI). Although not decisive, available research on the inter-rater reliability of the YASI may provide some useful information about the likely reliability of the adult model (see Jones, Brown, Robinson, & Frey, 2016).

Three independent teams have examined the YASI's inter-rater reliability. Based on assessment data collected by trained researchers, Brown, Geck, Harris, and Skilling (2012) reported

Table 9.1 Internal Consistency of SPIn and SPIn-W Full Assessment Domains

Domain	SPIn Custody Sample (N = 752)		SPIn Community Sample (N = 3,656)		SPIn-W Community Sample (N = 274)	
	Risk component	Strength component	Risk component	Strength component	Risk component	Strength component
	Cronbach's alpha (*n* items)	Cronbach's alpha (*n* items)	Cronbach's alpha (*n* items)	Cronbach's alpha (*n* items)	Cronbach's alpha (*n* items)	Cronbach's alpha (*n* items)
Criminal History	.79 (6)	—	.77 (6)	—	.51 (6)	
Response to Supervision	.69 (13)	—	.71 (13)	—	.78 (13)	
Aggression	.81 (4)	.84 (4)	.81 (4)	.84 (4)	.76 (3)	.78 (3)
Substance Use	—	—	—	—	—	—
Social Influences	.70 (6)	.64 (5)	.69 (6)	.56 (5)	.54 (5)	.57 (4)
Family	.62 (7)	.76 (7)	.48 (7)	.63 (7)	.65 (8)	.65 (8)
Employment	.82 (6)	.86 (5)	.79 (6)	.78 (5)	.75 (5)	.71 (4)
Attitudes	.81 (9)	.88 (9)	.82 (9)	.87 (9)	.75 (4)	.85 (4)
Social/ Cognitive Skills	.83 (8)	.90 (8)	.85 (8)	.87 (8)	.89 (10)	.89 (10)
Stability	.67 (4)	.66 (4)	.60 (4)	.46 (4)	.60 (6)	.50 (5)
Mental Health	.28 (4)	—	.21 (4)	—	.39 (3)	—
Overall	.85 (67)	.94 (42)	.86 (67)	.93 (42)	.82 (67)	.87 (42)

Note: There are only two items in the Substance Abuse domain, thus precluding the consideration of internal consistency. All other missing alphas refer to non-applicable values. For example, there is no strength component associated with the Mental Health domain.

high intra-class correlation coefficients (ICCs) ranging from .78 to .88 for risk/need domains and from .84 to .90 for strength domains. Yielding similar results, subsequent research conducted by the National Council on Crime and Delinquency (NCCD; Baird et al., 2013) reported an average percentage agreement of 85% for item scoring among a large sample of juvenile probation staff. By contrast, based on YASI assessments completed by staff across four custody sites in California, Skeem, Hernandez, Kennealy, and Rich (2012) obtained ICCs for total scores falling in the low to moderate range (.51 – .72). Notably, the four sites varied in reliability with the lowest ICC values attributed to one particular site.

Predictive Validity Research

The predictive validity of the SPIn has been evaluated with both the Alberta custody and community samples described above (Sample 1 and Sample 2). Results of each analysis will be described in turn, followed by sections on the predictive accuracy of SPIn Re-entry (Sample 3) and SPIn-W (Sample 4). We report the Area Under the Curve (AUC) as the primary criterion

Table 9.2 Predictive Validity of SPIn Over 3 Years Follow-up with a Custody Sample from Alberta, Canada

Recidivism outcome	Overall (*N* = 501) AUC (95% CI)	Male (*n* = 410) AUC (95% CI)	Female (*n* = 91) AUC (95% CI)	Non-Indigenous (*n* = 293) AUC (95% CI)	Indigenous (*n* = 208) AUC (95% CI)
		Demographic subgroup			
New offenses	.77*** (.73 – .81)	.78*** (.74 – .82)	.73*** (.62 – .83)	.77*** (.72 – .82)	.75*** (.68 – .82)
New convictions	.74*** (.70 – .78)	.76*** (.71 – .81)	.66** (.55 – .78)	.75*** (.69 – .80)	.72*** (.66 – .78)
New violent offences	.70*** (.63 – .76)	.71*** (.64 – .78)	.81** (.69 – .92)	.69*** (.58 – .78)	.68*** (.59 – .77)
New convictions for violent offences	.73*** (.66 – .80)	.73*** (.65 – .81)	.87*** (.78 – .96)	.74*** (.64 – .85)	.68** (.58 – .77)
New technical violations	.69*** (.63 – .74)	.70*** (.65 – .76)	.66* (.53 – .79)	.73*** (.66 – .80)	.64*** (.55 – .72)
New convictions for technical violations	.70*** (.65 – .76)	.71*** (.64 – .77)	.70** (.57 – .83)	.73*** (.65 – .80)	.66*** (.57 – .75)

*$p < .05$. **$p < .01$. ***$p < .001$.

for assessing predictive validity. According to the rubric proposed by Rice and Harris (2005), AUCs between .56 and .63 correspond to small effect sizes, AUCs between .64 and .70 to medium effect sizes, and AUCs of .71 and above to large effect sizes.

Alberta custody sample

Table 9.2 presents measures of predictive validity for the SPIn Pre-Screen total risk and strength scores over a three-year follow-up period for several outcome variables and for demographic subgroups (Jones & Robinson, 2016).[5] Results indicate that overall, the SPIn assessment protocol predicts technical violations, general recidivism, and violent recidivism among custody cases with AUCs ranging from .69 to .77 ($p < .001$). Importantly, Table 9.2 confirms that across all outcomes, levels of predictive accuracy are equivalent across male, female, non-Indigenous, and Indigenous clients. As such, these data provide support for the use of SPIn for prediction of post-release criminal justice outcomes across gender and ethnicity with custody populations.

Figure 9.3 presents rates of new offenses over the three-year follow-up period by risk and strength categories. Confirmed by logistic regression results provided in Table 9.3, the inclusion of the strength total in the assessment model provides incremental predictive validity; in other words, the consideration of strengths contributes to the prediction of recidivism above and beyond the consideration of risk/needs alone. Figure 9.3 illustrates the direct effect of strengths, whereby the presence of higher strength levels within each risk band lowers the resultant recidivism rate. With the current custody sample, the effect of strengths

---

5 Note that only those clients with at least a three-year follow-up period are considered here, reducing the original sample size from 752 to 501 cases.

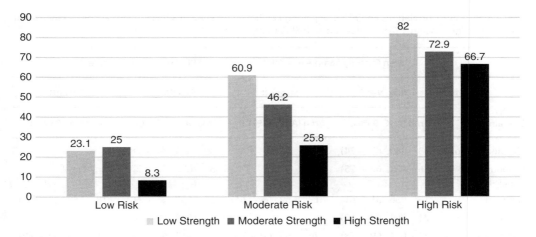

Figure 9.3 Rate of new offenses (%) over 3 years by SPIn Pre-Screen risk and strength categories (Alberta custody sample; *N* = 501). Overall recidivism rates by risk category are 18.3%, 49.3%, and 78.8% for low, moderate, and high, respectively.

Table 9.3 Results of Hierarchical Logistic Regression Analysis: Testing the Unique Contributions of SPIn Risk and Strength Pre-Screen Totals in Alberta Custody (N = 501) and Community Samples (N = 3,656)

SPIn Pre-Screen subscore	B(SE)	Wald Chi Square	OR (95% CI)
Custody sample			
Risk score	.03 (.01)	43.18***	1.03 (1.02 – 1.04)
Strength score	−.08 (.02)	13.48***	0.92 (0.88 – 0.96)
Community sample			
Risk score	.03 (.002)	245.15***	1.03 (1.03 – 1.03)
Strength score	−.06 (.01)	34.36***	0.94 (0.92 – 0.96)

***$p < .001$.
Note: Custody sample: R^2 associated with the Risk score alone is .25; R^2 associated with Risk + Strength as in the above model is .29. Community sample: R^2 associated with the Risk score alone is .20; R^2 associated with Risk + Strength as in the above model is .22.

is particularly pronounced among the moderate risk cases, whereby a "moderate-risk/high-strength" client is nearly 60% less likely to recidivate than a "moderate-risk/low-strength" client (25.8% vs. 60.9%).

The first half of Table 9.4 provides measures of predictive validity for each of the SPIn risk/need and strength domains vis-à-vis new offenses at three years post-release for the Alberta custody sample. All bivariate correlations and AUCs are significant and in the expected direction (save for the Mental Health domain). At the univariate level, the risk/need domains most predictive of recidivism include Criminal History, Response to Supervision, Social Influences, and Stability, with AUCs ranging from .69 to .74 (*p* < .001). Similarly, dynamic strengths in the

Table 9.4 Bivariate Correlations and AUCs Depicting Relationship Between SPIn Domains and New Offenses at 18 Months Follow-up and 3 Years Follow-up with SPIn Community and Custody Samples

	SPIn Custody Sample (*N* = 501)		SPIn Community Sample (*N* = 3,656)	
	Risk/Need	Strength	Risk/Need	Strength
Domain	*rho* (AUC, 95% CI)	*rho* (AUC, 95% CI)	*rho* (AUC, 95% CI)	*rho* (AUC, 95% CI)
Criminal History	.33*** (.69, .65 – .74)	—	.36*** (.76, .74 – .78)	—
Response to Supervision	.36*** (.71, .66 – .75)	—	.39*** (.75, .73 – .77)	—
Aggression	.15*** (.56, .51 – .61)	-.17*** (.59, .55 – .64)	.15*** (.57, .55 – .60)	-.18*** (.62, .59 – .64)
Substance Use	.24*** (.64, .59 – .69)	---	.18*** (.62, .60 – .65)	---
Social Influences	.41*** (.74, .69 – .78)	-.26*** (.65, .60 – .70)	.23*** (.65, .63 – .68)	-.21*** (.64, .62 – .67)
Family	.20*** (.61, .57 – .66)	-.21*** (.62, .57 – .67)	.08*** (.55, .53 – .58)	-.15*** (.60, .57 – .62)
Employment	.29*** (.65, .60 – .69)	-.27*** (.65, .61 – .70)	.17*** (.59, .57 – .62)	-.20*** (.63, .61 – .65)
Attitudes	.20*** (.60, .56 – .65)	-.20*** (.61, .56 – .66)	.07*** (.54, .52 – .57)	-.14*** (.60, .57 – .62)
Social/ Cognitive Skills	.27*** (.64, .59 – .69)	-.24*** (.64, .59 – .69)	.16*** (.59, .57 – .62)	-.18*** (.62, .60 – .65)
Stability	.34*** (.69, .65 – .74)	-.31*** (.68, .63 – .72)	.22*** (.64, .62 – .67)	-.21*** (.64, .62 – .67)
Mental Health	.04 (.52, .47 – .57)	—	.08*** (.54, .52 – .56)	—

***$p < .001$.

areas of Social Influences and Stability also yielded the highest levels of predictive accuracy (AUCs = .65 and .68, $p < .001$).

Alberta community sample

Jones and colleagues (2015) analyzed initial SPIn Pre-Screen assessments completed across Alberta, Canada, between January 2009 and May 2011. A total of 2,962 male and 694 female clients on community supervision (see Sample 2) were followed up for 18 months post initial assessment. As was the case with the custody sample, the predictive validity of the screening protocol was high irrespective of gender or Indigenous status (AUCs = .75 – .77, $p < .001$). The incremental predictive validity of strengths was also demonstrated across gender and ethnicity, suggesting that the quantitative inclusion of strength-based factors in the model serves to optimize the predictive potential of the assessment tool. Among female offenders, the strength score accounted for more unique variance than the risk score, with the latter rendered non-significant in a forced entry logistic regression model (for more information, please refer to Jones et al., 2015). Although this finding suggests that strengths may be particularly important in the assessment and classification of women, replication with additional samples is required. It is interesting to note, however, that the strong impact of strengths on the outcomes experienced by women is consistent with the strengths-based treatment and case management approaches endorsed for justice-involved females (e.g., Blanchette & Brown, 2006).

The SPIn Pre-Screen demonstrates excellent predictive utility with the Alberta community sample. As evidenced in Figure 9.4, high-strength scores are associated with reduced recidivism rates within each risk band. For example, among high-risk cases, there is nearly a 40% decrease in recidivism rates between low-strength and high-strength clients (58.7% vs. 35.7%).

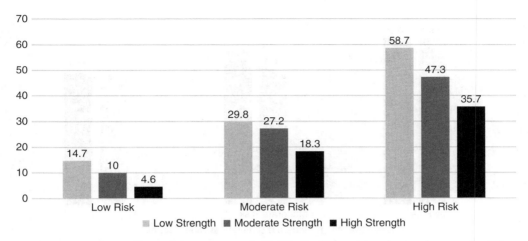

Figure 9.4 Rate of new offenses (%) over 18 months by SPIn Pre-Screen risk and strength categories (Alberta community sample; *N* = 3,656). Overall recidivism rates by risk category are 8.2%, 26.4%, and 52.3% for low, moderate, and high, respectively.

As such, an otherwise high-risk client with a number of strengths in place more closely resembles a moderate-risk case.

The second half of Table 9.4 provides measures of predictive validity for each of the SPIn risk/need and strength domains vis-à-vis new offenses at 18 months post-assessment for the Alberta community sample. All bivariate correlations and AUCs are significant and in the expected direction. At the univariate level, the risk/need domains most predictive of recidivism are Criminal History, Response to Supervision, Social Influences, and Stability, with AUCs ranging from .64 to .76 (*p* < .001). With respect to the dynamic strength domains, Social Influences and Stability yielded the highest levels of predictive accuracy (AUCs = .64, *p* < .001).

SPIn re-entry sample

Recall that SPIn Re-entry consists of a subset of 39 of the 90 items comprising SPIn. Accordingly, the validity of SPIn Re-entry was evaluated using the Alberta community sample prior to the implementation of the tool in a jurisdiction. Overall, the Pre-Screen SPIn Re-entry risk and strength measures yielded similar AUCs as those reported for the larger battery. SPIn Re-entry has yet to be validated with respect to its effectiveness in predicting recidivism with a new sample.

However, based on Dismas Charities clients (Sample 3), the SPIn Re-entry risk score successfully predicted successful program completion, disciplinary report rates, and proportion of late returns to reentry facilities following approved outings (Jones & Robinson, 2014). For example, 90% of low-risk cases successfully completed programming compared to just over 70% of high-risk cases. Success was defined as release from a Dismas reentry center following program completion without a return to Federal Bureau of Prisons. The mean disciplinary report rate was approximately 2.3 times greater for high-risk versus low-risk clients, and late returns were about 1.5 times more common for high-risk compared to low-risk cases. Levels of predictive validity met field conventions, with the highest accuracy associated with the prediction of successful completions (AUC = .65, *p* < .001).

Figure 9.5 shows the impact of strength on program completion across the three risk levels. The result is similar to the effects reported for recidivism in the Alberta custody and community samples. Program completion represents a highly relevant outcome measure for reentry programming, and one that has often been found to predict official measures of recidivism (e.g., Bouffard & Muftic, 2006).

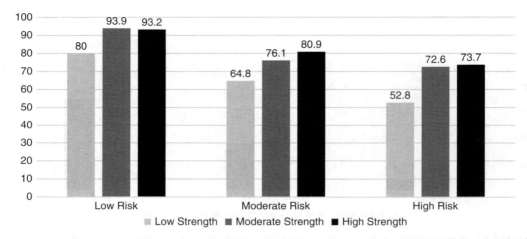

Figure 9.5 Percentage of successful program completions by risk and strength classification on SPIn Re-entry (Dismas Charities sample; $N = 4{,}110$). Overall rate of completions by risk category are 92.5%, 77.1%, and 67.6% for low, moderate, and high-risk categories, respectively.

SPIn-W Connecticut sample

Intake SPIn-W (Orbis Partners, 2006) and LSI-R (Andrews & Bonta, 1995) assessment data were available for the 274 female probationers from Connecticut, described above as Sample 4. Representing gender-specific and gender-neutral tools, respectively, the predictive validity of the two assessment protocols were compared (Robinson, Van Dieten, & Millson, 2012). Over a one-year follow-up period, respective arrest rates for those assessed as low, moderate, and high risk on SPIn-W were 12.9%, 25.3%, and 43.6% ($\chi^2 = 10.20$, $p < .01$), representing the desired increase between risk category and recidivism rates. In contrast, a non-linear relationship emerged between recidivism rates and risk level as defined by the LSI-R; new arrest rates over the same one-year fixed follow-up period with this gender-neutral tool were 29.9% for those in the 22–28 score range, 42.4% for those in the 29–38 score range, and 40.9% for those with scores of 39 or higher ($\chi^2 = 4.40$, $p = 11$). Overall, a moderate degree of predictive validity was reported for SPIn-W (AUC = .66, $p < .001$), whereas the AUC associated with the LSI-R fell in the low range at only .59. As such, the SPIn-W had higher predictive accuracy relative to the gender-neutral protocol among this sample of justice-involved females.

Although SPIn-W predicted criminal justice outcomes with moderate accuracy (AUC = .66, $p < .001$), the level of predictive validity yielded in this investigation was likely attenuated by the limited range of risk resulting from the selection criterion. Women were originally selected and assessed for participation in a case management model tailored to justice-involved females. In order to meet the eligibility requirement, potential participants had to achieve a score of 22 and above on the LSI-R, corresponding to medium or high risk. By eliminating those women scoring in the lower risk range, variability in the data was reduced and the predictive validity of SPIn-W was likely compromised.

Discussion

The quantitative inclusion of strengths in the SPIn protocol is a defining feature of the assessment model. Validation data collected to date demonstrate that SPIn strength scores contribute incrementally to the prediction of recidivism above and beyond the consideration of risks and needs alone. At the same time, our samples have consistently shown that risk/needs measures are inversely correlated with strengths. Indeed, some have argued that a strength measure is simply the absence or opposite of a risk factor (Baird, 2009; Harris & Rice, 2015) and has no contribution to make in predicting recidivism. However, the strength data presented for SPIn in this chapter challenge this assumption and provide compelling evidence that strengths have a recidivism reduction effect across risk levels.

Using SPIn and its variants, one is able to identify higher risk cases with a high level of strength and lower risk cases with a low level of strength. Such profiles might be serviced differently from their high-risk/low-strength and low-risk/high-strength counterparts. In addition, SPIn profiles will sometimes exhibit high need and high strength in the same domains. For example, in the Social Influences domain, some clients demonstrate a pattern whereby their need and strength scores are both in the moderate or high ranges. In such cases, one might have a combination of friends and associates who are antisocial, as well as members of their social networks who provide a positive influence. Such a mix of need and strengths is also commonly observed in the Family and Employment domains. In yet another indication that need and strength are not simply polar opposites, clients will sometimes exhibit low scores on both needs and strengths, a pattern suggesting neither problems nor identifiable assets within a given domain.

From a practical perspective, a more comprehensive profile of a criminal justice client emerges when assessment users have information about risk, needs, and strengths. In addition to optimizing predictive accuracy, knowing about an individual's strength profile can provide important responsivity information in the context of case planning. Moreover, when a case manager feels the need to override a risk classification, strengths can sometimes provide additional information for informing the decision. For example, consider a high-risk case that presents with high strengths or a low-risk case that presents with low strengths.

Although many case managers intuitively incorporate client strengths into their work, actually quantifying strengths through the assessment process draws attention to a number of advantages that emanate from strength-based approaches. Unless strengths are routinely included in the assessment process, many case managers are unlikely to generate or work with information about the positive attributes of their clients. Many case managers have learned that talking to clients about their strengths is a helpful engagement strategy and a critical tool for building rapport. The case planning model that SPIn users employ emphasizes that the provision of feedback on assessment results is one of the first steps in building a case plan. The feedback process begins with the assessment results that describe the client's strengths. Once positive elements have been reviewed, clients are more likely to be receptive to discussing the challenges (i.e., risk and needs) that should be addressed in the case plan.

Although research has indicated that including SPIn strength scores in statistical models serves to optimize predictive accuracy (Jones et al., 2015), there is a need to cultivate a greater understanding of how risk and strength factors interact to predict criminal outcomes. For instance, which specific strengths or strength domains are most influential in predicting recidivism? Do strength-by-risk interactions differ between demographic groups (e.g., race/ethnicity/culture, age, gender)? Such questions will be germane to the development of more effective assessment protocols and to the appropriate delivery of criminal justice services.

Notwithstanding the basic gender-responsive content of SPIn and its effectiveness with women, SPIn-W may be a preferable option for female offender populations given that the latter was expressly designed to assess factors that may uniquely impact women's outcomes. SPIn-W is used in a number of settings with female caseloads, including probation, custody, and community residential programs. Users of SPIn-W report positively on how the assessment tool provides in-depth profiles of the needs, strengths, and responsivity factors that are important in serving justice-involved women. At present, only one study featuring a relatively small sample of moderate to high-risk females has examined the predictive validity of SPIn-W (see Sample 4; Robinson et al., 2012). Although in the acceptable range (AUC = .65, p < .001), the predictive accuracy of the tool was likely hindered by the limited range of risk specified in the selection criterion (see earlier). Forthcoming samples will allow for the further exploration of SPIn-W's predictive validity.

As official recidivism records were unavailable, we were limited to examining the predictive accuracy of SPIn Re-entry using interim outcomes measures. These included successful program completion, disciplinary infractions, and late returns to a residential facility. There is evidence to suggest that interim or proxy outcomes of this nature, particularly treatment or program completion, are viable predictors of future reoffending (Bouffard & Muftic, 2006; Latessa, Lovins, & Smith, 2010; Rosenbaum, Gearan, & Ondovic, 2002). Moreover, construction test data from the Alberta community sample provided positive evidence to suggest that the abridged version of SPIn can also be effective for predicting outcomes among probation cases. SPIn Re-entry provides the key features of the larger model (strengths, Pre-Screen classification, dynamic scoring) with a substantially condensed battery of items. However, new samples will be helpful for further evaluating the usefulness of the brief version of the tool.

SPIn has performed consistently across different correctional sub-populations and demonstrates predictive validity across gender and ethnic groups. Additional samples will be needed to examine the utility of the protocol with African American and Hispanic clients. Inter-rater reliability studies will also be an important addition for future studies. Although further research is warranted (particularly on SPIn-W and SPIn Re-entry), there is evidence to suggest that the SPIn assessment model is a psychometrically sound protocol for predicting recidivism, guiding classification decisions, and informing case management strategies for justice-involved adults. Overall, the SPIn tools offer a viable risk/needs assessment alternative for jurisdictions that wish to include strengths in their assessment and case management models.

References

Anda, R. F., Felitti, V. J., Bremner, J. D., Walker, J. D., Whitfield, C., Perry, B. D., & Giles, W. H. (2006). The enduring effects of abuse and related adverse experiences in childhood: A convergence of evidence from neurobiology and epidemiology. *European Archives of Psychiatry and Clinical Neuroscience, 256*, 174–186. doi:10.1007/s00406-005-0624-4

Andrews, D. A., & Bonta, J. (1995). *LSI-R: The Level of Service Inventory–Revised*. Toronto, ON, Canada: Multi-Health Systems.

Andrews, D. A., & Bonta, J. (2010). *The psychology of criminal conduct* (5th ed.). New Providence, NJ: Anderson.

Andrews, D. A., Bonta, J., & Wormith, J. S. (2004). *The Level of Service/Case Management Inventory (LS/CMI): User's manual*. Toronto, ON, Canada: Multi-Health Systems.

Andrews, D. A., Bonta, J., & Wormith, J. S. (2006). The recent past and near future of risk and/or need assessment. *Crime & Delinquency, 52*, 7–27. doi:10.1177/0011128705281756

Baglivio, M. T., Wolff, K. T., & Piquero, A. R. (2015). The relationship between adverse childhood experiences (ACE) and juvenile offending trajectories in a juvenile offender sample. *Journal of Criminal Justice, 43*, 229–241. doi:10.1016/j.jcrimjus.2015.04.012

Baglivio, M. T., Wolff, K. T., Piquero, A. R., Bilchik, S., Joackowski, K., Greenwald, M. A., & Epps, N. (2016). Maltreatment, child welfare, and recidivism in a sample of deep-end crossover youth. *Journal of Youth Adolescence, 45*, 625–654. doi:10.1007/s10964-015-0407-9

Baird, C. (2009, February). *A question of evidence: A critique of risk assessment models used in the justice system*. Madison, WI: National Council on Crime and Delinquency.

Baird, C., Healy, T., Johnson, K., Bogie, A., Dankert, E. W., & Scharenbroch, C. (2013). *A comparison of risk assessment instruments in juvenile justice.* National Council on Crime and Delinquency (Award No.: 2010-JR-FX-0021; Document No.: 244477). Retrieved from https://www.ncjrs.gov/pdffiles1/ojjdp/grants/244477.pdf

Barnoski, R. (2003). *Changes in Washington State's jurisdiction of juvenile offenders: Examining the impact.* Olympia, WA: Washington State Institute of Public Policy.

Barnoski, R. (2009). *Positive Achievement Change Tool, Pre-Screen Instrument.* Tallahassee, FL: Florida Department of Juvenile Justice.

Belknap, J. (2015). *The invisible woman: Gender, crime, and justice* (4th ed.). Stamford, CT: Cengage Learning.

Blanchette, K., & Brown, S. L. (2006). *The assessment and treatment of women offenders: An integrative perspective.* Chichester, England: John Wiley & Sons.

Borum, R., Bartel, P., & Forth, A. (2006). *Manual for the Structured Assessment of Violence Risk in Youth (SAVRY).* Odessa, FL: Psychological Assessment Resources.

Bouffard, J. A., & Muftic, L. R. (2006). Program completion and recidivism outcomes among adult offenders ordered to complete a community service sentence. *Journal of Offender Rehabilitation, 43*, 1–33. doi:10.1300/J076v43n02_01

Brown, S. L., Geck, C., Harris, M., & Skilling, T. (2012). *Reliability and validity of the Youth Assessment Screening Inventory (YASI) in a sample of Canadian Youth* (Unpublished manuscript).

Daly, K. (1994). *Gender, crime, and punishment.* New Haven, CT: Yale University Press.

Felitti, J. J., Anda, R. F., Nordenberg, D., Williamson, D. F., Spitz, A. M., Edwards, V., . . . Marks, J. S. (1998). Relationship of childhood abuse and household dysfunction to many of the leading causes of death in adults. The Adverse Childhood Experiences (ACE) Study. *American Journal of Preventative Medicine, 14*, 245–258. doi:10.1016/S0749-3797(98)00017-8

Grasso, D. J., Dierkhising, C. B., Branson, C. E., Ford, J. D., & Lee, R. (2016). Developmental patterns of adverse childhood experiences and current symptoms and impairment in youth referred for trauma-specific services. *Journal of Abnormal Child Psychology, 44*, 871-886. doi:10.1007/s10802-015-0086-8

Hanson, R. K., & Morton-Bourgon, K. E. (2009). The accuracy of recidivism risk for sexual offenders: A meta-analysis of 118 prediction studies. *Psychological Assessment, 21*, 1–21. doi:10.1037/a0014421

Harris, G. T., & Rice, M. E. (2015). Progress in violence risk assessment and communication: Hypothesis versus evidence. *Behavioral Sciences and the Law, 33*, 128–145. doi:10.1002/bsl.2157

Jones, N. J. (2011). *Merging theoretical frameworks to inform risk assessment for the young female offender.* Unpublished doctoral dissertation, Carleton University, Ottawa, ON, Canada.

Jones, N. J. (2017). *Risk-need-responsivity, application to female offenders. Sage Encyclopedia of Criminal Psychology.* Thousand Oaks, CA: Sage.

Jones, N. J., Brown, S. L., Robinson, D., & Frey, D. (2015). Incorporating strengths into quantitative assessments of criminal risk for adult offenders: The Service Planning Instrument (SPIn). *Criminal Justice and Behavior, 42*, 321–338. doi:10.1177/0093854814547041

Jones, N. J., Brown, S. L., Robinson, D., & Frey, D. (2016). Validity of the Youth Assessment and Screening Instrument: A juvenile justice tools incorporating risks, needs, and strengths. *Law and Human Behavior, 40*, 182–194. doi:10.1037/lhb0000170

Jones, N. J., Brown, S. L., Wanamaker, K. A., & Greiner, L. E. (2014). A quantitative exploration of gendered pathways to crime in a sample of male and female juvenile offenders. *Feminist Criminology, 9*, 113–136. doi:10.1177/1557085113501850

Jones, N. J., & Robinson, D. (2014). *Validation of SPIn Re-entry with federal offenders served by Dismas Charities, Inc.* Ottawa, ON: Author.

Jones, N. J., & Robinson, D. (2016). *The validity of the Service Planning Instrument (SPIn) in an Alberta Custody Sample: A Brief Report*. Unpublished report prepared for Alberta Justice and Solicitor General, Canada.

Jones, N. J., Salisbury, E. J., & Kelly, B. (2016, October). Exploring the relationship between early trauma and negative outcomes in criminal justice clients. Workshop presented at the annual conference of the International Community Corrections Association (ICCA), Toronto, ON, Canada.

Latessa, E. J., Lovins, L. B., & Smith, P. (2010). *Follow-up evaluation of Ohio's community based correctional facility and halfway house programs – outcome study*. Cincinnati, OH: Center for Criminal Justice Research.

Lodewijks, H. P., Doreleijers, T. A., de Ruiter, C., & Borum, R. (2008). Predictive validity of the Structured Assessment of Violence Risk in Youth (SAVRY) during residential treatment. *International Journal of Law and Psychiatry, 31*, 263–271. doi:10.1016/j.ijlp.2008.04.009

Miller, W. R., & Rollnick, S. (2002). *Motivational interviewing: Preparing people for change* (2nd ed.). New York, NY: Guilford Press.

National Crittenton Foundation. (2013, May). *Summary of results: Crittenton Adverse Childhood Experiences (ACE) pilot*. Portland, OR: Author. Retrieved from http://nationalcrittenton.org/wp-content/uploads/2015/03/ACEresults.JJ_.pdf

Orbis Partners. (2000). *Youth Assessment and Screening Instrument (YASI)*. Ottawa, ON: Author.

Orbis Partners. (2003). *Service Planning Instrument (SPIn)*. Ottawa, ON: Author.

Orbis Partners. (2006). *Service Planning Instrument for Women (SPIn-W)*. Ottawa, ON: Author.

Orbis Partners. (2013). *Service Planning Instrument Re-entry (SPIn Re-entry)*. Ottawa, ON: Author.

Orbis Partners. (2016). *Collaborative Case Work*. Ottawa, ON: Author.

Rice, M. E., & Harris, G. T. (2005). Comparing effect sizes in follow-up studies: ROC Area, Cohen's *d*, and *r*. *Law and Human Behavior, 29*, 615–620. doi:10.1007/s10979005-6832-7

Robinson, D., Van Dieten, M., & Millson B. W. (2012, Spring). The Women Offender Case Management Model in the State of *Connecticut*. *Journal of Community Corrections, 7–25*.

Rosenbaum, A., Gearan, P. J., & Ondovic, C. (2002). Completion and recidivism among court- and self-referred batterers in a psychoeducational group treatment program: Implications for intervention and public policy. *Journal of Aggression, Maltreatment & Trauma, 5*, 199–220. doi:10.1300/J146v05n02_12

Rossegger, A., Wetli, N., Urbaniok, F., Elbert, T., Cortoni, F., & Endrass, J. (2009). Women convicted for violent offenses: Adverse childhood experiences, low level of education and poor mental health. *BMC Psychiatry, 9*, 1–7. doi:10.1186/1471-244X-9-81

Salisbury, E. J., & Van Voorhis, P. (2009). Gendered pathways: A quantitative investigation of women probationers' paths to incarceration. *Criminal Justice and Behavior, 36*, 541–566. doi:10.1177/0093854809334076

Serin, R. C., Chadwick, N., & Lloyd, C. D. (2016). Dynamic risk and protective factors. *Psychology, Crime & Law, 22*, 151–170. doi:10.1080/1068316X.2015.1112013

Skeem, J., Hernandez, I., Kennealy, P., & Rich, J. (2012). *CA-YASI reliability: How adequately do staff in California's Division of Juvenile Justice rate youths' risk of recidivism?* Irvine, CA: University of California.

Van Voorhis, P., Wright, E. M., Salisbury, E., & Bauman, A. (2010). Women's risk factors and their contributions to existing risk/needs assessment: The current status of a gender-responsive supplement. *Criminal Justice and Behavior, 37*, 261–288. doi:10.1177/0093854809357442

10

The Static Risk Offender Needs Guide – Revised (STRONG-R)

Zachary Hamilton, Xiaohan Mei, and Douglas Routh

Overview

The Static Risk Offender Need Guide – Revised (STRONG-R) was initially developed using a large sample of over 44,000 Washington State Department of Corrections (WADOC) offenders reentering the community. It was designed to provide an actuarial prediction of recidivism.[1] The STRONG-R is classified as a *general recidivism* prediction instrument; however, its scope has been expanded to provide a systems approach, predicting a variety of outcomes at multiple stages within the criminal justice system (e.g., failure to appear [FTA], infractions, recidivism, programming needs, and technical violations). This systems approach is a relatively contemporary concept within offender assessment, with the essential postulate that a fair amount of overlap and redundancies exist among the predictors of outcomes at each stage and those involved in the justice system. While outcomes of interest may vary at each stage of the system, many assessment items, such as age, prior convictions, and substance abuse are consistent predictors, whereas items such as prior FTAs, security threat group (STG), and current employment, are more (or less) predictive at different stages of the criminal justice system and for specific outcomes. Unique from other contemporary risk assessment systems, the STRONG-R attempts to make use of a large pool of predictor items, selecting and weighting measures dependent on the stage of the system, outcome of interest, gender of the offender, and jurisdiction. This ability to recreate and adjust each assessment according to agency specifications, makes the tool *customizable.*

Currently over 130 unique response items comprise the *pool* of STRONG-R items. Prediction models have been developed, making use of a selection of items from this pool to predict both general and more specified criminal justice outcomes of interest.[2] An example illustration of a truncated selection of items and models is provided in Figure 10.1.

Each model has a unique set of items selected and the weights of each response are allowed to differ for each model. Using both male and female samples of offenders, each *prediction model* is created separately for each gender in an effort to provide *gender specificity* of prediction model content. Collectively, each model predicts a given recidivistic outcome and makes

---

1 Although many definitions of recidivism exist, we have previously defined recidivism as a new conviction following an initial or re-assessment (Hamilton et al., 2016a).

2 The total pool of items is combined across all developed tools. Some items are not used in particular tools and others are collected for case management purposes and not scored. Readers should note that the exact number of items is presented for each tool as it is discussed throughout this chapter.

Handbook of Recidivism Risk/Needs Assessment Tools, First Edition. Edited by Jay P. Singh, Daryl G. Kroner, J. Stephen Wormith, Sarah L. Desmarais, and Zachary Hamilton.
© 2018 John Wiley & Sons, Ltd. Published 2018 by John Wiley & Sons, Ltd.

Item	Violent Model Weight	Property Model Weight	Drug Model Weight	Any Felony Model Weight
1. Total# of Felonies				
a. Zero	0	0	0	0
b. One	3	6	5	4
c. Two	6	12	10	8
d. Three +	9	18	15	12
2. Total# of Drug Felonies				
a. Zero	NA	0	0	0
b. One	NA	3	6	5
c. Two	NA	6	12	10
d. Three +	NA	9	18	15
Risk Model Scoring {	6	15	16	13

Figure 10.1 Example illustration of STRONG-R item selection and weighting. *Source:* Hamilton, Tollefsbol, Campagna, & van Wormer (2017).

up one of several STRONG-R *tools*.[3] The STRONG-R system of assessments, or collection of tools, represents the entirety of the *instrument*. The STRONG-R assessment system is designed to be an instrument that consists of multiple tools, derived from general and specific prediction models, used to assess a variety of criminal justice related outcomes. A comprehensive list of STRONG-R tool descriptives is provided in Table 10.1.

Depending on the stage of the system, agencies may wish to employ several tools. The result is a variety of outcomes, or scored categories, that assess the prediction of future events and assist decisions related to case management, classification, supervision contacts, and intervention needs. An illustration of the potential tool uses throughout the criminal justice system is presented in Figure 10.2.

Recidivism Prediction Spotlight

The current content has described the customizable models and flexibility of the STRONG-R assessment system. To describe the general design and background mechanics of the instrument, we highlight a single tool used to predict risk of recidivism. This tool was selected to spotlight, as the vast majority of analyses and supporting literature for the STRONG-R have been completed using this initial WADOC development sample.

Briefly, the STRONG-R recidivism tool uses a collection of statistical algorithms. With four outcomes (general, violent, property, and drug recidivism) and separate male and female algorithms constructed for each, the STRONG-R recidivism tool provides re-offense prediction using a total of eight uniquely constructed models (see Hamilton et al., 2016a). While most contemporary tools predict recidivism generally, ranking individuals as high, moderate, or low risk on a single continuous scale, one of the methodological advances of the STRONG-R is the use

---

3 We define *recidivistic outcomes* as reoffending and criminal justice events agencies seek to prevent, including FTAs, rearrests, reconvictions, infractions, and technical violations.

Table 10.1 STRONG-R Tool Descriptives

Tool	Target Population	Intent	Item Types	Outcomes Predicted
Pretrial	Defendants awaiting trail	Inform judges release decisions	Static, dynamic, risk, & protective	Failure-to-appear (FTA)
Recidivism	All criminal justice populations	Predict risk of recidivism for anyone currently, or to be, *released* to the community	Static, dynamic, risk, and protective	General, violent, property, and drug recidivism (i.e., rearrest or reconviction)
Need	All criminal justice populations	Intervention needs	Dynamic, risk, & protective	Domain needs: education, employment, family, peers, attitudes/behaviors, aggression, substance abuse, mental health, & residential
Classification	Prison and jail	Identify the custody designation of inmates (i.e., max, medium, minimum, etc.)	Static, dynamic, risk, & protective	Violent, serious, and non-serious infractions
Compliance	Community supervision (i.e., probation & parole)	Predict non-compliance with supervision conditions for anyone currently, or to be, *supervised* in the community	Static, dynamic, risk, & protective	Serious and non-serious technical violations
Low-Risk Screener	Reentry and those on community supervision	Short, static-only tool used to efficiently identify individuals for alternatives to or administrative supervision	Static risk, & protective	Low risk for general recidivism (i.e., rearrest or reconviction)

of qualitative distinctions that take into consideration outcome seriousness. This conceptual distinction indicates that, all things being equal, if two individuals are equally high risk to recidivate, the offender that is high risk for violent offending is a higher supervision priority than the individual at risk for a drug or property offense.

To apply this concept, the STRONG-R includes several scales, which identify and prioritize distinctions between recidivistic outcome types. In practice, the STRONG-R model makes use of a hierarchical classification system, combining the effects of one general and three specified risk scales. The classification hierarchy operationalizes risk category assignment as follows: (1) Low, (2) Moderate, (3) High Drug, (4) High Property, (5) High Violent, and (6) Criminally Diverse. The rules governing risk category placement are illustrated in Figure 10.3, where supervision contact and other conditions are set based on an individual's highest ranking among the four prediction models.

Each outcome of interest within the STRONG-R system has multiple layers of specificity to be predicted. Therefore, this same hierarchical classification system is used to categorize the seriousness of other outcomes for additional tools, such as those that predict infractions and technical violations. This novel categorization allows agencies to customize supervision strategies, noting that a general risk for any crime is not equal to the specified risk for particular offending patterns.

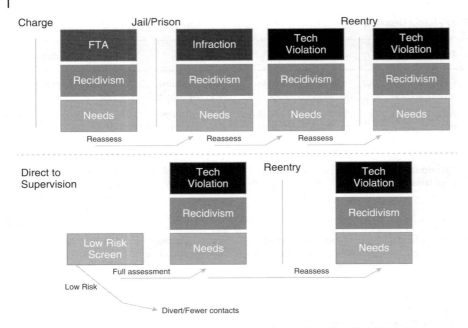

Figure 10.2 STRONG-R system tool outcome process. *Source:* Hamilton, Tollefsbol, Campagna, & van Wormer (2017).

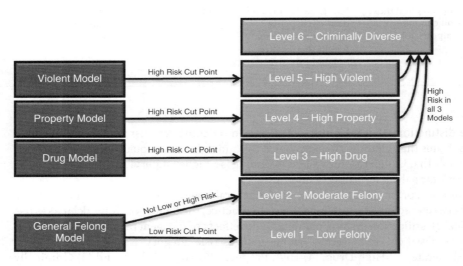

Figure 10.3 STRONG-R hierarchical risk categorization. *Source:* Hamilton, Kigerl, Campagna, Barnoski, Lee, van Wormer, & Block (2016a).

Item Types

The described collection of tools was crafted to identify reductions/increases in an individual's risk to commit recidivistic outcomes. As such, both static and dynamic items are utilized; where dynamic items allow assessed individuals to decrease, or increase, their level of risk following a re-assessment and over time. STRONG-R items are further categorized as either risk or protective; where affirmative responses to risk items identify increases in an individual's likelihood to commit a recidivistic event and protective items identify scoring reductions.

However, the STRONG-R uses a different framework than many contemporary tools. We contend that the intent of a *risk assessment* instrument is to measure an individual's risk to reoffend, which may include any, and all, measures (both static and dynamic) with the goal of providing a final summary score that indicates an individual's overall risk for the recidivistic outcome. However, the STRONG-R provides a separate *needs assessment* tool used for intervention selection, prioritization, and matching (Hamilton, Campagna, & Tollefsbol, 2016b). To develop the needs assessment, all static items in the STRONG-R item pool were removed, allowing an individual to be scored within nine broad domains of need. Needs assessment reports are then used by case management staff to plan and track an individual's progress. An example summary report is provided in Figure 10.4. The needs assessment development and application are further described in proceeding section.

Instrument Purpose(s)

While the STRONG-R does provide models and scores that predict any/all recidivism, a major feature of the tool is the provision of additional models and scores that predict violent, property, and drug recidivism, specifically. As previously indicated, models have also been created to predict a variety of infraction behaviors (violent, serious, and non-serious) while incarcerated, technical violations (violent, serious, and frequent non-serious) while on community supervision, as well as failure to appear for defendants awaiting trial. With regard to operational definitions of outcomes, as will be discussed, the STRONG-R allows definitions to vary based on jurisdiction preferences and need. This flexibility is a notable advantage, as a probation or a parole agency may have the same need to predict recidivism; however, the latter has a greater need to predict outcomes that will result in a possible return to prison (i.e., felony convictions) and the former may prefer a more general outcome prediction (i.e., any arrest, charge, or conviction).

Risk Level Classification: High Drug						
Risk level Classification From STRONG-R						
Need			**DOMAIN**	Protective		
Low	Moderate	High		Low	Moderate	High
			ALCOHOL/DRUG USE			
			EMPLOYMENT			
			FRIENDS			
			ATTITUDES/BEHAVIORS			
			RESIDENTIAL			
			FAMILY			
			AGGRESSION			
			MENTAL HEALTH			
			EDUCATION			

Case Management Information	
Additional Screening Needed	Alcohol/drug severity screening (completed)
Interventions Received	Theraputic Community (Completed)
Interventions Recommended	AA/NA in community, vocational training
Supervision Condition	3 CO contacts per month, I urine analysis per month
Potential Responsivity Barriers	No record of legal employment, felony record

Figure 10.4 STRONG-R summary report. *Source:* Hamilton, Tollefsbol, Campagna, & van Wormer (2017).

Target Population and Setting

As described, the STRONG-R makes use of a large general pool of predictive items. Those that are feasibly assessed and logically relevant to the outcome of interest are tested for their predictive strength. If predictive, the items are included in the instrument, and given the appropriate weight in the model's statistical algorithm. Described previously, each model is specifically crafted for male and female samples separately, allowing for gender specificity (see Hamilton et al., 2016a). As tools have currently been built to predict for pretrial defendants, incarcerated inmates, and offenders supervised in the community, the target population of the STRONG-R tool varies based on the population of interest and the jurisdiction in which it is applied. In theory, a STRONG-R tool is developed and recalibrated for each target population.

Time Frame of Prediction

Time frames of many contemporary assessments vary. Most focus on arrests while some focus on convictions (Hamilton, Tollefsbol, Campagna, & van Wormer, 2017). Some use a varying length of follow-up to track outcome occurrences, while others use a fixed time period (Hamilton et al., 2017). Because base rates (within a given time frame) of re-arrests are relatively larger than that of charges, reconvictions, or reincarcerations, the selection of the outcome type is important, as the models predicting re-arrest require a shorter prediction time-frame than those requiring further justice system involvement (e.g., reconvictions). However, like many elements of the STRONG-R, the duration of the prediction time frame is customizable. A probation jurisdiction primarily supervising misdemeanants may desire a tool that predicts arrests over a 12-month period. A felony supervision jurisdiction, such as the WADOC, may desire a multi-year felony reconviction prediction. Still further, an agency supervising pretrial release defendants, with varying sentence durations, may desire a censored follow-up period, examining time-to-event outcomes. Given that jurisdiction definitions and needs will vary, customizing the time frame of the prediction to the agency's need is a critical aspect of the STRONG-R.

Theoretical Framework

Over the last two decades, the use of offender assessments has expanded greatly; however, the theoretical framework of nearly all tools can be traced back to a relatively singular foundation. The theoretical underpinning of nearly all criminal justice assessment tools was derived from the risk, need, and responsivity (RNR) principles described in Andrews and Bonta's *Psychology of Criminal Conduct* (2010). The first "R" of the RNR principles refers to an assessment of offender risk. As indicated, a risk assessment is developed with all items that theoretically and logically predict the likelihood of the outcome of interest, typically recidivism. The "N" refers to an assessment of an individual's needs and a needs assessment serves a different purpose, prioritizing individuals for interventions and services. Responsivity is the final "R" of the RNR system, and describes the process of matching programs to individuals' needs. This process involves the utilization of assessed needs and the coordination and establishment of case planning, tracking an individual's use of agency resources to ameliorate criminogenic needs and, in turn, reduce an individual's risk to recidivate. These three principles fulfil the minimum requirements needed when building a RNR assessment system (Hamilton et al., 2016a).

Generally speaking, contemporary RNR assessments consist of algorithms of various complexities, which make use of predictive indicators of what can be several behavioral outcomes

(Falzer, 2013). From clinical judgment to the development of RNR models, Andrews, Bonta, and Wormith (2006) outlined four generations of tools. Each generation adds dimensions that improve an instrument's functionality (Baird, 2009).

Primarily, risk assessment instruments are developed to assist agencies in the management of correctional populations and to guide the frequency of contact and/or level of supervision in the community (Barnoski & Aos, 2003; Chadwick, DeWolf, & Serin, 2015; Viglione, Rudes, & Taxman, 2015). However, the RNR principles go beyond predicting recidivism, identifying key aspects of correctional management such as the provision of treatments and services, assistance in case management, and prioritization of offenders for interventions (addressing individuals' needs and responsivity). While the RNR principles have been applauded in contemporary corrections circles (Hamilton et al., 2016), consistent application of the concepts within offender assessments is a complex development process (Taxman & Pattavina, 2013).

The STRONG-R was founded on the RNR principles and classified as a fourth generation tool (Andrews, Bonta, & Wormith, 2006). As discussed, the STRONG-R predicts risk of recidivism generally and further specifies by type. A needs assessment is additionally computed for individuals via dynamic change measures, specifying programmatic needs by domain. Interventions and services are then recommended for the responsive provision of programming. The following section describes how RNR principles were integrated within the development of the STRONG-R and the advances made to extend their utility in practice.

History of Development

While additional STRONG-R tools for pretrial and prison classification have been developed, the current section addresses the development history of the most two prominent: recidivism and needs prediction tools. In particular, we describe the development of the subscales, methodological advances, customizable elements, and criminogenic needs domains. While relatively new in name, items and prior versions of the STRONG-R tool have been implemented and in use since 2006 (see Barnoski & Drake, 2007). The initial origins began in Washington State with the passage of the Offender Accountability Act (OAA). The OAA was critical to the history of risk assessment development in Washington, explicitly mandating that offenders be supervised in the community according to their level of risk. As it was the most widely used and easily accessible tool, the LSI-R was first adopted to meet statutory requirements. Following a Washington State Institute for Public Policy (WSIPP) review of the LSI-R's use in the initial years following implementation, it was determined that the lack of jurisdiction specificity and use of less-than-optimal predictive items reduced the performance and accuracy of the tool in Washington (Barnoski & Drake, 2007).

The Static Risk Assessment

Ultimately the state proceeded to craft a new tool using a localized WADOC population, analytic weighting item responses, and restricting the tool to 23 static criminal history measures (plus age and gender). The latter of these three elements was seen as a way to feasibly create a highly predictive instrument, in a short period of time, that required little training, and would return a reliable and valid offender risk score. The instrument created was termed the Static Risk Assessment (SRA) and is currently still used by California's Department of Correctional and Rehabilitation (CDCR) (Turner, Hess, & Jannetta, 2009), and several county probation and local court jurisdictions in California and Washington. Furthermore, in follow-up assessments, the SRA has been found to possess a strong predictive performance, serving as evidence in Washington as an improvement over the LSI-R (Barnoski & Drake, 2007). The instrument was eventually recalibrated into a second version, further improving its predictive accuracy and feasible use (Barnoski, 2010).

The Offender Needs Assessment

During the SRA's initial development, the WADOC recognized the new tool's restrictions pertaining to the assessment of offender needs. In conjunction with WSIPP, a team of WADOC SMEs were assembled and began the development of the Offender Needs Assessment (ONA). SMEs were tasked to assemble a collection of items that would form the common domain construction observed in other tools. Disappointed with the construction of the LSI-R and other contemporary tools, SMEs and the WSIPP assembled a list of items and domains that would assess similar content but be comprised of responses that were as *objective as possible* and, when feasible, confirmable through a record review. That is, instead of asking if "a hungry person has the right to steal," the ONA asks if "the offender respects personal property but not public/business property," where the latter can be potentially confirmed through a review of the offender's recent criminal behaviors and observed attitudes (Hamilton et al., 2016).

The initial version of the ONA was intended to be purely informative to case managers, with the intent of validating items following several years of data collection and analysis. The initial version of the tool was implemented in August of 2008 (see Hamilton et al., 2016). The secondary intent of the ONA was to establish a baseline, allowing SMEs and researchers to identify the reliability, content, and predictive validity of each item introduced by the ONA. The two tools (the SRA and ONA) were incorporated into a software medium and implemented in a similar, bifurcated model in several probation jurisdictions in California. This combined software provision of the two tools was then renamed the Static Risk Offender Needs Guide (STRONG).

The STRONG-R

Following five years of data collection, the WADOC partnered with the Washington State Institute for Criminal Justice (WSICJ) to develop and revise the instrument. As discussed, the revised version (the STRONG-R) selected and weighted predictive items from the SRA, ONA, and additional, routinely collected correction events to predict four types of felony reconvictions—violent, property, drug, and any (Hamilton et al., 2016). This initial version of the STRONG-R included a criminal record portion of 28 routinely collected criminal history items, and 78 additional assessment items collected via an interview by trained staff. The initial development sample for the risk and needs instruments was roughly 44,000 subjects, comprising offenders reentering from prison and others directly supervised in the community (i.e., felony probation). Following the initial sample creation, additional offenders have supplemented the development sample, which now comprises roughly 100,000 prison and community supervised offenders (Hamilton, Kigerl, & Routh, 2016).

Subscale Construction

The seminal concepts outlined in the *Psychology of Criminal Conduct* was based on work completed when the authors were developing the LSI-R (Andrews & Bonta, 1995). Specifically, Andrews and Bonta outlined their *Central Eight* domains, consisting of History of Antisocial Behavior, Antisocial Personality Pattern, Antisocial Cognition, Antisocial Associates, Family/Marital Circumstances, School/Work, Leisure/Recreation, and Substance Abuse (Andrews &

Bonta, 1995, pp. 58–59). In conjunction with their principles of Risk and Need, these eight domains describe clusters of assessment items that work together to describe characteristics of the offender and their environment that contribute to recidivism. Like many contemporary instruments (i.e., COMPAS, ORAS, IORNS, and WRNA), the STRONG-R also makes use of a domain structure, clustering items into 10 domains/distinct scales: (1) criminal convictions/correction events, (2) residential, (3) education, (4) employment, (5) peers/associates, (6) substance abuse/use, (7) mental health, (8) family, (9) aggression, and (10) attitudes/behaviors. While the items of these complementary domains differ from those originally formulated by Andrews and Bonta, their content and intended use are similar, yet expanded in both number of items and content.

As will be discussed, these domains are further aggregated into higher order constructs and broken down into several subscales and sub-subscales. A total of 28 items are contained within Domain 1, which includes all SRA items and added correctional events (i.e., infractions, technical violations, security threat group status, program participation). These criminal history items are intended to be automated via software integration (see Hamilton, Tollefsbol, Campagna, & van Wormer, 2017), while ONG items are collected via an interview, conducted by trained staff. The ONG comprises 78 items and the initial interview is typically completed in 45 to 60 minutes. Subsequent re-assessments are recommended to be completed every six to 12 months. However, software applications have been designed for re-assessments to address only those items that feasibly change from assessment to re-assessment. Using this automated process, re-assessments require roughly 10 to 20 minutes to complete. Readers should note that many of the ONG items are dynamic and therefore utilized in both the risk and needs assessment scoring.

Methodological Advances

Generally speaking, the majority of criminal justice assessment research can be attributed to two primary instruments—the Level of Service Inventory–Revised (LSI-R) (Andrews & Bonta, 1995) and the Correctional Offender Management Profiling for Alternative Sanctions (COMPAS) (Brennan & Oliver, 2000). While many other tools have come before and after their development, the bulk of contemporary tools' methodological foundations have been formulated around the concepts initiated by these two assessment instruments. In many respects, the STRONG-R is no exception.

Several years following the development of the LSI-R, Brennan and Oliver (2000) developed the COMPAS instrument. Using a similar construction of domains, the COMPAS advanced the methodological aspects of risk assessment development, creating models that utilize multivariate item selection, analytic weighting, outcome specific algorithms, improved validation metrics, and gender responsive assessment (see Hamilton et al., 2016). These advances form the basis of several of the design elements applied in the STRONG-R, allowing for greater predictive performance and a more consistent application of RNR concepts (see Hamilton, et al., 2016b).

Customization and the STRONG-R

While several of the theoretical concepts used in its construction were initially based on the prior works of notable assessment developers, a primary conceptual directive is central to STRONG-R tool development (see Hamilton et al., 2016). As indicated, many tools were built around psychological traditions, treating recidivistic outcomes similar to that of a mental health diagnosis. Analogous to a risk assessment, diagnoses are provided based on the confirmation of a list of key items, or symptoms. Thus, a diagnosis will manifest itself similarly in individuals indicating said symptoms, regardless of location, clinic, or hospital. Contemporary criminal justice instruments are commonly built on these concepts, attempting to make a single algorithm with a unified set of item weights that are generalizable to all jurisdictions (Andrews & Bonta, 1995; Brennan & Oliver, 2000; Latessa, Smith, Lemke, Makarios, & Lowenkamp, 2009).

In contrast, a primary postulate of the STRONG-R is that, when predicting any recidivistic outcome, both prediction items and their relative importance (item weight) should be tailored and designed to fit the local jurisdiction. We contend that this design provides an extension of Andrews and Bonta's concept of specific responsivity, directed toward the setting in which the tool is implemented. Each agency seeking to adopt a risk assessment tool has a notable, manifest outcome that can be predicted using their specified population. Noting differences in criminal justice populations (parole vs. probation), regional dereferences in both recidivism prevalence and types, alternate operational definitions of recidivistic outcomes of interest, agency's abilities/access to collect specific data elements (i.e., access to criminal records), and variants in local statutes and sentencing severities, the STRONG-R attempts to vary each tool's development with each implementation. Derived from a general pool of items, customized statistical procedures are used to select and weight items using data from each jurisdiction (see Hamilton et al., 2016).[4]

Although many of the reliability and validity statistics to be reported in the proceeding section were based on a single site (the WADOC), it is important to note that the STRONG-R name encompasses a suite of assessment tools that are remade with each implementation. This continual redevelopment is completed in an effort to provide the best fit for each tool to each jurisdiction.

Criminogenic Need Domains

Briefly mentioned previously, another unique feature of the STRONG-R is its use of dynamic items. Static risk factors are not amenable to change over time or altered through programming, while dynamic risk factors can change over time and be targeted for intervention (Chu, Thomas, Ogloff, & Daffern, 2013). Based on the RNR principles (see Andrews & Bonta, 1994, 2010), when addressing an offender's needs, one must focus efforts on those items that are dynamic or changeable. Many contemporary models that make use of both static and dynamic items are termed *risk-need* tools. This definition is true in that both risks and need, and for that matter static and dynamic, items are used to predict an individual's risk to recidivate. Research has routinely demonstrated that when both risk and needs are assessed, the prediction of recidivism is improved (Ashford & Lecroy, 1990; Cottle, Lee, & Heilbrun, 2001; Hamilton et al., 2016; Oliver, Stockdale, & Wormith; 2009; Ward & Stewart, 2003). This concept is one in which the STRONG-R developers share (Hamilton et al., 2016b).

Where the distinction lies is the use of static items in the assessment of an individual's needs. When developing a risk assessment, no distinction is needed regarding item type. That is, both risk and needs, and both static and dynamic, items may be included if identified to be predictive of the outcome(s) of interest. Furthermore, it is often the case that the static items are those that are found to be most predictive, and given the largest weight (Barnoski & Aos, 2003; Barnoski & Drake, 2007; Hamilton et al., 2016). However, when a tool is used to identify criminogenic needs, a domain-based structure is often applied. Assessing an individual's scoring

---

4 An illustration of this process was previously presented in Figure 10.1.

within content-specific categories of items identifies which areas are of highest need and direct the application interventions to reduce domain scores.

While many tools make use of domains that are a mix of both static and dynamic items, the STRONG-R has developed a separate needs assessment (Hamilton, Campagna, & Tollefsbol, 2016b). Using the same general pool of items, the development of needs scores first removes all static items, such as those that are based on an offender's criminal history and those within domains that are not changeable (e.g., a substance abuse problem in an individual's lifetime). Each of the nine criminogenic need domains was developed as a separate model predicting violent, property, drug, and general (any) offending. However, needs assessment responses are gathered simultaneously through the collection of items in the interview process of the STRONG. These item responses serve to score both the risk and needs tools and many items serve the dual purpose of assessing an individual's overall risk of recidivism and domain-specific levels of criminogenic needs. Through this approach, the needs assessment exists as a separate tool, applied strategically, assessing only items that are changeable, and targets an individual's most likely recidivistic outcome. Figure 10.5 displays series of example illustrations, diagramming the process.

To illustrate further with an example, an offender enters the system and is assessed on the items in the larger STRONG-R Assessment Item Pool, which contains all static and dynamic items/responses available. The STRONG-R algorithms for each of the four models are then scored for an individual, identifying the highest among the risk categories (e.g., Category 3—High Drug). The appropriate needs model algorithm is then applied and returns the offender's scores/classification needs (i.e., high, moderate, and low) within each domain that predicts drug offending. This filtering process from the general pool, to risk category, to needs scores, provides additional specificity for case managers. The added complexity allows case plans to focus intervention efforts on reducing an individual's assigned criminogenic needs category, which is designed to have the greatest strength in predicting an individual's specific recidivism risk type and is further outlined for placement among available interventions.

Administration and Training

Much of the administration training for the STRONG-R has been conducted via a software and training provider (Vant4ge), which has implemented juvenile and adult risk assessments both locally and statewide, as well as large and small jurisdictions throughout the United States for nearly 20 years. Generally speaking, training can be conceived of as covering two different areas. *Initial training* is delivered upon initial implementation of the tool. *Ongoing training* consists of regular measures of competency by assessment users and continued skills development. Like other aspects of the STRONG-R, training protocols were developed to be unique to a given jurisdiction and should be informed by agency-specific characteristics, including: available infrastructure resources, existing or historical departmental protocols or policies, and willingness to support training initiatives. Understanding the various jurisdictional characteristics allows those developing the training protocols to meet the jurisdiction where they are and work toward incremental change and sustainability.

Training at Implementation

One of the STRONG-R training customizations generally centers on who is trained. It is important to consider training not only for users but also for "consumers" of assessment results as well as other stakeholders. *Internal stakeholders* are those who are external to the organization

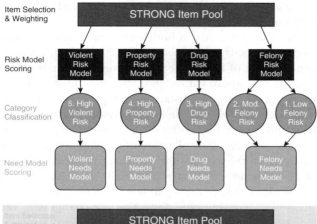

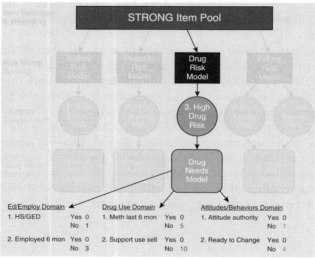

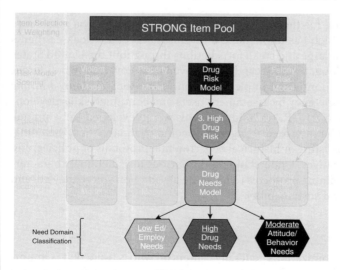

Figure 10.5 Illustration of STRONG-R risk & needs assessment process. *Source:* Hamilton, Campagna, & Tollefsbol (2016b).

housing the users who will administer the tool, while external stakeholders often include judges, prosecutors, defense counsel, treatment provider organizations, and law enforcement. Internal stakeholders are those who are employed within the agency, and may include: executives, mid-level management, first-line supervisors, and the assessment users themselves. STRONG-R customizes a specific training curriculum to work best for each stakeholder group.

At its most detailed, the protocol will be that for the actual assessment user group. A typical training protocol consists of a *2-by-2-by-2*, where users are trained three times, with each training consisting of two days, in the form of *initial* training, followed by *booster* training, and then a more in-depth Motivational Interviewing (MI) training. The initial two-day training emphasizes building a common knowledge base among all users, developing basic competencies to interview a subject, and gathering and inputting appropriate assessment information. The initial two-day training includes an overview the basics of Evidence-Based Practices (EBP) and MI. Then, skills training is completed, which includes four basic components: (1) a case file review, (2) the interview, (3) collateral sources, and (4) completing the assessment. The fourth component is completed using test cases in actual software, in a training software environment, exposing users to the software components themselves, including quality control features such as embedded *help screens*, which explain common issues that arise during administration.

Within approximately 60 to 90 days of the initial training, users are then given a one-day *booster training*. The booster includes an inter-rater reliability exercise and significant discussion of problem areas as well as clarification of item-level definitions within the assessment. An optional second day of the booster training is typically dedicated to a very basic case plan training that sufficiently instructs users in the process and software such that they can complete a case plan with a given subject. This additional case plan component is implemented for agencies with case planning resources and needs and includes four basic modules: (1) using assessment results for case planning, (2) collaborative case planning, (3) developing goals, and (4) software training.

Once basic skills for administering an assessment and building a case plan are developed, then it is important to create a protocol for continuous skills development or improvement. At this point a two-day MI training is provided, with emphasis on continued skills practice. An individual is considered STRONG-R "certified" following the completion of the two-day booster and may be given an additional certification for completion of the two-day MI training. Once someone is certified, protocols within the department are developed for users to maintain said certification.

Ongoing Training for Quality Assurance

Ongoing training for Quality Assurance (QA) is, perhaps, even more dependent on resources and priorities than the initial training, as it requires an ongoing resource investment from the agency. A menu of possible options are described herein, where departments work closely with assessment developers to create a sustainable set of protocols for ongoing training that allows users to maintain their certification. These can include the development of Subject Matter Experts (SMEs), the use of a train-the-trainer program, regular inter-rater reliability assessments, as well as individual taped critiques evaluating assessors' adherence to MI techniques. These types of taped critiques and coaching feedback sessions are completed (at least) annually. Readers should note that there are many methods for both initial training and ongoing training for quality assurance. The most important element is that it is tailored to the given jurisdiction and designed in a way that maximizes adherence and sustainability, and most efficiently using the resources available.

Reliability and Validity Research

Although relatively new, the STRONG-R has recently been examined for several forms of reliability and validity. Due to the extensive detail describing these testing procedures and findings, we provide a brief discussion of each and refer readers to source materials for more information. The WADOC initial development ($N = 44,010$), updated development ($N = 97,650$), and pilot sample ($N = 200$) were used to create and develop the risk and needs tools, as well as the latent structure and associated test of reliability and validity. This section describes the following instrument assessments: latent structure, content validity, internal consistency, convergent/divergent validity, predictive validity, and inter-rater reliability.

Latent Structure

We first start with the latent structure, as scales and analyses are used to derive many of the additional tests of reliability and validity. An instrument's latent structure provides an important component of the tool's construct validity. Latent modeling can be created to verify the existence of theoretical constructs. The examination of these constructs goes toward the assessment of internal consistency, convergent/divergent validity, and provides support for content validity. In 2016, the latent structure for the STRONG-R was examined and identified using a WADOC development sample (Mei & Hamilton, 2016a).

Based on the STRONG-R pool of items, there are 10 domains (or categories of items), that may then be conceptualized and operationally defined as measures of an individual's overall risks and needs. These 10 domains are effectively combined into five constructs *antisocial history*, *education & employment*, *antisocial propensity*, *substance abuse propensity*, and *reintegration needs*. Also, each of these constructs is further divided into scales and subscales.

To establish an instrument's latent structure, three basic aspects must be identified: dimensionality, measurement invariance, and reliability (Rios & Wells, 2014). The common method for establishing dimensional validation is Confirmatory Factor Analysis (CFA) for first order latent constructs/scales. CFA was used to confirm the number of factors based on model fit indices. If multiple factors were identified, and factors were substantially correlated with one and another, a higher order factor was constructed to explain the common variance among lower order factors (Chen, Sousa, & West, 2005).

Measurement invariance represents a lack of systematic bias resulting from group membership, which may lead to the misinterpretation of computed scale scores. The concept of measurement invariance is achieved at both the item and scale level. Invariance was analyzed by using Multiple Group Confirmatory Factor Analysis (MGCFA) (see Mei & Hamilton, 2016a). MGCFA identifies if a model possesses one of three levels of invariance: configural, metric, and scale (Dimitrov, 2010). Ultimately, the latent structure was examined and established within the framework of Item Response Theory (IRT) or Item Factor Analysis (IFA). IRT/ IFA were used because a majority of the STRONG-R items are ordinal in nature.

Table 10.2 displays the results of the global latent structure model on all total scores of the five constructs. All five constructs, independently, were identified to possess group invariance and item equivalence. Based on these findings, several conclusions were drawn. First, all the selected manifest items are statistically equivalent for both male and female offenders indicated by discrimination and threshold values. Second, factor scores of higher construct and scales were legitimate estimates of offenders' risk and needs, resulting from higher order modeling, subsequent measurement variance tests, and group invariance tests. All model fit indices values, including Comparative Fit Index (CFI), Tucker-Lewis Index (TLI), Root Mean Square Error of Approximation (RMSEA), and Standardized Root Mean Square Residual (SRMR)

Table 10.2 STRONG-R Latent Structure – CFA

Domain	No. of Item	Loading	Cronbach's Alpha	Model Fit Indices
Anti-Social History	14	.952	.720	CFI = .972
Education & Employment	8	.968	.723	TLI = .945
Anti-Social Propensity	46	.984	.770	*df* = 5
Substance Abuse	9	.899	.729	RMSEA = .059
Reintegration Needs	26	.930	.843	SRMR = .021
Overall Risk and Needs	103	—	.658	Omega Reliability = . 998

Source: Mei & Hamilton (2016a).

exceeded industry standard values indicating good model fit (Little, 2013). Also, the findings for the final G-Factor model demonstrated strong construct loadings for five identified constructs—ranging from .899 to .984—thus confirming the hypothesized internal latent structure of the STRONG-R.

Figure 10.6 provides an overview of the five constructs and their associated loadings.[5] Within the figure, arrows drawn to circles represent factor loadings, while arrows drawn to boxes represent the scale's alpha coefficients.

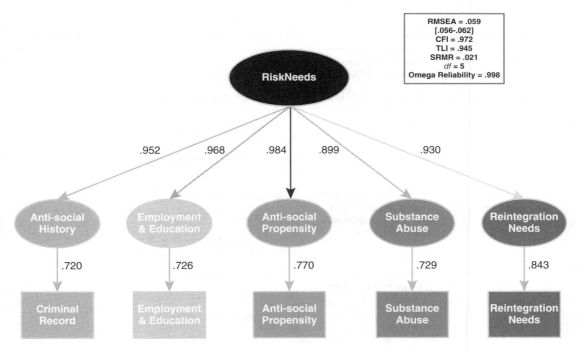

Figure 10.6 STRONG-R latent structure illustration. *Source:* Mei & Hamilton (2016a).

---

5 To conserve space, figures demonstrating individual construct, scale, and subscale loadings are not provided here but may be viewed in cited source material (see Mei & Hamilton, 2016a)

Content Validity

The STRONG-R items used to assemble the latent structure were further conceptualized, defined, and developed as latent constructs. These objects were completed to outline the structure's content validity, which is an assessment of how well items fit within the construct's conceptual definition and is achieved when a measure represents all aspects of said definition (Haynes, Richard, & Kubany, 1995; Kraska & Neuman, 2012). A full assessment of the STRONG-R's content validity examination was completed in 2016 (see Mei, Routh, & Hamilton, 2016a) using the development sample. A four-step process was used to determine the level of content validity for the STRONG-R (Sireci & Faulkner-Bond, 2014). First, we defined the constructs, including scales and subscales. Second, we identified and grouped the measurement items on the STRONG-R to illustrate how items represent and measure their respective scale and sub-scales. Third, we examined individual loadings to assess each item's measurement of the constructs and scales. Lastly, measurement and subject-matter experts (SMEs) assessed the test construction procedures.

To provide an example, the four-step process is illustrated for one of the STRONG-R constructs—the Anti-Social History Domain of the STRONG-R.[6] As seen in Table 10.3, the Substance Abuse construct is provided a conceptual definition, along with all of its subscales. From these conceptual definitions, measurement items of the STRONG-R designed to measure substance abuse, specifically its scales and subscales, were grouped to illustrate construct

Table 10.3 Content Validity Example

Construct, *Scale*, Sub-Scale	Definition	Measurement Item[†]	Item Loading
Substance Abuse	Extent of offender's substance abuse		
Recent Drug Use	Extent of an offender's substance use in past 6 months	Meth problem in previous 6 months (No/Yes)	.671
		Cocaine problem in previous 6 months (No/Yes)	.671
		Heroin problem in previous 6 months (No/Yes)	.671
Sharing and Exchange	Extent of an offender's substance use that is collective or used with associates	Drug support – share (No/Yes)	.671
		Drug support – barter (No/Yes)	.671
		Prior drug use (No issue/Drug use history/Drug use previous 6 months)	.671
Drug-Related Crime	Extent of offender's involvement in drug-related crime	Drug support – property crime (No/Yes)	.671
		Drug support – sell drugs (No/Yes)	.671
		Drug support – other criminal acts (No/Yes)	.671

[†]*Note:* – All item loadings are .671
Source: Mei, Routh, & Hamilton (2016a).

---

6 To conserve space only one construct is provided as an example of the content validity process. Each of the five construct definitions, item descriptions and loadings are further described in Mei, Routh, & Hamilton (2016a).

representativeness. Next, item loadings within the Substance Abuse construct were computed, where findings indicate that items provide substantive measurement of their larger subscales, scales, and construct. This evidence is indicative of the construct's domain representation and relevance.

Finally, the appropriateness of test construction procedures was reviewed. Beginning in 2014, a Comprehensive Strategy and Implementation Plan (CSIP) was implemented (Rist, Hosman, & Hamilton, 2014). As part of the CSIP, a development team was assembled, consisting of 45 WADOC SMEs from all areas of the agency (i.e., prisons, community, and health services), termed a "diagonal slice" of the Department's line staff, supervisors and managers, and executive staff. Through facilitated discussions, SMEs provided feedback regarding the technical accuracy of content and the sensitivity of responses as they pertain to the jurisdiction's population. In addition, measurement experts (Barnoski and Lee) reviewed items, scales, and scoring to determine the performance and conformation of standard psychometric principles.

Beginning in 2015, training and pilot testing of the risk and needs assessments were conducted (Hamilton, Kigerl, & Routh, 2016). As part of the pilot, a group of 45 WADOC staff members were trained using the new STRONG-R risk and need tools and completed assessments using a random sample of 200 offenders. A survey was also distributed and analyzed to provide stakeholder insight with regard to future STRONG-R implementation efforts. Pilot findings were used to identify items and responses with differential functioning and difficulty. Further examinations of the difficult items and differential item functioning among select subgroups (i.e., youthful/aging, prison, community, and sex offenders) are scheduled for further testing following additional data collection.

Internal Consistency

In a separate analysis, internal consistency was assessed for the STRONG-R scales (Mei & Hamilton, 2016b) previously described in the latent structure. Again, the development sample was utilized. To assess internal consistency of the STRONG-R, Cronbach alpha coefficients were computed for first and second order factor/scales, while Omega reliability was calculated for the overall model, or global factor (G-factor) solution. Internal consistency findings are presented in Table 10.4.

Overall, the STRONG-R scales demonstrate excellent internal reliability, demonstrated by the omega value of the global factor solution (.998). For higher order constructs/scales, Cronbach's alpha coefficients performed ranging from .429 to .852. With standardized loadings ranged from .714 to .894, the higher order constructs demonstrate acceptable-to-good reliability and account for considerable amount of common variance among lower order factors (George & Mallery, 2003). Cronbach's alpha coefficients for first order factor/scales ranged indicated a wide range (.631 to .151), although this finding is somewhat expected. The STRONG-R's first order scales possess as many as seven and as few as two items, which can result in substantial variation in alpha levels (Cortina, 1993). However, given the multi-dimensional aspects of the STRONG-R scales with demonstrated strong invariance natures, greater weight is given to the internal consistency demonstrated by the higher order scales and G-factor solution.

Inter-rater Reliability

Achieving a high level of inter-rater reliability (IRR) is an important performance metric for risk assessment tools. This metric is of particular importance for new tools like the STRONG-R, where training modules are recently established. A study of IRR was initiated in February of 2016. An implementation pilot was established to assess the effectiveness of a two-day

Table 10.4 STRONG-R Internal Consistency

Overall Model	Omega Reliability	CFI	TLI	RMSE (95%CI)	SRMR	No. of Items
G-Factor Solution	.998	.972	.945	.059 (.056–.062)	.021	

3rd Order Factor {3rd},(2nd), & [1st] order loading	3rd Order Cronbach's Alpha	2nd Order Factor	2nd Order Cronbach's Alpha	1st Order Factor	1st Order Cronbach's Alpha	
Anti-Social Hx. {.952}(.721) [.894]	.720	Criminal History	.677	Adult Criminal Record	.648	3
				Prison Infraction Record	.725	4
		Violence History	.489	DV & Violent Misd. Hx.	.445	4
				Aggression Hx.	.184	3
Educ. & Employ {.968} (.848) [.714]	.723	Education & Work Experience	.695	Juvenile Record	.625	4
				Education Level	.563	2
				Work Experience	.577	2
		Income	.542	Illegal Income	.408	2
				Legal Income	.723	2
Anti-Social Propensity {.984} (.720) [.877]	.770	Anti-social Influence	.429	Friend Anti-social	.229	3
				Partner Anti-social	.554	3
				Family Anti-social	.557	3
		Anti-social Personality	.852	Deceit	.582	2
				Empathy	.639	2
				Retreat	.636	3
				Stimulation	.404	7
		Anti-social Cognition	.728	Respect	.541	2
				Change	.738	2
				Thinking Error	.659	2
				Cognitive Skills	.731	2
		Aggressiveness	.665	Vulnerable Population	.582	3
				Resistant Population	.180	3
				Property	.546	2
				Relationship	.151	3
				Violence Out of Control	.333	4
Substance Abuse {.899}(−)[.927]	.729	—	—	Use Hard Drug[†]	.537	3
				Drug Use & Share & Barter[†]	.573	3
				Drug Related Crime[†]	.388	3

Table 10.4 (Continued)

Overall Model	Omega Reliability	CFI	TLI	RMSE (95%CI)	SRMR	No. of Items
Reintegration Needs {.930}(.727)[.726]	.843	Employment Barrier	.627	Physical & Mental Barrier[†]	.237	2
				Social & Working Skill[†]	.509	3
				Work Habit	.395	3
				Systematic Barrier	.510	3
		Mental Health	.588	Mental Health Issue - Past	.490	3
				Mental Health Issue - Recent	.631	3
		—	—	Basic living needs[†]	.843	9

[†]Scale does not possess a second order factor
Source: Mei & Hamilton (2016b).

training of 33 staff members. The training comprised a tutorial of item level definitions and interviewing techniques. IRR analyses were then completed for WADOC staff recently trained using the STRONG-R (Routh & Hamilton, 2016a). Video-recorded interviews were created for four offenders, one male and one female from both in-prison and community supervision. In June of 2016, raters (WADOC staff members) observed the recorded interviews. Each rater scored all four interviews. A two-way random-effects intra-class correlation (ICC) coefficient, with absolute agreement, was selected as the most appropriate analysis (Shrout & Fleiss, 1979).

The ICC results from the IRR test are presented in Table 10.5. Findings from each of the four interviews as well as an average ICC are provided. The level of agreement ranges between .87 and .91, indicating excellent consistency between raters. The average ICC was also found to be excellent (Mean ICC = .89). While this initial study demonstrated excellent reliability between raters utilizing the STRONG-R risk assessment tool, readers should note that the strength of

Table 10.5 ICC Coefficients for STRONG-R IRR

	ICC
Offender 1	.89
Offender 2	.88
Offender 3	.91
Offender 4	.88
Average IRR	.89

ICC magnitude: acceptable .40–.59, good .60–.74, excellent .75–1.00 (Cicchetti, 1994).
Source: Routh & Hamilton (2016a).

the results is grounded in the design of the item,; where item content is designed to be objective and, when feasible, verifiable via a record review.

Convergent/Divergent Validity

The ability for a tool to achieve a high level of construct validity is an essential indicator of performance. As empirical indicators of construct validity, convergent and discriminate validity are examined. Using a STRONG-R development sample, Mei, Routh, and Hamilton (2016b) demonstrated the instrument's ability to create both convergence of within-construct scales and the divergence of between-construct scales. Specifically, an exploratory factor analysis (EFA) was utilized to demonstrate the convergence and divergence of the STRONG-R constructs and its scales. For each of the STRONG-R scales, summary scores were computed. These scores were included as measures in the EFA analysis. Lastly, item loadings and cross-loadings were examined to demonstrate the convergent and discriminate validities. Rotated loading values and EFA model fit statistics are presented in Table 10.6.

Through an examination of the rotated loading values, theory, and prior findings, the five-factor solution was identified.[7] Specifically, scale measures loaded strongly on their

Table 10.6 STRONG-R EFA with Geomin Rotated Loadings

Construct	Anti-Social History	Education/ Employment	Anti-Social Domain	Substance Abuse	Reintegration Needs
Criminal History	**.467**	.062	−.029	.337	−.214
Violence History	**.789**	−.045	.042	.029	.021
Income	−.042	**.622**	−.043	.072	.001
Education & Working Experience	.121	**.574**	−.005	−.058	−.081
Anti-social Influence	−.046	**.254**	.193	.193	−.013
Anti-social Personality	.004	−.016	**.770**	.061	−.149
Anti-social Cognition	.054	.304	**.479**	−.046	.045
Anti-social Aggressive Characteristics	**.380**	.003	.337	.088	.179
Hard Drug	.045	−.092	−.038	**.861**	.058
Drug Use & Barter & Share	−.037	.146	.098	**.583**	.028
Drug Related Crime	−.009	.200	.075	**.436**	−.183
Mental Health	.011	.028	.004	.101	**.422**
Basic Living Needs	.096	**.311**	.024	.074	**.257**
Employment Barrier	−.018	**.347**	.286	.058	**.202**
Model Fit Indices	CFI	TLI	RMSE	SRMR	Eigen value
5 Factor Model	.942	.830	.066	.017	.941

Source: Mei, Routh, & Hamilton (2016b).

---

7 For additional analysis details see Mei, Routh, and Hamilton, 2016b.

hypothesized construct, with a few notable cross-loadings.[8] With this said, our findings provided substantial evidence of the existence of the five previously outlined STRONG-R constructs. Furthermore, multiple STRONG-R scales were found to similarly measure their higher order construct (convergent validity) and a considerable amount of evidence that subscales of differing constructs/scales diverge from one another (or divergent validity) (Kraska & Neuman, 2012).

Concurrent Validity

Concurrent validity of the STRONG-R scales, again using the updated development sample Mei and Hamilton (2016c). The intent of testing concurrent validity is an examination of the relationship, or the status, of scores with existing criteria. In contrast to predictive validity, concurrent validity attempts to examine if assessment scales predict their associated scores with regard to current/prior behaviors of interest.[9] To represent current/prior behaviors, the STRONG-R construct *Anti-Social History* was selected as the criterion of interest, as it provides a summary assessment of prior criminal and correctional history items.[10] Bivariate correlations were computed, identifying the relationship between each of the four remaining constructs with Anti-Social History. Multivariate analyses were then conducted to examine to what extent each of the four remaining constructs independently contribute to the variation of offenders' past antisocial behaviors.

As showed in Table 10.7, the Anti-Social History is highly correlated with all other domains, ranging from .990 to .998. This robust empirical evidence indicates that the four needs constructs not only concurred with each other but also concurred with the criterion

Table 10.7 STRONG-R Concurrent Validity – Correlations and Multivariate Findings

Domains	Anti-social History	Education & Employment	Anti-Social Propensity	Substance Abuse	Reintegration Needs
		Bivariate Correlations			
Anti-social History	1.00	—	—	—	—
Education & Employment	.997[***]	1.00	—	—	—
Anti-Social Propensity	.998[***]	.998[***]	1.00	—	—
Substance Abuse	.985[***]	.985[***]	.985[***]	1.00	—
Reintegration Needs	.990[***]	.990[***]	.992[***]	.976[***]	1.00
		Multivariate Scale Coefficients			
b (S.E.)	—	.291 (.013)[***]	.228 (.009)[***]	.112 (.030)[***]	.580 (.021)[***]
B	—	.080	.063	.031	.160
		Model R^2 = .924			

[***]$p < .001$
Source: Mei, Routh, and Hamilton (2016b).

---

8 Given that 14 first-order scales were used, some cross-loadings were anticipated, particularly when specific scales are conceptually and empirically strong predictors.
9 There are two methods to examine concurrent validity. The first attempts to examine if current instrument scales correlate with those of other, contemporary established tools for the same sample of offenders. Given the recent implementation of the STRONG-R, this method of assessing concurrent validity was not feasible.
10 This method was similarly employed by Brennan and Oliver (2000).

of offenders' Anti-Social History. Using the Anti-Social History construct as the dependent variable, multivariate analyses revealed that all four needs domains were statistically significant predictors. Furthermore, findings indicated that need domains explained 92.4% of the variance of Anti-Social History, providing strong evidence of the STRONG-R's concurrent validity.

Predictive Validity

Validation is a term that provides confidence for agencies selecting and using an assessment tool and predictive validity is the measuring stick that most instruments use to assure users of accuracy. This criterion of *predictive validation* is a relatively easy criterion to achieve by most cited standards. With that said, strength of validation can provide an important comparison between tools and versions of the same tool (Hamilton et al., 2016).

The development of the STRONG-R instrument was strategically focused on the creation of prediction models that optimize predictive validity. A customized code was created to select and weight items to predict each outcome of interest (Violent, Property, Drug, and any Felony reconviction) (see Hamilton et al., 2016). Using the initial development sample discrimination (Area Under the Curve [AUC]), calibration (the overall error [CALerr]), accuracy (ACC), and a combined metric (squared error, accuracy, and Receiver Operating Characteristic (ROC) area [SAR]) were assessed. These metrics and their use with the STRONG-R were previously described (see Hamilton, et al., 2016). Table 10.8 presents the described predictive validity findings for the eight recidivism prediction models.

AUC findings indicate strong predictive discrimination for all STRONG-R models (Rice & Harris, 2005). Furthermore, all STRONG-R models demonstrate satisfactory-to-strong levels of accuracy, calibration, and the combined SAR metric (see Tollenaar & van der Heijden, 2013). It is notable that all eight models demonstrated strong predictive validity, including specified and general outcomes, and for both males and females. Comparing the predictive validity to that of other contemporary tools, the STRONG-R has outperformed across a variety of metrics

Table 10.8 Measures of Predictive Validity for STRONG-R Models

Model	Discrimination AUC	Accuracy ACC	Calibration Entropy	Calibration Slope	Combined SAR
Male					
Violent	.74	.85	.30	.08	.76
Property	.78	.88	.26	.10	.79
Drug	.76	.87	.26	.08	.78
Felony	.74	.73	.49	.14	.69
Female					
Violent	.74	.94	.15	.07	.82
Property	.74	.88	.26	.09	.78
Drug	.73	.84	.31	.08	.76
Felony	.72	.75	.46	.11	.69

Source: Hamilton, Kigerl, Campagna, Barnoski, Lee, van Wormer & Block (2016a).

of discrimination, accuracy, calibration, and combined measures (see Drake, 2014; Hamilton et al., 2016). These comparisons were made to provide an understanding of the STRONG-R's predictive validity as it relates to other similarly created tools as well as to optimize the tools to create the best design fit for the WADOC population, serving as a baseline for predictive accuracy improvements. Additional research has been completed examining the predictive validity of the STRONG-R needs assessment (Hamilton, Campagana, & Tollesfbol, 2017) and prison classification tool (Hamilton & Kigerl, 2016) with further analyses to be completed in the upcoming year for the pretrial, supervision compliance, and screening tools.

Overall, our assessments of reliability and validity demonstrate excellent and substantive ratings for the STRONG-R. With a primary focus to optimize predictive validity, our current assessment in Washington demonstrates the results of these efforts. As additional data is gathered, newer versions will be created, with efforts to extend beyond the current performance gains. With regard to the internal constructs of the STRONG-R, we have identified the core latent structure of the instrument with items that fulfil stringent psychometric testing. Yet, even with the large pool of items available, the STRONG-R will continue to test new items, with the intent of incorporating additional predictors into scales and subscales to further improve its accuracy and functionality.

Although a substantial number of performance assessments have been presented here, there are several more that are planned for future study. For instance, for predictive validity, we are examining to what extent the change of offenders' needs is associated with the change in their future outcome measures. For convergent and discriminate validity, we planned to examine the construct validity of the STRONG-R by conducting longitudinal studies by using repeat measures, which allows for further examination of the stability of a variety of the performances of STRONG-R over time. Finally, future studies are planned to examine consistencies and variations of state performance in Nebraska, Tennessee, and additional implementation sites.

Implementation of the STRONG-R

The initial implementation of the STRONG-R, and its predecessors, were driven by legislative statutes, WADOC policy, and supporting research. Following the passage of the OAA, two important findings influenced the use of offender assessments in Washington. First, legislative statute explicitly added sentencing policy goals to (a) classify felony offenders according to their risk for future offending, and (b) deploy a greater amount of resources to high-risk offenders (Barnoski & Aos, 2003). Second, statute also directed that any changes to the WADOC's use of risk-need assessment tools be approved by the WSIPP.

In practice, this means that the WADOC employs minimum contact standards for offenders supervised in the community. Offenders classified by the STRONG-R as High Violent and Criminally Diverse are mandated to have a minimum of three contacts (i.e., office, home, employment) per month with their community corrections officer. Further, High Property and Drug offenders are to have two contacts per month, while legislatively mandated (i.e., sex offenders) Moderate and Low supervised offenders are to have one contact per month. A relatively radical change to the supervision of offenders occurred in 2009, where, due to a budget crisis resulting from the 2008 recession, approximately 12,000 low-risk and moderate-risk offenders were removed from community supervision (WADOC, 2012). Most notably, evaluations of these statutes and policy changes were completed, identifying a lack of impact to public safety (Drake, Aos, & Barnoski, 2010), or more specifically that the removal of lower risk offenders from supervision had no appreciable impact on recidivism.

The recently implemented STRONG-R is required to maintain these stipulations, outlining the frequency of supervision contacts in the community as well as the removal of the lowest risk offenders from supervision entirely. In its initial year of implementation in Washington, the WADOC and Washington State Institute for Criminal Justice (WSICJ) will examine a randomized control trial, piloting current and modified adjustments to contact standards over time.

Further, programming and service provision are based on state provided funds for evidence-based programming. Annual forecasting formulas are used to predict the anticipated WADOC supervision population as well as recidivism increases/reductions because of intervention provisions (Aos & Drake, 2013). Utilizing research created to support a recent legislative proviso, the Washington State Institute for Criminal Justice (WSICJ) in conjunction with the WSIPP identified a scale of evidence-based, research-based, and promising practices for interventions offered nationally and those provided by the WADOC (Hamilton, van Wormer, Campbell, & Posey, 2015). The created repository is now being integrated with Taxman and colleagues' CJ TRACK simulation software (Taxman, 2013) to provide a menu of programs to address offender needs, sequencing of interventions, and a gap analysis to identify additional programming allotments needs.

With regard to the approval of WADOC new tools used in the state, the legislature trusted the endorsement of the WSIPP to give provide final authorization. The 2014 WSIPP completed a systematic evaluation of risk-need tools utilized and/or compared within the state (Drake, 2014). The STRONG-R was revealed to possess the strongest level of predictive validity among the five tools examined and was approved for statewide implementation.

Similar to the OAA's mandates to utilize a risk-needs tool, states and jurisdictions are now keying in on the need to provide accurate risk and needs tools for both supervision and treatment provision. Two recent examples were observed in for the Department of Corrections of both Nebraska and Tennessee. In recently approved legislative statutes, each state outlined substantial modifications to their supervision and program delivery to supervised offenders, with strict mandates aimed at reducing recidivism over time (Nebraska Legislative Bill 605, 2016; Tennessee House Bill 2576, 2016). While still somewhat new to the field, the STRONG-R was selected by both jurisdictions to implement a system-wide approach, providing risk, need, and infractions assessments in an effort to meet legislative directives. Future research and planned evaluation will further demonstrate the effectiveness of the legislative directives and the tools' performance objectives, attesting to the STRONG-R's ability to assist in achieving state goals, as intended.

Current Issues and Future Directions

As new tools are created and contemporary tools continue to be used, and advance their methods and designs, several applications and developments will need to be considered. We direct this discussion around three central issues: (1) software applications, (2) responsivity, case management, and planning, and (3) methods of customization.

Software Applications

While initial assessments were designed to be completed with paper and pencil (Andrews, 1982), in the last two decades the use of software applications in criminal justice assessments has expanded rapidly. With the increase number of models, weighting structures, and links to services and programming, advanced software applications are becoming an ever-present need for adopting agencies. Several notable improvements to practices can be adapted from software applications, including integration and automation, matching and prioritizing interventions, and agency planning (Hamilton et al., 2017).

As new and contemporary tools adjust to create system-based approaches, integration and automation become critical. Many of the most predictive measures in an assessment are criminal history measures and other items routinely collected by criminal justice agencies. Software integration retrieves and enters agency records directly, reducing time and improving efficiency. As individuals progress from pretrial, to incarceration, reentry, and community supervision, responses collected from prior assessments are transferred forward via automation, reducing labor demands of re-assessments (Hamilton et al., 2017).

New software applications have also been developed to process risk and needs data in order to identify responsive programming. Simulation tools, such as Taxman's CJ TRACK tools, as well as STRONG-R applications have been created to address agency responsivity issues. These applications require research support (Hamilton et al., 2015; Taxman, Pattavian, & Caudy, 2014), identifying interventions that are evidenced-based via what works literature and linking said evidence to current programming provided. The outline of programming used and beds/seats available can be integrated, prioritizing individuals for interventions and organizing waitlists. Furthermore, by aggregating information compiled on the jurisdictions population, agencies may then identify program gaps, where additional and more efficient uses of programming resources are recognized.

Responsivity, Case Planning, and Management

As the STRONG-R is implemented in multiple jurisdictions and agencies, the focus is directed toward the case management and planning module. While many modules are available to improve practitioners' skills (i.e., Proactive Community Supervision [Taxman, 2008], Effective Practices in Community Supervision [EPICS]; Latessa, Smith, Schweitzer, & Labrecque, 2013); Integrated Behavioral Intervention Strategies [IBIS] [Lowenkamp, Holsinger, Flores, & Koutsenok, 2013]; Staff Training Aimed at Reducing Rearrest [STARR] [Office of Justice Programs, 2015]; and Strategic Training Initiative in Community Supervision [STICS] [Bonta et al., 2010]). Evidence supporting the effectiveness of these case management modules is still relatively unproven (Drake, 2013). The connection between the assessment's findings of an individual's risk and needs and the effectiveness of case planning and management is new territory to forge for criminal justice agencies. While large volumes of correctional publications discuss the application of the RNR model, the forgotten R (responsivity) is under-researched. Thought to be the final product initiated by the implementation of a risk-need tool, translating outputs of said tools into mechanics of reducing recidivism first requires assessments information to be accurate and the training of users regarding proper implementation and use (with fidelity). Participating in the Bureau of Justice Administration's (BJA's) Smart Supervision the WADOC has begun to develop methods of pairing effective case management training with the outputs of the STRONG-R risk and needs assessments. Furthermore, efforts in Nebraska and Tennessee used a similar approach to training of case management staff in the effective implementation of STRONG-R assessment tools.

Future research efforts will also endeavor to identify the relative efficacy and areas of needed improvement surrounding responsivity. Many instruments focus on concepts of general responsivity identifying programmatic barriers (e.g., language, health, and developmental issues), while the concepts of specific responsivity are relatively untested. Identifying the general patterns of offender needs and the best methods for addressing each is the next generation of research needed. Efforts such as Taxman's CJ TRACK simulation tool provide a method to link what were once disparate assessments, siloed in separate systems (see Figure 10.7).

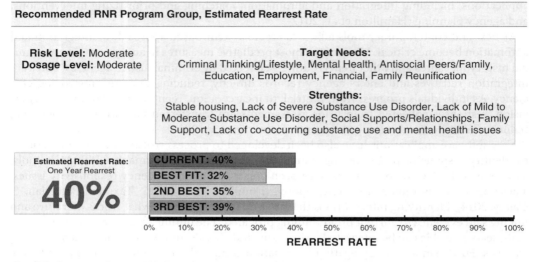

Best Fit Program Group: Criminal Thinking Interventions (B)
Recommended Dosage Level: Moderate

Group B programs primarily target criminal thinking/lifestyle by using cognitive restructuring techniques and interpersonal and social skills development. These programs use cognitive-behavioral or behavioral methods, offer a range of dosage levels across a continuum of care, and use an evidence-based treatment manual.

Example Programs:

- Cognitive-based criminal thinking curriculums
- Behavioral interventions
- Intensive supervision with treatment to address criminal thinking

Figure 10.7 Taxman CJ-TRACK illustration. *Source:* Taxman (2013).

Recognizing patterns of offender needs, their relative risk of recidivism, and the interaction of risk and needs with the provision of interventions is critical to the advancement of knowledge. Exploring the patterns and identifying offender typological structures are burgeoning areas of future research (Brennan, 2010; Routh & Hamilton, 2016b). Establishing these relationships will inform much needed policy efforts, forming a stronger connection between the criminal justice system and health and social policy.

Methods of Customization

As more jurisdictions identify the need for structured assessments, those agencies looking to adopt and apply risk assessment findings will soon realize that outcomes and populations of interest differ. Furthermore, tools applied to populations for which they were not designed can have detrimental consequences for accuracy, stakeholder buy-in, and extended use of the tool (Hamilton et al., 2016; Hamilton et al., 2017; Viglione et al., 2015). While the focus of this chapter, and the book generally, has been to examine and potentially compare risk assessment tools across similar psychometrics, we contend that the success of an instrument is directly related to its assessed accuracy (i.e., predictive validity) within the applied jurisdiction and the confidence that users have in an assessment's outcomes (i.e., ranking of risk). Risk assessment tools which are developed for a singular population with a distinct purpose will have difficulties when items, responses, and development populations differ from the one considering adoption. Recent research has demonstrated that agencies are often challenged to properly implement, transport, and sustain evidence-based practices and tools due to a number of issues and organizational characteristics (Taxman & Belenko, 2011).

Choosing an assessment is not a simple task. There are several issues for agencies to consider that will impact the instrument's accuracy within their jurisdiction and ultimately the buy-in of staff/stakeholders following implementation. While our discussion of the STRONG-R has outlined several elements of customization, such as outcome specificity, gender responsivity, and item weighting, these are but a few customization elements that should be considered and potentially developed for agencies seeking tool adoption. Hamilton and colleagues (2017) outlined 10 methods and elements of customization. Their discussion represents a potential trend for the future of criminal justice tool development and research surrounding effective implementation and best practices.

References

Andrews, D. A. (1982). *The Level of Service Inventory (LSI)*. Canada: Ontario Ministry of Correctional Services.

Andrews, D. A., & Bonta, J. (1994). *The psychology of criminal conduct* (1st ed.). Cincinnati, OH: Anderson Publishing.

Andrews, D. A., & Bonta, J. (1995). *The LSI-R: The Level of Service Inventory–Revised*. Toronto, ON, Canada: Multi-Health Systems.

Andrews, D. A., & Bonta, J. (2010). *The psychology of criminal conduct* (5th ed.). New York, NY: Taylor & Francis Group, Routledge.

Andrews, D. A., Bonta, J., & Wormith, J. S. (2006). The recent past and near future of risk and/or need assessment. *Crime & Delinquency, 52*(1), 7–27.

Aos, S., & Drake, E. (2013). *Prison, police, and programs: Evidence-based options that reduce crime and save money (Doc. No. 13-11-1901)*. Olympia, WA: Washington State Institute for Public Policy.

Ashford, J., & LeCroy, C. W. (1990). Juvenile recidivism: A comparison of three prediction instruments. *Adolescence, 25*(98), 441.

Baird, C. S. (2009). *A question of evidence: A critique of risk assessment models used in the justice system*. Madison, WI: National Council on Crime and Delinquency.

Barnoski, R. (2010). *Washington State Static Risk Assessment—Version 2.0*. Olympia, WA: Washington State Institute for Public Policy.

Barnoski, R., & Aos, S. (2003). *Washington's Offender Accountability Act: An analysis of the Department of Corrections' risk assessment (Document No. 03-12-1201)*. Olympia, WA: Washington State Institute for Public Policy.

Barnoski, R., & Drake, E. K. (2007). *Washington's Offender Accountability Act: Department of Corrections' static risk assessment*. Olympia, WA: Washington State Institute for Public Policy.

Bonta, J., Bourgon, G., Rugge, T., Scott, T.-L., Yessine, A. K., Gutierrez, L., & Li, J. (2010). *The strategic training initiative in community supervision: Risk-need-responsivity in the real world (User Report No. 2010–01)*. Ottawa, ON: Public Safety Canada.

Brennan, T. (2010). Taxonomies of delinquents. In R. J. R. Levesque, D. Farrington et al. *Encyclopedia of adolescence*. New York, NY: Springer.

Brennan, T., & Oliver, W. (2000). *Evaluation of reliability and validity of COMPAS scales: National aggregate sample*. Traverse City, MI: Northpointe Institute for Public Management.

Chadwick, N., DeWolf, A. H., & Serin, R. C. (2015). Effectively training community supervision officers: A meta-analytic review of the impact on offender outcome. *Criminal Justice and Behavior, 42*, 977–989.

Chen, F. F., Sousa, K. H., & West, S. G. (2005). Testing measurement invariance of second-order factor models. *Structural Equation Modeling, 12*(3), 471–492.

Chu, C. M., Thomas, S. D. M., Ogloff, J. R. P., & Daffern, M., (2013). The short- to medium-term predictive accuracy of static and dynamic risk assessment measures in a secure forensic hospital. *Assessment, 20*(2), 230–241.

Cicchetti, D. V. (1994). Guidelines, criteria, and rules of thumb for evaluating normed and standardized assessment instruments in psychology. *Psychological Assessment, 6*(4), 284–290.

Cortina, J. What is coefficient alpha? An examination of theory and applications. *Journal of Applied Psychology, 78*(1), 98–104.

Cottle, C. C., Lee, R. J., & Heilbrun, K. (2001). The prediction of criminal recidivism in juveniles: A meta-analysis. *Criminal Justice and Behavior, 28*, 367–394.

Dimitrov, D. M. (2010). Testing for factorial invariance in the context of construct validation. *Measurement and Evaluation in Counseling and Development, 43*(2), 121–149.

Drake, E. (2013). *Inventory of evidence-based and research-based programs for adult corrections (Document No. 13-12-1901)*. Olympia, WA: Washington State Institute for Public Policy.

Drake, E. (2014). *Predicting criminal recidivism: A systematic review of offender risk assessments in Washington State (Doc. No. 14-02-1901)*. Olympia, WA: Washington State Institute for Public Policy.

Drake, E., Aos, S., & Barnoski, R. P. (2010). *Washington's Offender Accountability Act: Final Report on Recidivism Outcomes*. Olympia: Washington State Institute for Public Policy.

Falzer, P. R. (2013). Valuing structured professional judgement: Predictive validity, decision-making, and the clinical-actuarial conflict. *Behavioral Sciences, 31*, 40–54.

George, D., & Mallery, M. (2003). *Using SPSS for Windows step by step: a simple guide and reference*. Boston, MA: Allyn & Bacon.

Hamilton, Z., Campagna, M., & Tollefsbol, E. (2016b). A more consistent application of the RNR model: the STRONG-R needs assessment. *Criminal Justice & Behavior*. Published online on November 19, 2016.

Hamilton, Z., & Kigerl, A. (2016). *Development and validation of the Nebraska Department of Correctional Services Prison Classification System*. Lincoln, NE: Nebraska Department of Correctional Services.

Hamilton, Z., Kigerl, A., Campagna, M., Barnoski, R., Block, L. Lee, S., & van Wormer, J. (2016a). Tailoring to fit: The development and validation of the STRONG-R Recidivism Risk Assessment. *Criminal Justice and Behavior, 43*(2), 230–263. doi:10.1177/0093854815615633

Hamilton, Z., Kigerl, A., & Routh, D. (2016). *The STRONG-R pilot assessment study*. Spokane, WA: Washington State Institute for Criminal Justice.

Hamilton, Z., Tollefsbol, E., Campagna, M., & van Wormer, J. (2017). Customizing criminal justice assessments. In F. S. Taxman (Ed.), *Handbook on risk and need assessment: Theory and practice, Volume 1* (pp. 333–377). New York, NY: Routledge.

Hamilton, Z., van Wormer, J., Campbell, C., & Posey, B. (2015). *Evidence-Based Practices Proviso (EBPP) – Final Report*. Olympia, WA: Washington State Department of Corrections.

Haynes, S. N., Richard, D., & Kubany, E. (1995). Content Validity in Psychological Assessment: A Functional Approach to Concepts and Methods. *Psychological Assessment, 7*(3), 238-47.

Kraska, P. B., & Neuman, W. L. (2012). *Criminal justice and criminology research methods*. Upper Saddle River, NJ: Pearson Education, Inc.

Latessa, E. J., Smith, P., Lemke, R., Makarios, M., & Lowenkamp, C. (2009). *Creation and validation of the Ohio Risk Assessment System: Final report*. Cincinnati, OH: Ohio Department of Rehabilitation and Correction.

Latessa, E. J., Smith, P., Schweitzer, M., & Labrecque, R. M. (2013). *Evaluation of the effective practices in community supervision model (EPICS) in Ohio*. Unpublished manuscript. Center for Criminal Justice Research, University of Cincinnati, OH.

Little, T. D. (2013). *Longitudinal Structural Equation Modeling*. New York, NY: Guilford.

Lowenkamp, C. T., Holsinger, A. M., Flores, A. W., & Koutsenok, I. (2013). Changing probation officer attitudes: Training experience, motivation, and knowledge. *Federal Probation, 77*, 54–58.

Mei, X., & Hamilton, Z. (2016a). *Latent structure of the STRONG-R*. Spokane, WA: Washington State Institute for Criminal Justice.

Mei, X., & Hamilton, Z. (2016b). *Reliability of the STRONG-R*. Spokane, WA: Washington State Institute for Criminal Justice.

Mei, X., & Hamilton, Z. (2016c) *Concurrent validity of the STRONG-R*. Spokane, WA: Washington State Institute for Criminal Justice.

Mei, X., Routh, D., & Hamilton, Z. (2016a). *Content validity of the STRONG-R*. Spokane, WA: Washington State Institute for Criminal Justice.

Mei, X., Routh, D., & Hamilton, Z. (2016b). *Convergent and discriminate validity of the STRONG-R*. Spokane, WA: Washington State Institute for Criminal Justice.

Nebraska Legislative Bill 605, LB605. (2016). Lincoln, NE: Nebraska Legislature.

Office of Justice Programs. (2015). Staff Training Aimed at Reducing Rearrest (STARR). *National Institute of Justice*. Retrieved from https://www.crimesolutions.gov/ProgramDetails. aspx?ID=236

Oliver, M., Stockdale, K., & Wormith, J. (2009). Risk assessment with young offenders: A meta-analysis of three assessment measures. *Criminal Justice Behavior, 36*, 329–353.

Rice, M., & Harris, G. (2005). Comparing effect sizes in follow-up studies: ROC area, Cohen's *d*, and *r*. *Law and Human Behavior, 29*, 615–620.

Rios, J., & Wells, C. (2014). Validity evidence based on internal structure. *Psicothema, 26*(1), 108–116.

Rist, M., Hosman, S., & Hamilton, Z. (2014). *STRONG-R Offender Change: Comprehensive Strategy and Implementation Plan*. Olympia, WA: Washington State Department of Corrections.

Routh, D., & Hamilton, Z. (2016a). *Inter-rater reliability (IRR) of the Static Risk Offender Need Guide for Recidivism (STRONG-R)*. Spokane, WA: Washington State Institute for Criminal Justice.

Routh, D., & Hamilton, Z. (2016b). *STRONG-R Offender Typologies*. Spokane, WA: Washington State Institute for Criminal Justice.

Shrout, P. E., & Fleiss, J. L. (1979). Intraclass correlations: Uses in assessing rater reliability. *Psychological Bulletin, 86*(2), 420–428.

Sireci, S., & Faulkner-Bond, M. (2014). Validity evidence based on test content. *Psicothema, 26*(1), 100–107.

Taxman, F. (2008). No illusions: offender and organizational change in Maryland's proactive community supervision efforts. *Criminology & Public Policy, 7*, 275–302.

Taxman, F. (2013). *The Risk-Need-Responsivity Simulation Tool*. Fairfax, VA: George Mason University.

Taxman, F. S., & Belenko, S. (2011). *Implementation of evidence based community corrections and addiction treatment*: New York, NY: Springer.

Taxman, F. S., & Pattavina, A. (Eds.). (2013). *Simulation strategies to reduce recidivism: Risk Need Responsivity (RNR) modeling for the criminal justice system*. New York, NY: Springer Science & Business. doi:10.10007/978-1-4614-6188-3

Taxman, F. S., Pattavina, A., & Caudy, M. (2014). Justice reinvestment in the United States: An empirical assessment of the potential impact of increased correctional programming on recidivism. *Victims and Offenders, 9*, 50–75.

Tennessee House Public Safety Act, House Bill 2576. (2016). Nashville, TN: State of Tennessee.

Tollenaar, N., & van der Heijden, P. (2013). Which method predicts recidivism best? A comparison of statistical, machine learning and data mining predictive models. *Journal of the Royal Statistical Society, 176*, 565–584.

Turner, S., Hess, J., & Jannetta, J. (2009). *Development of the California static risk assessment instrument (CSRA)*. Working paper. Irvine, CA: Center for Evidence-Based Corrections, University of California.

Viglione, J., Rudes, D., & Taxman, F. (2015). Misalignment in supervision: Implementing risk/needs assessment instruments in probation. *Criminal Justice and Behavior, 42*, 263–285.

Ward, T., & Stewart, C. (2003). Criminogenic needs and human needs: A theoretical model. *Psychology, Crime & Law, 9*(2), 125–143.

Washington State Department of Corrections (WADOC). (2012). *Warrants, detainers, and holds* [WADOC Policy No. 350.750]. Olympia: Washington Department of Corrections. Revised August.

Part III

Risk/Needs Assessment Abroad

11

Offender Group Reconviction Scale

Philip Howard

Overview

The Offender Group Reconviction Scale (OGRS) is a static actuarial risk assessment instrument, based on a narrow range of risk factors (age, gender, and official criminal history). It predicts the percentage probability of criminal recidivism in the community by offenders aged 18 and over who are discharged from custody or given non-custodial sentences, and has been used continuously since November 1996 within the criminal justice system of England and Wales. Its third version is currently used, with a fourth version awaiting implementation.

Originally owned and controlled by the Home Office, OGRS was transferred through government restructuring to Her Majesty's Prison and Probation Service (HMPPS; formerly the National Offender Management Service), an executive agency of the Ministry of Justice with responsibility for adult prison and probation services. The Crown Copyright and Licences team of HMPPS are responsible for licensing its use by other jurisdictions. OGRS needs to be fully recalibrated for use outside England and Wales. This is due to the absolute rather than relative risk nature of its predictions, and the use of a detailed current offense classification system.

History of Development, and Key Differences between the Versions

The prehistory of OGRS involves a number of predictors of English and Welsh recidivism created between the 1960s and 1990s, most often to inform the parole process (Kershaw, 1999). There have since been four versions of OGRS, all of which include predictors of recidivism intended to cover all offenses. These are referred to as OGRS1, OGRS2, OGRS3, and OGRS4/G. Version 2 also included a predictor of sexual and violent recidivism (OGRS2-SV). Version 4 also includes a predictor of non-sexual violent recidivism (OGRS4/V).

The development of version 1 of the OGRS (OGRS1; Copas & Marshall, 1998) involved several stages common to all versions. The criminal records of tens of thousands of offenders given sentences involving custody or probation management were retrieved from a central database to score risk factors and determine recidivism status within two years of community sentence or discharge from custody. A logistic regression model was then created, assigning weights to the various risk factors that reflect their relative contributions to the prediction of recidivism status. The criminal history domain was represented by the *Copas rate*, defined further later. At that time, the development data source was the now defunct Offenders Index (OI), a Home Office

Handbook of Recidivism Risk/Needs Assessment Tools, First Edition. Edited by Jay P. Singh, Daryl G. Kroner, J. Stephen Wormith, Sarah L. Desmarais, and Zachary Hamilton.

research database which listed only the dates of convictions for relatively serious offenses. Given the limited technology available to probation staff in 1996, the logistic regression parameter estimates were simplified into an integer scoring system (e.g., female = −3 points, male = zero points; seven offense groups are scored from −12 for sexual offenses to +6 for drugs offenses).

While the basic age, gender, and criminal history domains of risk remained, OGRS2 required assessors to input a more complex set of risk factors than OGRS1. The additional scale, OGRS2-SV, which estimated the combined risk of sexual and violent recidivism, was used only with offenders with a known history of these offenses (Taylor, 1999).

OGRS version 3 (OGRS3; Howard, Francis, Soothill, & Humphreys, 2009) introduced several substantial technical and practical improvements. The replacement of the OI with a central research copy of the Police National Computer (PNC) allowed the inclusion of more offenses, as detailed in "Operationalizing recidivism" later in the chapter. As exploratory analysis during OGRS3 development indicated that OGRS2-SV scores failed to predict proven sexual reoffending, this subscale was withdrawn and not replaced. The underlying algorithm was revised to model age separately for men and women, increasing predictive validity for female offenders. Efforts to lessen burdens on assessors led to a reduction in the number of data items required from nine to six, with trivial impact on predictive validity. Counts of previous convictions were replaced with *sanctions*: days on which the offender received a conviction and/or caution-type penalty. OGRS3 was the first version implemented in prisons as well as probation, improving the integration of sentence plans for released prisoners.

The predictive validity of OGRS4 (Howard, 2015a; Moore & Howard, 2015) benefited from various insights gained since the development of OGRS3. Within the logistic regression model, the use of the Copas rate was restricted to those with three or more sanctions, with separate terms indicating for first-time offenders (a simple binary variable) and second-time offenders (interacting with the number of years between first and current sanction). Learning the lessons of OGRS2-SV, the authors followed an empirical process (Howard & Dixon, 2011) to determine the range of offenses that should be operationalized as violent in order to optimize predictive validity, and concluded that sexual offenses should be excluded. This process informed the development of the static/ dynamic OASys Violence Predictor (OVP; Howard & Dixon, 2012) as well as OGRS4/V.

The Copas Rate, and Unusual Changes in OGRS Score

The criminal history Copas rate is the most complex part of each OGRS model. It is named after Professor John Copas, co-author of OGRS1, although the formula in OGRS3 is rather different. An offender's Copas rate, and thus their OGRS score, is higher when they have many criminal appearances and when their criminal career (i.e., from first to current appearance) is short. Younger, male offenders, and those with current offenses of burglary and theft also receive higher scores in all versions of OGRS.

In all versions of OGRS, the Copas rate is based on just two factors: the length in years of the offender's known criminal career (i.e., from their first conviction [OGRS1 and OGRS2] or sanction [OGRS3 and OGRS4] to the current conviction), and their total number of convictions or sanctions. Rates are at their highest when the criminal career is "quick"—that is, the length in years is short but the number of sanctions is high. Offenders receiving their first conviction or sanction have very low Copas rates, but it is possible for older offenders with very "slow" careers to have even lower rates (there is some data from which inferences can be made, unlike the first-time offender, who may be at the start of a prolific criminal career). In OGRS1 and OGRS2, a constant was added to the length of the criminal career; the number of convictions was then divided by this modified length, and the square root of the result taken. In OGRS3 and OGRS4, testing of different mathematical functions and possible constants led to the replacement of square roots with natural logarithms. For example, in OGRS2, the Copas rate formula is the square root of the quotient of the number of criminal convictions and (difference between age at first conviction and current conviction, plus 5), while in OGRS4/G it is the natural logarithm of the quotient of the number of criminal sanctions and (difference between age at first sanction and current sanction, plus 26).

In OGRS4, the Copas rate is only used for offenders with three or more sanctions, with separate model parameters for first-time offenders (a simple indicator variable) and second-time offenders (where the number of years between first and current sanction is also used). This recognizes that the value of the Copas rate is really in summarizing longer criminal careers, and that including these simpler alternatives for first- and second-time offenders improves overall model fit.

OGRS4/V includes a version of the Copas rate where only sanctions for violent offending are counted, in addition to the all-offenses rate. This is accompanied by a pair of "never violent" terms: one for women and one for men. These reflect the much lower likelihood of violent reoffending for those with no history of violence, especially among female offenders.

Occasionally, OGRS scores fall when an offender receives a new conviction. There can be two reasons for this. Firstly, the Copas rate balances number of sanctions and length of criminal career. It almost always rises as the number of sanctions in a criminal career increases, but can decrease in those rare cases where the increasing length of the career has a greater effect than the extra conviction. Secondly, offenders are placed in 11 age bands (four juvenile and seven adult), and moving up an age band will reduce the contribution of age to the predicted rate of reoffending for all but the youngest offenders. A few of these reductions are quite large (of these, the most frequently encountered in OGRS3 will be males moving from "18 to under 21" to "21 to under 25"), and so the predicted rate of reoffending may fall despite the new conviction. While these decreases in the OGRS score appear odd, they reflect the overall effect of reoffending with aging and previous long breaks in offending—and as with all OGRS scores, they should be interpreted in the context of the behavior and circumstances of the individual offender.

The Introduction of Offence-free Time and Violence Prediction in OGRS4

The use, for probation sentence planning, of a fixed OGRS3 score after sentence implicitly assumes that the probability of recidivism stays constant. Under this assumption, while a "first-two-year" estimate such as OGRS3 may not be strictly valid after the offender had spent some time offense-free in the community, it would be an acceptable proxy for their risk of proven reoffending over the next two years. Howard (2011) determined that this was not the case, as an offender's hazard (short-term probability) of future proven reoffending falls with time after community sentence or discharge from custody without reoffending. As such, OGRS4 presents a *next-two-year* probability, which could be recalculated during the community portion of an offender's sentence. An *offense-free time* term, measured in complete months since sentence/discharge, is the mechanism for these gradual reductions in score. This could therefore enable changes in tier (see Implementation in Correctional Practice below) over the course of a HMPPS sentence, and allow a more accurate comparison of offenders at different stages of community supervision when allocating scarce intervention resources.

OGRS3 lacks a predictor of violent recidivism. The recent direction of HMPPS' assessment policy and practice—with less comprehensive use of the Offender Assessment System (OASys) and thus the static/dynamic OVP—created a need for a cost-effective predictor of non-sexual violent recidivism. The only available such predictor, Risk Matrix 2000/v (Thornton et al., 2003), was designed for use with sex offenders. While it can be used with other offender groups, its simple scoring algorithm predicts non-sexual violent recidivism no better than the OGRS3 score (Howard & Dixon, 2012; Yang, Wong, & Coid, 2010). The OGRS4/V was created to fill this gap.

OGRS4 requires the same set of inputs as OGRS3, plus the addition of a count of sanctions for non-sexual violent offenses. As mentioned earlier, a second Copas rate for violent offenses, and a "never violent" term, were added to the logistic regression model.

Summary of Risk Factors Scored in Each Version

Table 11.1 sets out the risk factors that assessors are required to calculate and input, and other factors that are derived from these, in each version of OGRS (excluding OGRS2/SV, detailed in Taylor, 1999).

Operationalizing Recidivism and the Follow-up Period

The recidivism definition for all versions of OGRS includes only offenses brought to justice by the England and Wales criminal justice system. For offenders aged 18 and over, there are two routes to justice: being convicted at court or formally cautioned by the police. Offenders aged under 18 can also be convicted but have received alternatives to cautions in recent years: first reprimands and final warnings, then youth cautions or youth conditional cautions. For simplicity, all above outcomes other than convictions are henceforth labeled caution-type outcomes.

The scope of versions 1 and 2 was restricted because the OI did not record offenses resulting in caution-type outcomes and certain summary offenses (less serious offenses tried in magistrates' courts). As the OI also did not record offense date, reoffenses were included or excluded from the outcome based on their date of conviction. None of these limitations apply to the research copy of the PNC used in versions 3 and 4; as such, their recidivism measure refers to all offenses other than the most trivial parking and speeding offenses, including those with caution-type outcomes, and the PNC's record of offense date is used to determine whether a reoffense is within the follow-up period. Due to this broader outcome, the later versions of OGRS are described as predictors of *proven reoffending* rather than reconviction, despite the full name remaining unchanged.

The *follow-up* is the period of time during which the offender is at risk of proven reoffending. Conventionally, reoffending follow-ups start on the day of an offender's discharge from custody, or the date of conviction leading to a non-custodial sentence. Where the offender is in custody and their discharge date is uncertain, the assessor determines the earliest date upon which discharge is legally possible. A two-year follow-up period is standard, partly through historical precedent (Copas & Marshall, 1998) and also because most community sentences last either one or two years. OGRS versions 1 and 2 provided predictions based on two-year follow-ups, while versions 3 and 4 provide both one- and two-year predictions.

Versions 1, 2, and 3 of OGRS use these conventional follow-ups; these follow-ups, and the two-year predictions produced using them, are referred to in this chapter as *first-two-year* follow-ups or predicted rates, as they are based on the first two years in which offenders are at-risk in the community. By contrast, OGRS4 constructs predictors of proven reoffending which use the *next-two-year* follow-ups. These predictors estimate the offender's likelihood of proven reoffending specifically for the two years following the point they have reached in the post-sentence or post-discharge process.

Taylor (1999) did not operationalize OGRS2-SV's "sexual" and 'violent' offenses, but it is likely that these will have corresponded to the lists of sexual and violence against persons offenses maintained by contemporary official statisticians. As described earlier, OGRS4/V and OVP use an operationalization of "violent" offenses, excluding sexual offenses, that was founded upon detailed analysis of the impact of different options on predictive validity (Howard & Dixon, 2011).

Table 11.1 Sample Details and Risk Factors Included in Each Version of OGRS

	OGRS 1	OGRS 2	OGRS 3	OGRS4
Research sample				
Year offenders were sentenced/released	1990	1995	2002	2005-08; 2010
Number of cases	14,000	30,000	79,000	1,983,000
Factors included in the model: entered by assessor				
Gender	✓	✓	(AG)	(AG), (GV)
Age at / date of release or start of order			(AG)	(AG), (OFT)
Age at / date of sentence	✓	✓	(C)	(C)
Age at / date of first conviction	(C)	✓, (C)	(C)	(C)
Date of assessment				(OFT)
Number of previous convictions for all offenses	(C)	(C)		
Number of previous sanctions for all offenses (convictions, cautions, reprimands, & final warnings)			(C)	(C)
Type of offense (number of categories)	✓ (9)	✓ (27)	✓ (20)	✓ (20)
Is current sanction a conviction or another sanction?			(O)	(O)
Current or previous breach		✓		
Current or previous burglary		✓		
Number of previous youth custodial sentences	✓	✓		
Number of sanctions for violent offenses				(C), (GV)
Factors included in the model: calculated by hand (OGRS 1) or automatically (OGRS 2, 3, and 4)				
Offense-free time				✓
Combination of age and gender			✓	✓
"Copas rate": all offenses	✓	✓	✓	✓
"Copas rate": violent offenses				✓
Offending history status: all offenses				✓
Offending history status: violence, by gender			✓	✓

Note: OGRS4 was initially constructed and validated on 1,809,000 offenders released from custody or given other criminal justice disposals between April 2005 and March 2008 who had not reoffended before March 31, 2008. It was recalibrated on the HMPPS community caseload ($n = 174,000$) of March 31, 2010. "Offending history status" identifies offenders with especially short criminal careers. OGRS4/G excludes the violence-related factors, while OGRS4/V includes all factors in the "OGRS4" column.

Key:		
	✓	Included as a main effect
	(AG)	Part of age/gender interaction terms
	(C)	Part of "Copas rate"
	(GV)	Part of gender/violence history interaction term
	(O)	Part of offending history status
	(OFT)	Part of offense-free time.

Theoretical Framework

As an empirical actuarial tool, OGRS lacks an underpinning theoretical framework. Copas and Marshall (1998) stated that "it is an *explanation* rather than a *description*. It cannot be overemphasized that the OGRS does not attempt to explain why some offenders reoffend and others do not" (p. 170). In designing OGRS1, they built upon previous UK research identifying age, gender, current offense, and criminal history as significant predictors (Kershaw, 1999). The authors of subsequent versions have developed the algorithm by testing calibration and discriminative validity across offender groups (e.g., identifying that recidivism rates follow a different age pattern for female offenders and therefore introducing OGRS3's age/gender interaction). They also reviewed whether offense categorization schemes accurately reflect patterns of offending (e.g., offenses related to harassment, which have changed in character over recent years due to the rise in malicious electronic communications, were moved from the violence against the person category in OGRS3 to the public order category in OGRS4).

Administration

Among prison staff, formal training for OGRS is provided as part of the OASys assessor course. Learners are taught the difference between OGRS3 and other risk predictors used in HMPPS (e.g., OVP), that the scores equate to a percentage of proven reoffending over a one- and two-year period, and about the ways that scores are categorized for operational purposes (see "Implementation in Professional Practice" later in the chapter). Learners are required to accurately input information and calculate OGRS and OASys risk predictor scores successfully on two offender case studies to pass the course. A similar process is followed by staff studying for the Probation Qualification Framework. More junior staff, who may calculate OGRS scores without their being OASys assessments, are provided with "on the job" training and support from experienced staff.

Guidance notes for OGRS3 are available to all staff through internal information and communication technology (ICT) networks. These notes give an explanation of the purpose of the tool and how OGRS scores should be used, and instruct how each item should be scored. Particular attention is given to determining the effective assessment date[1] and the offense category. The MoJ Data Science Hub, which is responsible for OGRS development, maintains a spreadsheet which categorizes around 2,300 legally distinct, named and numbered, criminal offenses into the 20 OGRS3 categories and 20 OGRS4 categories, and updates it annually in response to changes in statute.[2]

When they are uncertain how to apply the OGRS guidance notes, or are concerned that the OGRS software may be in error, users can access a three-line support network. The first line focuses on ICT-related problems, the second line is a central team with a range of offender assessment and management support responsibilities, and the third line is the Data Science Hub.

OGRS scores can only be calculated when all items are scored. A criminal history summary report must be generated from the PNC in the course of the scoring process. This allows all current offense and criminal history items to be completed, and the offender's gender and date of birth will be readily available. Therefore, no mechanism to prorate missing items is required.

---

1 The effective assessment date is the date that the offender started a non-custodial sentence or was discharged from custody, or the assessor's best estimate of the date that one of these events will occur in the future. Such future dates will often not be known with certainty, and OGRS user guidance details the assumptions that assessors should make in a range of circumstances (e.g., if the offender will become eligible for parole in the future, the assessor should assume that they will be discharged on their parole eligibility date).

2 While the categorization schemes of versions 3 and 4 are similar, Howard (2015a), determined that around 7% of offenders would be placed into substantively different categories on the two versions.

Reliability and Validity Research

Given the intentional lack of a theoretical framework and the absence of subscales, no attempts have been made to measure internal consistency or discern latent structure within any version of OGRS. Similarly, content and face validity have not been measured, and there have been no inter-rater reliability studies.

Table 11.2 presents results on discriminative predictive validity. This table refers to a set of 153,562 offenders starting community case management in 2010, who had a timely and well-completed OASys assessment; lower-risk offenders may be underrepresented, as they were more likely to be among the 65,981 starters who were not assessed with OASys. It includes results for two sets of OGRS3 scores: those embedded within assessor-completed Offender Assessment System (OASys) records with the same offenders' scores calculated from central PNC data.

Table 11.2 Inter-Method Reliability and Discriminative Predictive Validity for OGRS Version 3

Offender group	N of offenders	Mean OGRS scores					AUC of OGRS score	
		Centrally coded	User-coded	Net difference (central score – user score)	Absolute difference	Correlation	Centrally coded	User-coded
All offenders	153,562	57.5	57.2	0.30	5.04	0.94	0.804	0.782
Sentence type								
License	47,400	63.0	62.5	0.52	5.69	0.93	0.817	0.794
Order	106,162	55.1	54.9	0.20	4.76	0.95	0.79	0.772
Age band								
18–20	22,785	68.0	67.1	0.93	5.35	0.90	0.752	0.731
21–24	29,050	61.9	61.8	0.13	5.69	0.91	0.774	0.747
25–29	29,124	62.4	62.2	0.25	5.23	0.93	0.802	0.777
30–34	22,482	60.5	60.4	0.08	5.08	0.94	0.819	0.794
35–39	18,519	55.6	55.3	0.31	4.75	0.95	0.821	0.795
40–49	23,027	46.1	45.9	0.28	4.43	0.95	0.818	0.793
50+	8,575	25.4	25.4	0.03	3.62	0.95	0.846	0.824
Gender								
Female	19,856	54.1	53.4	0.71	4.91	0.95	0.838	0.806
Male	133,706	58.0	57.8	0.24	5.06	0.94	0.798	0.778
Ethnicity								
Asian	7,245	47.9	47.0	0.86	5.51	0.93	0.793	0.777
Black	12,604	56.5	56.0	0.47	5.55	0.92	0.782	0.762
Mixed	800	50.0	48.7	1.30	5.69	0.93	0.822	0.821
Other	1,929	37.7	37.5	0.17	4.50	0.95	0.863	0.842
White	130,984	58.5	58.2	0.25	4.97	0.94	0.802	0.78
1-year reoffending status								
Non-reoffender	81,688	45.6	45.6	0.00	4.87	0.94	N/A	N/A
Reoffender	71,874	71.0	70.4	0.64	5.25	0.90	N/A	N/A

OGRS has strong discriminative predictive validity for most subgroups, with the user-calculated score achieving an Area Under Curve statistic one or two percentage points lower than the centrally-calculated score.[3] For all offenders, the user-calculated scores achieved an AUC of .78, compared with .80 for the centrally-calculated scores. In a prior study comparing centrally-calculated scores on different versions of OGRS, Howard (2015a) identified AUCs of .77 for OGRS4/G and .75 for OGRS3, predicting all proven reoffending. He also identified AUCs of .77 for OGRS4/V and .72 for OGRS3, predicting violent proven reoffending. While this was the original OGRS4 construction study, the above AUCs were calculated on a separate validation sample.

Inter-method reliability research can be conducted by comparing the two sets of OGRS3 scores. Table 11.2 details how these vary, including differences by a range of offender characteristics.

The two versions of the score are closely correlated, with $r \geq .90$ for all subgroups. User-calculated scores tend to be slightly lower than system-calculated scores, and the difference is greater for offender groups with higher mean scores. Not all differences in score will result from user error, as offenders' PNC histories can change between the dates of central and user calculation due to appeals against convictions or occasional late data entry. Nevertheless, the extent of the difference and lower AUC of user-calculated scores does suggest that users sometimes misunderstand the scoring guidance. The sizable residual for 18–20-year-old offenders indicates misinterpretation of the effective assessment date rules: given that 18 acts as a minimum age (below which offenders are not managed by HMPPS), any user error will have an asymmetric distribution (i.e., tend to incorrectly raise offenders' age) and thus lower risk, as greater age is associated with lower risk scores. As the mean absolute difference is five points, such score calculation errors would affect the tiers and program eligibility (see "Implementation in Correctional Practice" below) of a small but not negligible proportion of offenders.

Detailed analysis would be required to determine the cause of Table 11.2's variations in AUC between subgroups (it is higher for offenders on license, older offenders, women, and offenders of "other" ethnicity). AUC variation could occur because predictor scores discriminate differently for some groups.[4] However, as Howard (2017) demonstrates for sentence type and gender, substantial AUC variations between subgroups can also occur purely due to different score distributions (e.g., the population of female offenders genuinely consisting of a small proportion of high-risk offenders and many low-risk offenders, which naturally generates a high AUC).

Implementation in Correctional Practice

Assessments can be completed at any time after the offender has been convicted, and most are completed immediately after conviction. These post-conviction assessments inform the Pre-Sentence Reports (PSRs) with which probation staff advise judges and magistrates on the most appropriate type and duration of sentence. Whilst these sentencers have discretion in every case, the Sentencing Guidelines Council provides them with starting points, aggravating and mitigating factors for over 600 different offenses, and the OGRS score, as a standardized estimate of

---

3 Calibration is not reported, as the data set combines two-year predictions and one-year reoffending outcomes. The discriminative validity is unaffected by this, as the ranks of offenders' one- and two-year scores are identical.
4 For example, assuming a simplified population made up only of offenders scoring either 20% or 80% on OGRS, a subgroup whose reoffending rates were actually 22% and 78% respectively would achieve a lower AUC than a subgroup for which the 20% and 80% predicted reoffending rates held true.

recidivism risk, is one of a large number of such criteria (Sentencing Guidelines Council, 2016). Assessments can also be completed as necessary in custody or community settings.

HMPPS allocates resources such as probation officer supervision sessions and places on offending behavior programs according to the principles of Risk-Need-Responsivity (RNR; Andrews & Bonta, 2010). When allocating places on programs designed to address general—rather than violent or sexual—offending, the OGRS score is used to identify those presenting greater risk (Ministry of Justice, 2014), with places typically reserved for those scoring at least 50%.

Individuals on the HMPPS caseload are managed at one of seven levels of service tiers (National Probation Service, 2016). Those at higher tiers are managed by more senior staff and/or meet with staff more frequently. Offenders with OGRS scores of 75% or more will be managed at or above Tier B2, the third-highest tier, while those with scores of 50 to 74% will be managed at or above Tier C2, the fifth-highest tier. Other determinants of tier include structured professional judgment of risk of serious harm to others, vulnerability (e.g., risk of suicide or self-harm), and the offender's management level under multi-agency public protection arrangements (a combination of statutory duties and local partnerships that ensure coordination between police, probation, and other agencies such as health and social care).

The implementation of OGRS has not been subject to formal evaluation. Indeed, OGRS1 was introduced many years before the development of the kind of joined-up ICT systems necessary to any large-scale evaluation, nor was any smaller-scale qualitative evaluation conducted at the time.

However, OGRS has, in turn, been widely used in the evaluation of offender interventions. Travers, Mann and Hollin (2014) used OGRS and offense category to compare outcomes for 21,000 offenders receiving the Enhanced Thinking Skills program. The Ministry of Justice runs an evaluation service known as the Justice Data Lab (JDL; Ministry of Justice, 2016), which has been applied to over 100 interventions. The JDL applies a highly standardized method based around propensity score matching, in which the OGRS score is one of the matching factors.

Current Issues and Future Directions

The continued use of OGRS in England and Wales appears certain. The exact timing of the introduction to OGRS4 will depend on wider developments of the ICT available to prison and probation practitioners. When OGRS4 is launched, this will provide an opportunity to reinforce good practice and check that procedures for calculating scores are being followed correctly. The availability of OGRS4/V will allow every offender on HMPPS's caseload to receive risk scores for both general and violent reoffending: new versions of the OASys-specific predictors (Howard, 2015b), combining static and dynamic risk factors, will be used for those for whom sufficient data exist, but OGRS4 will provide a score with high discriminative validity for those who have received a less in-depth assessment.

The MoJ Data Science Hub is looking forward to a further generation of risk assessment tools, though no firm timescales yet exist. Alternative model-fitting methods such as Random Forests, stochastic boosting, and ensemble methods could be explored. If computing systems become more closely linked, allowing secure information exchange between HMPPS's systems and the PNC, then machine-scoring of static actuarial risk predictors such as OGRS may be enabled. This automatic processing would in turn allow larger sets of potential risk factors, such as offense-specific and/or time-limited criminal histories (e.g., burglary within the last three years) to be considered.

References

Andrews, D. A., & Bonta, J. (2010). The psychology of criminal conduct (5th ed.). Cincinnati, OH: Anderson.

Copas, J., & Marshall, P. (1998). The Offender Group Reconviction Scale. The statistical reconviction score for use by probation officers. *Journal of the Royal Statistical Society, Series C, 47*, 159–171.

Howard, P. (2011). Hazards of different types of reoffending. Ministry of Justice Research Series, 3/11. Retrieved from https://www.gov.uk/government/uploads/system/uploads/attachment_data/file/217377/research-reoffending-hazards.pdf

Howard, P. (2015a). OGRS4: the revised Offender Group Reconviction Scale. In R. Moore (Ed.), *A compendium of research on the Offender Assessment System (OASys) 2009–2012* (pp. 178–208). London, England: Ministry of Justice. Retrieved from https://www.gov.uk/government/uploads/system/uploads/attachment_data/file/449357/research-analysis-offender-assessment-system.pdf

Howard, P. (2015b). OGP2 and OVP2: the revised OASys predictors. In R. Moore (Ed.), *A compendium of research on the Offender Assessment System (OASys) 2009–2012* (pp. 178–208). London, England: Ministry of Justice. Retrieved from https://www.gov.uk/government/uploads/system/uploads/attachment_data/file/449357/research-analysis-offender-assessment-system.pdf

Howard, P. D. (2017). The effect of sample heterogeneity and risk classification on Area Under Curve (AUC) predictive validity metrics. *Criminal Justice and Behavior, 44*, 103–120. doi: 10.1177/0093854816678899

Howard, P. D., & Dixon, L. (2011). Developing an empirical classification of violent offenses for use in the prediction of recidivism in England and Wales. *Journal of Aggression, Conflict and Peace Research, 3*, 141–154. doi:10.1108/17596591111154176

Howard, P. D., & Dixon, L. (2012). The construction and validation of the OASys Violence Predictor: Advancing violence risk assessment in the English and Welsh correctional services. *Criminal Justice and Behavior, 39*, 287–307. doi:10.1177/0093854811431239

Howard, P., Francis, B., Soothill, K., & Humphreys, L. (2009). *OGRS 3: The revised Offender Group Reconviction Scale*. Ministry of Justice Research Summary, 7/09. Retrieved from http://webarchive.nationalarchives.gov.uk/20110201125714/http://www.justice.gov.uk/publications/docs/oasys-research-summary-07-09-ii.pdf

Kershaw, C. (1999). Interpreting reconviction rates. In M. Brogden (Ed.), *The British Criminology Conferences: Selected Proceedings. Volume 2.* Papers from the British Criminology Conference, Queens University, Belfast, 15–19 July 1997. Retrieved from http://www.britsoccrim.org/volume2/005.pdf

Ministry of Justice (2014). *Offender Behaviour Programmes (OBPs)*. Retrieved from https://www.justice.gov.uk/offenders/before-after-release/obp

Ministry of Justice (2016). *Justice Data Lab Statistics: May 2016*. Retrieved from https://www.gov.uk/government/uploads/system/uploads/attachment_data/file/522589/justice-data-lab-statistics-may-2016.pdf

Moore, R., & Howard, P. (2015). Compendium conclusions. In R. Moore (Ed.), *A compendium of research on the Offender Assessment System (OASys) 2009–2012* (pp. 290–295). London, England: Ministry of Justice. Retrieved from https://www.gov.uk/government/uploads/system/uploads/attachment_data/file/449357/research-analysis-offender-assessment-system.pdf

National Probation Service (2016). NPS Operation Model. Version 1.0. Retrieved from https://www.gov.uk/government/publications/nps-operating-model-version-10

Sentencing Guidelines Council (2016). *Imposition of community & custodial sentences: Definitive guidelines*. Retrieved from http://www.sentencingcouncil.org.uk/wp-content/uploads/Definitive-Guideline-Imposition-of-CCS-final-web.pdf

Taylor, R. (1999). *Predicting reconvictions for sexual and violent offences using the revised offender group reconviction scale*. Home Office Research Findings, 104. London, England: Home Office.

Thornton, D., Mann, R., Webster, S., Blud, L., Travers, R., Friendship, C., & Erikson, M. (2003). Distinguishing and combining risks for sexual and violent recidivism. *Annals of New York Academy of Sciences*, *989*, 225–235. doi:10.1111/j.1749-6632.2003.tb07308.x

Travers, R., Mann, R. E., & Hollin, C. R. (2014). Who benefits from cognitive skills programs? Differential impact by risk and offence type. *Criminal Justice and Behavior*, *41*, 1103–1129. doi:10.1177/0093854814543826

Yang, M., Wong, S. C. P., & Coid, J. (2010). The efficacy of violence prediction: A meta-analytic comparison of nine risk assessment tools. *Psychological Bulletin*, *136*, 740–767. doi:10.1037/a0020473

12

Forensic Operationalized Therapy/Risk Evaluation System (FOTRES)

Leonel C. Gonçalves, Astrid Rossegger, and Jérôme Endrass

Overview

This chapter describes the Forensic Operationalized Therapy/Risk Evaluation System (FOTRES; Urbaniok, 2004, 2007, 2016b), which is a web-based structured professional judgment (SPJ) tool designed to assess recidivism risk and to monitor treatment progress and intervention quality (Rossegger et al., 2011; Singh, 2016; Urbaniok, 2016b). The tool estimates the risk of pertinent reoffending, meaning new arrests, charges, or convictions for repeat offenses within the same offense category as the index offense without regard to a specific time frame. It includes static and dynamic items assessing risk factors rooted in the personality of the offender and situational factors that can influence the likelihood of reoffending. FOTRES was designed for use with offenders of either sex, aged 16 years or older, who have committed any type of crime. The tool can be used in community and institutional settings to assess people, excluding offenders with severe mental health disorders. It has been used mostly in Europe (Singh et al., 2014). Including two levels—Risk-Needs Assessment and Risk Management—the tool is useful in assessing recidivism risk as well as in identifying treatment targets and maximizing responsivity. FOTRES's history of development, theoretical framework, administration, validity and reliability research, implementation, case studies, current issues, and future directions are described in what follows.

History of Development

Description of FOTRES and its Subscales

FOTRES was developed in Switzerland in the late 1990s and is now routinely used by many forensic services nationally to estimate the recidivism risk of criminal offenders and to document treatment progress. The motivations for developing and implementing the tool in the Swiss criminal justice system were the limitations of actuarial risk assessment tools, such as the inability to apply group-based recidivism estimates to individual patients, errors in estimating recidivism rates when applied in different jurisdictions, and the inability to incorporate case-specific information to modify estimated recidivism rates (Rossegger et al., 2011; Singh, 2016). Although SPJ tools are susceptible to decision-making bias, may take longer, and be more difficult to administer, they are more focused on individual offenders and can thus take into consideration information not routinely included in actuarial tools. For this reason they are more useful in case formulation and risk management, thus being of greater interest to mental health

Handbook of Recidivism Risk/Needs Assessment Tools, First Edition. Edited by Jay P. Singh, Daryl G. Kroner, J. Stephen Wormith, Sarah L. Desmarais, and Zachary Hamilton.
© 2018 John Wiley & Sons, Ltd. Published 2018 by John Wiley & Sons, Ltd.

boards (Singh, 2016). Furthermore, despite their higher emphasis on prevention rather than prediction, it was found that SPJ tools produce assessments with a predictive validity comparable to actuarial tools (Fazel, Singh, Doll, & Grann, 2012).

In FOTRES, the risk of reoffending is estimated for a specific offense, which is called the "target offense." Users choose one out of 29 potential target offenses (e.g., violent offense) and then specify the offense within the selected category (e.g., homicide). If an offender committed several different offenses, a separate risk estimate can be derived for each target offense. The tool consists of two main levels: the Risk-Needs Assessment (RNA) level and the Risk Management (RM) level. Basically, the RNA level estimates the risk of reoffending and the offenders' treatability. Items included in this level explore the offender's personality disposition to committing crimes, specific areas of concern relevant to the offense, and the pattern of the offense itself. The RM level describes the treatment progress and changes in recidivism risk caused by interventions. Items included in this level measure the actual risk reduction achieved through therapy progress, through the implementation of coping strategies, and through the identification and management of offense-related personality patterns. Whereas RNA is only assessed once (at the time of the target offense before an intervention of any kind takes place), the RM level is scored periodically whenever the current risk of reoffending needs to be assessed (Rossegger et al., 2011; Urbaniok, 2016b). A flow diagram illustrating the basic structure of FOTRES v3 is presented in Figure 12.1.

Specifically, the RNA level includes a measurement of: (1) baseline risk, (2) plausibility of the baseline risk, and (3) baseline treatability. The baseline risk is composed of: (a) the risk profile, and (b) the relevance of the risk profile. The risk profile is based on a list of 97 different personal risk characteristics that the users select to describe the offense mechanism of the offender. Those risk characteristics are presented in nine groups: dissocial, violent, and dominant behavior; fantasies, arousal, and sexuality; responsiveness due to impulsivity/reactivity; reflationary dispositions; deficiency dispositions; schizophrenia and other psychiatric disorders; addiction, depression, and trauma; diverse dispositions; and basal perception patterns. The relevance of the risk profile quantifies how relevant the established risk profile is in explaining the offense mechanism. This includes four groups of items: readiness to act; circumstances of the offense; sustainable awareness of risk; and recidivism expectation.

The tool also includes two modules to assess the plausibility of the risk profile: (a) pattern of the offense, and (b) offense-related personality dispositions. The pattern of the offense is related to the behavior that the perpetrator showed when committing the offense. It includes five groups: planning of the offense; determination to offend; personal identification with the offense; proneness to offend and potential to damage; and offense progression and susceptibility. Offense-related personality dispositions are personality traits related to the offense that indicate a general affinity for criminal behavior. This module includes 11 dispositions, such as juvenile delinquency, criminal versatility, and lack of empathy. The score on those two modules should be similar to the score on the baseline risk. The rating of the scales related to the plausibility of the risk profile is optional and serves as an integrity check.

Baseline treatability measures the potential of the offender to change his/her criminal behavior through therapy and/or coping strategies. It includes two parts: (a) perspectives for treatment, and (b) personal resources. Perspectives for treatment include six characteristics such as resistance to change, expectation of success, and positive development. Personal resources are organized into four groups: taking responsibility; openness focus; potential to change; and change-enhancing factors.

The RM level includes: (1) current risk, (2) current treatability, and (3) current situational factors. Current risk is composed of: (a) self-control, (b) risk profile, and (c) relevance of the

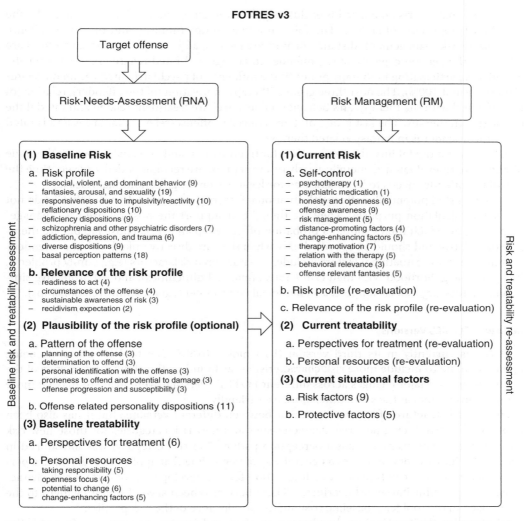

Figure 12.1 Diagram flow of the FOTRES v3 basic structure. FOTRES v3 = Forensic Operationalized Therapy/ Risk Evaluation System version 3.

The number of items included in each scale is presented in parentheses.

risk profile. When assessing current risk, the risk characteristics used to determine the risk profile of the offender and the relevance of the risk profile are re-evaluated.

Then, the self-control of the offender is measured. This scale is related to the capacity of the offender to compensate for his/her risk characteristics and includes 11 groups of items. The first group, related to psychotherapy, has three options referring to the type of psychotherapy the offender is engaged in: no psychotherapy, single and/or group psychotherapy, and single and/or group psychotherapy including elements to treat deviant fantasies. The second group is related to the influence of psychiatric medication on recidivism risk. Here, the rater determines what the importance of the medication in the risk-management strategy compared to the importance of psychotherapy is. The ratio of the importance of the medication to the therapy can be 0/100, 25/75, 50/50, 75/25, or 100/0. If the importance of the medication is 100%, the items regarding psychotherapy are not taken into consideration any more since it is assumed that the risk managed is exclusively determined by medication. This might be the case in schizophrenic offenders. The following five groups (honesty and openness, offense awareness, risk management, distance-promoting factors, and change-enhancing factors) are related to the general capacity of the offender to change and rated regardless of whether the offender is participating in therapy or not (if the influence of psychiatric medication on recidivism risk is not 100%). The next three groups (therapy motivation [of the offender], relation [of the offender] with the therapy, and behavioral relevance) are treatment related and rated if the offender is in therapy. The last group of items concerns offense-relevant fantasies and is rated when the offender is in fantasy-related therapy.

In the current treatability, the perspectives for treatment (a) and personal resources (b) of the offender are re-evaluated. Generally, yearly re-evaluations are recommended, or every time the risk of the offender needs to be re-assessed for legal reasons (e.g., conditional release).

Finally, a list of potentially influential situational factors is presented. Items of this list do not count for calculation purposes. They are thought to support the post-release case management (e.g., on which topics should a probation officer keep an eye?). Those factors are therefore descriptive and should be specified only when they are directly linked with the offender's criminal behavior. Situational factors include: (a) situational risk factors (e.g., family problems, living in a neighborhood with high crime rates, financial difficulties); and (b) protective situational factors (e.g., social support, a stable social environment, good family relationships).

Review of FOTRES Versions

FOTRES is currently in its third version (Urbaniok, 2016b). The tool is constantly being updated online to include more risk characteristics, as found by the clinical experience of the tool developers. Major changes across different FOTRES versions were made to make it more comprehensive and, at the same time, more user friendly.

The overall structure of the tool is similar between different versions, but it has also been improved by introducing new risk characteristics and new risk categories for those new risk characteristics. For example, "basal perception patterns" (a risk category) was introduced in version 3. This category describes a general way of perceiving that applies to everything a person experiences and can function as a foundation for the development of certain risk characteristics (e.g., authoritarian arbitrariness). There have also been several minor changes to the scales used in the tool (e.g., baseline treatability, or relevance of the risk profile).

Additionally, the terminology has been simplified and is now more straightforward. For example, "dynamic risk reduction" in FOTRES v2 has been renamed "self-control" in FOTRES v3; "unstable autonomous risk-relevant factors" was renamed "current situational factors"; and "structural risk for recidivism" is now called "baseline risk." The calculation of some scales has also changed. For example, the "pattern of the offense" or "offense-related personality dispositions" were previously included to calculate baseline risk, depending on which had the higher value. In FOTRES v3 both are optional modules used merely as an integrity check.

There were also some conceptual changes. For instance, versions 1 and 2 included psychiatric diagnoses. In versions 3, not the diagnoses but symptoms of psychiatric conditions are included as risk characteristics. In addition, for some risk characteristics there is now a distinction between affinity and preference when describing whether a risk characteristic is of a primary nature (e.g., pedophilia as a preference would mean that the offender is interested in children only) or is of a secondary nature (e.g., pedophilia as an affinity would refer to an offender who, besides children, is also interested in adults).

There were other minor changes. For example, in FOTRES v1, the users had to write the name of the target offense. In subsequent versions, this requirement was removed due to pejorative descriptions and the disparity in the terminology used to describe the target offense. Users now need to select one of the target offenses available in the software. The technical basis of the tool's web application also has changed between versions. Finally, because FOTRES v3 is more user friendly, the training workshops are now shorter.

Theoretical Framework

Scope of Application

FOTRES has primarily been developed for assessing and managing recidivism risk in violent and sex offenders, although it is not limited to offenses of that nature. Despite including situational risk factors, FOTRES is especially focused on personal risk characteristics and associated treatment needs. In fact, violent crimes committed solely because of a highly specific situation are very rare (e.g., honor crimes). In the case of offenses that are exclusively triggered by the situational context, there are different implications for risk management and, in most cases, ordinary sanctions are sufficient to achieve an adequate outcome.

Risk Characteristics

As there are general salient personality traits used to describe a person (e.g., authentic, shy, or intelligent), there are also specific personality traits that are directly linked to criminal behavior (e.g., dominance or violence affinity). In FOTRES, these traits are conceptualized as risk characteristics. These risk characteristics are closely related to individual behavior and should not be confounded with psychiatric disorders according to taxonomic classification systems such as the DSM-IV-TR (American Psychiatric Association, 2000) or the ICD-10 (World Health Organization, 1993), even if those can overlap.

Target Offense

In FOTRES, risk is always specified as the risk for committing a certain type of crime. This specification is operationalized as the target offense and is made during the first step of the assessment. The target offense does not necessarily need to correspond with legal classifications. For example, killing a person would be considered a homicide legally but such an offense is sometimes sexually motivated (e.g., sexual murder). Therefore, the selection of the target offense always takes into consideration the motivation of the offender. The risk of committing the target offense must directly result from the characteristics of the offender's risk profile.

Offense Mechanism Hypothesis

Recidivism risk is estimated based on an hypothesis regarding the offense mechanism. The offense mechanism is specific to every case and explains the process of how the relevant personal and situational risk characteristics led to the perpetration of the target offense. The goal is not to develop an etiological model about how and why the person became an offender, but rather to develop a model that describes how the risk characteristics interacted and influenced a specific criminal behavior. The offense mechanism hypothesis is therefore very descriptive and close to individual behavior. In building the offense mechanism hypothesis, the user has to combine two sources of information: information about the perpetrator and information about the pattern of the offense. Because the offense mechanism is conceptualized as an hypothesis, it is checked by criteria of plausibility including the value of the explanation (i.e., consistent integration of the central findings on the perpetrator with as many facets of the offense as possible), its plausibility (i.e., it has to be internally consistent and plausible according to forensic-psychiatric standards), and evidence (i.e., consideration of all available information so that the offense mechanism has sufficient reliability) (for more information on FOTRES theory see, for example, Endrass & Rossegger, 2012; Urbaniok, 2016b).

Administration

If case information is collected (file information and personal interview) the rating of FOTRES takes approximately 60 minutes. As in other SPJ tools, in FOTRES the evaluator must identify the relevant personal and situational factors that lead up to the offender's criminal behavior from a larger set of available risk characteristics that were developed to reflect the state of the art with respect to scientific knowledge and professional practice. The evaluator then conceptualizes the causal role of these risk characteristics, speculates about possible future behavior, and develops individual case management plans. This is contrary to the assessment made based on actuarial tools which include only a small set of risk factors, that are optimized to predict a specific outcome in a specific population over a specific period of time, and which the evaluator must, generally, simply code as present or absent (Hart & Logan, 2011).

After selecting and coding the relevant items, the RNA level of FOTRES v3 provides four scores: (a) one score for baseline risk, (b) one score for baseline treatability, and (c) two scores for the plausibility of the risk profile modules (i.e., offense-related personality dispositions and the pattern of the offense). The scores for the offense-related personality dispositions and the pattern of the offense are compared with the score for baseline risk. There is no specific rule to evaluate if the scores on the scales of plausibility of the risk profile match the score on baseline risk, but when the scores in these scales are higher than the score on baseline risk it may signal potential problems with the assessment of baseline risk. Regarding baseline risk, individual items comprising the scales included in the risk profile and the relevance of the risk profile are rated on a Likert scale ranging from 0 to 4. The score on each item is then combined to produce a score for each scale composing the risk profile and the relevance of the risk profile. The sum of the scores for each of those scales is then combined to produce a total score for the baseline risk, also ranging between 0 and 4. The total score produced for the baseline treatability is computed in a similar way. That is, individual items included in the scales composing the perspectives for treatment and personal resources are combined to produce a score for these same scales. The scores on the scales composing the general perspectives for treatment and personal resources are then combined to produce the total baseline treatability score.

For the RM level, four scores are produced: (a) risk profile and relevance, (b) self-control, (c) current risk, and (d) current treatability. Scores of the individual items and scales, and of the resulting totals, are computed and interpreted in the same way as in the RNA. The risk profile and relevance score is a combination of the scores for the current risk profile and the current relevance of the risk profile. Current risk is a combination of the scores on the risk profile and relevance and the self-control scales. Current treatability is a combination of the scores on the perspectives for treatment and personal resources scales.

Single risk characteristics are rated 0 to 4 in one-unit increments. Items scores of the RNA level can be interpreted in the following way: 0 = the risk characteristic is not present, 1 = present to a low extent, 2 = present to a moderate extent, 3 = present to a high extent, and 4 = present to a very high extent. Items scores of the RM level also range between 0 and 4 in one-unit increments and are interpreted in a similar way: 0 = no/very low treatability, 4 = very high treatability. Total scores for baseline and current risk are rated 0 to 4 in .5-unit increments and are interpreted as: between 0 and .5 = there is a very low risk for committing crimes in the domain of the assessed target offense, 1 = low risk, 1.5 = low to moderate risk, 2 = moderate risk, 2.5 = moderate to high risk, 3 = high risk, 3.5 = high to very high risk, and 4 = very high risk. The scores on the baseline and current treatability are also rated 0 to 4 in .5-unit increments and are interpreted as: 0 = no treatability, .5 = very low treatability, 1 = low treatability, 1.5 = low to moderate treatability, 2 = moderate treatability, 2.5 = moderate to high treatability, 3 = high treatability, 3.5 = high to very high treatability, and 4 = very high treatability.

Based on the results, specific interpretation of the recidivism risk and indications for treatment, as well as specific recommendations for treatment and its prospects are presented to the user. FOTRES do not provide expected recidivism rates for the different risk scores or categories. However, a theoretical Stanine distribution (normal distribution divided into nine categories) is presented to compare the actual scores of different offenders.

All total scores are calculated automatically by the web application. The details of the algorithm are not shown to the user to avoid human errors and manipulation of the results. FOTRES includes a manual (Urbaniok, 2016b) that should be used to better understand the theory, application, and interpretation of the tool, although guidelines and descriptions of the items are also available online. One-day standardized workshop training is promoted regularly (see the FOTRES webpage at http://www.fotres.ch/; Urbaniok, 2016a). Although not mandatory, this training is recommended due to the complexity of the tool. There are no required qualifications, but knowledge of forensic psychology and/or psychiatry is recommended.

Validity and Reliability Research

Research regarding FOTRES's psychometric properties has been scarce. Until now, only a couple of studies investigated its predictive validity and inter-rater reliability. In a study investigating the predictive validity of the tool with 109 violent and sex offenders released from a prison in Switzerland between 1994 and 1999, and who were followed in the community for an average of nine years, Rossegger et al. (2011) found that both the total score (OR = 1.74, $p < .010$) and the risk categories (OR = 3.74, $p = .010$) of FOTRES v2 were significantly associated with repeated offending, and discriminated well between recidivist and non-recidivist (AUC = .81, .76, respectively). Compared with the Psychopathy Checklist-Revised (PCL-R; Hare, 1991), the Violence Risk Appraisal Guide (VRAG; Quinsey, Harris, Rice, & Cormier, 2006), the Historical, Clinical, Risk Management-20 (HCR-20; Webster, Douglas, Eaves, & Hart, 1997), and the Level of Service Inventory–Revised (LSI-R; Andrews & Bonta, 2001), FOTRES presented the highest odds ratio (OR) for both the total score and risk categories. Only the PCL-R presented a higher area under the curve (AUC; .84 for the total score). The inter-rater reliability among three raters for 20 cases was good (Kappa > .65; Altman, 1991).

In another study, 15 patients from a German forensic psychiatry unit were rated on FOTRES by three independent raters based on the official records of the penitentiary. Keller et al. (2011) found that the intraclass correlation (ICC) for structural risk, the main scale of FOTRES v2, was poor ($r = .23$; Cicchetti, 1994). For the likelihood of successful treatment scale, the ICC, was fair ($r = .53$). Both scales included subscales with high and low agreement.

Based on these results, FOTRES appears to have predictive validity but the results regarding its reliability have been mixed. Besides methodological differences between studies, divergent findings regarding the reliability of the baseline risk of offenders may be explained by the nature of the tool. Unlike actuarial tools, where users rate every item of the tool, users of FOTRES only rate the items that they select to make the risk profile of the offender. Due to the number of potentially selectable factors and different possible combinations, the results on inter-rater reliability may be low because a high level of subjectivity is introduced into the ratings. That is, the tool has the advantage of being very specific and comprehensive but the rating of the baseline risk may differ substantially across raters. Such problems may be attenuated in the perspectives for treatment part of the tool, where every item is rated.

Users of FOTRES working in different settings throughout the Swiss cantons have described the tool as very useful in the development and monitoring of risk management plans (Manhart et al., 2014). This indirectly attests to the face validity and clinical utility of the tool.

Implementation Research

One of the most important developments in prison and sentencing measures in recent years in Switzerland is the Risk-Oriented Enforcement of Sentence (ROES) project, funded by the Federal State and launched jointly in four cantons from 2010 to 2013. The motivations for the project were the critical events and recidivism rates observed during previous years, as well as the obligation to plan the criminal sanctions introduced in 2007 by the PG-CP law, art. 75 CP (Bundesversammlung der Schweizerischen Eidgenossenschaft, 1937). ROES is a structured risk-based process that includes the principles of risk-needs-responsivity, early identification of high-risk offenders, assessment of individual risk characteristics, recommendations for appropriate interventions, monitoring of the process with regular evaluation and adjustment, and cooperation between the various entities of the criminal justice system. It aims at reducing recidivism and easing the social reintegration of offenders through the implementation of standardized processes and tools, and by providing a common language for professionals of the correctional facilities, probation services, therapeutic institutions, and offenders themselves, thus promoting scientifically supported and transparent legal decision-making in the criminal justice system (Fink & Bruni, 2013; Keller, 2016; Manhart et al., 2014).

The ROES process includes four steps: (1) screening, (2) assessment, (3) planning, and (4) correctional process. FOTRES is implemented with every violent and sex offender and used in the assessment and planning phases as a standardized risk assessment and case formulation guide, including standardized information on the target offense, personal and situational characteristics related to the offense, and risk management plans. The cost-benefit analysis with the ROES was positive. The results obtained up until 2013 showed that ROES substantially improved the quality and efficiency of the execution of penal sanctions and work process through a strong division of tasks between the different authorities of the criminal justice system, improved treatment efficiency, and better assistance for offenders after their release into the community. In addition, this methodology was well accepted by the different entities of the criminal justice system who also evaluated FOTRES as a useful tool for the assessment, treatment, and follow-up of offenders. The evaluation of recidivism rates before and after the introduction of the ROES will be undertaken with a complementary study, which can only take place after an observation period of several years (Manhart et al., 2014).

Since May 2013, following the preliminary evaluation of the ROES project, the canton of Zurich has made it mandatory to use FOTRES to assess high-risk offenders. This was later extended to all German cantons and is planned to be extended to the French cantons as well. It will probably be extended to the entire country at a later stage. From a practical point of view, ROES allows the establishment of a uniform process across the entire country with common steps and terminologies to achieve better harmonization, standardization, and technical execution of penal sanctions, to encourage collaboration between the cantons, and to facilitate the transmission of criminal cases from one cantonal agency to another (Manhart et al., 2014).

Case Studies

Urbaniok, Rossegger, and Endrass (2006) conducted a study investigating the assessment of high-risk offenders and the establishment of post-sentence preventive detention for offenders identified as very high risk during imprisonment in Switzerland. The authors identified a total of nine offenders that were released from prison (from 1997 to 2005 in the canton of Zurich) due to legal reasons despite their evident level of dangerousness. The authors evaluated the progress of eight of these released offenders in a follow-up study. They found that these high-risk offenders re-offended with severe violent and sex offenses—seven within a year of their release—resulting in a total of 24 victims being harmed. The authors also found that although incarcerated violent and/or sex offenders frequently score high on risk assessment tools, what distinguished this group of high-risk offenders was the combination of a high recidivism risk with a lack of treatability and unsuccessful attempts at therapy and/or other kinds of coping strategies training. Specifically, all nine offenders had a very high score of 3.5 or 4 in structural risk of recidivism, and very low scores of 0 or .5 in mutability and dynamic risk reduction, as assessed by FOTRES v1 (Urbaniok, 2004). The results of this study showed that at least some categories of very dangerous offenders can be reliably detected with FOTRES (Urbaniok, Rossegger, & Endrass, 2006).

Current Issues and Future Directions

FOTRES has been implemented into the forensic practice of different Swiss cantons and was used in the development of a structured risk-based process, ROES, that improved the quality and efficiency of the execution of penal sanctions and the work process of the criminal justice system. The tool has been regarded as useful in the assessment, treatment, and follow-up of offenders, as well as in the establishment of a uniform process and terminology across the different entities involved in the criminal justice system of different cantons of Switzerland. Though FOTRES has proved to be a useful tool for the criminal justice system, especially when used as one tool among a more comprehensive array of risk assessment tools and diagnostic scales, there is limited empirical data available regarding its psychometric properties. More studies on FOTRES properties are therefore necessary to better conclude about its validity, reliability, and usefulness in forensic settings. A large-scale evaluation study is planned.

As with most SPJ tools, FOTRES does not provide recidivism rates. Therefore, it is not possible to assess the calibration properties of the tool in other jurisdictions and countries. A further limitation of FOTRES is that it is a relatively long and complex tool. However, unlike the reductionism of actuarial scales (which include few items and are mostly of a static nature), SPJ tools attempt to assess the complexity of a case and allow professionals in the field to better understand the offender and thus to better plan suitable treatment interventions (Rossegger et al., 2011). FOTRES can, therefore, be used for monitoring offender treatment and for providing information on treatment goals, level of security, recommendations for early release, and therapeutic progress in offense-oriented treatment plans. The complexity of the tool requires considerable effort for translations. Despite this, translations of the tool and the manual into English and French are being made.

Note: The present manuscript has not been published elsewhere and is not currently under consideration by any other outlet. The authors received no funding for this research and have no conflict of interest. The authors thank BioScience Writers, LLC. for editing the final version of the manuscript.

References

Altman, D. G. (1991). *Practical statistics for medical research*. London, England: Chapman & Hall/CRC.

American Psychiatric Association. (2000). *Diagnostic and statistical manual of mental disorders – DSM-IV-TR* (4th ed.). Washington, DC: American Psychiatric Association.

Andrews, D. A., & Bonta, J. (2001). *LSI-R. The Level of Service Inventory – Revised. User's manual.* Toronto: Multi-Health Systems.

Bundesversammlung der Schweizerischen Eidgenossenschaft (1937). Schweizerisches Strafgesetzbuch [Swiss Criminal Code], 311.0 C.F.R.

Cicchetti, D. V. (1994). Guidelines, criteria, and rules of thumb for evaluating normed and standardized assessment instruments in psychology. *Psychological Assessment, 6*(4), 284–290.

Endrass, J., & Rossegger, A. (2012). Forensisches Operationalisiertes Therapie-Evaluations-System 2.0 (FOTRES 2.0). *Forum Strafvollzug – Zeitschrift für Strafvollzug und Straffälligenhilfe, 61*(2), 90–94.

Fazel, S., Singh, J. P., Doll, H., & Grann, M. (2012). Use of risk assessment instruments to predict violence and antisocial behaviour in 73 samples involving 24 827 people: Systematic review and meta-analysis. *British Medical Journal, 345*, e4692.

Fink, D., & Bruni, H.-U. (2013). Switzerland. In A. van Kalmthout & I. Durnescu (Eds.), *Probation in Europe* (pp. 1047–1076). Utrecht, The Netherlands: Wolf Legal Publishers.

Hare, R. D. (1991). *The Hare Psychopathy Checklist – Revised*. Toronto, ON: Multi-Health Systems.

Hart, S. H., & Logan, C. (2011). *Formulation of violence risk using evidence-based assessments: The Structured Professional Judgment approach*. Chichester, England: Wiley-Blackwell.

Keller, A. (2016). Focused sentenced management: A multidisciplinary and joint task. In F. Dünkel, J. Jesse, I. Pruin, & M. von der Wense (Eds.), *European treatment, transition management and re-integration of high-risk offenders* (pp. 171–176). Mönchengladbach, Germany: Forum Verlag Godesberg GmbH.

Keller, F., Kliemann, A., Karanedialkova, D., Schnoor, K., Schuett, U., Keiper, P., . . . Schlaefke, D. (2011). Interrater reliability in the Forensic Operationalized Therapy/Risk Evaluation System. *Nervenheilkunde, 30*(10), 813–817.

Manhart, T., Patzen, H.-J., Schilling, A., Mayer, K., Treuthardt, D., Weiss, S., ... Dvorak, A. (2014). Projet pilote – Exécution des sanctions orientée vers les risques (ROS): Rapport final. Zurich, Switzerland: Services de probation et d'exécution de Zurich.

Quinsey, V. L., Harris, G. T., Rice, M. E., & Cormier, C. A. (2006). *Violent offenders: Appraising and managing risk* (2nd ed.). Washington, DC: American Psychological Association.

Rossegger, A., Laubacher, A., Moskvitin, K., Villmar, T., Palermo, G. B., & Endrass, J. (2011). Risk assessment instruments in repeat offending: The usefulness of FOTRES. *International Journal Offender Therapy Comparative Criminology, 55*(5), 716–731.

Singh, J. P. (2016). *International perspectives on forensic risk assessment: Measuring use, perceived utility, and research quality.* PhD thesis, University of Konstanz. Retrieved from http://nbn-resolving.de/urn:nbn:de:bsz:352-0-322142

Singh, J. P., Desmarais, S. L., Hurducas, C., Arbach-Lucioni, K., Condemarin, C., de Ruiter, C., ... Otto, R. K. (2014). Use and perceived utility of structured violence risk assessment tools in 44 countries: Findings from the IRiS Project. *International Journal of Forensic Mental Health, 13,* 193–206.

Urbaniok, F. (2004). *FOTRES: Forensisches Operationalisiertes Therapie-Risiko-Evaluations-System* (1st ed.). Bern, Switzerland: Zytglogge.

Urbaniok, F. (2007). *FOTRES: Forensisches Operationalisiertes Therapie-Risiko-Evaluations-System* (2nd ed.). Bern, Switzerland: Zytglogge.

Urbaniok, F. (2016a). FOTRES. Retrieved from http://www.fotres.ch/

Urbaniok, F. (2016b). *FOTRES: Forensisches Operationalisiertes Therapie-Risiko-Evaluations-System* (3rd ed.). Bern, Switzerland: Zytglogge.

Urbaniok, F., Rossegger, A., & Endrass, J. (2006). Can high-risk offenders be reliably identified? A follow-up study on dangerous offenders in Switzerland released from prison for legal reasons. *Swiss Medical Weekly, 136*(47–48), 761–768.

Webster, C. D., Douglas, K. S., Eaves, D., & Hart, S. D. (1997). *HCR-20: Assessing risk for violence* (Vol. 2). Burnaby BC: Simon Fraser University.

World Health Organization (1993). *The ICD-10 classification of mental and behavioural disorders: Diagnostic criteria for research.* Geneva, Switzerland: World Health Organization.

13

The RisCanvi: A New Tool for Assessing Risk for Violence in Prison and Recidivism

Antonio Andrés-Pueyo, Karin Arbach-Lucioni, and Santiago Redondo

Introduction

The "prison bubble" phenomenon (Petersilia, 2011) is not exclusive to the U.S. In many ways, it also applies to the significant increase in the number of people incarcerated during the last 25 years in Europe. Many Western European countries, especially the U.K., France, and Spain, have been witness to a trend similar to that seen in the U.S., though admittedly not on the same scale (Aebi et al., 2014). It has been well documented that the presence of a large prison population pushes up the rates of recidivism (Petersilia, 2003; Zara & Farrington, 2016). In this chapter, we will examine the issue of prison recidivism in Catalonia, briefly summarize the studies of recidivism carried out in recent years, and present a new instrument for assessing the risk of recidivism, the RisCanvi or "Risk Change" protocol, which has made an important contribution to the management and rehabilitation of offenders in the Catalan prison system. The RisCanvi was designed to assess the risk of violence in prisons in Catalonia and, since 2009, it has been the main tool both for preventing prison violence and for managing rehabilitation and recidivism. It has been empirically tested and its metric parameters are similar to those of other recidivism risk assessment tools like the Level of Service Inventory–Revised (LSI-R) and Post-Conviction Risk Assessment (PCRA) (see Desmarais & Singh, 2013).

A Brief Overview of the Catalan Correctional System

Catalonia is a region in northeastern Spain that is a fairly typical European region in terms of its levels of social development and industrialization with a relatively high-quality social services and welfare system. This region has its own regulations in criminal and correctional laws and in technical norms. In Catalonia, crime rates are very similar to those in the rest of Spain. Currently crime rates in Spain are low, below the EU average. After Portugal and Greece, Spain is the country with the lowest crime rates in Europe. In 2015, the Spanish Ministry of the Interior reported a rate of 44.3 crimes per 1,000 inhabitants, compared with 147.9 in Sweden and 64.6 in the UK, and an average for the European Union as a whole of 61.3 (Andrés-Pueyo, 2015).

Despite these low crime rates, however, the prison populations in Catalonia and Spain are among the highest in Europe. In recent years, the prison population in Catalonia has fluctuated between 6,095 inmates in 2000 and 10,009 in 2013, the latter representing a rate of 129.7 prisoners per 100,000 people. Between 1990 and 2010, the number of inmates in Catalan prisons rose steadily; since 2010, there has been a clear reduction in the rate of incarceration, although

Handbook of Recidivism Risk/Needs Assessment Tools, First Edition. Edited by Jay P. Singh, Daryl G. Kroner, J. Stephen Wormith, Sarah L. Desmarais, and Zachary Hamilton.

it is still considered excessively high. Thus, Catalonia has a high rate of incarceration but one of the lowest crime rates in Europe.

The Catalan prison service authorities originally designed their policies in the 1980s and 1990s and took as their reference point the rehabilitation programs in operation in other countries, especially Canada. Over the last 30 years, various correctional programs have been developed in Catalonia. Today, these programs range from health-based systems to cognitive behavioral treatments for different types of offenders (for a review, see Redondo, 2008). In this professional context, the RisCanvi tool was designed in 2008 at the request of the Catalan prison service to introduce new techniques to the management procedures for offenders.

Since the later 1990s, the research center at the Department of Justice in Catalonia, which is responsible for the Prison Service, has carried out a series of four continuous studies of prison recidivism and other more specific studies in young populations, with sex offenders, and with partner abusers and traffic offenders (see Table 13.1). The first study of prison recidivism was by Redondo, Funes, and Luque in 1991 (Redondo, Funes, & Luque, 1994) and consisted of a four-year longitudinal analysis of a random sample of 485 prisoners who had completed their prison sentences in 1987 and had reentered prison at any time since their release until the end of 1991. This study obtained a recidivism rate of 37.9% (Redondo, Funes, & Luque, 1994). The second study, conducted between 1997 and 2001, covered a much wider sample of 1,555 cases with the same conditions as the previous study and obtained a similar recidivism rate of 37.2% (Luque, Ferrer, & Capdevila, 2004). The third study, with a sample of 1,303 cases and a five-year follow-up period, recorded a recidivism rate of 40.3% (Capdevila & Ferrer, 2009). The fourth and most recent study was conducted between 2010 and 2013 and included all cases released in 2010 who returned to prison before the end of 2013. The recidivism rate obtained in this study was 30.2%, but it was the most accurate study because it included many methodological improvements (Capdevila et al., 2015). An executive report of this fourth research study is accessible online in English.[1] All of these analyses registered the return to prison for a recidivating ex-inmate within a three- to four-year time period.

The RisCanvi: A New Tool for Risk Assessment of Prison Recidivism

The RisCanvi was developed in response to the concern of prison system authorities in Catalonia regarding violent recidivism among offenders (especially sex offenders) after serving their sentences. In 2007, a commission of experts created by the Catalan Department of

Table 13.1 Prison Recidivism in Catalonia (Spain): A Historical View

Years	N	Rate (%)	Notes
1987–1991	485	37.9	Sampling/general recidivism
1997–2001	1,555	37.2	Sampling/general recidivism
2002–2007	1,303	40.3	Sampling/general recidivism
2010–2013	3,414	30.2*	Penitentiary recidivism (without technical violations)

*General Recidivism: 30.2%; Violent Recidivism: 27.6%; Technical Violation: 23.3%

---

1 http://cejfe.gencat.cat/web/.content/home/recerca/cataleg/crono/2015/taxa_reincidencia_2014/prison_recividism_rate_executive_report.pdf

Justice recommended the implementation of a protocol for assessing risk in prisons to manage recidivism in dangerous offenders. The measures adopted by the committee included the recommendation that a specific procedure, to be used by the judicial system, the prison service, and the police, be introduced to evaluate the risk of future violence among released prisoners. In 2009, the RisCanvi, a multi-level risk assessment protocol for prison violence prevention, was created and was introduced in the prison system in Catalonia. The RisCanvi was launched at a time when Catalan prisons were becoming overcrowded due to the lengthening of prison sentences and had to find a balance between maintaining treatment programs, introducing new alternative penal measures, and responding to society's constant demands for security and safety both at home and in Europe as a whole.

Today, there are numerous protocols designed specifically for use in a prison context for assessing the risk of recidivism. In a recent review, Singh, Desmarais, & Van Dorn (2013) described 19 of these protocols used in the U.S. Others have been used in the U.K., Australia, Germany, and elsewhere, although many of them are the same as those used in the U.S. In Catalonia and Spain until the creation of the RisCanvi (in 2009), no such protocols were available for professional use in prisons. Some experimental studies have been conducted with the Violence Risk Appraisal Guide (VRAG) and the Self-Appraisal Questionnaire (SAQ), (Andreu-Rodriguez et al., 2016) but none of these has been adopted for professional application in Spanish prisons.

Currently in Spain, the most internationally recognized tools for the assessment of violence risk, such as the Psychopathy Check List – Revised (PCL-R), the Historical Clinical Risk Management-20, Version 3 (HCR-20^{v3}), the Sexual Violence Risk-20 (SVR-20), the Spousal Assault Risk Assessment Guide (SARA), or the Structured Assessment of Violence Risk in Youth (SAVRY), are available for professional use in Spanish translations; there are also experimental adaptations of the Level of Service Inventory–Revised (LSI-R), the Self Appraisal Questionnaire (SAQ), and the Violence Risk Appraisal Guide (VRAG) (see Andrés-Pueyo & Echeburúa, 2010). Most of these tools have been adapted by the GEAV at the University of Barcelona. At the same time, in Spain—and above all in Catalonia—new tools for risk assessment have been developed for use in forensic and clinical contexts, in prisons, by the police, and by the social services for the prevention of serious crimes. Among these instruments are a series of original protocols: the RisCanvi, the "Risc de Violencia contra les Dones-Barcelona" (RVD-BCN), the "Escala de Prevencion de Violencia–Revisada" (EPV-R), and the "Sistema de Valoración Policial integral de Violencia de Género" (VIOGEN) (Arbach-Lucioni & Andrés-Pueyo, 2016). All of these violence risk assessment tools, both the adapted ones and the ones originally created in Spain, provide reasonable reliability and predictive validity (see Arbach-Lucioni & Andrés-Pueyo, 2016). Currently in Spain, the police and mental health professionals account for between 60 and 80% of risk assessment tool use, with lower rates among correctional and general psychiatric care professionals (Arbach-Lucioni & Andrés-Pueyo, 2016).

The RisCanvi was designed to achieve two main objectives. The first objective was to improve individualized predictions of the risk of future violence in the form of new violent crimes, self-directed aggression, and violent behavior inside the prison facilities, and to predict the likelihood of breaches of prison furloughs or parole. The RisCanvi was to offer support for professionals by providing prognostic data to help standardize the decision-making process and to minimize errors and ensure the transparency of the decisions made. Second, the implementation of RisCanvi was intended to generalize the use of tools for risk assessment as a habitual procedure among prison professionals and thus to introduce best practices in the management of the information for decision-making, sharing information between professionals, ensuring constant updates of the information and consolidating the use of technical instruments of empirically proven validity and utility.

The implementation of the RisCanvi sought to introduce "risk management" as a new resource for expanding and increasing the effects of rehabilitation programs. Successful risk management depends on the incorporation of individualized interventions that assess the risk of violence and recidivism, and the dynamic adaptation of these interventions in response to this risk, the potential for personal change, and the criminogenic needs of offenders.

The RisCanvi was designed and developed in a joint project involving prison services and the Group of Advanced Studies on Violence at the University of Barcelona between 2007 and 2009. This collaboration is ongoing, and the RisCanvi remains a protocol "in construction." Currently, the RisCanvi is fully incorporated in several procedures of prisoners' management and is a resource at the disposal of professionals in Catalan prisons to enhance effective decision-making in all areas in which the assessment and management of the risk of violence are important.

Through a structured assessment of various risk factors (criminal, biographical, social, medical, and psychological), the RisCanvi determines the level of risk present for each inmate relative to three possible future violent behaviors: (a) self-directed violence (self-injury, suicide); (b) violence in the prison facilities (directed at other inmates or prison staff); and (c) committing further violent offenses (violent recidivism). The RisCanvi also estimates the risk of breaking prison permissions or leaves and other similar situations, which are particularly important in prison management in Catalonia where probationary periods are often granted during the course of a sentence. The RisCanvi has specific scales for each of these criteria.

The construction and implementation of the RisCanvi followed a three-phase process: (a) a case-control study to identify elements of the protocol, especially the formulation of risk factors and the construction of scales; (b) training for users, in both the basics of risk assessment and the use of RisCanvi; and (c) the implementation of the protocol according to a predesigned plan that allowed its widespread use over a one-year period in all prisons in Catalonia and their associated services (about 25 facilities with about 9,000 inmates at any one time). The RisCanvi has been incorporated into the regular prison management procedures and is included in the computer applications of the rehabilitation programs. Since its implementation, the central services have provided guidance for improving the protocol's use and have set up important resources, such as the SOS RisCanvi office, team validators, actions with the GEAV in the form of psychometric analysis and calibration, training sessions, and so on. All of these measures have helped to maintain a high level of quality control.

During 2008–2009, the initial RisCanvi protocol and the instructions for its application inside the correctional management system were prepared. Since 2010, the evaluations completed with the RisCanvi have been applied in all the prisons in Catalonia. To date, approximately 15,000 assessments have been administered, many of which are reassessments. In 2011, a document entitled "The rehabilitation model in Catalan prisons"[2] was published, which contains a wealth of detail regarding the RisCanvi's objectives and functions.

The RisCanvi: Structure and Some Psychometric Properties

The starting-point for the development of the RisCanvi was a retrospective case-control study with a sample of 643 cases and 428 controls. The study analyzed the prevalence of four risk criteria related to violence in prisons and identified the factors relevant for each one (Andrés-Pueyo, Arbach-Lucioni, & Redondo, 2010). Hundreds of prison records were selected and analyzed

---

2 http://justicia.gencat.cat/web/.content/documents/publicacions/model_rehabilitacio_presons_catalanes.pdf

and formed the empirical basis for the development of the instrument. Its creation included a retrospective analysis of 106 criminal and violence risk factors in cases and controls obtained from four sources: other preexisting prison risk assessment protocols (LSI-R, COMPAS, FOTRES, OASYS, HCR-20, etc.); more specific violence risk assessment guidelines (SVR-20, SARA, etc.); clinical and personality tests (GHQ and NEO-PI-R); and other risk factors (based on the staff's professional experience). From this extensive initial draft and through a case/control study, we were able to identify 43 risk factors that allowed us to determine the probability of committing a new violent act or of breaching parole. Once these factors were identified, we used binary logistic regression to select the risk factors that were specific to predicting each criterion. We then designed a unique scale (i.e., predictive algorithm) for each criterion, which took into account the loading of each risk factor.

In addition to the risk factors themselves, all scales incorporated four grouping variables which moderated in different ways the effect of risk factors included in the algorithm. These factors were age (above or below 30), sex (male or female), the country of origin (Spanish or foreign), and the prison status or situation (remanded in custody or incarcerated). As a result, for each criterion there is an algorithm that includes various risk factors with their weighted effect and four group factors moderating the risk, which together produce a highly individualized, standardized score of the risk assessed for each inmate.

After the creation of the basic structure, two versions of the protocol were made: one for screening and the other for diagnosis. Therefore, two formats were designed: the RisCanvi Screening (RisCanvi-S), comprising 10 risk items, and the full version, the Riscanvi Complete (RisCanvi-C), comprising 43 risk items grouped into five different categories. In the RisCanvi-S, for all four criteria, there are always two levels of risk—high and low—which are obtained using a fully actuarial procedure. In the RisCanvi-C, on the other hand, there are three risk levels: high, medium, and low. These levels are initially calculated actuarially; then, after using the structured clinical judgment method, the rater indicates which level is appropriate. Both versions include the four modulating factors of age, sex, criminal status, and national origin (Andrés-Pueyo et al., 2010). Cutoff points for converting the continuous risk scores into discrete assessments of the level of risk were also obtained from the retrospective study. The cutoffs were initially reviewed eight months after the introduction of the RisCanvi, because the professionals considered that they were overestimating risk.

One of the features that most clearly identifies a risk assessment protocol is the composition of its items, that is, the risk factors that must be evaluated and encoded by a professional. The items in the RisCanvi were obtained through a combination of an empirical selection and rational decision, and include static factors (age of onset of violent behavior, family history of crime, etc.) and dynamic factors (membership of groups of social exclusion, procriminal attitudes, etc.). These items varied and are heterogeneous but are quite common in protocols of this kind. They are defined in terms of risk factors to facilitate their coding and their use by professionals. The full version of the RisCanvi comprises 43 risk factors while the screening version contains only 10 (eight of which are also in the full version, and two are a combination of different items from the full version). In the screening version, items requires "yes/no" responses, while the full version has three levels: "yes/??/no." Table 13.2 displays the items from the screening version and the items from the full version.

The screening version is designed for use only in accordance with an actuarial procedure. In the full version, the user applies a structured clinical judgment procedure and can therefore add specific risk factors that determine the final level of risk in the cases evaluated. From a criminological point of view, the risk factors of the RisCanvi scales constitute a full representation of the explanatory variables that appear in different criminological models and theories

Table 13.2 Risk Factors of RisCanvi Screening and Complete Versions

RisCanvi Screening	RisCanvi Complete	
Risk Factors	**Risk Factors**	
1. Start of the criminal or violent activity.	*Group 1* Criminal/ Penitentiary	1. Violent index offense.
2. History of violence.		2. Age at the time on index offense.
3. Institutional/prison misconduct.		3. Intoxication during the perpetration of the index offense.
4. Escapes, infringements, or non-fulfillments.		4. Victims with injuries.
5. Problems with drug or alcohol use.		5. Length of criminal convictions.
6. Limited response to psychological and/or psychiatric treatments.		6. Time served in prison.
		7. History of violence.
		8. Start of the criminal or violent activity.
7. Self-injury attempts or behavior.		9. Increasing of the frequency, seriousness, and diversity of the offenses.
8. Lack of financial resources.		10. Conflict with other inmates.
9. Lack of family and social support.		11. Failure to accomplishment of penal measures.
		12. Disciplinary reports.
		13. Escapes or absconding.
		14. Grade regression.
10. Hostile attitudes or procriminal values.		15. Breaching prison permission.
	Group 2 Biographical	16. Poor childhood adjustment.
		17. Distance from residence to prison.
		18. Educational level.
		19. Problems related with employment.
		20. Lack of financial resources.
		21. Lack of viable plans for the future.
	Group 3 Family/Social	22. Criminal history of family or parents.
		23. Difficulties in the socialization or development in the origins family.
		24. Lack of family or social support.
		25. Criminal or antisocial friends.
		26. Member of social vulnerable groups.
		27. Relevant criminal role.
		28. Gender violence victim (only women).
		29. Dependent family charges.
	Group 4 Clinical	30. Drug abuse or dependence.
		31. Alcohol abuse or dependence.
		32. Severe mental disorder.
		33. Sexual promiscuity and/or paraphilia.
		34. Limited response to psychological and/or psychiatric treatments.
		35. Personality disorder related to anger, impulsivity, or violence.
		36. Poor stress coping.
		37. Self-injury attempts/behavior.
	Group 5 Attitudes/ Personality	38. Procriminal or antisocial attitudes.
		39. Low mental ability.
		40. Recklessness.
		41. Impulsiveness and emotional instability.
		42. Hostility.
		43. Irresponsibility.

of crime, especially the most serious and chronic forms of violent crime (Andrés-Pueyo & Redondo-Illescas, 2007).

The information used to encode the risk factors in both forms of the RisCanvi come from different sources—as is usual in such protocols (Hart, Michie, & Cooke, 2007)—such as administrative, judicial and criminological records, interviews with offenders and informants, psychological evaluations, information from professionals who deal with the inmates on a daily basis, and so on. Most of the information obtained through interviews is directly generated by the inmates and recorded by social workers, lawyers, health professionals, psychologists, and also from relatives or staff who come into contact with the offenders and are familiar with their biographical and social circumstances. Another important source of information is the judicial and correctional official documentation and files regarding the criminal acts for which the inmate has been sentenced, which is usually handled by lawyers and criminologists. Other information on inmates' incarceration, such as "uninterrupted time in prison," sanctions, transfers, and so on, is dealt with electronically and is introduced automatically into RisCanvi before evaluation by the staff and regularly updated.

An important resource for professionals using the RisCanvi is a warning automatically generated by the computer program in the presence of certain combinations of risk factors and type of index offense, indicating that another risk assessment protocol should be added and used alongside the RisCanvi-C. These recommendations are provided for six combinations and correspond to six "special risk groups" for violent recidivism; these require a complementary assessment with a more specific instrument, like PCL-R or HCR-20, to refine the prediction of future violent recidivism. Among these special groups are sex offenders (both extra- and intra-familial), perpetrators of violence against women (domestic and/or partner violence), chronic offenders with long-term criminal histories, and offenders with a psychopathic personality disorder or mental illness.

In the professional assessment of the risk of violent recidivism using the RisCanvi, the evaluation can be supplemented with other, more specific instruments depending on the criminological characteristics of the offense and the offender. In the case of sex offenders, it is common practice to use the SVR-20/RSVP alongside the RisCanvi, and in the case of IPV offenders the SARA, a more specific evaluation tool, is often added. With chronic offenders and/or offenders with a history of mental disorder, the HCR-20^{V3} is frequently used, and in the case of young offenders with high risk and less serious crimes, the RisCanvi is often combined with the PCL-SV to avoid false positives for violent recidivism; these offenders may have less serious criminal records but have a high potential risk of recidivism. The e-RisCanvi (the electronic version of the protocol) has a program that advises users to complement the risk assessment offered by the RisCanvi with these protocols, which have adaptations in Spanish.

The RisCanvi is still "under construction." We are currently performing analyses of the inter-observer reliability and are working on the creation of a new risk assessment scale for general recidivism. Naturally, though, when the RisCanvi was created, the outcome scales were validated to guarantee an acceptable level of quality that would allow their application in the day-to-day management of a prison.

In the case-control study carried out for the construction of the RisCanvi, the correlations between the global scale scores of the RisCanvi and the results of the predictions were analyzed to obtain a first assessment of the protocol's predictive validity. Since 2010, the GEAV and the Department of Justice's research and training section have carried out partial studies of the RisCanvi scales and their metric properties and have presented their results at specialized meetings or in specialized publications in the field of violence risk assessment

(Andrés-Pueyo et al., 2015). The results generally provide good evidence of the quality of the RisCanvi in both its formats.

In the first case-control analysis, the point-biserial correlations of the global scores of the RisCanvi-C were .249 ($n = 465$; $p < .001$) for the scale of self-directed violence, with the presence or absence of self-injury attempts or suicide, .228 ($n = 568$; $p < .001$) for intra-institutional violence, .106 ($n = 138$; $p < .007$) for violent recidivism, and .328 ($n = 201$; $p < .001$) for breach of prison leave or parole. The time lag between the risk assessments made by each of the RisCanvi scales and the recording of each outcome was 36 months.

For the RisCanvi-S using the same study, the following point-biserial correlations were obtained: $r = .247$ ($n = 465$, $p < .001$) for self-directed violence, $r = .187$ ($n = 568$; $p < .001$) for intra-institutional violence, and $r = .177$ ($n = 138$; $p < .001$) for violent recidivism. The correlation between the breach of prison leave or parole scale on the RisCanvi-C and the real breach of parole committed by inmates was $r = .115$ ($n = 201$; $p < .005$) (Andrés-Pueyo et al., 2010).

The most recognized predictive validity parameter is calculated from the AUC of the ROC curves. For the scale of self-directed violence (suicide, suicide attempts and threats, self-harm, etc.), this parameter was estimated for the screening and complete formats of the RisCanvi, obtaining respective AUC values of .83 (95% CI: .56–.97) and .87 (95% CI: .67–.98) (Andrés-Pueyo et al., 2010). These AUC values are very high for this scale; thus, they are currently under review in a prospective study using another sample to assess the AUC for self-directed violence (Andrés-Pueyo et al., 2015)

For the scale of intra-institutional violence, which assesses violent behavior in prisons either against other inmates or against the prison staff, we also achieved positive results. Initial estimations of the predictive validity of the intra-institutional violence scale offered an AUC of .82 (95% CI: .74–.91) for the RisCanvi-S and .83 (95% CI: .75–.88) for the RisCanvi-C. In a later prospective study, the AUC values were .82 (95% CI: .78–.86) for the RisCanvi-S and .82 (95% CI: .76–.87) for the RisCanvi-C (Arbach-Lucioni, Martinez-García, & Andrés-Pueyo, 2012).

In relation to violent recidivism, this scale is discussed in the greatest depth due to its relationship to an inmate's behavior outside prison. The 2014 study of recidivism (Capdevila et al., 2015) provided a better estimate of the RisCanvi-C's parameters of predictive validity, since it was based on a prospective study of 3,414 cases with a follow-up of three years. As in the previous cases, the first parameters of the predictive capacity of these scales were obtained from the case-control study and offered the following results: the AUC of the RisCanvi-S was .80 (95% CI: .786–.907) and of the RisCanvi-C was .79 (95% CI: .676–.805). An AUC of .750 was obtained (95% CI: .690–.811) and an OR of 4.72 (95% CI: 2.83–7.95) (Capdevila et al., 2015).

In the initial case-control study, we observed that the AUC of the breach of prison furlough scale in the RisCanvi-S was .46 (95% CI: .386–.570), which was clearly inadequate. In the RisCanvi-C the AUC of this scale was .84 (95% CI .686–.970), a much better value. In a new study (Ferez-Mangas and Andrés-Pueyo, 2015), we improved the predictive ability of this scale in both the complete and the screening versions. The authors of this study found AUCs for this scale of .628 (95% CI: .586–.670) for the RisCanvi-S and .738 (95% CI: .656–.795) for the RisCanvi-C.

The first opportunity to reliably test the quality of the RisCanvi came with the comparison of its predictions with the violent recidivism rate recorded in the prison recidivism study of 2014 (Capdevila et al., 2015). Since the inmates in that study had been released from prison during 2010, a small group (17.8% $n = 654$) had already been administered the RisCanvi (some in both its versions) before leaving prison; this made it possible to obtain data on the predictive validity of the scale of violent recidivism. In addition to this subsample from the study of recidivism, the Department of Justice later provided data for all the inmates who had been released from prison in Catalonia between 2010 and 2013, and their level of recidivism was recorded over a variable time period. With these prospective data, a study of predictive validity was performed using survival analysis for both the RisCanvi-S (which identifies two levels of risk: high and low) and the RisCanvi-C (which identifies three levels of risk: low, medium, and high). With the help of Julio Vega from the University of Yucatan in Mexico, we applied the survival analysis technique to see how the prediction of the risk of recidivism evolved over time. The data we used were the 3,454 inmates released from Catalan prisons between January 2010 and December 2013. The longitudinal follow-up period lasted 1,460 days. During that time, recidivists were registered when they returned to prison for a new offence.

The survival analysis was based on the risk assessment data obtained from the RisCanvi-S and the RisCanvi-C with the presence and absence of violent recidivism as the outcomes. As in many studies with censored data, the Kaplan-Meier procedure was used, and the Cox regression method was used to calculate the RR (Risk Ratios). The results are shown in the two survival charts shown in Figure 13.1. As can be seen, the curves of low-risk cases indicate that they will take longer to recidivate and, in the end, their level of recidivism is lower than that of their high-risk peers. In the RisCanvi-S (for a sample of 4,631 inmates released from prison), low-risk inmates took an average of 295 days to commit a new violent crime and an average of 393 days to commit a new non-violent crime. Cases with a low risk of committing a new violent crime ended up with a recidivism rate of 37%, while high-risk cases had a rate of 48%. In the case of the RisCanvi-C (with a sample of 2,250 inmates released from prison), the mean time until subjects committed a new violent crime was 443 days, and the mean time until they committed a new non-violent crime was 622 days. The comparison between groups indicated violent recidivism in 32% of high-risk, 16% of medium-risk, and 9% of low-risk individuals. The hazard ratio for the comparison of low and medium levels was RR = 1.95 (95% CI: 1.51–2.51) and RR = 4.33 (95% CI: 3.38–5.55) between high and medium levels.

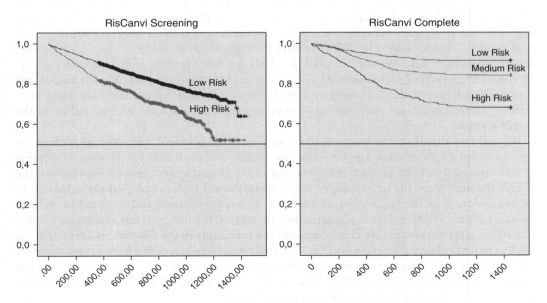

Figure 13.1 Survival analysis of recidivism and RisCanvi (see details in text).

Using the RisCanvi in Practice

The RisCanvi was designed for universal application in prisons for both individuals remanded in custody and those already sentenced, regardless of the crime involved. Since its implementation, the RisCanvi has been applied at different moments in an inmate's sentence and for reassessments. The official recommendation is at six months or at the discretion of the case manager (for example, if an inmate changes center, if his/her personal situation has changed significantly, and so on). The screening version is administered to all inmates in Catalan prisons and allows rapid, reliable, and valid detection of the risk for self-injury, intra-institutional violence, violent recidivism, and breach of parole. For its part, the RisCanvi-C is often applied to inmates evaluated as high risk by the RisCanvi-S, offenders convicted of serious violent crimes, and others who, in the view of the prison experts, require this attention due to their criminal history records or behavior in prison.

The RisCanvi-S is applied to all inmates on entering prison, both first-timers and those with a previous criminal record. If the evaluation finds the risk levels to be low for all four criteria assessed, the same protocol is repeated after six months. If there is any substantial change in the inmate's situation, or if the risk levels are found to be high, then the RisCanvi-C version is applied relatively quickly; it is applied immediately in the case of inmates incarcerated for violent and serious crimes and within four weeks if the inmate has high-risk scores on the RisCanvi-S. If the RisCanvi-C scores show a medium- or high-level risk, the next evaluation will be conducted with the RisCanvi-C; if not, the RisCanvi-S will be used. The RisCanvi-C is also administered to violent offenders (perpetrators of sexual or domestic violence, etc.) before they are released from prison or leave on parole.

Because two forms of the RisCanvi exist and are used in combination, the RisCanvi-S scores often being used as predictors of the RisCanvi-C scores, it is important to examine their interaction at the predictive level. Having a short and a long version of the same protocol has its advantages and disadvantages. The main advantage is the possibility of estimating the risk of an inmate, calculated with the RisCanvi-C (43 risk factors), by using the shorter version with only 10 risk factors. The relationships between the two protocols, Screening and Complete, were explored. Analyzed using correlation coefficients in a sample of 3,945 cases, the Pearson correlations between the scores on the different scales of risk on the RisCanvi-S and the RisCanvi-C were $r = .763$ ($p < .001$) for self-directed violence, $r = .755$ ($p < .001$) for intra-institutional violence, $r = .810$ ($p < .001$) for non-violent recidivism, and $r = .183$ ($p < .005$) for breach of permission. As can be seen, except for the breach of permissions, the correlations between the Screening and the Complete formats of RisCanvi are fairly consistent. These results are only partial at present and more data are sure to follow in the coming years.

We will now discuss certain aspects of the quality of the protocol, its modes of application, and its utilities. One of these aspects is the face validity and credibility for its users. Given that it was created jointly by professionals working in the prison system and by members of the GEAV research team, the terminology used to create the risk factors and their extended definitions (contained in the application manual) was widely understood and accepted by users, a fact that greatly facilitated its implementation. In general, the RisCanvi has a high face validity in part because its contents are consistent with the subculture of the Catalan prison system. As for its content validity, the creation of the RisCanvi model was based, to a large extent, on other recognized and validated protocols which have been well contrasted in numerous empirical studies of risk factors (Kroner, Mills, & Reddon, 2005) but, as described earlier, the items of the protocol were obtained from the case-control pilot study.

Both versions of the RisCanvi are administered through the e-RisCanvi software program which is included in the management software system in use in the Catalan prison service. The e-RisCanvi is used to complete individual assessments of inmates and is integrated into the prison system computer network, which receives official updated information related to the inmates. The e-RisCanvi software offers substantial advantages in terms of the management of the information recorded: for example, it can store changes in risk factors in a database for later use, and it aids the computation of prediction algorithms. In the context of computer protocols, the RisCanvi evaluation is of particular help to experts, as it indirectly allows the accumulation of an enormous body of historical and epidemiological information. In fact, the RisCanvi is now a database of risk factors and other variables of great professional interest and is permanently accessible and revisable.

The prison professionals who complete this protocol come from a variety of academic backgrounds—they are lawyers, social workers, criminologists, psychologists—and they code the risk factors according to their specialization. They are supervised by a team leader, usually a deputy director of the prison, who reviews and validates the final assessments of the RisCanvi outcomes. The e-RisCanvi also helps to prepare reports and provides warnings which are particularly useful in prison management.

All the users of the RisCanvi received an initial training course that included extensive practice with the instrument in its natural context of application and with the e-RisCanvi software. After this training and after applying the scale for at least six months, users were sent an anonymous satisfaction survey in which they were asked about their degree of agreement with the predictions made by the RisCanvi and with other elements of the instrument in general. The responses were relatively positive but also revealed a certain distrust of the protocol; users also complained that the protocol increased their daily workload. Even so, they did not express any significant disagreements regarding the nature and definition of the risk factors included. This survey has not been repeated and it would be of great interest to see how the opinion of professionals who habitually use the RisCanvi has changed, and in what direction.

Since its introduction in Catalan prisons in 2010, the RisCanvi has helped to standardize the risk assessment of inmates and to reduce the variations between staff at different prisons. This relationship between risk assessment and professional tasks has strengthened institutional coordination in the detection and monitoring of cases, in the selective sharing of information at internal levels, and in the prioritization of resources and adaptation of other legal instruments.

Thus far, the RisCanvi has been used only within the prison context. However, given that prison services are closely related to other legal services and criminal enforcement bodies, it has many external applications as well. For example, RisCanvi evaluations have been used to design a procedure called "the process of release of high-risk inmates" in which prison staff inform the judicial authorities and the police that a high-risk prisoner is about to be released; these services then prepare community safety actions to prevent or reduce the risk of recidivism.

The impact of the RisCanvi on judges, lawyers, and prosecutors who receive the information generated by the protocol is very interesting. Until now, risk assessment in forensic practice in Catalonia has been largely based on the use of non-structured clinical judgments, which inevitably tend to reflect subjective opinions. The initial response was a certain skepticism and disbelief that this protocol could actually change the way prison service experts report information to other agents in the legal system. Recently, the protocol has also received criticism; some authors have noted the "excessive reliance on quantification" in the assessment of the risk of recidivism and demand more rigorous and individualized forecasts.

However, the risk reports based on RisCanvi are no longer seen as a novelty and are beginning to gain widespread acceptance.

Risk assessment of violence is playing an increasingly important role in the decisions regarding the adequacy of criminal sentencing, prison classifications, the granting of permits, psychological treatment, and rehabilitation (Andrews & Bonta, 2006; Heilbrun, 1997). The general objective of violence risk assessment in prisons is to prevent criminal violence and its consequences. Specifically, accurate assessment will help to keep offenders with a high risk of recidivism under rigorous monitoring inside the prison and will also mean that less stringent control can be applied to low-risk criminals.

The RisCanvi assessments individualize the work of prison service experts by providing information on specific inmates at particular moments in their prison career. In these cases, prognostic decisions are constantly being made. The RisCanvi helps prison service experts in this task. Scientific studies of groups of subjects (criminals, women inmates, prisoners with personality disorders, sex offenders, etc.) provide general overviews of these group, which would only be fully valid if offenders were all identical. The great difficulty in applying scientific knowledge to professional practice in prisons is the heterogeneity of the inmates, and this is where the professional competence of the expert comes into play.

Conclusions

In the law and criminal enforcement field's, the ability to predict the behavior of inmates and ex-prisoners is of enormous value. Attempts to anticipate recidivism began in the 1920s but did not achieve much success (Glueck & Glueck, 1959). By the 1960s, little progress had been made, though prestigious criminologists like the Gluecks claimed: "in our view the moment has arrived in the history of criminology when, based on the evidence, the predictive approach opens up a promising path through the dense forest of guesswork, hunch, and vague speculation concerning theories of criminal behavior" (Glueck & Glueck, 1959). With the arrival of the 21st century, these new approaches, such as the RisCanvi protocol, have become an essential part of professional prison practices for assessing the risk of violence in prison populations.

Today, prison management professionals use protocols to assess the risk of recidivism to apply the most appropriate preventive measures for the criminogenic needs of prison inmates. This approach eschews two (probably mistaken) beliefs: at one extreme, the belief that stricter criminal measures are the way to resolve the problems of recidivism, and at the other, the notion that the treatments applied in prison will be sufficient for the rehabilitation of offenders. The advances in evidence-based studies, among them studies of recidivism, should persuade prison managers to try to improve the services they provide by addressing the individual needs and characteristics of ex-offenders.

In this chapter, we have analyzed the series of longitudinal studies of prison recidivism that have been carried out in Catalonia. We have described the most recent study of recidivism, which refers to the period between 2010 and 2013 and shows the lowest rate of recidivism of the last 20 years (30.2%, Capdevila et al., 2015). We stress the finding in that study that 39.0% of inmates with a high level of risk of reoffending, according to the RisCanvi protocol (a higher rate than the average), return to prison after a shorter period of time. In turn, those identified as having a lower level of risk by the RisCanvi had a recidivism rate of 17.4%, and those who returned to prison did so after a longer period.

In the past six years, the RisCanvi protocol has helped to improve many of the risk management processes implemented by prison service professionals and other agents in the penal system and the health service. However, the protocol remains under construction and still needs to improve several psychometric characteristics and its prognostic accuracy. These needs are particularly pressing bearing in mind that the protocol is used to determine matters of real consequence, such as whether an ex-prisoner is likely to re-offend.

Acknowledgments

This chapter and research was funded by Grant PSI2009-13265, through Spain's Ministry of Science and Innovation, and by Grant PSI2013-47043-C2-2-R, through Spain's Ministry of Economy and Competitiveness. Financial support was also provided by the Direcció General de Presons de la Conselleria de Justicia de la Generalitat de Catalunya in relation to the RisCanvi project.

References

Aebi, M. F., Aubusson de Cavarlay, B., Barclay, G., Gruszczyńska, B., Harrendorf, S., Heiskanen, M. . . . Þórisdóttir, R. (2014). *European Sourcebook of Crime and Criminal Justice Statistics* (5th ed.). Helskinki, Finland: Akateeminen Kirjakauppa.

Andrés-Pueyo, A. (2015). ¿Cuantos presos retornan a prisión? Análisis y utilidad de los estudios de la reincidencia delictiva. *Boletin ATIP, 31*, 3–21.

Andrés-Pueyo, A. Arbach-Lucioni, K., & Redondo, S. (2010). *Informe de elaboración del protocolo de valoración y gestión del riesgo de violencia en las prisiones RisCanvi.* Dep. de Justicia Generalitat de Catalunya.

Andrés-Pueyo, A., & Echeburúa, E. (2010). Valoración del riesgo de violencia: instrumentos disponibles e indicaciones de aplicación. *Psicothema, 22*(3), 403–409.

Andrés-Pueyo, A., & Redondo-Illescas, S. (2007). Predicción de la violencia: entre la peligrosidad y la valoración de riesgo de violencia. *Papeles Del Psicólogo, 28*(3), 157–173.

Andrés-Pueyo, A. et al. (2015). *RisCanvi: A new multi-scale protocol for violence risk assessment and management in the correctional system in Catalonia (Spain).* Paper presented at XV Annual Meeting IAFMHS, Manchester, England.

Andreu-Rodriguez, J., Peña-Fernández, M. E., & Loza, W. (2016). Predicting risk of violence through a self-appraisal questionnaire. *The European Journal of Psychology Applied to Legal Context, 8*(2), 51–56.

Andrews, D., & Bonta, J. (2006). *The psychology of criminal conduct* (4th ed.). New York, NY: Lexis Nexis.

Arbach-Lucioni, K., & Andrés-Pueyo, A. (2016). Violence risk assessment practices in Spain. In J. Singh, S. Bjørkly, & S. Fazel (Eds.). *International perspectives on violence risk assessment* (pp. 280–293). New York, NY. Oxford University Press.

Arbach-Lucioni, K., Martinez-García, M., & Andrés-Pueyo, A. (2012). Risk factors for violent behavior in prison inmates: A cross-cultural contribution. *Criminal Justice and Behavior, 39*(9), 1219–1239.

Capdevila, M., & Ferrer, M. (2009). *Tasa de reincidencia penitenciaria 2008.* Barcelona, Spain: Centro de Estudios Jurídicos y Formación Especializada. Departamento de Justicia. Generalitat de Catalunya.

Capdevila, M. et al. (2015) *Tasa de reincidencia penitenciaria en Cataluña 2014.* Informes de investigación del CEJFE. Generalitat de Cataluña.

Desmarais, S., & Singh, J. P. (2013). *Instruments for assessing recidivism risk: A review of validation studies conducted in the U.S.* Lexington, KY: Council of State Government.

Ferez-Mangas, D. F., & Andrés-Pueyo, A. (2015). Predicción y prevención del quebrantamiento de los permisos penitenciarios. *Revista Española de Investigación Criminológica, 13,* 7–28.

Glueck, S., & Glueck, E. (1959). *Predicting delinquency and crime.* Book, MA: Harvard University.

Hart, S. D., Michie, C., & Cooke, D. J. (2007). Precision of actuarial risk assessment instruments: Evaluating the "margins of error" of group v. individual predictions of violence. *British Journal of Psychiatry, 190* (Suppl 49), s60–s65.

Heilbrun, K. (1997). Prediction versus management models relevant to risk assessment: The importance of legal decision-making context. *Law and Human Behavior, 21*(4), 347–359.

Kroner, D. G., Mills, J. F., & Reddon, J. R. (2005). A Coffee Can, factor analysis, and prediction of antisocial behavior: The structure of criminal risk. *International Journal of Law and Psychiatry, 28*(4), 360–374.

Luque Reina, M., Ferrer Puig, M., & Capdevila i Capdevila, M. (2004). *La reincidència penitenciària a Catalunya.* CEJFE. Generalitat de Catalunya.

Monahan, J., & Skeem, J. L. (2016). The evolution of violence risk assessment. *Violence in Psychiatry, 17,* 1–9.

Petersilia, J. (2003). *When prisoners come home: Parole and prisoner's reentry.* New York, NY: Oxford University Press.

Petersilia, J. (2011). Beyond the prison bubble. *The Wilson Quarterly, 11,* 50–55.

Redondo, S. (2008). *Manual para el tratamiento psicológico de los delincuentes.* Madrid, Spain: Pirámide.

Redondo, S., Funes, J., & Luque E. (1994). *Justicia penal y reincidencia.* Barcelona, Spain: Centre d´Estudis Jurídics i Formació Especialitzada de la Generalitat de Catalunya y Fundació Jaume Callís.

Singh, J. P., Desmarais, S. L., & Van Dorn, R. A. (2013). Measurement of predictive validity in violence risk assessment studies: A second-order systematic review. *Behavioral Sciences & the Law, 31*(1), 55–73.

Zara, L., & Farrington, D. (2016). *Criminal recidivism.* New York, NY. Routledge.

Part IV

Conclusion

14

Risk Assessment: Where Do We Go From Here?

Faye S. Taxman

Within the last decade, most major reforms emphasize the importance of using objective, validated risk assessment tools to support criminal justice decisions. The value placed on standardized, validated tools that predict the likelihood of certain behaviors varies. Depending on the decision points of the criminal justice system, the validated tool may be used to: 1) structure decisions to reduce arbitrary, discretionary decisions; 2) to increase fairness and justice in the system; and, 3) to better allocate resources. And these tools focus on factors that are related to the desired outcome. Reforms at all stages of the criminal justice system—arrest decisions, prosecution decisions, pretrial release, probation, parole, early release from prison/jail—are decisions that can be supported by risk assessment tools. While no recent surveys have been conducted regarding how many agencies use risk assessment tools, it is almost impossible to find any reform that does not begin with an emphasis on the need for such tools to standardize decision-making (Taxman, 2016).

The attention to risk assessment, as demonstrated in the chapters in this book, and the recent *Handbook of Risk and Need Assessment* sponsored by the Division of Corrections and Sentence of the American Society of Criminology (Taxman, 2016), has led to the expansion of both the number of different tools available as well as the different purposes for which tools can be applied. The proliferation of the number and type of tools, in turn, has resulted in the growing list of unanswered questions regarding risk assessment tools for criminal justice decisions. The unanswered questions range from the adequacy of the procedures to develop and validate the instruments, to the implementation challenges associated with using the results of risk assessments, and to inform various criminal justice decisions. This chapter is devoted to highlighting these issues, and to discussing the importance of making significant headway to ensure that risk assessment instruments and procedures will lead to improved criminal justice decisions. The current experience with risk and need assessment instruments raises concern whether the methods used ensure the reliability and predictive validity of the instruments; whether the instruments contribute to fairness and justice; how practitioners use the instruments which reflects challenges in improving decision-making; and the political and sociolegal environments that affect risk-based decisions. Given the enormity of the challenges ahead, it is appropriate to call for an Oversight Review to ensure that risk assessment fulfills its promise. Seven pressing areas are identified in what follows; these are needed to advance the field including enhancing the utilization of risk assessment tools.

Handbook of Recidivism Risk/Needs Assessment Tools, First Edition. Edited by Jay P. Singh, Daryl G. Kroner, J. Stephen Wormith, Sarah L. Desmarais, and Zachary Hamilton.
© 2018 John Wiley & Sons, Ltd. Published 2018 by John Wiley & Sons, Ltd.

What Are Major Issues Affecting the Development and Evaluation of Risk Assessment Tools?

The proliferation of risk assessment tools to support criminal justice decisions has resulted in the realization that each tool has the capacity to predict different outcomes, and that the ingredients (variables) in a tool are selected based on those outcomes. Tool designers typically use the term "risk" as a generic concept attached to a myriad of behaviors. Risk can refer to the likelihood or probability of failure to appear (FTA) in court (pretrial), arrest for any new crime (pretrial to reentry to probation/parole), arrest for a new felony offense, failure to comply with conditions of release (pretrial, probation, parole), reincarceration, reconviction, dangerousness, violence, and so on. The concept of risk is broad, and therefore tools can be developed to predict different outcomes.

Different researchers use different methods to develop, test, and validate their risk assessment tool. For the most part, risk assessment tools are designed to estimate the likelihood of an outcome, but as discussed above, the outcomes vary across tools. This means that the variables or scales used to estimate risk in any given instrument will also vary, and in fact, there is no standard method for defining key concepts. Consider three recent studies:

1) Mayson (2016), in a recent review of pretrial risk assessment tools, notes that the outcome variable ranges from any new criminal arrest to FTA to criminal filing (including traffic and municipal ordinances) to violent crime to domestic violence with injury during a pretrial period ranging from six months to two years (depending on the instrument). And, the base rate of "reoffending" during this period of time, depending on the jurisdiction(s) participating in the development of the tool ranges from 8% to 42%. The number of items in the tool ranges from seven to 15, some of which are individual factors and others are scales. Only one instrument focuses on static factors (criminal history) while the other combine criminal history with dynamic factors (which range from residence, employment, substance abuse, available working phone, educational level, etc.).

2) Desmarais, Johnson, and Singh (2016) conducted a meta-analysis of 19 recidivism risk assessment instruments and reported similar findings regarding the variations in the instruments and the implications for prediction of risk. They report that: (1) the number of items in the instrument ranged from four to 100; (2) the validation population varied from all offenders to parolees; (3) the outcome variable ranged from any recidivism (i.e., rearrest, reconviction, reincarceration, etc.) to new charges; (4) the instruments included protective factors, 19 instruments included static factors, 15 instruments included dynamic factors, and 19 instruments included substance abuse (and the contents varied in terms of which other domains were included); and (5) various statistical procedures were used to identify predictive validity.

3) Via, Dezember, and Taxman (2016) reviewed five instruments to examine the contents of the instruments in the static and dynamic risk factors and domain areas. The domain areas include criminal history, criminal personality, criminal cognitions, social support, antisocial associates/peers, substance use and abuse, education, employment, accommodations/place/housing, leisure time activities, and mental health. No one domain contained similar items used. The domains are the same (i.e., substance abuse, criminal thinking, etc.) even though they measure different concepts and ideas. That is, there is no consistency in terms of what key terms mean, including Andrews and Bonta's (2010) classic eight domains of criminal personality, antisocial peers, antisocial values, criminal cognitions, substance abuse, employment, family dysfunction, and leisure. The wide variation in meaning suggests that each risk assessment tool is defining its own concepts. The impact on the instruments' predictive validity and utility have not been assessed.

These three reviews, along with countless individual studies, highlight the methodological issues at this stage of the evolution of using risk assessment tools in criminal justice decisions. The unanswered question is: Where is the field of risk assessment in terms of validity and methodological consistency? The field is way past the developmental stage, but it has not reached an advanced stage or achieved methodological rigor. The assessment of the stage of our methodology is crippled by the lack of clarity and frequent lack of transparency in the development and validation of tools. Another added issue is that there are insufficient standards to guide the development and validation of the risk assessment tools, including the core meaning behind common scales such as criminal history, substance use disorders, criminal cognitions, criminal values, and so on. But, it is clear that few developers follow the basics in test development (see Gottfredson & Gottfredson, 1988 or Gottfredson & Moriarity, 2006 for a description of the application to criminal justice; American Educational Research Association, American Psychological Association, and National Council on Measurement in Education, 2014). A consensus group has developed the Risk Assessment Guidelines for the Evaluation of Efficacy (RAGEE) Statement to address this problem but it is generally recommended for risk assessment tools for violent behaviors (Singh, Mulvey, Yang , & RAGEE Group, 2014).

Do Risk Assessment Tools Accurately Identify the Probability of Recidivism (Predictive Validity)?

The premise behind using a risk assessment instrument is that doing so will identify the probability of recidivism with accuracy—accuracy that exceeds subjective judgment of practitioners. In fact, the generational evolution of risk assessment assumes that this is the case: (1) the first generation is subjective, clinical judgment; (2) the second generation is the use of static risk items to summarize historical, actuarial factors that predict involvement in the criminal justice system or risk for reoffending (regardless of the definition); (3) the third generation is the use of static and dynamic risk factors to improve the prediction of recidivism based solely on historical factors; and (4) the fourth generation is the use of risk assessment tools for another purpose beyond the prediction of recidivism, such as case management, programming/treatment decisions, and other uses (Andrews & Bonta, 2010). With each generation, there is an implicit assumption that the predictive validity and, thus, utility of the risk assessment knowledge increases, especially from the first to second generation tools. That is, each generation is believed to advance the utility of the tools (and the information generated), although this has not necessarily been found to be accurate.

There are statistical measures to help us determine the predictive validity of information gleaned from any given risk assessment tool. The recognized statistical measures are the area under the receiver operating characteristic curve (AUC) (probability that a recidivist event would have received a higher rating than a non-recidivist), the point biserial correlation coefficient (strength of association between risk rating and recidivism), the odds ratio (OR) (the odds of a higher classification for those recidivist) , and Somers' d (direction and strength of the risk category and a dichotomous outcome) (Singh, Desmarais, & Van Dorn, 2013). Based on a review by Desmarais and Singh (2013, see Table 8), five of the instruments assessed with the AUC have good performance, three have excellent, and one poor; for those that use the point biserial correlation, two have fair performance, three are good, and six have excellent performance; for those that use the odds ratio, four instruments have poor performance and one has good performance; and for those that use Somers' d, three have good performance and one has excellent performance. Collectively, there is a lot of variation in the predictive validity of the risk assessment instruments, and even when there are multiple studies of the same instrument, there are variations in performance.

As shown by these reviews there is insufficient validation of the instruments. The standard in the field is that each tool should be validated on its own population. This would lead to an assumption that there would be a greater number of prediction studies than the 72 unique studies identified by Desmarais and Singh (2013) and Desmarais et al. (2016). In contrast, these reviewers found relatively few studies overall, with some instruments having a very limited number of validation studies. Further, this review found that only two examined inter-rater reliability, which is important because it indicates that the tool can be delivered consistently across different users. Kennealy, Skeem, and Herandez (2016) recently noted:

> In this study, we assess the extent to which 78 staff members' scoring of juveniles on the California-Youth Assessment and Screening Instrument (CA-YASI; Orbis Partners, Inc., 2008) agree with experts' criterion scores for those cases. There are 3 key findings. First, at the total score level, practitioners manifest limited agreement (M ICC = .63) with the criterion: Only 59.0% of staff scores the tool with "good" accuracy. Second, at the subscale level, practitioners' accuracy is particularly weak for treatment-relevant factors that require substantial judgment—like procriminal attitudes (M ICC = .52)— but good for such straightforward factors as legal history (M ICC = .72). Third, practitioners' accuracy depended on their experience—relatively new staff's scores were more consistent with the criterion than those with greater years of experience.

The lack of inter-rater reliability negatively affects the performance of the instrument. Even if the tool has predictive validity, if the frontline staff do not apply the risk assessment tool consistently (i.e., inter-rater reliability), then the utility of the risk assessments is undermined overall.

The work of Desmarais and colleagues (2016) revealed that there is considerable variation in the predictive validity of each tool and that few studies reached the standard of .70 or a threshold of excellence. When instruments are reviewed by different performance measures, there is variation in their results. Furthermore, it is unclear that the third or fourth generation tools outperform second generation (static risk) tools in terms of their predictive validity. Austin (2006) noted in a review of the Level of Service Inventory–Revised (LSI-R; Andrews & Bonta, 1995) (a third generation risk assessment tool) that the static risk items (the first 10 items) account for most of the predictive validity of the instrument. Others have noted the same with other instruments (see Brennan, 2016; Brennan, Dieterich, & Ehret, 2008 for a discussion of issues). This, of course, begs the question about the added value of the dynamic risk items, a question that is often raised by enthusiasts of machine learning algorithms (Berk & Bleich, 2013). Some empirical evidence exists that demonstrates the incremental predictive validity of dynamic risk factors over solely static factors.

More importantly, we are unsure of the drivers of this variability in predictive validity. The reasons for the variability can be driven by: (1) study population such as the type of population (pretrial defendants, probationers, parolees, reentry, etc.); (2) outcome variable used and the length of follow-up; or (3) the instruments are used by practitioners in various settings, such as the setting, practitioners, or the way in which the instrument is administered. We need to better understand the factors that detract from the predictive validity of an instrument. This is important because we cannot improve the performance of these instruments if we are unsure of what factors affect dilution of their predictive validity. We also need to address the needs of practitioners regarding the assurances that risk assessment instruments are worth the time and effort, and to address concerns that instruments are valid (see Miller & Maloney, 2013 and Viglione, Rudes, & Taxman, 2015 for a review of the perspectives of practitioners on the use of risk assessment tools).

Do the Risk Assessment Instruments Differentiate Between Those in the Justice System and Those That Are not in the Justice System?

For the most part, risk assessment instruments have been developed on populations involved in the justice system and/or mental health facilities (for various psychiatric disorders). While this makes sense, insofar as it provides a mechanism to assess risk *within* the justice-involved or mental health populations, it begs the question regarding how the justice-involved population compares to a non-justice-involved population. Risk assessment instruments should be able to differentiate between those involved in the justice system (i.e., presumably criminals) compared to those that are not involved in the justice system. If the tool development does not include a non-justice-involved population, then the discriminant validity of the risk assessments may be limited.

Blumstein and Nakamuri (2009) examined cohorts of individuals that are involved in the justice system and then are "clean" (i.e., not involved in the justice system). This well-regarded study illustrates that there is a redemption point, or a time when an individual presents the same risk for arrest (proxy for criminal behavior) as the general population at the same age; that is, age becomes a function of risk for reoffending. To summarize briefly, depending on the age of first arrest, there is a different point of redemption for different types of offenses. For example, those individuals who commit a first offense of robbery at 16, 18, or 20 have different redemption points which are 8.5 years, 7.7 years, and 4.4 years respectively. That means that a 16-year-old robbery offender needs 8.5 years' clean time (no offenses/arrests) to be equivalent to the general-population, non-arrested individual. Or if the robbery offender is 25 years old and has not been arrest free for 8.5 years, they have not approached the risk for recidivism for an individual in the general population. The study found that certain offenders (violent) have a different trajectory than other offenders (property) to reach the same developmental point as those that have never been arrested—violent offenders take longer to cease their behaviors than property offenders. However, Blumstein and Nakamuri (2009) identify a number of qualifiers and areas for further development, which means that the actual redemption years are largely hypothetical at this point.

The point of redemption concept is challenging to our current methods for risk assessment tools. The Blumstein and Nakamuri (2009) study suggests that our assessment of a person's risk for recidivism should consider factors that differentiate the justice and non-justice-involved population. Risk assessment tools that are validated on a short period of time (for example, under two years) might not consider the redemption point which is tied to the year of first offense and the number of years clean. Not to mention that most risk assessment tools do not "clean the slate"—that is the historical, static risk factors consider "any arrest/offense" regardless of the age of the individual or the lapse between arrest/conviction events.

Are the Methods to Score Items and Categorize Risk Appropriate?

A similar concern regarding the interpretation of the risk assessment is that there is a lot of variability in the information used in determining a risk category and how agencies create risk levels or categories. First, the scoring of the instrument. In most second generation instruments, the scoring is more simple with the total score related to the individual's past history. But, in third and fourth generation instruments, many combine the static and dynamic risk items together to compute a total score. Baird (2009) has indicated that this procedure serves to inflate risk level, with many low risk in the criminal history category elevated to a moderate risk due to dynamic factors, such as education, employment, attitudes, etc., some of which are tangentially related to recidivism. For example, in a study of parolees in Pennsylvania, 43% of the parolees are ranked low risk using the full LSI-R total score (including static plus dynamic factors) and 34% are ranked low risk when only the static risk factors are used. By placing individuals in a higher risk category, they have more liberty restrictions which increases the potential for technical violations or non-compliance with the conditions of release. From this perspective, there is concern that the scoring process may create unfairness as well as disparity problems in the criminal justice system. This issue of a total score or individual scores by domain is a topic of discussion in the field, with little research, or even more so, little exploration, of how one approach versus the other affects predictive validity or how it affects implementation of a risk assessment instrument in the field (Hamilton, Tollefsbol, Campagne, & Van Wormer, 2016a).

Another area lacking research is how best to categorize risk scores. Risk categories provide for the opportunity to label groups based on their likelihood to recidivate. The typical categorization is three levels of low, medium, and high risk. But the Ohio Risk Assessment System (ORAS; Latessa, Smith, Lemke, Makarios, & Lowenkamp, 2009) (third generation tool) proffered the use of a five-point system of very low, low, medium, high, and very high risk. This spreads the distribution of risk into finer categories which distinguishes the polar extremes (very low and very high). There is no well-subscribed method to create the categories, although the area under the curve statistics provides the best methodology to do so, since it allows one to differentiate the risk level by the within-group recidivism level. However, AUCs are often not reported or used in the validation process. The categorization is often used as a resource allocation tool where agencies can adjust the risk level based on the distribution of supervision and/or treatment resources available in the system. Of course, distorting the risk level to "match the data" affects the face validity of labels. Staff may not agree with the categorization based on their clinical assessment which creates a distrust of the instrument (Viglione, Rudes, & Taxman, 2015).

A new movement is afoot to identify a methodology to assign meaning to risk categories. The strategy of assigning risk categories varies considerably which means that it is impossible to compare individuals across jurisdictions—a low-risk individual in one jurisdiction could be high risk in another jurisdiction and vice versa. The Council of State Government (CSG) Justice Policy Center is sponsoring a workgroup to identify a methodology for creating meaningful categories. The concept of "meaningful" is that the risk categories would be consistent across jurisdictions and be linked to levels of supervision and intervention. To do so, the low risk category would be graded on the likelihood of an individual at a given age to commit a crime. This then adjusts the risk level on the basis on the likelihood of recidivism based on criminal history and age (and perhaps gender). This would serve to reduce the inconsistencies across jurisdictions as well as to ensure that there is a uniform meaning to the terms used to describe risk levels. The basic premise is to have five categories where the very low category echoes the likelihood of an arrest given the age of the individual, a mechanism resembling the work of Blumstein and Nakamuri (2009). For more details on the five-level concept see Hanson and Bourgon (2016).

Another related issue has to do with high-stake offenses that do not conveniently fit within general recidivism risk assessment instruments. High-stake offenses are those crimes that are high profile, such as sex offenses, driving while intoxicated, or domestic violence. Usually individuals that commit these offenses tend to engage in specialized offending, but this is an untested assumption. In fact, operational definition of recidivism measures for sex offenders used to be considered different than general offenders (see Hanson & Bourgon, 2016 for a discussion of this issue). Sex offender researchers generally report low base rates of sexual recidivism, which makes detection more difficult. For example, sex offenders tend to be rated low risk when sex offending is the main outcome variable (low detection) with an estimated recidivism rate at 2%. When all offending is examined, the rate of recidivism is 40% which suggests that sex offenders also engage in other offending behaviors (Hanson & Bourgon, 2016). More research is needed, including whether specialized risk assessment tools are necessary given the rate of offending.

Are Instruments Neutral on Race, Gender, and Other Key Demographic Issues?

Within the last year, a continuous issue has been raised about the degree to which risk assessment instruments are neutral on race, gender, and other key demographic issues. Given recent concerns raised in the U.S. regarding the potential racial bias of justice policies and practices, the ability to demonstrate that the tools are racially neutral is critical. As noted by Desmarais and colleagues (2016), many risk assessment instruments have not been examined for differential validity or using specificity analyses which would rule out any problems related to age, race, gender, or cultural biases in the instrument. They found a few studies that illustrated predictive validity was better for men than women with some risk assessment instruments, but this is not conclusive because of the few studies that actually examine differential validity. The same is true for race/ethnicity—too few studies exist to verify that the risk assessments are racially or culturally neutral. This is of major concern because of the prior studies that have found potential areas of racial bias (see discussion in Desmarais et al., 2016), but more work is needed in this area.

The complexity of examining differential validity has to do with the interaction of criminal history with some of these demographic variables of race/ethnicity and gender. Most scholars indicate that static criminal history, which has the greatest predictive validity in most risk assessment instruments, is the domain that protects against instrumentation bias. That is, sources of bias that should be assessed are the prior history of criminal justice experience, i.e., arrests, convictions, incarceration, prior probation violations, etc.; these areas may be more sensitive to being racially or gender neutral since it is a summary of an individual's experience. Skeem and Lowenkamp (2016) in an examination of the issues regarding race and criminal history in the Federal Post Conviction Risk Assessment tool (PCRA; Johnson, Lowenkamp, VanBenschoten, & Robinson, 2011) (third generation tool) note that nearly 66% of the racial difference in PCRA scores is attributable to criminal history. However, they indicate that criminal history "partially mediates the relationship between race and future violent arrest" (p. 29). As noted by Hannah-Moffat (2016), Harcourt (2015), Starr (2015), and others, there is a need to recognize that criminal histories are experiences that are the product of the war on drugs and mass incarceration policies over the last four decades, and that these criminal histories depict the institutional bias of the justice system. The debate regarding whether criminal history is a proxy for race is ongoing, and more work is needed to address this issue. It might be helpful if the measures of criminal history focused more on crime-specific behaviors (i.e., violent offenses, property offenses, felonies) instead of generic criminal conduct (such as total arrests, convictions, or incarceration). That is, how we measure criminal history may have an impact on the ability of the tools to be neutral on racial/ethnic issues. Not enough research exists on these critical measurement issues.

The issue of gender neutrality also needs further work (see Salisbury, Boppre, & Kelly, 2016). Van Voorhis and colleagues (2010) demonstrate that female offenders have different needs that should be included in gender-responsive risk assessment instruments, and that these needs should be incorporated in the design and utilization of risk assessment tools that are more appropriate for women. This developmental work by Van Voorhis, Wright, Salisbury, & Bauman (2010) identified a number of domains that, while not "criminogenic," affect the stabilization of the individual, as well as their ability to benefit from various treatment interventions, such as parental stress, family support, educational assets, housing safety, anger/hostility, child abuse, and adult victimization. Given the high victimization rates for those in the criminal justice system, it is likely that these domains are relevant for men and women, which means that there is potentially another set of variables that might be useful in third and fourth generation risk assessment tools that are not currently used.

Do the Domains on the Risk Assessment Instruments Have Construct and Content Validity?

A major challenge to the field is in the area of dynamic risk measures. According to Andrews and Bonta (2010), there are seven categories of dynamic risk factors that should be considered: antisocial peers, antisocial values, antisocial personality, substance abuse, employment, education, and leisure time activities. These are considered "criminogenic" since they are related to offending behaviors. But, in a recent review, it was noted that in five of the most prominent risk assessment instruments (i.e., Wisconsin Risk & Needs, ORAS, LSI-R, COMPAS, and STRONG-R), these dynamic risk factors are measured differently (Via, Dezember, & Taxman, 2016). That is, each instrument has a different way to measure the construct and this then means that there are differences in the meaning attributable to results of the risk assessment. This presents problems because it signifies the lack of construct and content validity. Construct validity is the degree to which inferences can be made from the operationalizations of theoretical constructs, whereas content validity is the degree to which the operationalizations measure all aspects of the construct. If there is inconsistency about what a construct means, then this affects content validity. Take, for example, the construct of substance use disorders which can refer to behaviors linked to alcohol and drug use. If the intent is to examine problem substance use disorders, then the content needs to cover aspects of the disorders that are associated with poorer functionality.

A major issue in the measures of these dynamic risks is whether the variables are measured to reflect current issues. That is, some instruments use lifetime measures and some use measures that indicate the last 12 months, last 30 days, or some other increment. Lifetime measures are problematic because they could indicate that the person had an issue in the past but it might not be a current problem. If it is not a current problem, then lifetime experience may not be useful in identifying problem behaviors. The wording of the items or scale in the risk assessment instrument is critically important because the wording defines the degree to which a problem is contemporary and affects current behavior, as well as the degree to which the factor is dynamic. Mixing static with dynamic factors only serves to undermine the overall confidence that the domain is relevant to case planning and recidivism reduction efforts. This could be part of the reason that probation officers and treatment providers are dubious about

Table 14.1 Measuring Criminal Cognitions or Thinking

	COMPAS	LSI-R	ORAS	STRONG-R	Wisconsin
Unfavorable towards convention		X			
Attitude toward sentence		X			
Attitude toward supervision		X			
Supportive of Crime		X			
Engages in risk-taking behavior			X		
Walks away from a fight			X		
Attitudes towards authority figures				X	
Attitudes towards property				X	
Do things without thinking	X				
Lose your temper	X				
Can be dangerous when you lose your temper	X				
Never intensely dislike anyone	X				
Has a short temper	X				
Number of items	8	4	2	3	0

using the results from risk assessment instruments since it might not reflect the issues that a person currently presents (see Hamilton et al., 2016a; Viglione, Rudes, & Taxman, 2015). The nature of the items and the way that the factors are measured may affect overall face validity of the instrument which may complicate implementation of the risk assessment instrument as part of case planning, treatment referral, or treatment placement.

For example, Via and colleagues (2016), in their analysis of five tools, explored the different questions used to measure different constructs. In Table 14.1 (summarized from Via et al., 2016) the different ways to ask questions about criminal cognitions or thinking are measured. Each instrument also measures the items differently, from a five-point Likert scale (COMPAS; Brennan et al., 2008), no items (Wisconsin), to points assigned to different response categories. The different ways criminal cognitions are measured range from anti-authority attitudes, callousness to criminal behavior, impulse control, to perception of fairness. This means that the concept of criminal cognitions may not be the same across the various instruments but, even more importantly, the measured construct might be different than the original research that identified antisocial values or antisocial cognitions as being "criminogenic."

Substance abuse is another area that displays the disparity across the risk assessment instruments. Many of the risk assessment instruments use measures that capture lifetime use, which may not identify current substance use problems. As shown in Table 14.2, the ways in which the substance abuse is measured demonstrates that some risk assessment instruments may not be able to capture contemporary drug use or the way in which substance abuse may affect behavior. And, risk assessment instruments often do not differentiate among mild, moderate, or severe substance use disorders. That is, risk assessment instruments often do not integrate the Diagnostic Statistical Manual (DSM; APA, 2013) definition for frequency and physical tolerance for substances in these specific domains.

Table 14.2 Measures of Alcohol/Drug (Substance) Use

	COMPAS	LSI-R	ORAS	STRONG-R	Wisconsin
Age at first use			X	X	
Longest period of abstinence from alcohol			X		
Drug of choice				X	
Ever used drugs			X		
Has/history of drug problem		X		X	
Disruption of functioning					X
Currently in formal treatment	X			X	
Ever been in formal treatment	X			X	
Current/past legal problems due to drugs	X	X	X	X	
Under the influence when arrested for current offense	X			X	
Drugs caused problems with family/partners/spouse		X		X	
Drugs caused problems with employment		X	X	X	
Would you benefit from treatment	X				
Use heroin, cocaine, crack, or methamphetamines as a juvenile	X				
Method of supporting substance use				X	
Number of items	9	9	5	7	2
Sensitive to substance use problems within last 12 months	Yes	Yes	No	Yes	Yes

How to Implement Risk Assessment Instruments so They Are Useful in Practice Including Case Planning, Resource Allocation, Treatment Referral or Placement, and Clinical Progress?

Risk assessment tools are only as valuable as the application of their results in practice to promote just and fair decisions. The evolution of risk assessment tools from first to fourth generation is premised on the utilization of the results to improve decision-making. With each generation there is also an expansion of how the tools can be used, including using the tools for justice decisions regarding release or placement in a supervision level, to case planning, to treatment placement. That is, the added domains (particularly from second to third generation tools) are designed to improve the utility of the risk assessment instruments by including both static and dynamic risk factors. A number of scholars have noted that risk assessment tools are not well respected or well used in the field (see Hamilton et al., 2016a; Miller & Mahoney, 2013; Miller & Trocchio, 2016; Taxman, 2016b; Viglione, Rudes, & Taxman, 2015).

Most evaluations of the implementation of risk assessment instruments, or other evidence-based practices more broadly, note the lack of confidence frontline staff have in the instrument (Hamilton et al., 2016a; Viglione, Rudes, & Taxman, 2016). The issues related to confidence have a lot to do with the staff member's assessment of whether a given risk assessment instrument improves *their own* decision, which is affected by how much the offender before them resembles, in their view, the risk score and categorization produced by the instrument. Viglione and colleagues (2015), in their observations of the use of risk assessment tools in practice, found that there were many instances in which the staff member doubted results of the risk assessment tool—the stakes of the offense committed were too great, the individual did not resemble a "low risk" offender, the needs did not reflect the instability of the individual given their housing, mental illness, or other factors that are not assessed on the instrument, etc. That is, the risk score and categorization did not resemble the offender, and therefore officers rely upon their own (subjective) judgment. While overrides are encouraged to allow for clinical/expert judgment, a general concern is that if overrides are being used frequently (over 10% of the cases), then the issue is less about professional judgment and more about the utility of the tool from the perception of staff.

Another common implementation issue is that the risk assessment instruments are seldom customized for a jurisdiction. Hamilton and colleagues (2016a) have identified a number of areas where customization could build user confidence in the risk assessment tools, including the language used, the visual representation of data and scores, the systems approach, use of screening assessments to decide who to use a risk assessment tool on, scoring adjustments (e.g., weighting and tailoring the scores), gender responsivity, case management and planning, supplemental assessments, special populations, and software. Miller and Trocchio (2016) discuss how more implementation analyses are needed to fully understand the organizational or agency factors that serve as a barrier to the use of risk assessment instruments in practice; there is a need to examine work processes that staff use to manage their workload and to deal with the complex needs of those involved in the criminal justice system. Implementation studies should focus on assessing the risk assessment tools and how they fit within a socio-political environment (i.e., political philosophy, resources, priorities, etc.). Understanding the environment, and how different agency and stakeholder factors affect the uptake risk assessment tools in practice, is an understudied area (see Taxman, 2016b for a discussion).

Evaluations of implementation also need to address which of the various uses of a given risk assessment tool are plausible in different environments. The expanded utilization of a risk assessment tool—from guiding decision-making to case planning to treatment placement to assessing progress—adds complexity to the implementation of the tool. This complexity may weaken the perceived value of the tool to staff and its effectiveness, or it might identify areas where staff are more comfortable using the tool. That is, expanding the potential areas where risk assessment information is used may undermine how the tools are used by staff.

Conclusion

Advances in criminal justice practice have relied upon risk assessment tools as a first step to altering practice. For example, many evidence-based practices begin with the use of a risk assessment tool before advancing to other reforms. System reform efforts tend to focus on using risk assessment tools to reduce disparity in decision-making or to increase efficiency. But the current state of methods to develop, test, validate, and refine the risk assessment tools, as previously discussed, leaves open the potential to undermine the ability of risk assessment tools to improve justice decision-making. A few studies have been done on the results of using risk assessment tools, but a review of the literature illustrates that there is more work to be done to ensure that the potential for increasing fairness and justice through the use of risk assessment tools has not been met. A new iteration of risk assessment tools is occurring in the form of machine learning tools instead of pen-and-pencil survey instrument tools which offer the potential for both a new generation of tools and a new way of putting a risk score in the hands of users. This is an emerging area where more work is needed, including the methodological issues related to the creation and validation of the tools.

This chapter has identified seven areas where more work needs to be done. A priority should be placed on improvements in the methods used to construct and validate risk assessment tools. A proposed Oversight Committee consisting of criminal justice research and practitioner communities would serve to advance methods and practice in this area. This review has highlighted a number of areas that have been poorly addressed by researchers, practitioners, and policymakers. The Oversight Committee could be used to oversee the construction, validation, and implementation of the risk assessment tool. The advantage of an outside body is that the Committee can provide an objective oversight to the tools which should result in increasing the reliability and validity of a tool, as well as the utility of the implemented tool. As noted by Taxman (2016b) there are a number of unanswered implementation issues that need more attention if we are going to advance the field of practice using risk assessment tools. At this point, without such oversight, risk assessment tools are developed and implemented in the field without attention to many of the reliability and predictive validity issues that have affected the current state of the art. And, the current state of the art is in need of advancements to better the science and practice of risk assessment.

References

American Educational Research Association, American Psychological Association, and National Council on Measurement in Education. (2014). *The standards for educational and psychological testing*. Washington, DC: AERA Publications.

American Psychiatric Association. (2013). *Diagnostic and statistical manual of mental disorders* (DSM V) (5th ed.). Washington, DC: American Psychiatric Association.

Andrews, D., & Bonta, J. (2010). The psychology of criminal conduct. New York, NY: Anderson.

Andrews, D. A., & Bonta, J. (1995). *The Level of Service Inventory–Revised*. Toronto, ON, Canada: Multi-Health Systems.

Austin, J. (2006). How much risk can we take? The misuse of risk assessment in Corrections. *Federal Probation, 70*(2). Retrieved from http://www.uscourts.gov/sites/default/files/fed _probation_sept_2006.pdf

Baird, C. (2009). *A question of evidence: A critique of risk assessment models used in the justice system*. San Francisco, CA: FOCUS Views from the National Council on Crime and Delinquency. Retrieved from http://www.jdaihelpdesk.org/intersiteconf2012/A %20Question%20of%20Evidence%20A%20Critique%20of%20Risk%20Assessment %20Models%20Used%20In%20The%20Justice%20System%20(NCCD%20February%202009).pdf

Berk, R. A., & Bleich, J. (2013). Statistical procedures for forecasting criminal behavior. *Criminology and Public Policy, 12*(3): 513–544.

Blumstein, A., & Nakamura, K. (2009). Redemption in the presence of widespread criminal background checks. *Criminology, 47*(2), 327–359.

Brennan, T. (2016). An alternative scientific paradigm for criminological risk assessment: Closed or open systems, or both? In F. S. Taxman (Ed.), *Risk and need assessment: Policy and practice*. New York, NY: Routledge.

Brennan, T., Dieterich, W., & Ehret, B. (2008). Evaluating the predictive validity of the COMPAS risk and needs assessment system. *Criminal Justice and Behavior, 36*, 21–40.

Desmarais, S. L., Johnson, K. L., & Singh, J. P. (2016). Performance of recidivism risk assessment instruments in U.S. correctional settings. *Psychological Services, 13*(3), 206–222.

Desmarais, S. L. & Singh, J. P. (2013). *Risk assessment instruments validated and implemented in correctional settings in the United States*. New York City: Council of State Government.

Retrieved from https://csgjusticecenter.org/wp-content/uploads/2014/07/Risk-Assessment-Instruments-Validated-and-Implemented-in-Correctional-Settings-in-the-United-States.pdf

Gottfredson, M. R., & Gottfredson, D. M. (1988). *Decision making in criminal justice: Toward the rational exercise of discretion* (2nd ed.). New York, NY: Plenum Press.

Gottfredson, S. D. & Moriarty, L. J. (2006). Statistical risk assessment: Old problems and new applications. *Crime and Delinquency, 52*(1), 178–200.

Hamilton, Z., Kigerl, A., Campagna, M., Barnoski, R., Lee, S., Van Wormer, J., & Block, L. (2016b). The development and validation of the STRONG-R recidivism risk assessment. *Criminal Justice and Behavior, 43*(2), 230–263.

Hamilton., Z., Tollefsbol, E., Campagna, M., & Van Wormer, J. (2016a). Customizing criminal justice assessments. In F. S. Taxman (Ed.), *Risk and need assessment: Policy and practice.* New York, NY: Routledge.

Hannah-Moffat, K. (2016). Purpose and context matters: Creating a space for meaningful dialogues about risk and need. In F. S. Taxman (Ed.), *Risk and need assessment: Policy and practice.* New York, NY: Routledge.

Hanson, K., & Bourgon, G. (2016). Advancing sexual offender risk assessment: Standardized risk categories based on psychologically meaningful offender characteristics. In F. S. Taxman (Ed.), *Risk and need assessment: Policy and practice.* New York, NY: Routledge.

Harcourt, B. (2015). Risk as a proxy for race: The dangers of risk assessment. *Federal Sentencing Reporter, 27,* 237–243.

Johnson, J. L., Lowenkamp, C. T., VanBenschoten, S. W., & Robinson, C. R. (2011). Construction and validation of the Federal Post Conviction Risk Assessment (PCRA). *Federal Probation, 75*(2), 16–29.

Kennealy, P. J., Skeem, J. L., & Hernandez, I. R. (2016). Does staff see what experts see? Accuracy of front line staff in scoring juveniles' risk factors. *Psychological Assessment.* Retrieved from http://psycnet.apa.org/doi/10.1037/pas0000316

Latessa, E., Smith, P., Lemke, R., Makarios, M., & Lowenkamp, C. (2009). Creation and validation of the Ohio Risk Assessment System Final Report. Cincinnati, OH: University of Cincinnati School of Criminal Justice, Center for Criminal Justice Research.

Mayson, S. G. (2016) *Dangerous defendants.* University of Pennsylvania Law School, Public Law Research Paper No. 16-30. Retrieved from http://ssrn.com/abstract=2826600

Miller, J., & Maloney, C. (2013). Practitioner compliance with risk/needs assessment tools: A theoretical and empirical assessment. *Criminal Justice & Behavior, 40,* 716–736.

Miller, J., & Trocchio, S. (2016). Risk/need assessment tools and the criminal justice bureaucrat: Reconceptualizing the frontline practitioner. In F. S. Taxman (Ed.), Risk and need assessment: Policy and practice. New York, NY: Routledge.

Salisbury, E., Boppre, B., & Kelly, B. (2016). Gender-responsive risk and need assessment: Implications for the treatment of justice-involved women. In F. S. Taxman (Ed.), *Risk and need assessment: Policy and practice.* New York, NY: Routledge.

Singh, J. P. (2013). Predictive validity performance indicators in violence risk assessment: A methodological primer. *Behavioral Sciences & the Law, 31,* 8–22.

Singh, J. P., Desmarais, S. L., & Van Dorn, R. A. (2013). Measurement of predictive validity in violence risk assessment studies: A second-order systematic review. *Behavioral Sciences & the Law, 31*(1), 55–73.

Singh, J. P., Mulvey, E. P., Yang, Z., & RAGEE Group (2014). Reporting guidance for violence risk assessment predictive validity studies: The RAGEE Statement. *Law and Human Behavior.* doi:10.1037/lhb0000090

Skeem, J., & Lowenkamp, C. (2016). Race, risk, and recidivism: Predictive bias and disparate impact. *Criminology, 54*(4): 1745-680–712.

Skeem, J., Monahan, J., & Lowenkamp, C. (in press). Gender, risk assessment, and sanctioning: The cost of treating women like men. *Law & Human Behavior*. Retrieved from http://papers.ssrn.com/sol3/papers.cfm?abstract_id=2718460

Starr, S. B. (2015). The new profiling: Why punishing based on poverty and identity is unconstitutional and wrong. *Federal Sentencing Reporter, 27*, 229–236.

Taxman, F. S. (2016a). *Risk and need assessment: Policy and practice*. New York, NY: Routledge.

Taxman, F. S. (2016b). The value and importance of risk and need assessment (RNA) in corrections and sentencing: An overview of the handbook. In F. S. Taxman, *Risk and need assessment: Policy and practice*. New York, NY: Routledge.

Van Voorhis, P., Wright, E. M., Salisbury, E., & Bauman, A. (2010). Women's risk factors and their contributions to existing risk/need assessment: The current status of a gender-responsive supplement. *Criminal Justice and Behavior, 37*(3), 261–288.

Via, B., Dezember, A., & Taxman, F. S. (2016). Exploring how to measure criminogenic needs: Five instruments and no real answers. In F. S. Taxman (Ed.), *Risk and need assessment: Policy and practice*. New York, NY: Routledge.

Viglione, J., Rudes, D. S., & Taxman, F. S. (2015). Misalignment in supervision: Implementing risk/needs assessment instruments in probation. *Criminal Justice & Behavior, 42*(3), 263–285. doi:0093854814548447.

Appendix

Ex02: Example, Cecil (DOB: 5/11/2001)   Printed: 6/11/2013

Client/Case ID:	Ex02
Youth:	Example, Cecil
Assessment Date:	6/11/2013

Completed By:	Katie Meyer
Last Update:	6/11/2013

Primary Case-planning Approach

Scores

Selective Intervention	46
Casework Control	79
Environmental Structure	22
Limit Setting	61

Scored Category: CC

The predominant characteristic of this group is a general instability in their life situation (e.g., changing jobs frequently, school problems, family problems, chemical dependency, etc.). They experience a lot of failure in their lives due to their lack of goal-directedness. Offenses tend NOT to follow a consistent pattern but to include both felonies and misdemeanors of various types. The goals for these youth include increasing stability in all areas of their lives; overcoming negative self-concepts; and substituting self-affirming behavior for self-defeating behavior, especially with regard to substance abuse. The caseworker should bring them down to reality when they are unrealistically positive and encourage them when they are discouraged. Resist the temptation to transfer or revoke simply because they are so frustrating. They expect you to give up on them like most others in their lives have. Although they seem to be so needy and have frequent crises, a balance must be maintained between extending help and insisting that they put forth reasonable effort. Beware of quick, superficial solutions to lifelong problems, which these youth often seek. Reinforce sustained and consistent involvement in long-term interventions.

Educators Should Know

- An inability to cope with chronic individual and family problems coupled with generalized hostility make CC youth very frustrating to work with in the classroom. It is important to consider the following when working with these youth in school:
- Cognitive skills are impaired due to emotional problems and/or chemical abuse.
- Whenever possible, limit transitions in school. Consider self-contained classrooms until behaviors are stabilized.
- Establish clear routines in the classroom that are easy for the student to follow.
- Set attainable short-term goals for behavior management.
- Work on reasoning skills.
- Set up a reward system that reinforces positive behaviors versus consequences for negative behaviors.

Handbook of Recidivism Risk/Needs Assessment Tools, First Edition. Edited by Jay P. Singh, Daryl G. Kroner, J. Stephen Wormith, Sarah L. Desmarais, and Zachary Hamilton.
© 2018 John Wiley & Sons, Ltd. Published 2018 by John Wiley & Sons, Ltd.

- These youth will lie to shift blame to others or to sabotage success.

Reintegration Considerations

CC youth will often minimize their problems and claim that all issues are resolved. Stress a need for stability in housing and relationships prior to returning to the community.

Other Considerations

CC youth tend to disrupt attempts at rational discussion of their behaviors. They have difficulty seeing the self-defeating nature of their responses and attitudes, so the focus of any work with these youth must be persistently redirected to the behavior of the juvenile. Agency workers, counselors, educators, and parents should emphasize the youth's responsibility to examine alternative behaviors prior to acting rather than allowing the youth to blame others for his poor choices. Sexual aggression may be present; this must be addressed. General health and hygiene issues may stem from substance abuse. Additionally, these youth may be at risk for sexually transmitted diseases. A thorough health evaluation is recommended. CC youth are at high risk for running away from home or any out-of-home placement.

Risk Level

Ranges:	Low	-4 to 2	**Score:**	16
	Moderate	3 to 8	**Scored Level:**	High
	High	9 to 18		

The risk level represents the potential for the youth to commit subsequent offenses.

Youth with a high risk level have the greatest potential for recidivism. Typically, 45-55% of high risk youth nationwide are either revoked or experience a new felony conviction within 24 months of placement on probation or parole supervision.

Override: [X] None

[ ] Policy

[ ] Discretionary (reason): _____

Final Level: [ ] Low [ ] Moderate [X] High

Supervisor Approval of Override: _____ **Date:** _____

Principal Service Needs

Strength: School Performance

It should be noted that school performance is a strength for this youth. Most members of this group lack strength in this area. Workers may use the strength in this area as a building block for interventions in other areas. Youths' strength in academics may provide insight into ways to have them examine their choices regarding behaviors that lead to trouble.

Need: Emotional Factors as Highly Significant

CC youth will often exhibit widely fluctuating moods and exaggerated responses to problems and conflict. They will often present as depressed, and may target naïve professionals who will foster their own sense of victimization and refusal to accept responsibility for their behavior. Staff should persist in redirecting these youth towards accepting responsibility for and consequences of their actions. Intense reactions to a crisis will often lead to volatile or aggressive behavior. CC youth are often at high risk for suicidal ideation. They may also be at risk for self-mutilation or "cutting." Chemical abuse is seen frequently among these youth, and this should be examined as a contributor to emotional responses. These youth will often tantrum or display out-of-control behaviors for the benefit of spectators. Workers should handle outbursts calmly with the awareness that reasoning will generally be ineffective and physical control may escalate behaviors. When these youth do tantrum, the best intervention is to remove the audience and allow the tantrum to subside naturally.

- Focus on addressing aggression through anger management classes.

- Address or rule out substance abuse issues prior to or in conjunction with addressing emotional factors.

- Consider behavioral therapy models only after substance abuse issues are addressed.

- Residential therapeutic communities may be ideal settings for these youth.

Need: Family History Problems as Highly Significant

A CC youth's family may mirror many of the youth's personal and adjustment problems. Family members may demonstrate hostility towards authority while at the same time expecting outside agencies and schools to take responsibility for the youth's behavior and to solve the family's problems. Home situations are likely chaotic and inconsistent. Families often have a history of chemical abuse, and there may be a history of foster care placements. Workers should note that crisis intervention and direct services will most likely be required for these families.

- If there are current concerns regarding abuse/neglect, referrals should be made to all necessary social services agencies.

- Expect multiple agency involvement with the family and a need to coordinate services.

- Family members are not good candidates for family therapy. However, individual members may need mental health services.

- The youth may benefit from residential or therapeutic foster care placement. However, placements should be closely monitored, as the youth is a likely runaway risk.

Need: Drug Abuse as Significant

Drug use and abuse are common among CC youth. Interventions in other areas should include some aspect of drug treatment if those interventions are to be effective. Workers should be aware that there may be an extensive history of substance abuse in the family. Therefore, any treatment of the youth's issues should also include an examination of substance abuse in the family unit. Emotional outbursts, poor school performance, and criminal behavior may all have roots in the youth's drug abuse. There may also be excessive bragging about drug use that requires close examination in order to determine the extent of the problem. Criminal behaviors may include trafficking in drugs. Chemical use may result in reduced cognitive ability and compromised physical health. As a result of substance abuse, all threats of self-harm or harm to others should be taken seriously.

- Complete a substance abuse assessment.

- Provide family members with detailed print and electronic information on the specific drugs used by the youth.

- Consider referral to a residential treatment program.

- Following completion of residential or detox programs, refer to ongoing 12-step programs and monitor attendance closely.

- Administer frequent and random urinalyses with clear consequences for any positive tests.

Ex02: Example, Cecil (DOB: 5/11/1996) Printed: 6/11/2013

Need: Abuse/Neglect and Trauma as Significant

The trauma of sexual abuse is long lasting. The ability to trust others is impaired, as is self-esteem. This boy is more likely to become depressed, or a substance addiction. He can also display aggressive and hostile tendencies and show problems at home, school, and in the treatment setting. He may have a pattern of school truancy, dropout, running away from home, and prostitution. Referral for counseling with a qualified professional is critical.

- Determine if the boy meets the criteria for post-traumatic stress disorder (PTSD).
- Determine the extent of trauma in the boy's life.
- Teach ways to cope safely by helping him to identify past situations and old coping skills that did not serve him well. Rehearse new ways to cope with similar situations. Have boys rate how safe the old coping skill was and how safe the new way of coping will be.

Need: Relationships as Significant

It is important for staff to observe and explore the lives of boys in the context of relationships. In evaluating relationships, assess whether the relationships value or devalue him. Are the relationships safe or unsafe? To address issues of self-worth, in addition to social manipulation, boys also engage in self-protective insecurity. This coping strategy serves to protect them from criticism and hurt by others, but also serves to stifle self-expression and suppress their skills and talents. Boys who use this coping strategy are particularly vulnerable because they do not have a strong sense of self, and are particularly at risk when they are devalued or rejected by peers because everything is subsumed by the relationship. These boys allow others to determine their self-esteem and self-worth.

- Provide positive opportunities for connections to self, family, and community that can serve as an anchor for boys during adolescence.
- Teach skills associated with personal responsibility, empathy, trust, and loyalty, all of which are critical for maintaining friendships.
- Identify which friendships are worth the investment and which are not. Discuss the importance of friends who genuinely make him feel good about himself and are trustworthy and loyal. Authentic friendships support boys in being themselves.
- Provide opportunities for boys to interact with positive male role models from diverse backgrounds.
- Do not tolerate bullying or exclusionary behaviors; teach boys that they could be the target of such behaviors.

Special Concerns

Q20: Youth admits gang affiliation.

Q41-43: Youth reports history of abuse and/or neglect; follow up with child welfare.

Q44: Youth reports experiencing a traumatic event. Determine if youth meets the criteria for post-traumatic stress disorder (PTSD).

Q49c: Youth reports that mother/stepmother has a history of probation, jail, or prison.

Q49f: Youth reports that mother/stepmother has a history of drinking and drug problems.

Q62: Youth admits to prior placement in juvenile justice facilities; ensure accuracy of report and document incarceration history.

This report includes information disclosed to you from records protected by federal confidentiality rules (42 CFR Part 2). The federal rules prohibit you from making any further disclosure of this information unless further disclosure is expressly permitted by the written consent of the person to whom it pertains or as otherwise permitted by 42 CFR Part 2. A general authorization for the release of medical or other information is not sufficient for this purpose. The federal rules restrict any use of the information to criminally investigate or prosecute any alcohol or drug abuse patient.

Questions and Answers

General Information

1 A. How did you get involved in your most recent offense?

B. How did you decide to do it?
- ● emotional reasons (e.g., anger, sex)
- ○ both emotional and material reasons
- ○ material (monetary) reasons

2 A. Could you tell me more about the circumstances that led up to this offense?

B. How did you get caught?
- ● admits committing and doesn't attempt excuses
- ○ admits committing but emphasizes excuses
- ○ denies committing

3 A. Have you been in trouble before? (List arrests and discuss individually.)

B. * What else have you been arrested or referred to juvenile court for?
- ○ nothing prior to current offense
- ○ mainly status offenses
- ○ mainly criminal offenses
- ● no consistent pattern

4 A. In these offenses, have you ever been armed or hurt someone?

B. Did you ever threaten anyone during an offense?
- ● yes, non-sexual offenses
- ○ yes, sexual offenses
- ○ no

5 How did you decide to commit these offenses?
- ○ planned
- ● impulsive
- ○ no consistent pattern

6 Were you with someone when you got in trouble?
- ○ no consistent pattern
- ○ with accomplices
- ● alone

7 Were you drinking or on drugs when you got in trouble?
- ● 50% or less
- ○ never
- ○ more than 50%

Ex02: Example, Cecil (DOB: 5/11/1996)   Printed: 6/11/2013

8	Have you ever been arrested for offenses against your family, like stealing or running away?
	○ never
	○ sometimes
	● usually
8a	Has youth been assaultive with family member?
	○ no
	● yes

School Adjustment

9	A. Do (did) you have any problems with schoolwork?
	B. Do (did) you ever receive any special help in school?
	○ no problems
	● other achievement problems
	○ problems primarily due to lack of intellectual capacity
10	Did youth ever receive special education for learning deficiencies?
	● no
	○ yes
11	Did youth ever receive special help for emotional or behavioral problems in school?
	○ no
	● yes
12	Do (did) you go to class regularly?
	○ minor truancy
	● extensive truancy
	○ no truancy
13	Generally, do (did) you get your homework done?
	○ generally no problem
	● major problem
14	How do (did) you generally get along with your teachers and principals?
	○ no problem
	● authority problems
15	Do (did) you have any other problems in school?
	● major truancy or dropped out; suspended three or more times; considered seriously disruptive
	○ enrolled, attending regularly, no suspensions; or graduated/received GED
	○ suspended one to two times; considered somewhat disruptive
16	Current school status:
	● enrolled
	○ suspended
	○ dropped out/not enrolled
	○ expelled
	○ graduated

Ex02: Example, Cecil (DOB: 5/11/1996)   Printed: 6/11/2013

17	How far do you plan to go in school?
	• post-high school training
	○ high school diploma
	○ no further education
	○ GED
18	Do (did) you like school?
	○ generally positive
	• neutral or mixed
	○ generally negative

Interpersonal Relationships

19	Do you like to hang out with a group, or one or two friends at a time?
	○ prefers individual friends
	○ prefers groups
	• mixed
20	Have your friends been in trouble?
	○ mixed
	• gang member/associate
	○ essentially not in legal trouble
	○ mostly in legal trouble
21	A. How much do your friends drink?
	B. *How much drugs do they do?
	○ sometimes
	○ rarely
	• frequent or abusive
22	A. How much drinking and/or drugs do you do?
	B. (For youth who score b or c, ask) How do you get money to pay for it?
	○ no problems or experimentation only
	• use sometimes interferes with functioning
	○ frequent/chronic use or abuse
22a	Type of drugs used?
	○ methamphetamine
	○ heroin
	○ other
	○ none
	• marijuana
	○ cocaine
	• alcohol

Ex02: Example, Cecil (DOB: 5/11/1996) Printed: 6/11/2013

23	How do your parents feel about your friends?
	● mixed or neutral
	○ approve
	○ disapprove

24	When you're with your friends, who generally decides what to do (where to go, etc.)?
	○ friends usually decide
	● mixed
	○ youth usually decides

25	A. Do you have a closest friend?
	B. What do you like best about him/her?
	● do things together (less emphasis on talking or sharing feelings)
	○ talk (share feelings) or help each other
	○ has none

26	A. Do you have a significant/special partner?
	B. Can you describe your relationship?
	C. Are you sexually active with this partner?
	○ partner is significantly older
	○ bisexual relationships
	○ partner is similar in age to youth
	○ not disclosed
	○ feels emotionally threatened in relationship
	● no partner
	○ feels physically threatened in relationship
	○ same-sex relationships

27	Have you had sexual relationships with anyone other than your significant partners?
	○ two
	○ one
	○ three or more
	● none

Feelings

28	A. What kinds of things get you depressed?
	B. What do you do when you're feeling depressed?(If he denies getting depressed, how does he avoid depression?)
	○ seeks someone to talk to about the problem or tries to figure it out
	● seeks an activity to distract himself
	○ isolates himself
	○ drinks, uses drugs, and/or self-mutilates
	○ denies getting depressed

29	Have you ever tattooed or cut on yourself?
	○ yes
	● no

30	A. Have you ever thought seriously about killing yourself?
	B. (If youth says yes to above) Have you ever tried it?
	○ never seriously contemplated it
	○ attempted it
	● had definite thoughts

31	A. What do you do when you're feeling angry with people?
	B. *Have you ever hurt anyone when you were angry?
	○ avoids expressing anger
	○ responds appropriately
	● physically aggressive toward people
	○ trouble expressing anger appropriately

32	A. Can you describe your personality?
	B. What do you like and dislike about yourself?
	○ emphasizes inadequacy
	● emphasizes strengths
	○ can't describe himself

33	In general, do you tend to trust or mistrust people?
	○ basically trusting
	○ mixed or complex view
	● basically mistrusting

Family Attitudes

34	A. Are you living at home?
	B. *How many different houses or apartments have you lived in?
	○ five to nine
	● ten or more
	○ zero to four

35	A. Can you describe your living environment now? (current or prior to residential placement)
	B. Are there other people who live in your home for periods of time?
	○ has housing, some basic living needs unmet
	○ family is homeless and/or needs serious family resources
	● suitable
	○ youth has left home

Ex02: Example, Cecil (DOB: 5/11/1996)   Printed: 6/11/2013

36	A. How do (did) you get along with your mother?
	B. How do you feel about her?
	○ mixed or neutral
	● close
	○ hostile
37	A. Since about age 12, if you did something wrong, how did your mother handle it?
	B. What kind of discipline did she use?
	○ verbal or privilege withdrawal
	● physical
	○ permissive (generally let youth do as he pleased)
	○ not applicable
38	A. How do (did) you get along with your father?
	B. How do you feel about him?
	○ close
	○ hostile
	● mixed or neutral
39	A. Since about age 12, if you did something wrong, how did your father handle it?
	B. What kind of discipline did he use?
	○ physical
	○ not applicable
	○ permissive (generally let youth do as he pleased)
	● verbal or privilege withdrawal
40	Can you describe your father's personality? (If answer is unclear, ask youth to describe another person he knows well.)
	○ multifaceted
	● superficial
41	A. Were you ever abused by your parents?
	B. Did they ever go overboard on punishment?
	● yes
	○ no
42	Were your parents ever reported to the child welfare system for physically or sexually abusing or neglecting you?
	● yes, physical abuse
	○ yes, both physical and sexual abuse
	○ yes, sexual abuse
	○ no

43	A. Have you ever been abused by anyone else? B. Have you ever been abused sexually? ○ yes, both physical and sexual abuse ○ yes, physical abuse ○ yes, sexual abuse ● no
44	Have you ever experienced a traumatic event that significantly impacted your life? ○ none ○ sexual abuse ● death of parent, sibling, friend ● divorce ● other major disruption ○ domestic violence ○ rape ● physical abuse ● witnessing violence ○ serious accident
45	A. How would your parents have described you when you were younger (prior to age 10)? B. *Did they both see you the same way? ○ parents differed ● good kid (normal) ○ problem child
46	How would you describe yourself during that time (prior to age 10)? ● good kid (normal) ○ problem kid
47	Would you describe your early childhood (prior to age 10) as happy or unhappy? ○ happy ● unhappy
48	Are you satisfied with your early childhood? ○ basically satisfied (little change) ● dissatisfied with family ○ dissatisfied with material aspect ○ dissatisfied with self
49b	Does any parent have a history of criminal behavior? ○ father/stepfather ● neither parent ○ mother/stepmother ○ both parents
49c	Does any parent have a history of probation, jail, or prison? ○ father/stepfather

Ex02: Example, Cecil (DOB: 5/11/1996)

	● mother/stepmother
	○ both parents
	○ neither parent
49a	Does any parent currently receive TANF?
	○ mother/stepmother
	○ both parents
	○ father/stepfather
	● neither parent
49d	Does any parent have a history of psychiatric hospitalization?
	○ mother/stepmother
	● neither parent
	○ both parents
	○ father/stepfather
49e	Does any parent have a history of suicide attempts?
	○ mother/stepmother
	○ both parents
	○ father/stepfather
	● neither parent
49f	Does any parent have a history of drinking and drug problems?
	● mother/stepmother
	○ both parents
	○ father/stepfather
	○ neither parent
49g	Does any parent have a history of physical disablity and/or major illness?
	○ mother/stepmother
	○ both parents
	○ father/stepfather
	● neither parent
49h	Does any parent have a history that is free of the problems in items 49a-g?
	● father/stepfather
	○ neither parent
	○ mother/stepmother
	○ both parents
50	Have siblings (include step- and half-siblings) ever been arrested?
	○ some
	○ not applicable
	○ none
	● most
51	Has any sibling or parent ever been placed on probation or in jail or a correctional institution within the last three years?
	○ no

Ex02: Example, Cecil (DOB: 5/11/1996) Printed: 6/11/2013

	• yes
51a	Which sibling or parent has been placed on probation or in jail or a correctional institution?
	• mother or stepmother
	• adult sibling
	○ none
	○ father or stepfather
51b	Is any sibling or parent currently incarcerated?
	○ mother or stepmother
	• adult sibling
	○ none
	○ father or stepfather
52	Does youth have any children?
	○ yes, and has custody of one or more children
	• no
	○ yes, but does not have custody
53	A. How do you feel about being a dad?
	B. What are some of your baby's needs?
	○ parent (or expectant father), can meet basic needs of child and self
	○ parent (or expectant father), shows disregard for self and child(ren)
	• no child(ren) and is not an expectant father
	○ parent (or expectant father), cannot meet basic needs of child and self
Plans and Problems	
54	Aside from trouble with the law, what is the biggest problem in your life now?
	• vocational/financial
	○ relationships
	○ no big problems presently
	○ education
	○ personal issues
55	A. What goals do you have for the future?
	B. *How do you expect to accomplish those goals?
	○ short-term goals (most goals can be fulfilled within about six months)
	• long-term goals
56	Are there any places/programs or people that can help you when you leave here/or when you are off of supervision?
	• barriers exist that limit ability to access resources
	○ yes, has knowledge of existing resources and is willing to use them
	○ denies needing any social support
	○ resources do not exist

57	How will being on supervision (institution or field) affect your life?
	○ no effect
	○ counseling or program help
	● negative
	○ will keep him out of trouble
	○ mixed or unclear

Objective History

58	Age of earliest arrest or referral to juvenile court intake:
	● 12 or younger
	○ 14
	○ 15-16
	○ 13
	○ 17 or older

59	Number of arrests for criminal (non-status) offenses:
	○ none
	○ two or three
	● eight or more
	○ one
	○ four to seven

59a	Number of arrests for drug offenses:
	● one or more
	○ none

60	Number of court referrals for violent/assaultive offenses:
	○ one
	○ none
	● two or more

61	Number of arrests for status offenses:
	○ none
	○ five or more
	● one to four

62	Number of placements in correctional institutions:
	○ one
	○ none
	● two or more

63	Total number of prior out-of-home placements:
	○ none
	○ one
	● two or more

64	Time spent under prior probation/parole supervision:
	○ none (this is the first time)
	● more than 12 months
	○ seven to 12 months
	○ six months or less
65	Medical history (note all applicable choices):
	○ drug/alcohol treatment
	○ psychological/psychiatric treatment
	○ prior major illness (recovered)
	○ serious head injuries
	○ major current illness
	○ sexual offender treatment program
	● none of the above
66	What generally happens when you are feeling sick or have a health problem?
	○ has a regular doctor, or caregiver coordinates adequate health care
	○ undiagnosed health problems, recurring symptoms, rarely or never seeks medical care
	● poor health conditions reoccur, inconsistent with self-care

Behavioral Observations

67	Appearance and hygiene:
	○ below average
	○ average
	● above average
68	Comprehension:
	○ below average
	○ above average
	● average
69	Affect:
	● average
	○ depressed (sluggish)
	○ animated (hyper)
70	Self-disclosure:
	○ evasive
	○ very open
	● average

Interviewer Impressions

71	Social inadequacy:
	○ significant
	● not significant
	○ somewhat significant
	○ minor significance
	○ highly significant

Ex02: Example, Cecil (DOB: 5/11/1996)   Printed: 6/11/2013

72	School inadequacy:
	○ significant
	○ minor significance
	○ highly significant
	○ somewhat significant
	● not significant
73	Basic living needs:
	● not significant
	○ highly significant
	○ somewhat significant
	○ significant
	○ minor significance
74	Parental supervision:
	○ minor significance
	● somewhat significant
	○ not significant
	○ significant
	○ highly significant
75	Criminal orientation:
	○ highly significant
	○ somewhat significant
	○ not significant
	○ significant
	● minor significance
76	Emotional factors:
	○ somewhat significant
	○ significant
	○ minor significance
	● highly significant
	○ not significant
77	Family history problems:
	○ not significant
	● highly significant
	○ somewhat significant
	○ significant
	○ minor significance
78	Abuse/neglect and trauma:
	○ somewhat significant
	○ not significant
	● significant
	○ highly significant

Ex02: Example, Cecil (DOB: 5/11/1996) Printed: 6/11/2013

	O minor significance
79	Physical safety: O highly significant O significant ● minor significance O somewhat significant O not significant
80	Relationships: O highly significant O somewhat significant O not significant ● significant O minor significance
81	Isolated-situational or temporary circumstances: O minor significance ● not significant O significant O highly significant O somewhat significant
82	Interpersonal manipulation: O somewhat significant O not significant O significant ● minor significance O highly significant
83	Alcohol abuse: O significant O minor significance O highly significant ● somewhat significant O not significant
84	Other drug abuse: O highly significant ● significant O somewhat significant O minor significance O not significant
85	Vocational skills: O highly significant O somewhat significant ● not significant

	O significant
	O minor significance

Index

Page numbers annotated with 'n', 't', and 'f' refer to notes, tables, and figures respectively.

Handbook of Recidivism Risk/Needs Assessment Tools, First Edition. Edited by Jay P. Singh, Daryl G. Kroner, J. Stephen Wormith, Sarah L. Desmarais, and Zachary Hamilton.
© 2018 John Wiley & Sons, Ltd. Published 2018 by John Wiley & Sons, Ltd.